MASS TORTS IN A
WORLD OF SETTLEMENT

MASS TORTS

IN A WORLD OF

SETTLEMENT

RICHARD A. NAGAREDA

The University of Chicago Press • *Chicago & London*

Richard A. Nagareda is professor of law at Vanderbilt University
Law School, where he serves as the director of the Cecil D. Branstetter
Litigation & Dispute Resolution Program.

The University of Chicago Press, Chicago 60637
The University of Chicago Press, Ltd., London
© 2007 by The University of Chicago
All rights reserved. Published 2007
Printed in the United States of America
16 15 14 13 12 11 10 09 08 07   1 2 3 4 5
ISBN-13: 978-0-226-56760-0 (cloth)
ISBN-10: 0-226- 56760-5 (cloth)

Library of Congress Cataloging-in-Publication Data

Nagareda, Richard A.
    Mass torts in a world of settlement / Richard A. Nagareda.
        p.   cm.
    Includes bibliographical references and index.
    ISBN-13: 978-0-226-56760-0 (cloth : alk. paper)
    ISBN-10: 0-226-56760-5 (cloth : alk. paper)
    1. Torts—United States. 2. Class actions (Civil procedure)—United
States. 3. Complex litigation—United States. I. Title.
    KF1250.N34 2007
    346.7303—dc22

                                                    2006037824

CONTENTS

INTRODUCTION

When lawyers first encounter the subject of torts in law school, the cases they study typically involve bizarre, idiosyncratic events. The word "tort" derives from the Latin *torquere,* meaning to twist. A tort literally involves a twisting—an injuring—of another that the law empowers the injured person to straighten out by way of a lawsuit.[1] In one famous case read by generations of lawyers, a passenger attempts to board a moving train. A railway employee comes forward to assist but knocks a package that happens to contain fireworks from the passenger's arms. An explosion results, dislodging from the other end of the railway platform some heavy scales that fall and injure Helen Palsgraf.[2] In another tort classic, George Kendall raises a stick in an effort to separate two fighting dogs and inadvertently pokes the eye of George Brown, a bystander.[3] In a third case, waitress Gladys Escola suffers lacerations to her hand from an exploding Coca-Cola bottle.[4] These are the stories that have long introduced new lawyers to the law of torts.

The settings of these cases are extraordinary. But their essential structure is both simple and typical of tort litigation as traditionally conceived. A single, identified plaintiff with some sort of physical impairment sues the specific defendant she believes to have wrongfully caused that malady. "Mass torts" diverge from traditional tort litigation, grounded in what Oliver Wendell Holmes described as "isolated, ungeneralized wrongs."[5] The mass tort phenomenon is all too familiar in recent decades, not only to lawyers but also to the public at large. Examples include the claims of industrial workers who inhaled high concentrations of asbestos fibers on the job; soldiers exposed to Agent Orange during the Vietnam War; women who received silicone gel breast implants; dieters who consumed the drug combination popularly known as fen-phen; smokers of tobacco products; and, in a recent variation, the government itself, suing to recoup the additional outlays from the public fisc said to result from smoking and firearm misuse.

These accumulated examples have made "mass torts" into a term of art in the law—something understood not merely to involve tortious misconduct on a mass scale but, more specifically, a kind of mass tortious misconduct that is especially difficult for the legal system to address. As a working definition, "mass torts" involve allegations of tortious misconduct affecting large numbers of broadly dispersed persons. These persons, in turn, complain of injuries that may remain latent for years or even decades but, when they do emerge, present a limited set of factual variations. As I shall discuss, each of these characteristics—numerosity, geographic dispersion, temporal dispersion, and factual patterns—poses its own challenges for a tort system designed primarily for idiosyncratic events, one-on-one litigation, and present-day injuries. The subject matter of this book is not tort doctrine, however, though its components bear discussion along the way. The subject, instead, is the institutional transformation wrought by the mass tort phenomenon.

Simply put, the evolving response of the legal system to mass torts has been to shift from tort to administration. With the term "administration" I invoke the notion of an ongoing, institutionalized regime that sees its subject matter not as a series of isolated events but, instead, as suitable for systematized treatment. The features that define a mass tort have precipitated a convergence, in practical operation, of tort litigation—lawsuits at the behest of private parties represented by private attorneys—and the administrative functions of public agencies. The sheer numbers of claims, their geographic breadth, their reach across time to unidentified future claimants, and their factual patterns, together, demand the kind of systematized treatment characteristic of administrative processes.

It would be an overstatement, nevertheless, to suggest that tort litigation, even in the early years of the twentieth century, lacked any semblance of administration, in the sense I use that term here. Before the emergence of mass torts, the law confronted a spate of injuries in industrial workplaces. Lawyers for injured workers and industrial employers developed gridlike schemes for the settlement of claims. And the law ultimately built upon those arrangements in the form of public administrative regimes for workers' compensation.[6] This book explains how similar administrative regimes have emerged for mass torts—this time, not primarily through public legislation but through ad hoc experimentation by private lawyers.

To imply that the transformation from tort to administration has proceeded along a clear, linear path for mass torts would also be an overstatement. Much of this book is the story of tentative experimentation — including several notable failures — that chafe at conventional boundaries, whether of tort doctrine or of institutional categories. As for any world in flux, there have been choices made, foregone, deferred, or only dimly perceived. There is a surprising degree of consensus today about the basic parameters for the comprehensive resolution of mass tort disputes. The hard questions center not on whether the law should move from the traditional tort system to some manner of privatized administrative regime but, instead, how the law may do so with legitimacy.

In casting mass torts today as a problem of dispute resolution, this book locates its subject matter within broader trends in civil litigation. With rare exception, the resolution of a plaintiff's tort claim will come by way of a settlement, not a trial.[7] The settlement agreement describes a business transaction. The defendant effectively purchases from the plaintiff her right to sue based on the underlying events in the case. And the terms of that transaction — the price for the sale, for example — have only a remote bearing upon the terms of settlement for other pending suits. The settlements that conclude the vast majority of ordinary tort suits, moreover, are transactions crafted by agents: lawyers on the defense side (who generally bill their clients on an hourly basis) and lawyers on the plaintiff's side (who typically have a financial stake in the outcome of the case due to their retention on a contingency-fee basis).[8]

Mass torts accentuate the role of lawyers as agents. As in traditional tort litigation, the endgame for a mass tort dispute is not trial but settlement. But the scope of the settlement differs. Here, the most ambitious settlements seek to make and enforce a grand, all-encompassing peace in the subject area of the litigation as a whole. Lawyers, once again, act as the designers of these deals, and the strategic motivations of lawyers on both sides shape the design of the peace.

One significant facet of the mass tort phenomenon consists of the emergence and operation of an elite segment of the personal injury plaintiffs' bar. These lawyers specialize in the identification, development, and comprehensive resolution of whole categories of mass tort disputes. The story of this mass tort plaintiffs' bar — indeed, the intense, competitive relationship among such law firms — is as much a part of the mass tort world as legal doctrine.

In effect, mass torts have endowed with a power of governance the agents who design the transactions to resolve mass tort disputes on a comprehensive basis. As used here, the term "governance" embraces two related features: the power to alter preexisting legal rights and the power to make those alterations binding upon individuals in order to advance the greater good. As in the world of government itself, the power of governance wielded by peacemaking lawyers encompasses a power to undertake law reform, to make trade-offs between conflicting goals, and to impose the chosen trade-off with finality. This book seeks to expose this governing power, to assess its operation, and to develop a framework for the resolution of mass tort disputes that includes appropriate constraints upon the designing agents.

I ultimately argue that a proper set of constraints requires the law to question some of the most deeply engrained ideas about mass torts today. Specifically, the law should conceive of the constraints upon the peace designers less in terms of lawyer-client relationships and more along the lines of representation in other areas where agents wield governing power. If making peace involves an act of governance — if it involves altering preexisting rights and making difficult trade-offs — then it should not surprise us that the world of government should have lessons to teach.

At the outset, one might ask: Why regard comprehensive peace as the endgame for mass torts? Two answers shall emerge over the course of this book. The first rests upon observed behavior. Across a wide range of subject areas, lawyers in mass tort litigation have sought to craft and enforce comprehensive settlements of various sorts — peace plans that seek to lend binding force to various negotiated parameters for the resolution of future claims. That the behavior of people at the forefront of mass tort litigation has coalesced around a particular endgame is an indication, in itself, that the endgame is worthy of evaluation. There is, however, a deeper importance to peace as the endgame for mass torts.

Savvy lawyers on opposing sides have not hit upon the ideal of comprehensive peace by happenstance; rather, observed behavior reveals an underlying truth. The prospect of mass liability extending over years or decades — especially, liability of such a scope as to threaten the viability of the defendant as a business firm — generates huge uncertainty. For plaintiffs, the main uncertainty concerns the availability of resources to compensate persons who happen to develop disease later rather than sooner. For defendants, uncertain and potentially firm-threatening liability can cripple their ability to draw upon the capital markets to support their continued business operations.

Efforts at comprehensive peace reveal that uncertainty is as much a spur for creativity as it is a cause for consternation. The attraction of peace lies in its tremendous potential literally to generate value—to reduce dramatically the uncertainties of continued litigation and, in so doing, to call forth additional resources that would not otherwise be on the table. Peace, in short, can be a value-creating business transaction. But this value-creating potential turns crucially upon the very thing that pushes the peacemaking lawyers toward something akin to government: the power to make the peace terms binding for the future. Many of the problems associated with peacemaking flow from the use of private agents to wield a power of governance. As we shall see, the value created by peace calls for decisions about how to allocate that value, and the recurring pathology of peacemaking in mass tort litigation consists of the inadequate provision of resources for future claims. For the law, the challenge lies in lending a structure to peacemaking that affords latitude for creativity to generate value but, at the same time, inhibits plaintiffs' lawyers and defendants from largely appropriating that value for themselves.

In casting this book in the foregoing terms, I seek to reorient in two respects the way that we think about mass torts. First, the vantage point of this project—an examination of the mass tort phenomenon as a whole—contrasts with the perspective of most previous books that have addressed particular mass tort disputes.[9] Those accounts have proven invaluable, and I draw upon their richness of detail here. With rare exception, however, book treatments have eschewed analysis of mass torts as a whole.[10] This reluctance was commendable—certainly, understandable—in earlier decades, when the boundaries of mass tort litigation and the institutional dimensions of mass tort settlements remained unclear. The time now has come to envision the forest that encompasses the many trees.

Second, this book speaks across conventional dividing lines in its audience: among others, the division between private-law scholars interested in the development of torts and public-law scholars concerned with administration and the allocation of governing power; the division between readers versed in the processes of civil litigation (class action lawsuits and evidence law, for instance) and those focused on the bodies of substantive law (like tort) that civil litigation enforces; and, perhaps most importantly, the division between the scholarly community and the practicing bar. One recurring theme of the book consists of how innovation by lawyers and judges in the real world of mass tort litigation has driven the academic dialogue on the subject, not vice versa. As a result, one cannot speak realistically about mass torts in a world of settlement without a rich sense of lawyers as settlement designers and wielders of a privatized power of governance.

The Characteristics of a Mass Tort

Each of the defining features of a mass tort—numerosity, geographic dispersion, temporal dispersion, and factual patterns—poses challenges for the conventional tort system. Before I discuss each feature in its own right, a brief word is helpful to distinguish the category of mass torts from two related categories of civil litigation: "mass accidents" and "toxic torts." The term "mass accidents" describes tortious misconduct that affects large numbers of persons in similar ways. The most familiar torts of this type arise from localized disasters involving a particular physical structure—say, a hotel fire or an airplane crash. Mass accidents exhibit numerosity and, often, geographic dispersion and injury patterns. The physical impairments typically produced by a hotel fire or an airplane crash—burns, broken bones, or death—nonetheless tend to become apparent immediately or shortly after the accident. The absence of temporal dispersion makes mass accidents simply a more wide-ranging variation on the chain of events that befell Helen Palsgraf.

The term "toxic torts" describes tortious misconduct involving toxic substances said to produce latent disease. Residents near an industrial facility, for example, might sue in tort based upon their exposure to a toxic chemical released into the groundwater. The residents' claims may well entail some manner of present-day harm—say, to their property values. But an even more challenging component of their claims likely will center on allegations of latent disease. The key feature of latent disease is a gap of time between exposure to the defendant's misdeed (here, the wrongful release of the toxin) and the emergence of impairment on the part of any given claimant. Cancer is the classic example of a latent disease, though other noncancerous diseases also can give rise to a temporal gap between exposure and impairment. At the time of litigation, scientists simply may be unable to specify which residents will go on to develop cancer as a result of their exposure. At most, scientists may be able to estimate the relative risk of cancer—the difference between the risk of cancer among the plaintiff residents *collectively* in our example and the risk of cancer for a comparable group of persons not exposed to the toxin.[11] In the meantime, the individual residents stand as players in a macabre lottery. Only some of those exposed ultimately will suffer impairment, understood as some medically verifiable diminution in bodily function. Others, perhaps the vast majority, may go on to develop no impairment at all.

For all the difficulties posed by latent diseases such as cancer, however, toxic torts tend to remain relatively confined in their geographic reach. The plaintiffs consist of persons in proximity to the industrial facility—persons unlikely to sue in courts spread across the country. Toxic torts, then, are mass torts minus the high degree of geographic dispersion.

Given the conceptual overlap in mass tort, mass accident, and toxic tort litigation, much of what this book says will have implications across each category. All involve torts of a mass scope. All are mass torts in a literal sense. In deploying the term "mass torts" as more of a term of art, however, the law today speaks of litigation that gathers together the defining features found in the other two categories. Numerosity, geographic dispersion, temporal dispersion, and factual patterns in mass tort litigation, together, create enormous difficulties for the resolution of claims within the traditional tort system.

Numerosity and Factual Patterns

The first and last of the characteristics that define mass torts have related consequences. The sheer number of claims belies any aspiration for an individualized "day in court," if for no other reason than the scarcity of judicial resources. The move from retail to wholesale administrative resolution of claims, in other words, is driven in part by raw numbers. In addition, when claims exhibit a limited set of factual variations, there is no good reason for any system of justice to commit itself to the rehashing of those matters in each individual case. Unlike tort claims arising from idiosyncratic events, moreover, individual mass tort suits are highly interdependent in value. "[C]laims are so similar that the prospective value of many claims will rise or fall sharply with a large plaintiff award, a defense verdict or even a signal discovery event or evidentiary decision in a single case that is part of the mass of pending claims."[12]

Geographic Dispersion

Geographic dispersion of claims poses problems of its own that stem from the structure of the court system in the United States and the structure for lawmaking in the tort area specifically. In keeping with concepts of federalism in our government generally, the judiciary in the United States consists of a system of federal courts and fifty different systems of courts in the various states. The relationship among the various judicial systems is complex, forming the subject of its own field commonly described as the law of federal courts. Putting aside the caveats and qualifications found in that body of law, one may say in broad-brush terms that state judicial systems enjoy substantial autonomy vis-à-vis both the courts of the federal government and those of other states. It generally is not possible to swoop down and carry off into a single judicial system the claims of all mass tort plaintiffs pending in different court systems across the country.[13]

The existence of multiple judicial systems does not merely inhibit the coordination of pending claims. In addition, it has more subtle implications for the timing and dynamics of efforts at comprehensive settlement. Given the difficulty of coordinating thousands of pending lawsuits across multiple judicial systems, the tendency will be to search for some means to set in advance the terms for the resolution of mass tort claims anticipated to arise in the future — specifically, to set those terms before the persons holding such claims have filed traditional, individual lawsuits in tort. Two of the most important cases on mass tort settlements — the Supreme Court's landmark class action decisions in *Amchem Products, Inc. v. Windsor* and *Ortiz v. Fibreboard Corp.*[14] — involved bold efforts to craft grand transactions that would have set, in advance, the settlement terms for future asbestos claims.

Geographic dispersion dovetails with claim numerosity. As geographic dispersion increases, the likelihood decreases that any given law firm within the mass tort plaintiffs' bar will succeed in identifying and developing conventional lawyer-client relationships with all would-be claimants. Waiting for mass tort claims to be filed thus inhibits judicial coordination while also spurring competition for the control of the litigation as a whole among multiple law firms on the plaintiffs' side — each with its own inventory of pending cases. Comprehensive settlements thus seek not merely to avoid problems of judicial coordination later on, but also to enable the plaintiffs' law firms spearheading peacemaking effort to assert control of the litigation as against their competitors. To analyze mass tort settlements simply in terms of their effects upon plaintiffs and defendants thus would be to miss the interfirm competition that often underlies the deal. As I shall detail later, the successful legal campaign to derail the class action settlements in *Amchem* and *Ortiz* stemmed from precisely such interfirm competition within the asbestos plaintiffs' bar.[15]

Geographic dispersion also has implications for the choice of substantive law in a mass tort dispute. Substantive law on many subjects has become increasingly federalized during the past century. But tort law remains overwhelmingly the province of state law. Geographic dispersion of claims across the country raises the prospect that a multiplicity of state substantive laws, not the tort law of any single jurisdiction, will govern the various individual claims that comprise an area of mass tort litigation. An entire branch of legal doctrine — what lawyers describe as "choice-of-law" principles — seeks to address situations where more than one body of substantive law potentially applies to a given dispute. The prospect of having to resolve difficult choice-of-law questions in order to adjudicate mass tort claims on a collective basis contributes to the interest in comprehensive settlement without trial. Fine-grained variations in substantive law rarely have practical significance for the design of settlements, as distinct from trials. Settlement designers need to account only for those features of tort law across the various states with a potential to make for gross, dramatic differences in the value of the claims to be resolved.

Temporal Dispersion

Numerosity and geographic dispersion, by themselves, would make mass tort litigation primarily a problem of procedural design. The challenge would lie simply in the design of processes to address large numbers of claims spread across the country. The temporal dimension of mass torts adds more complications, however.

Mass tort litigation does not await the passing of the latency period between exposure and impairment for all persons who ultimately might suffer harm. Nor does it behoove any mass tort plaintiffs' law firm to wait while its competitors make inroads in a given subject area for litigation. Mass tort lawsuits instead arise at times when one can know the ultimate fate of only some exposed persons: those who, by sheer chance, happen to have become impaired early rather than late. Temporal dispersion means that any resolution of mass tort litigation inherently entails the making of contestable trade-offs between the present and the future. It involves the allocation of both resources and risk between persons who are sick now and those expected to become sick years or decades later. Because no defendant has unlimited resources, generous compensation terms for early claimants threaten to produce inequitable treatment for later ones who are identical, except for the fortuity of when their impairments happen to emerge.

Resource limitations are important not just from the perspective of would-be plaintiffs. The gap in time produced by latent disease is what contributes to the uncertainty of mass tort litigation for defendants and the consequent drag on their business operations. As suggested earlier, the value to be generated by the reduction of this uncertainty supplies the primary inducement for serious peacemaking efforts on defendants' part.

One could attempt to address temporal dispersion simply by changing the content of tort law. The gap in time between exposure and impairment has formed the subject of several ambitious proposals to rethink the concept of injury in tort law. One strand of the scholarly literature seeks to recast injury in terms of exposure itself and the risk of future disease that it entails, rather than the actual emergence of impairment on the part of a particular plaintiff.[16] Risk-based theories of this sort come in various forms — for instance, claims for emotional distress in the present day arising from the risk of disease at a future time and claims for ongoing medical monitoring to detect the emergence of disease, if any. A related line of commentary calls for liability predicated not upon the emergence of disease but, instead, upon the difficulties of proof in tort litigation encountered by exposed persons due to the lack of appropriate precautions — say, proper product testing — by the defendant.[17]

Risk-based theories of injury would smooth the path to comprehensive resolution of mass tort disputes, essentially by conceptualizing away the gap in time between exposure and impairment. Albeit with some difficulty, the law conceivably might ascertain all persons exposed to a given harmful product who have present-day tort claims, reframed in risk-based terms. The enterprise of this book, nonetheless, is not to rehash the long-standing scholarly debate over the merits of risk-based claims in tort.

As I shall elaborate, the process of peacemaking in mass tort litigation has largely bypassed the scholarly debate about risk-based claims. In seeking to set the compensation terms for persons expected to become impaired years or decades in the future, peace designers effectively act *as if* those persons have tort claims today — whatever the content of substantive law might be. The difficult questions for mass torts center not upon whether to encompass persons expected to manifest disease in the future but, instead, how to hew the loyalties of the peace designers to the welfare of such persons. Solutions centered on the reformulation of tort doctrine, in other words, cannot answer the questions of institutional design posed by mass tort settlements. This book accordingly frames those questions as problems of governance — of how to constrain the law reform power that settlement designers inherently wield — not as problems of tort doctrine.

The Plan of the Book

With a working definition of mass torts in hand, I now turn to the plan of the book. Part I — composed of the first three chapters — frames the difficulties posed for the civil justice system by mass torts. Chapter 1 explains the origins of the mass tort phenomenon, tying together the effects of industrialization, changes in tort theory, and changes in the procedures for civil litigation during the twentieth century. Chapter 2 discusses the development of mass tort litigation, linking its progress to the economic underpinnings of mass tort claims from the perspective of lawyers on both plaintiffs' and defendants' sides. The basic notion of developmental phases in mass tort litigation stems from the scholarship of Francis McGovern.[18] Chapter 2 builds on this insight in two new respects.

First, the chapter traces the movement in mass tort litigation from an immature stage to a mature one in which the parameters of the litigation become well established—McGovern's insight—and then goes on to pinpoint the potential for dysfunctions to emerge at the mature stage. Avoidance of these dysfunctions comprises an important and underappreciated impetus for comprehensive settlement. Second, the chapter links this richer conception of mass torts to the challenges posed for settlement design. Matters of timing and structure are intertwined. *When* within the litigation process lawyers attempt to resolve mass tort litigation on a comprehensive basis can affect the *structure* of the likely bargain—in particular, the relationship between the compensation plan those lawyers create and the preexisting tort litigation system.

Chapter 3 considers the transition from the immature to the mature stage. Specifically, the chapter draws a conceptual connection between two developments previously seen as separate by scholars: the Supreme Court's landmark 1993 evidentiary decision in *Daubert v. Merrell Dow Pharmaceuticals, Inc.*[19] and the ongoing controversy over whether certification of nationwide class actions in the mass tort area exerts inappropriate pressure upon defendants to settle. The chapter explains how both of these matters involve efforts to forestall or, sometimes, to precipitate the development of mass tort litigation beyond the immature stage.

Part II analyzes the shift from ongoing litigation—what one might dub as "muddling through" in the tort system—to the design of a comprehensive peace that will entail the processing of future claims under predetermined grids. This part describes the shift in terms of a transition from tort to administration. Chapter 4 starts by observing that the use of gridlike arrangements does not represent as much of a departure as one initially might think. The kinds of comprehensive settlements ultimately attempted in cases like *Amchem* expose and generalize the settlement practices used to resolve large numbers of pending tort claims brought by a common law firm—what have come to be known as aggregate settlements. Chapter 4 goes on to analyze a notable judicial effort to build on the aggregate settlement process through court-administered statistical sampling of pending claims.

Chapter 5 chronicles the next step in the transition from tort to administration: the search for an institutional vehicle to address both pending claims and future ones. Here, the idea is to switch future claims from the conventional tort system to some form of private administrative framework.

As noted earlier, this book is as much a story of failures as of successes, as much of consequences unforeseen as those anticipated. The rise and fall of the mass tort class settlement—the story of *Amchem* and *Ortiz*—bears close attention, as it continues to shape the world of mass torts to the present day.

Part III traces the meandering course of mass tort litigation after *Amchem* and *Ortiz*. The period has been marked by a halting search for some legitimate and practicable alternative for peacemaking. These alternatives have taken many forms: the emergence of legislative measures to switch particular kinds of claims out of the tort system and into an administrative regime (for instance, the compensation legislation enacted after the September 11, 2001, terrorist attacks and proposed legislation for asbestos litigation); the use of contractual arrangements with leading plaintiffs' law firms to generalize the process of aggregate settlement; efforts to salvage some manner of class action treatment; and the use of reorganization proceedings in bankruptcy to make binding trade-offs between present and future claimants.

Chapter 6 discusses the limitations of the two most straightforward alternatives that have emerged: public legislation and private contracts. Chapters 7 and 8 analyze the divergent efforts to salvage the device of the mass tort class action. Specifically, chapter 7 considers both the scholarly case for mandatory class treatment of mass tort claims and a notable, real-world attempt to achieve such treatment for punitive damage claims against the tobacco industry. Chapter 8 covers other efforts to draw upon class settlements as vehicles for peace, whether by expanding or constraining in practical effect the opportunity of persons within the class to opt out of the peace plan and thereby to preserve their opportunity to bring a conventional, individual tort action. Chapter 9 turns to bankruptcy, discussing how the defeat of the class settlements in *Amchem* and *Ortiz* has led to even more problematic efforts to replicate those arrangements through "prepackaged" reorganizations of asbestos defendants under § 524(g) of the Bankruptcy Code.

Chapter 10 addresses a further development that, at first glance, might seem distinct from efforts at peacemaking by private lawyers. The chapter focuses on litigation by the government itself—at the federal, state, or local level—to recover the additional increment of expenditures from the public fisc said to be caused by a defendant industry's wrongful conduct. Government reimbursement actions have occupied a central role in litigation against the tobacco and firearms industries, for example. In fact, reimbursement litigation brought by state governments against the tobacco industry resulted in the largest civil settlement in history. If peace for a mass tort involves a kind of governance, then one initially might think that situating the government as plaintiff might make for an improvement in the law. Chapter 10 explains why this is not so. Government reimbursement lawsuits actually replicate the deficiencies of representation observed in peacemaking through private channels.

Part IV points the law of mass torts in a new direction. Chapter 11 begins by gathering together the lessons learned in the period since *Amchem*, identifying three suppositions that pervade current thinking. The first speaks to the appropriate structure for legal representation—specifically, the notion that the simultaneous representation of persons with present-day disease and persons at risk of future disease poses an inherent conflict of interest. This first supposition is deeply entrenched in the law of class actions, especially after *Amchem*, and has made significant inroads in bankruptcy law as well. The second supposition concerns the parameters for compensation of mass tort lawyers—here, the idea that the fee for a plaintiffs' lawyer should depend exclusively on the outcome that her efforts produce for someone whom the law considers her client. The third supposition pertains to mass tort claimants themselves—in particular, the notion that the legitimacy of any peace arrangement rests chiefly on its respect for the individual autonomy of claimants.

Chapter 11 argues that developments since *Amchem* should lead us to question each of the foregoing suppositions. Rather than avoid the perceived conflict of interest involved in the representation of present and future claimants, the law actually should build upon that conflict to inhibit mass tort plaintiffs' lawyers from embracing self-serving peace terms. The law, in short, should *leverage* conflicts of interest for the protection of mass tort claimants. If anything, such an approach would build upon the leveraging that mass tort plaintiffs' lawyers themselves wield to obtain a place at the bargaining table for any grand peace. They use their capacity to represent present claimants in large numbers as the basis for their assertion of a power to set the compensation terms for future ones.

Rather than think about fee arrangements in strictly lawyer-client terms, the law should approach the subject of fees from the standpoint of what lawyers actually do when they make peace. They assert a power of governance not only with respect to their clients but also over future claimants, many of whom may never become their clients. The compensation terms for peacemakers should track what we want them to do—to design a fair and practicable peace for the future—rather than adhere to the outlines of their present-day lawyer-client relationships. Chapter 11 explains how the law may turn the leveraging by plaintiffs' lawyers into its own source of constraint. The key move consists of tying the contingency fees to be garnered from the representation of present claimants to the real contingency about which we care: whether the peace arrangement ends up affording equitable treatment for future claimants.

These changes, in turn, portend a change in how we think about the legitimacy of peace arrangements in the mass tort area. Rather than attempt to legitimize the peace by reference to claimant autonomy, the law instead should look to how other regimes of administration have garnered legitimacy: by using institutional structure to align the interests of the administrators with those of the people whom they are supposed to serve, not by empowering affected persons to opt out. Chapter 12 links this notion to foundational premises of the modern administrative state in the public sphere.

The legal regime that I envision would not involve the creation of a vast new public bureaucracy. Congress, moreover, need not intervene time and time again to create a public compensation regime for each mass tort of the twenty-first century in the manner of the 9/11 Fund. The law instead may build innovatively upon existing experiments in the administrative sphere — for example, negotiated rulemaking involving the representatives of private parties and public agencies — to effectuate the transition from tort litigation to administration with regard to new mass torts. There is, in short, an important role for government, not as just another mass tort plaintiff but, instead, as the means to enforce a superior alignment of interest between peacemaking lawyers and the claimants — both present and future — over whom they wield governing power.

The specifics of its prescriptions aside, this book seeks to alter the terms of debate about mass torts by counseling a fundamental change of perspective. Mass torts do not present problems primarily of tort doctrine or litigation procedure. They present problems of governance — of representation and administration familiar to the realm of modern government itself. The time has come to address them in precisely those terms.

PART I

THE MASS TORT PROBLEM

CHAPTER I

ORIGINS

W hy did mass torts emerge as a pressing concern in the late twentieth century? Relationships of cause and effect are complex. My objective here is not to present clean lines of causation where none exist. I suggest, instead, that a confluence of economic, intellectual, procedural, and political developments during the twentieth century have contributed to the mass tort phenomenon. These developments have produced an environment in which litigation over mass torts and demands for their comprehensive resolution are virtually inevitable — certainly, are matters that will challenge the legal system for the foreseeable future.

I discuss each development in its own right and do not mean to imply the existence of any single force behind all of them. The connection of each to the emerging shift from tort to administration nonetheless bears notice at the outset. Each development — industrialization, intellectual trends in tort theory, reform in civil procedure, and political dimensions of mass torts — has raised questions about the proper relationship between private and public institutions for the resolution of disputes.

Economics and the Making of Markets

The economic developments behind the mass tort problem are easily stated, their implications less so. Mass torts are the by-products of industrialization, with its systematized processes for production and sale on an unprecedented scale. As in any complex process, there is a potential for error, however inadvertent. The scale of production and sale simply expands the adverse effects of any error. Mass torts stand as an awkward reminder of humanity's imperfect mastery of the world. One strand of tort scholarship

goes a step further, arguing that the demands of mass marketing create incentives for manufacturers to mislead consumers about the risks associated
with their products.[1] Whatever the accuracy of this claim as a general matter, one need not look far in the annals of mass torts to identify instances in
which such a characterization finds ample support.[2]

To focus merely upon the spread of harm through the mass marketing
of products, however, is to miss the full implications of modern markets for
mass tort litigation. The concept of market relationships also sheds light on
the origins of mass torts in a more subtle way — one that turns not upon
the presence of markets but, rather, their absence. For most mass torts,
markets spread harm across large numbers of persons who lack preexisting
relationships with one another. Two observations — one directed to litigation in the present day, the other to events of yesteryear — help to pinpoint
the importance of this nonmarket dimension of mass torts.

Mass torts are not the only example of litigation on a mass scale to arise
from the industrial revolution in the United States. Modern industrial activity takes modern finance. One significant vehicle for capital accumulation today entails the sale of securities — in ordinary parlance, shares of
stock that provide investors with equity interests in the business firm. Like
tort law for product consumers, securities law for investors embraces notions of liability for fraud. And, like doctrines of fraud generally, the federal
cause of action for securities fraud includes reliance by the plaintiff investor
on the fraudulent misstatement or omission by the defendant as one of its
elements.[3] Yet, for all its continuing challenges, securities litigation has not
proven as vexing for the civil litigation system as mass torts. Part of this difference undoubtedly stems from the retrospective nature of the injury in a
typical securities fraud case. The classic form of injury in a securities case
consists of financial loss in the past as a result of the fraud. But another,
underappreciated difference relates to the market concept itself.

The shareholders in a given business firm typically do not have any preexisting relationship with one another. But their status as shareholders in
the securities market, in itself, operates to link one investor with all others.
In broad terms and with economic subtleties suppressed here, the Efficient
Capital Market Hypothesis posits that, in an efficient market, the price of a
security will reflect all investors' evaluations of the publicly available information about the firm.[4] Building on this hypothesis, federal law embraces
the concept of "fraud on the market" in its treatment of the reliance element of securities fraud.[5]

Fraud on the market amounts to a legal presumption that, in the event
of a misstatement or omission, the market price for the security in question

was affected thereby. The implication is that any investor who purchased or sold at the fraudulently induced price did so in reliance on the misstatement or omission.[6] Securities law may presume reliance based upon the preexisting relationship between investors in an efficient capital market, a relationship brought into being by that market itself. Courts are able to handle securities fraud claims on a mass basis, because the mechanism of the share price enables one to allocate compensation—albeit, with some tedious number-crunching—upon proof or settlement of the liability question. Share price in an efficient capital market provides the organizational frame for plaintiff investors who otherwise lack relationships with one another. No comparable organizational frame exists for mass tort plaintiffs, as a further observation underscores.

Developments in mass tort litigation stand in contrast to those from a much earlier crisis of the industrial age at the intersection of tort and administration. In an important book, John Fabian Witt traces the development of modern tort law itself to the phenomenon of rampant workplace injuries in nonlatent forms at the dawn of the twentieth century.[7] Witt situates tort law as merely one of several approaches to workplace accidents. Others, such as cooperative insurance arrangements administered by labor unions, bear more than a passing resemblance to modern efforts at comprehensive solutions in particular areas of mass tort litigation.[8] Both amount to forms of privatized administration. Union-run cooperative insurance could arise as an alternative to tort law, however, only because of the preexisting relationship among industrial workers that the workplace itself provided and that unionization cemented.

With regard to workplace accidents, the story arc that Witt details has been from administration (in the form of union-run cooperative insurance) to tort *and then back* to administration in a more public form (modern public programs for workers' compensation), rather than simply from tort to administration. The trend, in short, has been for public programs to draw upon, modify, and institutionalize the experimental arrangements crafted by the private sphere to address workplace accidents. This book calls for a similar transformation in the resolution of mass torts built upon private experimentation. The major point of difference consists of who the experimenters are and what problems those experimenters introduce.

Entrepreneurial lawyers with business interests of their own create the organizational framework whereby mass tort plaintiffs come to be connected with one another. Unlike their individual clients, plaintiffs' lawyers involved in mass tort litigation gain familiarity with the nature of claims in a given subject area—most importantly, the price at which legal claims of various types may be sold to the defendant through settlement. Lawyers involved in the subject area know, if only roughly, the implicit compensation grid that arises from the presentation of large numbers of claims that exhibit factual patterns.

This is not to deny the role of lawyers in the representation of injured workers on a mass basis, both before and after the implementation of workers' compensation. It is simply to observe that, for mass torts, lawyers often *make* a market where no relationships previously existed among would-be plaintiffs. The legal claims brought in plaintiffs' names are the mass-marketed "product" that entrepreneurial plaintiffs' lawyers sell to defendants in settlements. Mass tort litigation is a matter of dealing with the consequences of industrialization not only in product manufacture but also in litigation itself. Industrialization and its discontents, in short, have given rise to an industrialization of litigation that presents discontents of its own.

Trends in Tort Theory

The rise of mass torts is more than an economic story. It also embraces an intellectual dimension that stems from a reorientation of tort law itself. That mass tort litigation rose to the forefront of concern in the last decades of the twentieth century is no accident of timing when one considers the intellectual history of tort law. Mass marketing extends the reach of modern products beyond simple one-to-one contractual relationships between seller and buyer. By the late twentieth century, tort doctrine had embraced a similar expansion of perspective. The scholarly literature treats in depth the principal manifestation of that expansion: the products liability revolution.[9] Two of its many features created a hospitable legal environment for mass tort litigation. I discuss these features in turn and then position them within a larger shift in tort theory.

First, by the mid-twentieth century, courts had swept away limitations on the scope of tort liability grounded in contractual relationships. In 1966, William Prosser declared "the fall of the citadel of privity."[10] In practical terms, the liability of manufacturers in tort, whether strict or fault-based, no longer would depend upon the existence of direct contractual relationships with product consumers. A consumer now could sue not only the firm that sold her an injurious product but also those—more remote in the chain of production and, in all likelihood, wealthier—who designed and manufactured the product. The fall of privity limitations expanded the sheer numbers and locations of persons positioned to sue the manufacturer of a widely marketed product—hence, the problems of numerosity and geographic dispersion in mass tort litigation.

Second, in roughly the same period, the Restatement (Second) of Torts set forth the notion of strict liability—that is, liability without regard to fault—for any product "in a defective condition unreasonably dangerous to the user or consumer."[11] As its title suggests, the Restatement largely described developments in doctrine already afoot in courts across the country. The concept of product defect embraced not just anomalous errors like the manufacturing defect that led to the Coca-Cola bottle explosion in Gladys Escola's case. The defect concept also extended to systematic errors in the design of a product or inadequacies in the provision of risk information to the ultimate consumer. A design defect or a failure to warn made a product defective; and defectiveness made for strict liability under the Restatement.[12] Indeed, as to product warnings, tort law would go even further, applying a presumption that any given plaintiff would have remained unharmed by avoiding the product entirely, had an adequate warning accompanied it.[13]

The precise theories of tort liability asserted in mass tort litigation vary somewhat from one context to another. But the most common formulation stems directly from the changes wrought by the products liability revolution. Persons exposed to a product sue its ultimate manufacturer. And the crux of their allegation typically is that the manufacturer failed to provide adequate warnings concerning some risk associated with the product.

The fall of privity limitations and the focus on systematic product defects, together, positioned tort litigation to call for wide-ranging inquiries that resemble the regulatory determinations made by administrative agencies. The key question surrounding an alleged product defect asks whether the utility of the product outweighs its risks[14]—what administrative agencies often ask about new products in regulated industries, such as pharmaceuticals. The inquiry into an alleged failure to warn looks, in no small part, to whether the product, in fact, posed an undisclosed risk to consumers—an often complex question of risk assessment similar to those encountered in environmental or toxic substance regulation.

The tendency of modern products liability to resemble regulatory policymaking comes as no surprise. The changes in tort doctrine that facilitated mass tort litigation are much in keeping with a larger reorientation of tort theory over the span of the twentieth century. A comprehensive history of tort theory is not the enterprise of this book. The connection between changes in tort theory and the rise of mass torts as problems of administration, however, remains underappreciated.

Tort theory over the past century encompasses a multiplicity of approaches. Taking a bird's eye view, however, one may say that the dominant theoretical account of tort law today conceives tort litigation as an occasion for regulatory policymaking[15] — as an opportunity for the formulation of tort doctrine to achieve, among other policy objectives, the optimal deterrence of risk-taking by manufacturers and the optimal compensation of product users.[16] This regulatory perspective has a lengthy pedigree, dating at least to Oliver Wendell Holmes's discussion of tort law as a vehicle for social regulation in his 1881 work *The Common Law*. In his 1941 *Handbook on the Law of Torts*, Prosser included an introductory section that described tort law as a matter of "Social Engineering."[17] In 1959, Leon Green similarly touted tort law as a form of "public law in disguise" for the achievement of regulatory ends.[18]

By the early 1970s, scholars such as Richard Posner and Guido Calabresi sought to lend precision to the regulatory force of tort law by subjecting its doctrines to the conceptual rigor of economics. For Posner, tort litigation could subject risky activity to an examination that would compare the marginal cost to manufacturers of additional precautions with the marginal benefits of such precautions in terms of accident avoidance.[19] Here, Posner drew upon a similar formulation of the tort inquiry in a 1947 opinion of the famous federal appellate judge Learned Hand.[20] For Calabresi, litigation could provide the occasion for courts to target liability in tort so as to place the costs of accidents on the "least cost avoider" — that is, the party best positioned to undertake appropriate precautions and to spread their costs throughout society.[21] This notion, too, had roots in judicial writings — here, by California Supreme Court Justice Roger Traynor.[22] Capturing the zeitgeist of the period, one commentator observes that "[a]mbitious judges and scholars viewed tort rules not as a direct reflection of the mores of the citizenry, but as a means of implementing social policy decisions arrived at through the application of philosophical, scientific, and technical knowledge to social problems."[23]

The goal of this abbreviated intellectual history is not to suggest that the regulatory conception of tort law somehow stands unchallenged. The major rift in tort theory in recent decades has pitted the intellectual heirs of Holmes, Posner, and Calabresi against a competing camp of scholars. This rival camp insists upon analysis of tort law not primarily in light of the regulatory ends it might pursue but, instead, in rights-based terms, as a vehicle for the achievement of corrective justice between the particular parties to the lawsuit.[24]

The prevailing account of tort law in regulatory terms creates a conceptual opening—at the very least, a comfortable receptiveness—for mass tort litigation. All of this is not to suggest that mass tort claimants or their lawyers somehow read Holmes, Posner, and Calabresi and then suddenly decided to sue en masse. It is simply to point out that the rise of mass tort litigation is in keeping with larger intellectual trends that conceive tort law itself as an adjunct or complement to regulation by administrative agencies. If tort law is regulatory policymaking for an industrialized world, then it is all the better to turn the attentions of that body of law to the most sweeping sorts of problems generated by industrialization. On this account, the mass nature of mass torts merely exposes to view the operation of tort law as a vehicle for social engineering.

The Transformation of Civil Procedure

The potential for widespread injury in an industrial economy and the framing of tort law in regulatory terms explain the emergence of mass torts only in part. The transformation of civil procedure in the late twentieth century forms another feature of the landscape. This, too, is a multifaceted story. Three aspects stand out, however: the gearing of civil procedure generally toward settlement rather than trial, the facilitation of representative litigation, and the effects of these and other procedural changes on litigation finance. I introduce briefly these three features and then turn to their collective contribution to the mass tort phenomenon.

First, the dominant trend in modern civil procedure has been to facilitate the resolution of civil litigation across the board by way of settlement.[25] One may situate many changes in civil procedure during the twentieth century within this broad theme: for example, the emergence of pretrial conferences as occasions for judges to nudge the parties toward settlement.[26] Some commentators doubt the wisdom of designing civil procedure to induce settlement,[27] but the existence of the trend in that direction appears beyond dispute. Empirical research confirms the impression that civil trial "is a disease, not generally fatal, but serious enough to be avoided at any reasonable cost."[28] The transformation of civil procedure into a framework primarily for settlement has changed the role of judges, turning them from neutral umpires at trial to "managerial" figures who oversee deals and administer their implementation over time.[29] Indeed, judges themselves have an interest in settlement as a means of easing pressure on crowded court dockets.

Second, beginning in the 1960s, amendments to the Federal Rules of Civil Procedure expanded dramatically the vehicles for civil litigation on a mass basis. The most salient development among several — one that, by the 1990s, would find itself unexpectedly on a collision course with tort law — consists of the drafting of Rule 23 along its current lines in 1966.[30] The rule expanded the grounds for certification of civil litigation to proceed on a classwide basis. This is not to say that mass torts necessarily start as class actions. Nor is it to imply that class actions were unknown to civil litigation prior to the 1966 amendments. The intellectual origins of the modern class action date back centuries.[31] Rule 23 nonetheless broke new ground by recognizing the possibility of class treatment where "questions of law or fact common to the members of the class predominate over any questions affecting only individual members" and where a class action would be "superior to other available methods for the fair and efficient adjudication of the controversy."[32] The upshot is that courts could certify a class action not just in situations of compelling circumstance — say, to facilitate the orderly disposition of a limited fund for recovery[33] — but also when desirable on grounds of fairness and efficiency, relative to the other procedural tools at hand.

The ripples from the adoption of Rule 23 in 1966 remain a topic of considerable controversy in procedural scholarship today. But there is no dispute about one bedrock point: The drafters of Rule 23 in its modern form did not aspire to facilitate, much less to foment, tort litigation. Their gaze extended principally to the kinds of civil rights, institutional reform, and antitrust matters that had given rise to procedural difficulties in the surrounding time period.[34] Insofar as the rule drafters took cognizance of tort matters, they did so by cautioning, in passing, that a "'mass accident' resulting in injuries to numerous person is ordinarily not appropriate for a class action because of the likelihood that significant questions, not only of damages but of liability and defenses to liability, would be present, affecting individuals in different ways."[35] That the twain of mass torts and the modern class action rule should meet in the Supreme Court by the late 1990s thus stands as the unexpected outgrowth of procedural innovation.

Third, procedural changes for civil litigation shaped law practice. As in business generally, new opportunities invite investment and risk taking. The opportunities created by procedural reform in the twentieth century would have the same effect. In what Stephen Yeazell dubs the "refinancing" of civil litigation, the practicing bar on the plaintiffs' side would become both better capitalized and more specialized.[36] Improved capitalization gave plaintiffs' law firms the financial wherewithal to undertake the kinds of lengthy, expensive discovery campaigns permitted by the rules of civil procedure and essential as a strategic matter in litigation against large-scale corporate defendants.[37] The structure of plaintiffs' law firms changed as well. They tended not to be solo practitioners with local clients across many substantive areas of litigation. They more often consisted of law firms with a national orientation and with a specialization in particular subject matter.

One must take care when pointing to the confluence of a prosettlement ethos, expanded vehicles for representative litigation, and the refinancing of civil litigation as explanations for mass tort litigation. Procedural transformation did not create the material conditions that led to mass torts. But it does explain why a rich account of mass torts must be as much about settlement as it is about litigation in a literal sense. The transformation of civil procedure in the twentieth century brought into being a new legal environment, one in which sophisticated lawyers on both sides of mass tort disputes could begin to conceptualize the endgame of their clashes in terms of grand settlements on an aggregate basis. The class action reveals much in this regard, not because it dominates the mass tort landscape today but, instead, because it usefully frames the questions for the future in terms of a shift from tort to administration.

By the terms that begin Rule 23, the class action device enables "[o]ne or more members of a class" to sue "as representative parties on behalf of all."[38] The nature of the class action as a vehicle for representative litigation has significant business implications for lawyers. For a plaintiffs' law firm, the class action raises the possibility of representing large numbers of persons as a formal matter but not having to expend resources to meet them in person or to secure their agreement to representation on a conventional lawyer-client basis. In terms of any one firm's relationship with its competitors, moreover, the class action offers the further prospect of keeping those competitors from reaping financial rewards — of using civil procedure as a vehicle to establish a kind of client relationship en masse with the persons affected by a given mass tort.

For the defense side, the class action would offer a tantalizing prospect of a different sort, one that defense lawyers would come to recognize decades after the 1966 amendments. The court-issued judgment in a class action — in particular, a judgment approving a class settlement[39] — might serve as the means to give binding force to a comprehensive settlement in a given area of mass tort litigation. With some technicalities suppressed for the moment, this binding force would derive from another principle of civil procedure — labeled today as "claim preclusion" or, earlier, as the Latin *res judicata* — that prevents the parties to a given judgment from relitigating claims that were, or might have been, raised in the underlying litigation.[40]

The desire for peace on the defense side would dovetail with the attractiveness of the class action on the plaintiffs' side as a technique of interfirm competition.

Politics and Litigation

Economics, intellectual history, and procedure still leave untouched one final point of context. The rise of mass tort litigation in the last decades of the twentieth century corresponded in time with two developments in the political realm: the dwindling of the New Deal faith in government as a source of bold solutions to social problems and the growing resistance of the public to taxation as a means to fund new government initiatives. Upon entering office in 1981, President Ronald Reagan famously declared that "[g]overnment is not the solution to our problem; government is the problem."[41] Less than two decades later, President Bill Clinton observed that "[t]he era of big Government is over."[42] Notwithstanding their considerable policy differences, both the Reagan and the Clinton administrations embraced measures that called for close examination of the costs and benefits of regulatory initiatives.[43] Ambitious regulatory programs, in short, would be harder to obtain through the ordinary channels of public legislation and administrative regulation.

In such an environment, tort litigation — conceived as regulation in disguise and brought in a procedural system geared to settlement — emerged as an alternative means to address the human costs of risk-taking by product manufacturers. Some of the examples discussed in subsequent chapters — litigation over asbestos and the diet drug combination fen-phen, for instance — arise from arguable shortcomings in the regulatory processes of government. Still other examples — lawsuits over tobacco and firearms — involve conscious efforts to precipitate through the settlement of litigation major changes in the marketing of products that ordinary political channels had shown little inclination to impose by way of regulation.

The relationship of law and politics in mass tort litigation is complex. The overarching point, for now, remains that mass tort litigation could emerge as a rival regime for law reform, in part, because government itself had effectively ceded a portion of that terrain by the later decades of the twentieth century.[44] Mass torts could present a problem of governance only because government had — for better or worse — become more limited in its own ambitions.

CHAPTER II

THE DEVELOPMENT
OF A MASS TORT

Mass torts do not start as occasions for the reform of people's legal rights in a manner to rival public legislation. Efforts to fashion a comprehensive peace, instead, grow out of the way in which mass tort litigation often develops. At the outset, it bears emphasis that a particular developmental pattern is not necessary for the emergence of mass tort litigation. There is no single mold here, only the observation that mass tort litigation frequently comes by way of stages that one may identify. Existing scholarship recognizes these stages, but their full implications remain relatively unexplored.[1] This chapter sets forth the major stages, connecting them to the economic underpinnings of mass tort lawsuits and the challenges of settlement design. Those subjects, in turn, implicate the strategies and objectives of mass tort lawyers on both plaintiffs' and defendants' sides.

Three themes permeate the discussion in this chapter. First, the emergence of mass tort litigation relates closely to the defining features of mass torts themselves and the elements of a tort cause of action. Each element has financial implications for the development of a viable subject area for mass tort litigation.

Second, the stages often exhibited by mass tort litigation influence settlement design. The time when one pursues a comprehensive solution affects dramatically the content of the peace terms that the contending sides will find palatable. In general, the later one proceeds in the development of mass tort litigation, the less attractive defendants will find solutions that posit some manner of continued litigation in the tort system and the more they will seek measures to replace tort litigation with some privatized administrative system. As I shall explain, this phenomenon is not merely the by-product of negotiation strategy; it also stems from the conception of meritorious claims in the law of torts.

Third, the different stages of mass tort litigation form a continuum over time; they do not come in discrete, black-and-white categories. Gray areas exist between the stages and comprise focal points for contention. The discussion here sets the stage for the treatment of these gray areas in the chapter that follows.

Briefly summarized, mass tort litigation frequently proceeds from an immature stage to a mature stage and, thereafter, to what one might call a peacemaking stage, where efforts focus on the crafting of a comprehensive settlement. Progress is by no means inevitable. To the contrary, the objective of defendants throughout remains to block the advance of the litigation from one stage to the next. In practical terms, the differences between the various stages represent the playing out of the economic investment made by plaintiffs' law firms in the development of the litigation. A treatment of this economic dimension introduces the analysis. It also provides the necessary background for later analysis of the relationship between the progress of mass tort litigation and settlement design.

The Immature Stage and the
Economics of Mass Tort Litigation

Contingency fees have long served as the underwriting device on the plaintiffs' side for tort litigation as a whole, and mass torts are no exception. The effect of the contingency fee is to give the lawyer a financial stake in the lawsuit—not only a share of any recovery that might result but also, as its antecedent, the incentive to invest in the development of the lawsuit in the first place.[2] I use the phrase "plaintiffs' law firm" and similar terminology to describe law firms in the business of representing plaintiffs with regard to personal injuries. Ethical limitations on the representation of multiple clients with conflicting interests tend to keep any given law firm predominantly on one side or the other of the plaintiff-defendant divide in tort litigation.[3]

For a tort law practice centered on idiosyncratic events, investments in the development of any given lawsuit will not transfer extensively to others, except at a high level of generality. A practice focused on automobile accidents, for instance, does give rise to an expertise in the sorts of physical injuries likely to result and the kinds of insurance policies likely to be implicated for defendants. Practice along these lines remains a viable business model, as countless law firms on the plaintiffs' side continue to demonstrate. The investment outlook differs dramatically for mass torts, however.

At the level of doctrine, successful tort litigation of any sort depends on a credible threat to precipitate favorable determinations as to each of the elements of a tort cause of action: duty, breach, causation, and damages. These elements organize the lawyer's investment strategy. Development of a credible threat to precipitate findings as to each element comprises a valuable business asset. The numerosity and factual patterns that define mass torts mean that assets developed for purposes of one client's lawsuit often will be transferable, with little or no modification, to other lawsuits involving the same subject matter.

A distinction between what one might label "generic assets" and "specific assets" forms the backdrop for the development of mass tort litigation. Generic assets come in many forms, but their defining characteristic remains their high degree of transferability from one case to many others. Generic assets may concern legal or factual matters. In legal terms, a plaintiffs' law firm must advance a credible threat to garner favorable judicial resolution of any open questions of law. Commentators trace the origins of litigation over asbestos on a mass scale, for example, to successful efforts in the early 1970s to establish a legal duty on the part of asbestos product manufacturers—not just companies in charge of industrial workplaces—to warn workers of the health hazards associated with asbestos exposure.[4] Some areas of mass tort litigation today—say, government suits against the firearms industry on a theory of public nuisance—seek new applications or extensions of tort principles over which there remains serious dispute.[5] Efforts to achieve judicial recognition for these applications or extensions, at a minimum, entail brainstorming by a plaintiffs' law firm, perhaps assisted by sympathetic scholars within the legal academy.

Even when the legal underpinnings for the litigation are beyond question, a plaintiffs' law firm also must make a credible threat to prove the applicable tort elements as a factual matter. Development of this threat entails an elaborate process of historical reconstruction. To make out liability for failure to warn—a typical ground for mass tort litigation—a plaintiffs' law firm will need to ascertain the progress of medical knowledge about the risk at issue in order to show that the defendant breached its duty to warn. In addition, the firm will need to undertake lengthy civil discovery to find sources of information—corporate documents and employees, past and present—from which to construct a narrative of the defendant's business decisions concerning the product.

The causation element also may demand considerable investment. The

firm must credibly threaten to precipitate findings of both "general causation" and "specific causation." General causation entails a showing that
the product in question is capable of causing a particular disease in humans
generally. Specific causation calls for a demonstration that the product
caused the particular plaintiff's individual case of the disease.[6] The next
chapter shall return to the causation element when discussing movement
between the stages of mass tort litigation. For now, causation bears attention as yet another drain upon the investment resources of a plaintiffs' law
firm. A credible threat to show both general and specific causation with
regard to latent disease will entail the retention of experts versed in toxicol-
ogy—indeed, may involve the development of research on the causation
element in a manner not already addressed in the available scientific literature.

The development of generic assets takes money. Experts generally do
not work for free; indeed, some may regard consultation as a major source
of outside income. And law firm associates or paralegals tasked with the
heavy lifting of civil discovery must be paid to do so. The use of contingency fee arrangements means that a plaintiffs' law firm will see no financial return from its investment until the first plaintiff obtains some manner
of recovery. A plaintiffs' law firm, in short, must incur considerable fixed
costs to develop generic assets long before it can threaten credibly to precipitate a favorable verdict or settlement in a single case. To shoulder these
costs, multiple plaintiffs' law firms might enter into arrangements to share
the burden of developing a given area of litigation at the immature stage.
Indeed, firms might wish to form such arrangements early on, for fear that
they otherwise might lose control over at least some of the information they
develop—for instance, through court documents that are open as a matter of public record and, hence, potentially accessible to competitor firms
within the plaintiffs' bar. For that matter, even in the absence of previous
arrangements, the pioneering law firms literally might package and sell—
for a fee, of course—a collection of pertinent documents, sample legal papers, and other useful materials, touting the collection as a virtual "trial in
a box" for a given area of mass tort litigation.[7]

The immature stage marks the period for exploration of the legal and
factual questions surrounding the merits of the litigation. The ultimate
success of the litigation remains fraught with uncertainty, and lawyers on
both sides will attempt to resolve that uncertainty in the direction desired
by their respective clients. Some individual lawsuits typically will proceed
through full-scale trials to test the quality of proof gathered on the plaintiffs' side and to gauge the reactions of jurors to the allegations presented.

Defendants, in particular, will be on the lookout for arguments with the potential to knock out the entire subject area of litigation — a lack of general causation as a factual matter or the absence of some other necessary element as a matter of law.

The choice of rhetoric here — the emphasis on "credible threats" to precipitate findings of liability and the distinction between proof on the merits and the "reactions" of jurors — is not accidental. Investment by a plaintiffs' law firm will not necessarily track the substantive merits of the litigation, strictly defined. The firm, of course, would prefer to assemble irrefutable proof of liability under legal theories well grounded in existing doctrine. The investment objective nonetheless remains to develop a credible threat to prevail at trial — an outcome correlated with substantive merit, but only imperfectly. In fact, the next chapter discusses developments outside the realm of tort law that serve as brakes — albeit, highly imperfect ones — upon movement beyond the immature stage for reasons unrelated to the merits of the litigation.

The transition to the mature litigation stage comes only when the threat to prevail is such that defendants face a substantial probability of loss in the event of trial. The usual way to establish the credibility of this threat, not surprisingly, is through actual plaintiff victories in some early cases. As Francis McGovern defines the term, mature mass torts consist of those "where there has been full and complete discovery, multiple jury verdicts, and a persistent vitality in the plaintiffs' contentions," such that "little or no new evidence will be developed" and "significant appellate review of any novel legal issues has been concluded."[8] All of this is not to say that every plaintiff at the mature stage necessarily has a winning claim. As I discuss later in this chapter, defendants at the mature stage may well face a mixture of cases with varying merit as a matter of prevailing tort doctrine. The important point is that, by the mature stage, defendants will no longer have ways to knock out the entire area of litigation.

The transition to the mature litigation stage alters the strategies pursued by lawyers on both sides. Before turning to those changes in strategy, however, a brief word is in order about the connection between the litigation stages sketched here and the sheer number of claims put forward in the tort system. Awareness of the way in which mass torts often develop has come to affect when plaintiffs' lawyers engage in significant client recruitment efforts. I do not mean to suggest that plaintiffs' lawyers somehow study the scholarly literature on mass tort litigation and alter their behavior accordingly. To the contrary, theory follows practice here, not vice versa. Still, awareness of the developmental process — if only in a rough intuitive sense—has prompted changes in the timing of client recruitment in the mass tort setting.

Client Recruitment

In early examples of mass tort litigation, the move from the immature to the mature stage corresponded with a massive influx of similar claims in the tort system. Asbestos lawsuits in the 1970s established the existence of a legal duty running from product manufacturers to industrial workers. With defendant manufacturers unable to fend off all liability to workers based on the duty element, asbestos lawsuits would enter the tort system in large numbers by the 1980s. I start by explaining the reasons for this influx and then turn to what lawyers on the plaintiffs' side have come to learn from it. To anticipate the argument that follows: The transition to the mature stage in early examples of mass torts, such as the asbestos litigation, corresponded with a surge in the sheer number of claims. Having seen this process at work, plaintiffs' lawyers often engage in substantial client recruitment even earlier in the developmental process. They might not await the completion of the immature stage but, rather, might combine the recruitment of clients in large numbers with efforts to establish a credible threat to prevail at trial.

The relationship between generic and specific assets on the plaintiffs' side of mass tort litigation made it especially likely that early successes in the asbestos litigation would prompt an influx of similar claims. Development of evidence concerning general causation for purposes of one case means that, if it or others like it generate positive returns, a plaintiffs' law firm readily can redeploy that same evidence in subsequent cases. So, too, with other generic assets that a plaintiffs' law firm has assembled, at considerable fixed cost, through discovery at the immature stage. Having invested in the development of a valuable array of generic assets, a plaintiffs' law firm will have every reason to search for the one thing that stands between it and the maximizing of its returns from that investment: additional clients. In economic terms, the goal is to spread the fixed costs of generic assets over ever more units and, in so doing, to achieve economies of scale.[9]

Client recruitment is not costless. A plaintiffs' law firm nonetheless may pursue a variety of strategies to that end. One involves the development of franchiselike relationships. The firms that have succeeded in developing generic assets at the immature stage might join forces with other firms within the plaintiffs' bar positioned to identify and to recruit clients within their respective geographic spheres. Developments at the mature stage of the asbestos litigation illustrate this approach. Through lengthy civil discovery, the firms that pioneered the asbestos litigation succeeded in assembling devastating evidence against the defendant manufacturers that led, in turn, to early victories at trial. Those firms then developed ties with other plaintiffs' law firms across the country able to produce streams of new asbestos clients. The pioneering firms would handle proof of liability on the part of defendant companies; the firms supplying new clients would handle proof of the particular plaintiffs' injuries; and the two firms would share the fees from successful claims.[10] This phenomenon is much in keeping with the industrialization of litigation discussed in the preceding chapter. The various firms effectively engage in specialization, much like one firm might supply the engine for a car while another supplies the metal frame. The use of franchiselike arrangements by pioneering firms in the asbestos litigation proved to be ingenious. The arrangements effectively enabled those firms to spread the fixed costs of their generic assets and to place upon their franchisees much of the marginal cost for development of specific assets in the form of new clients.

Yet another means for coordination across multiple plaintiffs' law firms arises from the efforts of the litigation system itself to bring some degree of order to the handling of similar claims in large numbers. Within the federal court system, the Judicial Panel on Multidistrict Litigation (MDL Panel) has authority to consolidate related lawsuits pending in federal courts across the country for purposes of pretrial proceedings.[11] As chapter 11 shall discuss, the MDL Panel might form a useful means for improved coordination of tort and administrative institutions with regard to mass torts. In its current form, pretrial consolidation of pending federal lawsuits by the MDL Panel typically results in the appointment — often, the judicial rubber-stamping — of a steering committee for the consolidated proceedings composed of the leading plaintiffs' law firms involved.[12] Participation in such a steering committee may serve as the springboard for coordination by the various firms in other regards.

Aside from the efforts of lawyers, intermediaries might have reasons of their own to assist in the identification and recruitment of new clients. One practice at the mature stage of the asbestos litigation, for instance, consists of coordination between labor unions and plaintiffs' law firms to conduct mass medical screenings at industrial workplaces, essentially as a prelude to referrals of workers to those firms for purposes of litigation.[13] These mass screenings have garnered considerable controversy in the asbestos litigation, but the point for now remains simply that they are yet another form of client recruitment.

These strategies, together, amount to what Howard Erichson dubs the "informal aggregation" of claims.[14] Coordination among firms within the plaintiffs' bar inherently entails a sharing of the wealth from further litigation. But a plaintiffs' law firm that has achieved success at the immature stage might not necessarily wish to share. Such a firm instead might attempt to use formal mechanisms of aggregation as a substitute for informal aggregation and the wealth sharing likely to accompany it. Client recruitment, in short, might not necessarily call for coordination with other lawyers, much less the meeting of new clients in the flesh. It instead might involve formal aggregation by way of the certification of a class action, whereby all would-be plaintiffs would become the clients of the firm by operation of procedural rule.

Thus far, I have couched the connection between the developmental process and the sheer number of claims in terms of early examples of mass torts, such as the asbestos litigation. There, early lawsuits at the immature stage established the credibility of the litigation, and claims in large numbers followed at the mature stage. The influx of claims, however, need not correspond with the change in litigation stage. The dividing line between the stages stems from the credibility of plaintiffs' threats to prevail at trial, not from the raw numbers of pending cases. A rough awareness of the litigation process on the part of plaintiffs' lawyers might well lead to significant client recruitment efforts even at the immature stage. In effect, plaintiffs' law firms might seek simultaneously to establish a credible litigation threat and to position themselves to take a leading role in any comprehensive peace negotiation that may ensue, once the threat is demonstrated.

Put less formally, the point is that plaintiffs' firms may organize their conduct at the immature stage with an eye to what may transpire at later stages. In ongoing litigation over the prescription pain reliever Vioxx, for example, plaintiffs' law firms across the country filed thousands of lawsuits even before the first Vioxx case had gone to trial.[15] Multiple plaintiffs' law firms, moreover, might engage in a division of labor as part of an effort to establish a credible threat to prevail in the first place, not as its outgrowth. A pooling of efforts at the outset has the advantage of adding to the resources the joint enterprise can devote to lawsuits at the immature stage.

The Mature Stage and the Transformation of Strategy

The mature litigation stage marks a transformation in the strategies of lawyers on both sides. When litigation at the immature stage has established a substantial probability of success for plaintiffs in the event of trial and when large numbers of similar claims have entered the tort system, defendants have little reason to seek trials as test vehicles. They, instead, would prefer to delay.

To cast defendants' stance as a strategy of delay is not to impugn its grounding in the law. Tort law offers no basis to treat defendants any better at the mature stage due simply to the sheer number of claims pending against them, but neither does tort law supply a reason to treat them any worse. One role of tort law—some say, its defining feature[16]—is to provide an avenue by which an aggrieved person may seek redress for mistreatment at the hands of another by invoking the coercive power of the civil justice system. The use of this avenue for private redress remains contingent upon satisfaction of the elements of tort liability. The openness of the tort system—the freedom of the plaintiff and her lawyer to initiate suit without first seeking the government's permission, for example—exists only with corresponding constraints. Tort doctrine serves as a limitation on the coercive power that litigation stands to exert on the defendant to defend itself and, potentially, to pay a judgment for damages. Most importantly, for present purposes, tort law requires proof of a causal link between the product of a particular defendant and the injury suffered by a particular plaintiff before the latter may compel the defendant to pay damages.[17] At the mature litigation stage, defendants thus may insist strictly upon such proof in each individual case. And, in fact, many did just that in the asbestos litigation by "repeatedly contest[ing] . . . every contestable issue involving the same products, the same warnings, and the same conduct."[18]

The law of civil procedure has long constrained relitigation through doctrines labeled today as "claim preclusion" and "issue preclusion." But, even in their modern form, preclusion principles afford only modest grounds on which a plaintiff might prevent the defendant from revisiting matters addressed in earlier lawsuits. Those earlier suits necessarily involved different plaintiffs whose circumstances—at least the defendant would speculate—might differ.[19] Claim preclusion operates only between the particular parties to the earlier judgment said to have preclusive effect,[20] and issue preclusion depends on the existence of the same factual issue in both the current lawsuit and the previous one.[21]

The incentives of plaintiffs' law firms and defendants at the mature stage make for a devastating combination for the civil litigation system. The success of early plaintiffs continues to attract large numbers of similar claims into the tort system. But defendants have no reason to prefer prompt payment over the delay that comes with insistence on individualized proof of liability in each case. In the face of defendants' intransigence, mass tort plaintiffs' lawyers have only one real bargaining chip, but it is a big one: their power to take cases to trial.[22] Trial dates are scarce resources. Their availability is limited by the capacity of the judicial system. But when they do approach, trial dates create conditions ripe for settlement — typically, in the form of aggregate settlements whereby the defendant resolves multiple pending cases represented by the same plaintiffs' law firm. These aggregate settlements may take a variety of forms.[23] One common form consists of a lump-sum payment by the defendant, with the plaintiffs' law firm then responsible for the division of that sum among its individual clients.

The trial queue is not a constraint that lies entirely outside the control of mass tort plaintiffs' law firms. Rather, plaintiffs' lawyers can increase the likelihood that trial dates will arise for the cases they represent by increasing the sheer number of cases they have pending on court dockets. The gambit is to increase the percentage of one's cases within the overall run of pending civil lawsuits and, thereby, to increase the likelihood of receiving an available trial date. In fact, empirical research documents precisely such a rise in the percentage of asbestos cases among all new federal civil cases filed during the 1980s.[24]

For plaintiffs' lawyers, the response to a defense strategy of delay is more cases; but, for defendants, the response to more cases is still more incentive to delay. The resulting stalemate, if allowed to fester, has the potential to lead to dysfunctions of its own. This is not to suggest that mass torts typically proceed so far in the litigation cycle that these dysfunctions actually emerge. To the contrary, lawyers may well undertake efforts at comprehensive settlement beforehand. A clear picture of the dysfunctions possible at the mature stage nonetheless is essential to an understanding of settlement design. Settlement efforts of all sorts take place in the shadow of expectations about what might happen if litigation should continue.

The Potential for Dysfunctions at the Mature Stage

When mature mass tort litigation is allowed to continue, the resolution of claims in the tort system has the potential to become dysfunctional. Simply put, the claims of exposed but presently unimpaired persons can start to exhibit settlement values out of line with current tort doctrine. At the outset, it bears emphasis that my point here is not one about legal technicalities. Any legal system that does not implement accurately the standards of applicable substantive law hardly would be a system worthy of applause. But there is a human cost here that goes beyond finicky insistence upon doctrine. The devotion of resources at a given time to pay exposed but presently unimpaired persons has the potential to endanger the availability of resources to pay persons who manifest severe forms of disease at later times. Paying people who are not sick now is problematic — whatever the content of tort doctrine — for it can endanger the capacity also to pay people who become sick later.

As I shall explain, the most vivid illustration of the foregoing phenomenon consists of developments in the asbestos litigation. When invoking any particular area of mass tort litigation for purposes of illustration, one must take care to avoid overgeneralization.[25] Features of the asbestos litigation undoubtedly lend to that example a scale and persistence that mass torts of the twenty-first century are unlikely to replicate. The sheer breadth of exposure to asbestos explains much of the potential for ongoing streams of claims — at least, if one includes exposures at low concentrations on an incidental basis, such as are thought widespread in the United States.[26] One nonetheless can identify aspects of the asbestos experience that stem from the features that define a mass tort and thus carry a potential for replication, if not necessarily to quite the same "elephantine" proportions.[27]

The significance of unimpaired persons at the mature stage stems, in part, from the nature of latent disease. If one were to play out in full the relevant latency periods, the kinds of products that are the subject of mass tort litigation stand to impair only a modest fraction of the persons exposed to them. To take one stark example, consider the well-established causal link between cigarette smoking and lung cancer — a matter widely thought to present a public health issue of major proportions. Smoking ultimately causes lung cancer in only about 5 to 10 percent of smokers, a fact obscured by the usual presentation of risk information in terms of the additional lung cancer risk faced by smokers above that of nonsmokers.[28] Now add a latency period into the picture. The result is that the fraction of persons who actually are impaired at a given stage of mass tort litigation declines still further. The upshot for the mature litigation stage is this: Plaintiffs' lawyers who wish to bring forward large numbers of claims will run up relatively quickly against a hard medical fact. Persons with present-day impairments at any given time are likely to be significantly smaller in number than the persons exposed to the relevant product or substance who are presently unimpaired. Raw numbers, in short, push the search for additional clients in the direction of exposed but presently unimpaired persons.

A second consideration pushes plaintiffs' law firms in the same direction. Once mass tort litigation enters the mature stage, plaintiffs' lawyers understandably might anticipate an endgame to the litigation as a whole through reorganization of the defendant company under the Bankruptcy Code, not through settlement within the tort system. The asbestos litigation has led to a spate of bankruptcies in recent years,[29] but the interplay between bankruptcy and mass tort litigation is far from unique to the asbestos example. Litigation over the Dalkon Shield contraceptive device and over silicone gel breast implants wound its way through bankruptcy as well.

The bankruptcy justification for claim filings on behalf of presently unimpaired persons turns on one simple point. As a condition for approval of a reorganization plan, the Bankruptcy Code calls for an affirmative vote by at least one-half of those who hold two-thirds of the claims, by dollar amount, within each category of creditors.[30] The upshot is that control of one-third of the pending claims in dollar terms will confer upon a mass tort plaintiffs' law firm an effective veto power over any reorganization plan. Chapter 9 will discuss in greater depth the problems that stem from the voting structure in bankruptcy. For now, the point is simply that the possibility of bankruptcy will contribute to the impetus for claim filing in large numbers. Underlying medical facts then direct the attention of plaintiffs' lawyers to unimpaired persons.

Two further observations help to frame the dysfunctions possible in mature mass tort litigation. The first concerns the current conception of a cognizable injury as a matter of tort law. The second deals with advances in technology that enable modern medicine to detect minute changes in the body that nonetheless fall short of actual impairment—that do not, in other words, produce some objectively verifiable diminution in bodily function.

Scholars have long debated whether people who lack a present-day impairment but who are at an elevated risk of future disease have a cognizable injury in tort—in practical terms, whether they can bring a tort suit now or must wait until some manner of impairment, if any, actually emerges. In chapter 6, I will have more to say about this debate—in particular, how developments in mass tort litigation have largely bypassed the scholarly disagreement about what should count as a cognizable injury in tort. For now, it suffices to note that the resolution of claims on the part of unimpaired claimants has the potential to become dysfunctional by reference to existing tort doctrine.

Tort law in its present form is highly ambivalent, at best, toward the claims of exposed but unimpaired persons. These claims can come in different varieties. The ones of greatest significance here consist of claims for the emotional distress associated with the increased risk of future disease—colloquially, fear-of-cancer claims—and claims for medical monitoring to detect and mitigate the effects of future disease, if any should emerge.[31]

Conveniently enough, the Supreme Court in recent years has had occasion to canvass the prevailing common law in the United States concerning these kinds of risk-based claims.

The setting for the Court's discussion of current tort doctrine has not been tort cases proper but rather — one step removed — litigation under the Federal Employers' Liability Act (FELA). This statute affords compensation for workplace injuries in the railroad industry, among others. The relevant statutory language entitles workers to compensation for any "injury" resulting from the negligence of their employers.[32] When interpreting the reference to "injury," the Court has accorded "great weight" to the content of prevailing common law.[33]

In its 1997 decision in *Metro-North Commuter Railroad Co. v. Buckley*, the Court observed that "[c]ommon-law courts do permit a plaintiff who suffers from a disease to recover for related negligently caused emotional distress," and that "some courts permit a plaintiff who exhibits a physical symptom of exposure to recover." But, the Court emphasized, the vast majority of jurisdictions "deny recovery [for emotional distress] to those who . . . are disease and symptom free."[34] As to medical monitoring, the Court noted that even those jurisdictions that recognize claims of that sort still "do not endorse a full-blown, traditional tort cause of action for lump-sum damages." Rather, they "have suggested, or imposed, special limitations on that remedy," such as the use of a court-supervised fund for the medical monitoring regimen.[35] Relying heavily on these features of common law, the *Metro-North* Court ultimately denied FELA compensation to workers "negligently exposed to a carcinogen (here, asbestos) but without symptoms of any disease."[36]

It is no coincidence that workplace exposure to asbestos should have prompted the Court's exploration of risk-based claims under FELA. In the asbestos litigation, the drive for client recruitment dovetailed with the sophistication of modern medical science. By the early 1990s, commentators estimated that "up to one-half of asbestos claims" were being brought on behalf of persons with "little or no physical impairment," and that "[m]any of these claims produce[d] substantial payments (and substantial costs) even though the individual litigants will never become impaired."[37] By 2005, research by the RAND Institute for Civil Justice lent empirical support to these suggestions, documenting that "a large and growing proportion of the [asbestos] claims entering the system in recent years was submitted by individuals who had not at the time of the claim filing suffered an injury that had as yet affected their ability to perform the activities of daily living" — in short, who are unimpaired.[38]

Scientists have long associated extended exposure to asbestos in many industrial workplaces during much of the twentieth century with a variety of malignant and nonmalignant diseases.[39] The sophistication of medical science, however, extends beyond the detection of actual disease. Many persons who remain unimpaired nonetheless exhibit observable "markers of prior asbestos exposure" in their bodies consisting of pleural thickening, a condition in the lung that does not independently enhance the progression of asbestos-related disease and may well not impair the functions of the lung.[40]

Revisiting the treatment of asbestos-exposed workers under FELA in its 2003 decision in *Norfolk & Western Railway Co. v. Ayers*, the Supreme Court held FELA compensation to be available for workers diagnosed with asbestosis, a disease the Court described as accompanied by "symptoms includ[ing] shortness of breath, coughing, and fatigue"[41] that amount to "real physical harm."[42] But the Court also took care to note that FELA compensation is not available to asbestos-exposed workers with detectable medical conditions in their lungs — such as pleural thickening — that nevertheless do not cause workers to "suffe[r] current pain."[43] Such persons, in practical terms, are equivalent to those merely exposed to asbestos and, as such, ineligible for FELA compensation under the reasoning in *Metro-North*.

The category of persons with observable conditions in their bodies that nonetheless do not rise to the level of impairment is by no means unique to the asbestos litigation. More recent lawsuits alleging the existence of a causal link between the diet drug combination fen-phen and heart valve abnormalities have brought to light a similar phenomenon. "[T]oday's echocardiography technology is so sensitive that it can detect even trivial amounts of [heart valve] regurgitation that require no medical treatment and are not a precursor of any disease."[44] As medical technology becomes increasingly sophisticated in other areas, the potential for fine-grained detection short of the emergence of an actual impairment will only grow. The central point remains that impairment — not some condition that a doctor can detect in the body with the aid of modern technology but that does not inhibit bodily functions — serves as the touchstone for injury under tort law in its present form.

Why would defendants, even with trial dates pending at the mature stage, agree to settle claims about which tort law is skeptical, at best? The explanation lies in a combination of litigation psychology, settlement strategy, and distortions introduced by the insurance arrangements commonly used by large-scale business enterprises. Recent work on the civil litigation process from the standpoint of cognitive psychology has important implications throughout the development of mass tort litigation. The next chapter, for example, considers the implications of that literature for the transition from immature to mature litigation. For now, the literature on cognitive psychology sheds light on the settlement value of unimpaired claims at the mature stage.

Speaking to the general phenomenon of frivolous claims in civil litigation — defined as those having a low probability of success on the merits — the literature predicts that settlements for such claims are likely to involve dollar amounts "greater than the expected value of the litigation."[45] The reason, Chris Guthrie explains, is that the strategies of plaintiffs and defendants in frivolous litigation are "likely to be diametrically opposed to litigant behavior in ordinary litigation." Plaintiffs "are likely to prefer the risk-seeking option — trial — while defendants are more likely to prefer the risk-averse option — settlement." In turn, "[b]ecause trial is more attractive to plaintiffs than defendants, plaintiffs are likely to demand more, and defendants are likely to offer more, than the expected value of plaintiffs' claims."[46] The boost in settlement payouts above expected value and the large absolute number of unimpaired persons relative to impaired ones, together, make for a powerful combination. A further point about settlement strategy adds to the tendency to pay unimpaired claims.

At the immature stage, plaintiffs' law firms have reason to remain relatively selective in the individual cases they press forward, so as to present the strongest chance of precipitating damage awards. To be sure, plaintiffs' lawyers may also have on file large numbers of claims. The point here is simply that they have reason to be selective about the ones they press vigorously to trial as test cases. Indeed, some firms may continue this selective approach into later litigation stages. When defendants come to understand that trial carries a substantial risk of loss, however, many plaintiffs' lawyers may take a different approach. They may threaten to take the most meritorious cases to trial, with potentially disastrous consequences for defendants, unless the claims of exposed but unimpaired persons are also included in an aggregate settlement. Indeed, acting with an eye toward continued recruitment of clients in the future, a plaintiffs' law firm will have reason to structure aggregate settlements so as to enable the firm later to say truthfully that it has a track record of obtaining substantial dollars for unimpaired claims.

The willingness of some courts to consolidate large numbers of individual claimants — sometimes with widely disparate physical conditions[47] — enhances further the settlement value of claims brought on behalf of exposed but unimpaired persons.[48] In this regard, genuine judicial concern for docket clearance in the short term — not to mention for the plight of impaired persons stuck in the trial queue — can have the perverse effect over the long term of inviting additional unimpaired claims. The phenomenon resembles the oft-noted consequence of additional highway construction: simply to attract more drivers on the highway.[49]

Thus far, discussion of the defense side of mass tort litigation has assumed a vaguely monolithic tone, suggesting the existence of a single, undifferentiated unit. In fact, the defense side frequently involves multiple defendant manufacturers and, for each of them, multiple insurers. This multiplicity of insurance coverage manifests itself along both horizontal and vertical dimensions. The horizontal dimension relates to the latency period between exposure to a given firm's wares and a resulting manifestation of impairment. The vertical dimension concerns the relationship between different types of insurance coverage, implicated for a given time period.

Prior to the mid-1980s, the standardized language used in the sorts of "comprehensive general liability" (CGL) policies purchased by corporate manufacturers provided coverage for liability arising from an "occurrence" or "accident" during a specified period of years. Application of this policy language is relatively straightforward for conventional kinds of injuries where there was little, if any, gap in time between the "occurrence" or "accident" and resulting harm. The insurer that issued the CGL policy for the relevant year would indemnify the insured in the event of any liability. The same standardized language, however, gave rise to formidable difficulties of interpretation with regard to the sorts of latent diseases associated with mass torts. The crucial question concerned when one should understand a covered "occurrence" or "accident" to have occurred. The answer to that question then would determine which insurers' CGL policies would be "triggered." Several points in time presented themselves as candidates, ranging from the time of exposure all the way to the time of impairment.[50] In the asbestos litigation, courts largely finessed the question, often adopting a "continuous" trigger of all policies that provided coverage from the time of exposure.[51] The practical effect of this continuous trigger was to increase the insurance resources potentially available to settle any given asbestos-related tort claim — quite arguably, the underling objective of courts that adopted such a construction of the standard CGL policy language. Any attempt by an insured to settle claims on a comprehensive basis thus effectively called for involvement of all the implicated insurers.

By the mid-1980s, the insurance industry changed its standard CGL policy language, shifting to coverage simply for "claims made" against the insured during a specified time period.[52] The result is that the mass torts of the early to mid-twenty-first century are less likely than those of the late twentieth to present difficulties along the horizontal dimension of insurance coverage. The vertical dimension still remains, however; and it stands to affect the incentive to monitor the quality of claims settled as a matter of their grounding in tort doctrine.

Even as to a single defendant, the typical insurance arrangement consists of multiple layers of policies "stacked" on one another for any given time period. A primary insurer might cover, say, the first $100 million of liability, an excess insurer the next $20 million, another excess insurer the next $30 million, and so on, with the insured responsible for any remaining liability. The various insurers themselves purchase insurance of their own from "reinsurers" on the international market, such as the underwriters collectively known as Lloyd's of London. The distinctive feature of primary insurance policies is that they generally include not only coverage for liability but also a duty to defend the insured in litigation raising a potential for liability, a matter to which I shall return.[53]

The stacking of insurance on top of insurance, and reinsurance thereon, has the well-recognized virtues of spreading risk. Stacking, however, has unexpected consequences in mass tort litigation. The reason is that mass torts frequently give rise to expectations that the total liability of the defendant ultimately will exceed the dollar limits on multiple layers of its insurance coverage for a given time period.[54] This expectation, in turn, affects the incentive of insurers at lower rungs of the stack to expend resources to monitor closely the nature of claims settled in litigation. The insurer itself must expend the costs for monitoring — manpower and expertise to evaluate the quality of settled claims — but stands to capture little, if any, of the gains from such monitoring in terms of the discouragement of unimpaired claims at later times. Those benefits will redound to insurers higher in the stack who, in turn, face the same disincentive to monitor claim quality in the settlement process insofar as they too anticipate that the liability of the insured will exceed the dollar limits on their own policies. The more massive the mass tort in financial terms, the more extensive the disincentive to monitor claim quality will be.

Primary insurers' duty to defend adds to the foregoing disincentives for claim monitoring. The incentive of the primary insurer will be to minimize the defense costs expended in litigation by embracing the kinds of aggregate settlements sought by plaintiffs' lawyers — again, with minimal, if any, monitoring of claim merit. The long-term consequence of this approach is to create a hospitable environment for the filing of additional unimpaired claims. But that consequence falls not upon the primary insurer whose policy limits will be exceeded but, again, upon other insurers higher in the stack.

During the mature stage, in short, outcomes in mass tort litigation have a considerable potential to become increasingly dysfunctional from the standpoint of existing tort doctrine. The use of aggregate settlements to resolve cases as trial dates approach comes only at the cost of doctrinal tension, for its tendency is to inflate settlement values through the inclusion of claims about which current tort law is skeptical, at best. The larger implication of this observation speaks to the interplay between the developmental process for a mass tort and the structure of any comprehensive solution. The particular stage within the mass tort litigation process influences the degree to which replication of aggregate settlements on some more regularized basis will be attractive to defendants.

By highlighting defendants' strategic interests, I do not mean to suggest that their interests somehow stand above those of plaintiffs. I merely mean that comprehensive peace agreements for any area of mass tort litigation — like the tango — take two cooperative partners. When the dysfunctions of the mature stage emerge, defendants have no reason to set in stone, by way of any all-encompassing peace plan, a process by which they must continue to pay cash up front for unmeritorious claims from the standpoint of current tort law. Rather, defendants will embrace any alternative to the tort system only insofar as it promises a cure for the dysfunctions of the mature litigation stage. The incentive will be to use any comprehensive resolution of the litigation as a way to streamline the processing of claims and to align payouts more closely with existing tort doctrine.[55] *When* one tries to make peace, in short, will shape the content of the peace itself.

Unlike the asbestos litigation, the mass torts of the future are unlikely to proceed far into the mature litigation stage. With the outlines of the developmental process in mind, one may identify other features of the legal landscape that serve as brakes upon the movement from one litigation stage to the next. The next chapter focuses on the first gray area: the transition between the immature and mature stages. Two seemingly unrelated developments in the law — one focused on matters of evidence, the other on class certification — operate to regulate this transition.

CHAPTER III

REGULATING
DEVELOPMENT
INDIRECTLY

To make the transition from immature to mature mass tort litigation, plaintiffs' lawyers must establish a credible threat to prevail at trial. One way to make this transition is to establish the merits of the litigation. But that is not the only way. Additional claims may come into the tort system for other reasons: due to inaccurate information about the merits of the litigation sent by early lawsuits at the immature stage or through the aggregation of litigation at that stage, through the certification of a class action. The workings of this process and the efforts of the civil litigation system to regulate it form the subject of this chapter.

The story of mass tort litigation over the safety of silicone gel breast implants illustrates the problem of inaccurate information about claim merit. A useful starting point for discussion of aggregation focuses on litigation over HIV-contaminated blood products. In casting the discussion along these lines, this chapter ties together two topics that have garnered much attention in scholarship on civil litigation in recent decades: first, the rise of a "gatekeeper" role for trial judges with respect to the admissibility of expert scientific testimony, as described in the Supreme Court's 1993 evidentiary decision in *Daubert v. Merrell Dow Pharmaceuticals, Inc.*;[1] and, second, concern over the capacity of litigation on an aggregate basis—most prominently, class actions—to exert undue or illegitimate pressure upon defendants to settle. Each of these topics has spawned a rich literature of its own, and each has repercussions beyond the world of mass tort litigation.[2] At bottom, however, both topics arise from the mass tort setting.

A lawsuit over the morning sickness drug Bendectin provided the occasion for the Court's decision in *Daubert,* though contemporaneous litigation over silicone gel breast implants lays out even more clearly the implications of that decision for mass torts. *Daubert* and its progeny comprise an important device to regulate, in practical effect, the accuracy of information conveyed about claim value by early cases. A 1995 opinion by Judge Richard Posner in the blood products litigation — In re *Rhone-Poulenc Rorer, Inc.*[3] — gave renewed impetus to discussions of aggregation and settlement pressure.

Examination of these two topics in light of the previous chapter helps to reveal a conceptual connection that existing commentary has not identified. Both the debate in evidence law over admissibility standards for expert scientific testimony and the debate in procedural law over the settlement pressure exerted by aggregation center on the appropriate regulation of efforts to amplify — whether by claim information or by civil procedure — preexisting imperfections in the system of tort adjudication. The discussion that follows identifies the pertinent imperfections, traces their implications for the transition to the mature litigation stage, and then assesses the regulatory responses implemented, in practical effect, by *Daubert* and *Rhone-Poulenc*.

Cast in their best light, both *Daubert* and *Rhone-Poulenc* are on to something important for mass torts. Both seek to reassert the primacy of tort doctrine over the distorting effects that litigation dynamics or aggregative procedure may have on the progress of litigation. Both aspire for substance to drive the movement of mass tort litigation to the mature stage, not vice versa. That said, however, both *Daubert* and *Rhone-Poulenc* raise serious concerns of institutional capacity and legitimacy when seen as vehicles to regulate the development of mass tort litigation. The discussion that follows is far from a paean to the two decisions. My treatment stands, more properly, as an effort to pinpoint the reason why one should regard the operation of both decisions only with a degree of ambivalence in the mass tort setting.

Cognitive Psychology, Litigation Investment, and Imperfections in the Tort System

Courts have long understood that tort actions trigger the right to trial by jury enshrined in the Seventh Amendment.[4] The behavior of juries is a notoriously murky subject prone to exaggeration on all sides. Neither jury bashing nor jury touting is my goal here. My focus, instead, is on decision making by humans generally and its effect upon the decisions made by plaintiffs' lawyers in the development of mass tort litigation.

An emerging branch of scholarship in recent years speaks to the relationship between litigation and cognitive psychological research on human decision making under conditions of uncertainty.[5] Building on the Nobel Prize–winning work of Amos Tversky and Daniel Kahneman on "prospect theory,"[6] among other sources, commentators at the intersection of litigation and cognitive psychology advance two observations that shed light upon both decision making in tort litigation and the investment opportunities for mass tort plaintiffs' lawyers.

First, the literature observes that human decision making under conditions of uncertainty exhibits identifiable cognitive biases — tendencies to rely on analytical shortcuts or suppositions that facilitate the making of decisions but only at the cost of predictable, systematic errors in terms of accuracy.[7] Most notable for present purposes is what commentators describe as "hindsight bias," the tendency after-the-fact to overestimate the ability of decision makers to foresee the outcome of events.[8] If anything, the temporal orientation of a tort lawsuit plays into hindsight bias. A tort suit inherently presents a known, tragic outcome for the plaintiff, who then invites the jury to find a causal connection to wrongful conduct on the defendant's part.[9]

Second, other portions of the same literature point to the human tendency to arrange complex factual information presented at tort trials into a coherent narrative or story, often with melodramatic elements of blame.[10] One prominent version of this hypothesis holds that jurors tend to side with the litigant whose position best accords with this story model as a whole, rather than as considered strictly according to each legal element that the plaintiff must prove in order to prevail.[11] This holistic process of reasoning raises the potential for jurors to commingle different legal elements of a given case — in the tort context, to overlook relatively weak evidence of causation when presented with evidence of blameworthy conduct by the defendant.[12] Still other contributions to the literature suggest more broadly that, "with respect to risks of injury or harm, vivid images and concrete pictures of disaster can 'crowd out' other kinds of thoughts, including the crucial thought that the probability of disaster is very small."[13]

Speaking in the criminal context and without reference to cognitive psychology, the Supreme Court has lent credence to a vision of trials in terms of the presentation of competing stories. The Court has noted that evidence at trial can be relevant not simply for the specific legal element to which it speaks but also for the coherence it lends to the larger narrative its proponent wishes to present to the jury. In *Old Chief v. United States,* the Court noted that evidence offered by a prosecutor to prove a particular element of a crime may have the secondary effect of making more believable the prosecution's case with regard to other, closely disputed elements.

A defense offer to stipulate with regard to the particular element thus does not, in itself, render the prosecutor's evidence irrelevant.[14] Rather, in the words of Justice David Souter for the Court, evidence "has force beyond any linear scheme of reasoning, and as its pieces come together a narrative gains momentum, with power not only to support conclusions but to sustain the willingness of jurors to draw the inferences, whatever they may be, necessary to reach an honest verdict."[15]

All of this is not to suggest that cognitive biases or commingling necessarily redound to the benefit of plaintiffs in all instances or that human decision making exhibits those tendencies in every case. The point, instead, is that expectations about the potential for decision making along such lines—perhaps, in only a portion of cases at the immature stage—can influence mass tort plaintiffs' lawyers' selection among competing investment opportunities. The selection of subject areas for mass tort litigation is likely to favor systematically contexts in which plaintiffs' lawyers have reason to believe that they may channel cognitive biases and commingling in their favor. And it is plaintiffs' lawyers, not defense lawyers, after all, who retain the crucial power of case selection for the initiation of mass tort litigation.

In framing the investment decisions of plaintiffs' lawyers in terms of the scholarly literature on litigation and cognitive psychology, I do not mean to imply that lawyers read that literature and strategize accordingly. Quite the opposite: The literature itself builds, in substantial part, on the observed behavior of lawyers. Scholarly examination of actual argumentation in tort trials, for example, bears out the practicing bar's intuitive grasp of what scholars have modeled in formal terms.[16] Here, practice drives theory, not vice versa. The scholarly literature nevertheless helps to explain the tendency for mass tort litigation to focus not simply on situations of legally meritorious claims but also on what might be described as scenarios of "outrageous fortune"—situations that combine story elements of blameworthy behavior on the defendant's part with closer questions concerning other aspects of the litigation, such as doubt about the existence of general causation as a scientific matter.

Blameworthy conduct—say, a corporate effort to suppress questions about product safety, even if those doubts ultimately prove to be unfounded—will increase the potential upside of an investment in litigation concerning that product. Claims for punitive damages in mass tort litigation often are predicated upon allegations of the defendant's willful suppression of safety concerns.[17] Moreover, as the term "commingling" suggests, elements of blameworthiness may lead decision makers examining events in hindsight to overcome their doubts about other contested elements of the plaintiff's case. Evidence of blameworthy conduct accordingly can prove helpful not just in its own right, as a predicate for punitive damages, but also as part of the larger story that a plaintiff's lawyer seeks to tell.

Any tort case, even of a conventional sort arising from idiosyncratic events, carries the potential for the foregoing imperfections to surface in the adjudicatory process. Their significance for mass tort litigation lies in the possibility of efforts to amplify those imperfections[18] and, in so doing, to precipitate a transition from the immature litigation stage (with its focus on exploration of claim merit) to the mature stage (where attention shifts to the challenges of comprehensive settlement design). The silicone gel breast implant litigation illustrates one avenue for amplification: inaccurate information provided by lawsuits at the immature stage.

Daubert and the Accuracy of Information about Claim Value

In terms of the elements for a tort claim, the silicone gel breast implant litigation centered on a dispute over general causation. Implant plaintiffs argued that silicone leaking from a breast implant can turn the human immune system against itself. The result, plaintiffs contended, was the development of connective tissue disease, either as conventionally conceived or in some atypical form involving a constellation of symptoms not previously defined by medical science.[19] Claims of a causal link to connective tissue disease carried the potential for formidable damage awards, in contrast to claims — ultimately, borne out by scientific research — of local complications consisting simply of the hardening or rupturing of the implant.[20]

The challenge for tort adjudication lay in determining whether the connection between silicone gel breast implants and diagnoses of connective tissue disease consisted of a causal relationship or a mere coincidence. Approximately one in every hundred women will develop some form of connective tissue disease for reasons that science has yet to understand fully; and roughly the same ratio of women in the United States received silicone gel breast implants. One thus would expect "on the basis of chance alone" that some ten thousand women would have both connective tissue disease and implants.[21]

The immature stage of the implant litigation saw multimillion-dollar verdicts in early individual lawsuits: first, for plaintiff Marcia Stern in 1984 and, later, for plaintiff Mariann Hopkins in 1991.[22] At the time, scientists had yet to initiate epidemiological studies on the relationship between silicone gel breast implants and connective tissue disease — that is, studies to compare systematically the incidence of connective tissue disease in women with and without implants. In the absence of epidemiology, the plaintiffs relied on the testimony of several expert witnesses based on other types of scientific research: a published hypothesis of a causal relationship between silicone and connective tissue disease that, nonetheless, provided no evidence to confirm that hypothesis; studies of animals exposed to silicone; and clinical observations of patients with both connective tissue disease and implants.[23] These sources do not lie wholly outside the realm of consideration for scientists who study the causes of disease in humans. The plaintiffs' experts had not relied on a Ouija board. They nevertheless had been prepared to opine about the possibility of a causal relationship based on highly speculative and preliminary information within the panoply of research methods on human disease.

The Stern and Hopkins lawsuits were noteworthy for their outcomes and for the revelation of conduct on the part of implant manufacturers — particularly, the leading implant maker, Dow Corning Corporation. The gist of these revelations was that manufacturers, based on their own internal experiments on laboratory animals during the 1960s and 1970s, had reason to suspect that silicone might trigger some sort of response in the immune systems of mammals. Manufacturers nonetheless proceeded forward with the marketing of silicone gel breast implants.[24] The Stern case also featured evidence suggesting that Dow Corning had altered experimental data to deflect attention from the results of one internal study indicating that silicone implants had produced a response in the immune systems of laboratory dogs.[25]

The generation of a response in the immune system does not necessarily amount to the causation of disease. The point of the immune system, after all, is to keep the body healthy precisely by responding to intrusions of various sorts. Likewise, risks identified in laboratory animals do not necessarily translate into similar risks for humans.[26] At the same time, however, it is one thing to press forward with the marketing of a product while warning consumers of any lingering uncertainties about its effects. It is quite another to do so while saying nothing in the face of one's own research that raised if not red flags then, at least, yellow ones. From the apportionment of compensatory and punitive damages in the early implant suits, one can sense the impact that these revelations of manufacturer conduct had upon jurors, as compared to the more murky issue of general causation. Stern received $211,000 in compensatory damages coupled with $1.5 million in punitive damages;[27] Hopkins received $840,000 in compensatory damages plus $6.5 million in punitive damages.[28]

In the meantime, national media attention brought the implant controversy to the public eye, "[c]onveying the clear message that implants were dangerous devices foisted off on unsuspecting women."[29] The evidence concerning manufacturers' conduct soon found its way by back channels—notwithstanding the sealing of case records by court order—to federal Food and Drug Administration (FDA) Commissioner David Kessler. The FDA subsequently imposed a moratorium on sales of silicone gel breast implants that the agency would revisit—but still not lift—more than a decade later.[30] The moratorium was by no means a declaration of general causation by the FDA. As Dr. Kessler underscored at the time, the link—"if any"—between implants and connective tissue disease remained "unknown."[31] In a subsequent television interview, Dr. Kessler described his agency's action simply as an attempt "to say, 'Time-out.'"[32]

Time-out for the FDA, however, did not mean time-out in the development of mass tort litigation. The attention garnered by suggestions of a causal link between implants and connective tissue disease meant that "women who had both . . . would be bound to consider whether they, too, should sue."[33] The understandable concerns of women with implants coincided with the economic opportunity that implant litigation offered to plaintiffs' lawyers, some of whom set up "assembly line" office procedures to represent implant recipients.[34] The litigation also presented an economic opportunity for doctors, some of whom would go on to earn millions of dollars for the handling of "bulk referrals" from plaintiffs' lawyers.[35] The result was for mass tort litigation over breast implants to leap from the immature to the mature stage. Within two years of the FDA moratorium and the revelations of manufacturers' behavior, approximately 16,000 women filed lawsuits nationwide.[36] And the question for lawyers quickly shifted from the assessment of claim merit to the selection of a suitable vehicle for comprehensive resolution of the litigation.

The sheer number of actions led initially to the consolidation of federal implant suits by the MDL Panel. Later, in 1994, the contending forces attempted to resolve all present and future implant claims through a $4.2 billion class action settlement. The legal basis for such a class action aside, the settlement fell apart for a much more practical reason. An unexpectedly large number of claims—by then, some 440,000—quickly made it apparent that the fixed sum of $4.2 billion set by manufacturers for the class settlement would be insufficient to fund the compensation payments described therein.[37] Shortly before the collapse of the settlement, Dow Corning sought protection under Chapter 11 of the Bankruptcy Code. Indeed, secondary reports subsequently implied that Dow Corning might have desired to proceed by way of Chapter 11 rather than to continue with the class settlement on the hope that the bankruptcy proceeding might enable it to get a quick up-or-down ruling on the causation question in the breast implant litigation.[38] That hope—if it existed—proved to be misplaced, with the bankruptcy court declining to place the initial focus of the reorganization proceeding on the valuation of pending tort claims against the debtor corporation.[39] After five more years of wrangling, Dow Corning ultimately garnered judicial approval for a corporate reorganization plan—one that, like the defunct class settlement, contemplated substantial payments to implant recipients with connective tissue disease.[40]

The content of the Dow Corning reorganization plan is all the more striking when one considers what happened in the meantime on the scientific front. A wealth of epidemiological research failed to show an elevated incidence of connective tissue disease in women with implants as compared to those without. The overwhelming scientific consensus behind that conclusion ultimately included a review of the scientific literature by FDA scientists (including Dr. Kessler) in 1996,[41] a panel of neutral scientific experts appointed by the federal court supervising MDL-consolidated litigation in 1998,[42] and the National Academy of Sciences in 2000.[43]

The civil justice system is unlikely to witness a replay of the process that made immature litigation over breast implants into mature mass tort litigation. The reason why lies in the consequences of the Supreme Court's 1993 evidentiary decision in *Daubert*. The nuances of *Daubert* and its progeny have spawned whole treatises,[44] but one easily may summarize the basics of the Court's decision. *Daubert* concerns Rule 702 of the Federal Rules of Evidence, the major rule on the admissibility in federal court of testimony based on "scientific, technical, or other specialized knowledge." Writing for the Court, Justice Harry Blackmun posited a "gatekeeping role"[45] for trial judges to distinguish scientific knowledge from mere "subjective belief or unsupported speculation" masquerading as science.[46] The Court held that the grounding of expert testimony in scientific knowledge does not depend exclusively upon its "general acceptance" within the scientific community.[47] In so holding, the Court seemingly departed from the admissibility standard applied in an influential lower-court decision from 1923—*Frye v. United States*[48]—which the Court itself acknowledged as "the dominant standard for determining the admissibility of novel scientific evidence" prior to *Daubert*.[49]

Reading the *Daubert* opinion, some observers took the Court to call for judicial scrutiny of the expert's "principles and methodology" but not of the expert's "conclusion"—that is, her ultimate opinion on a contested factual issue at trial.[50] One passage in the *Daubert* opinion appeared to say exactly that.[51] Shortly thereafter, in 1994, a federal appellate court upheld the multimillion-dollar damage award to implant plaintiff Mariann Hopkins, pointing out that her expert witnesses came with plausible scientific credentials and had looked to sources within the canon of scientific inquiry on human disease.[52] Elaborating on the trial judge's gatekeeping role in later decisions, however, the Supreme Court cast the *Daubert* inquiry in broader terms that have consequences for the development of mass tort litigation.

In its 1997 decision in *General Electric Co. v. Joiner,* the Court noted that "[t]rained experts commonly extrapolate from existing data" in an analytical process such that "conclusions and methodology are not entirely distinct from one another." The trial judge must ask whether "there is simply too great an analytical gap between the data and the opinion proffered."[53] A judicial conclusion that the content of the expert's opinion — her bottom line as to general causation, for example — is not generally accepted in the scientific community is not necessarily fatal to the admissibility of that opinion testimony at trial. But an unexplained or implausible analytical process leading to that conclusion will be fatal to admissibility. "[T]oo great an analytical gap" between the data considered by the expert and the opinion ultimately proffered serves as a warning that the expert seeks to testify based on speculative faux science, not scientific knowledge. Along similar lines, the Court in 1999 added that the trial judge must "make certain that an expert . . . employs in the courtroom the same level of intellectual rigor that characterizes the practice of an expert in the relevant field." The trial judge must ensure that the expert's testimony does not fall "outside the range where experts might reasonably differ."[54] In the breast implant litigation, the directive to scrutinize "analytical gaps" distinguishes the decision to uphold the admission of the plaintiff's expert testimony in *Hopkins* from later federal cases that proved inhospitable to similar testimony.[55]

The Court's emphasis on the scrutiny of analytical gaps, if anything, makes better sense of the outcome in *Daubert* itself than a strict methodology-conclusion distinction. *Daubert* arose relatively late in the sequence of lawsuits over an alleged causal connection between the morning sickness drug Bendectin and deformities in children whose mothers had ingested that drug during pregnancy. Birth defects remain a tragically familiar phenomenon, even in the absence of Bendectin ingestion by the expectant mother. The question of general causation in the Bendectin litigation — like that in the implant litigation — centered on the distinction between a mere coincidence and a causal relationship.

In contrast to the early implant lawsuits, *Daubert* was not an instance of litigation pursued in the absence of scientific research on the general causation question but, rather, litigation pursued in its face. By the time of the *Daubert* trial, the scientific literature included some thirty published epidemiological studies on Bendectin, none of which had found the drug to be a human teratogen — that is, a substance capable of causing malformations in fetuses.[56] The Bendectin litigation already had turned largely in favor of the defendant manufacturer Merrell Dow Pharmaceuticals and, within a few years, the litigation as a whole would be virtually dead.[57] In the face of the published epidemiological literature, the *Daubert* plaintiffs sought to admit expert testimony that relied on other techniques of toxicological inquiry: studies on cells in the laboratory, animal studies, comparison of the chemical structure of Bendectin with that of known teratogens, and "reanalysis" of the data assembled in the published epidemiological studies.[58] Like the experts in the early implant cases, the *Daubert* plaintiffs' experts did not seek to rely on information completely beyond the pale for scientists interested in human disease. Again, no Ouija board. The real problem lay in the experts' willingness to conclude that Bendectin "could possibly" cause birth defects in the face of the thirty published epidemiological studies showing no elevated incidence of such defects, not in the nature of the sources considered by those experts.[59]

On remand from the Supreme Court in *Daubert*, the United States Court of Appeals for the Ninth Circuit upheld the exclusion of plaintiffs' experts and, accordingly, upheld the entry of judgment for the defendant Merrell Dow. Writing for the court, Judge Alex Kozinski wryly observed that "no one in the scientific community" outside the context of the Bendectin litigation had deemed the views of the *Daubert* plaintiffs' experts "worthy of verification, refutation or even comment." This silence, he inferred, reflected "a tacit understanding within the scientific community that what's going on here is not science at all, but litigation."[60] The Supreme Court's own subsequent elaboration in *Joiner* — calling for judicial scrutiny of the analytical leap made by the expert from the data she has considered — is entirely in keeping with the outcome on remand in *Daubert*.

Empirical research on federal civil litigation confirms the significance of *Daubert* and its progeny, not only for lawsuits raising questions of medical science but also for those implicating other bodies of expertise. The Court's decision in *Daubert* undoubtedly focused the attention of both judges and lawyers on the importance of scrutiny for expert testimony. Based on a systematic review of federal trial-level opinions from 1980 to 1999, researchers at the RAND Institute for Civil Justice concluded that, "[a]fter *Daubert*, the proportion of challenged evidence in which [expert] reliability was discussed and the proportion of expert evidence found unreliable rose." Challenges to the admissibility of expert testimony "increasingly resulted in summary judgment after *Daubert*," with "nearly 90 percent" going "against plaintiffs." The same research also suggests a deterrent effect from the Court's decisions, with litigants withdrawing or not proposing expert testimony in light of the *Daubert* standard.[61] Other commentary indicates that, at the state level, numerous jurisdictions have adopted the federal *Daubert* standard as a matter of state evidence law, though the *Fyre* "general acceptance" test remains the majority view at the state level today.[62] But even there, practical application appears to dominate over differences of terminology. A close analysis of the published decisions reveals that "case law under *Frye* is slowly converging with *Daubert* jurisprudence."[63]

The consequences of *Daubert* and its progeny remain vast. The Court has called for analogous scrutiny of expert testimony grounded in all manner of "specialized knowledge," not just in science.[64] For mass tort litigation specifically, however, one may understand *Daubert* in regulatory terms. The regulated industry, if you will, consists of the industrialized approach to litigation and legal representation spawned by the nature of mass torts. As to that industry, *Daubert* regulates efforts to amplify preexisting imperfections in tort litigation through the dynamics of mass torts.

In focusing on the jump from the immature to the mature stage, my argument here does not turn upon the attribution of particular intentions on the part of plaintiffs' lawyers, other than the obvious objective of winning. One need not necessarily assume a grand, behind-the-scenes plan to push litigation to the mature stage. One need only assume that substantial damage awards at that stage tend to garner attention from other plaintiffs' law firms across the country. The awards are not trade secrets.

In terms of the developmental process for mass torts, *Daubert* regulates the transition from the immature to the mature stage by reducing the likelihood of inaccurate information from early lawsuits concerning the merits of the litigation. Against the tendency toward hindsight bias, *Daubert* effectively enables the defendant to concede the existence of a tragic outcome — the plaintiff's diagnosis of disease — and to focus attention, instead, on whether that known outcome is merely coincidental with exposure to the defendant's product or its causal result. Against the tendency toward the commingling of blameworthiness with general causation, *Daubert* enables the defendant effectively to carve out the latter for separate judicial consideration at the pretrial stage as a question of admissibility. In so doing, *Daubert* reinforces the insistence of tort law upon the satisfaction of its elements as distinct concepts. The question that tort law asks is not a holistic one of whether the defendant is more likely than not liable to the plaintiff in some overall, gestalt sense. Rather, the question is a disaggregated one: whether the defendant more likely than not breached an applicable tort duty, more likely than not caused the plaintiff's injury, and so on—all leading to the ultimate conclusion of liability, if each element is found by a preponderance of the evidence.[65]

Where the analytical gap between available information and any conclusion about general causation is simply "too great," *Daubert* enables evidentiary determinations to bring about, in practical effect, the kind of time-out that the FDA desired but could not deliver with regard to silicone gel breast implants. To see *Daubert* as regulating the development of mass tort litigation nonetheless is to raise as much concern as praise. One familiar critique of *Daubert* points to the awkward position in which it casts judges—persons who are learned in law, not science. Even while upholding the exclusion of the Bendectin plaintiffs' experts in *Daubert* itself, Judge Kozinski lamented that the Supreme Court had placed upon judges the "daunting" enterprise of "resolv[ing] disputes among respected, well-credentialed scientists about matters squarely within their expertise, in areas where there is no scientific consensus as to what is and what is not 'good science.'"[66] Cognizant of judges' shortcomings in scientific expertise, both commentators and prominent judges themselves have called for the use of expert scientific panels—like the one appointed late in consolidated federal litigation over breast implants—to assist trial judges in the evaluation of *Daubert*-related issues.[67] This is a sensible development within the parameters of current law, but it highlights two concerns about *Daubert* as a regulatory device for mass torts. The first concern goes to the scope of the *Daubert* inquiry. The second speaks to the authority of judges to undertake that inquiry in the form of admissibility determinations where tort law is overwhelmingly the province of state law, not federal law.

The operation of *Daubert* as a regulatory device rests on the identification of some body of scientific research—understood both qualitatively and quantitatively—that shall constitute the minimum corpus on which an expert may base any opinion on the existence of general causation. Judges, in short, must differentiate outright analytical gaps from analytical leaps that the scientific community nonetheless would regard as the subject of reasonable disagreement. The situation presented in *Daubert* masks the nature of this challenge, however. The case involved a scenario far removed from the regulation of the transition from immature to mature litigation. That transition involves expert witnesses who wish to opine not in the face of contrary epidemiological research (as in the Bendectin litigation by the time of *Daubert*) but, instead, in *advance* of such research (as in the early breast implant trials). There is a seemingly infinite number of points between the two extremes of the Ouija board and, say, the huge volume of research that makes scientists confident of the general causal relationship between smoking and lung cancer—so much research that one hardly could describe a conclusion on the latter point as involving much of an analytical leap at all.

The crucial point is that judges cannot look to science to say how much research must exist on a question of general causation before an expert should be permitted to invite a jury finding on that score. Unlike the search for truth at trial, the search for truth in science operates under no presupposed obligation to generate an answer by a particular time. To the contrary, the norms of scientific discourse counsel both a reluctance to reach firm conclusions and an inclination to identify additional avenues for further inquiry.[68] The question of how much, and what kinds of, scientific research is enough for an expert to form any opinion about general causation at the immature stage is not a question internal to science itself. Nor, for that matter, is the question one that science has reason to ask for its own purposes. To answer that question, judges applying *Daubert* necessarily must look outside of science. But to what?

As a regulatory regime for the progress of mass tort litigation, *Daubert* acts within the backdrop of a commitment to state law as the dominant source of tort doctrine. Existing commentary recognizes the tendency of the *Daubert* admissibility inquiry to shade into an inquiry into the sufficiency of expert testimony—here, its capacity to enable the jury to find, more likely than not, the existence of a general causal relationship as opposed to a mere coincidence.[69] Sufficiency in this sense is a matter not of evidence law but of civil procedure—specifically, motions for summary judgment. A defense motion for summary judgment effectively asks whether there is enough of a dispute on the facts to justify putting the defendant to the burden of a full-fledged trial.

The question of how much scientific research should be enough to permit an analytical leap about general causation verges into sufficiency-like terms in its very formulation. The question effectively asks when, within the sequence of ongoing research, a scientist knows enough—in short, has a *sufficient* body of information—to find a general causal relationship. Any court would be hard pressed to say that what is sufficient for an expert to form a conclusion in these regards—what amounts to a dispute within "the range where experts might reasonably differ"—somehow could not constitute a sufficient basis for a jury finding along the same lines.

At first glance, the admissibility-sufficiency distinction looks like just another instance of semantic hair-splitting. A mass tort plaintiff who loses because the court excludes her expert witnesses on the causation element is no worse off, in practical terms, than one who loses because the court grants summary judgment to the defense. In legal terms, such a grant of summary judgment would rest upon the absence of a genuine issue as to the causation element, on which the plaintiff bears the burden of proof. The judge would be finding that a reasonable jury could come out only one way — for the defense — notwithstanding the plaintiff's causation evidence. The couching of the analysis in terms of admissibility or sufficiency, however, has considerable bearing on the institutional authority of the judge and the mode of legal reasoning that she must employ.

Federal courts have authority to hear tort actions grounded in state law only on the basis of their diversity jurisdiction — that is, their authority to hear cases brought between citizens of different states. In diversity cases, federal courts have authority to apply federal evidence law.[70] But, as the Supreme Court made clear in 1938 in *Erie Railroad v. Tompkins*, the federal courts enjoy no authority to create a federal common law of torts.[71] If the inquiry into what counts as an analytical gap in expert testimony partakes of an inquiry into sufficiency — if it is an inquiry that science cannot answer — then the legitimacy of *Daubert* as a means to regulate the transition to the mature litigation stage is open to real doubt. In determining the quantity and quality of information needed to support an expert opinion on general causation under the rubric of a ruling on admissibility, the trial judge necessarily decides a question of tort law. Casting the question in terms of admissibility, however, misdirects the court's attention to science rather than tort, to a single federal evidentiary standard rather than the multiplicity of approaches to tort law that the various states might take, and to the interpretation of an evidence rule (a form of statutory interpretation) rather than common-law cases. When a state court makes the admissibility determination — whether under *Daubert*, as adopted by state law, or under the *Frye* test, increasingly converging therewith — the inquiry is even more miscast. Unlike federal courts post-*Erie*, state courts *do* have authority to engage in common-law decision making when confronted with an open question of state tort law, whereas the same courts typically enjoy less flexibility with regard to the interpretation of state evidentiary rules.

In highlighting the foregoing concerns about *Daubert*, I do not mean to dismiss lightly the Court's decision. The *Daubert* Court rightly identifies a pressing need within the civil justice system for some way to regulate the transition from immature to mature litigation — to call time-out in mass tort litigation so that superior information might emerge. There is a need to constrain the amplification of preexisting imperfections in tort adjudication. By casting this regulatory function in terms of an admissibility question to be answered by reference to science, *Daubert* sets the courts on a harrowing enterprise—into a "brave new world" where they are unlikely to find answers supplied by science and will tend to press at the bounds of their own institutional authority to generate answers themselves.[72]

Regulation of the transition from immature to mature litigation, nonetheless, is not the exclusive province of *Daubert*. The same concern over amplification of imperfections in civil adjudication provides the most plausible justification for a brake on the use of aggregation procedures to achieve the same end. At the same time, even more than *Daubert*, the regulation of aggregation by way of judicial standards for the certification of class actions also raises serious questions of institutional capacity and legitimacy.

Rhone-Poulenc, Aggregation, and Amplification

In the breast implant litigation, the information generated at the immature stage about the value of claims precipitated an influx of similar lawsuits. The sheer mass of cases then took on its own dynamic, shifting attention from claim merit to the challenges of settlement design. Aggregation played a role in the breast implant litigation, but only as the vehicle for comprehensive settlement—initially, through the ill-fated effort to craft a class settlement for implant recipients and, later, by way of Dow Corning's reorganization in bankruptcy. Aggregation, however, need not act merely as the vehicle for peace after mass torts litigation already has progressed to the mature stage. Considerable attention has focused in recent years on the capacity of aggregation itself—chiefly, judicial decisions to certify litigation to proceed on a classwide basis—to generate pressure on defendants to settle comprehensively. The question, in short, is whether one can do by way of procedures for the aggregation of civil claims what the breast implant litigation did by way of a deluge of individual cases.

The effects of class certification have enjoyed renewed attention from scholars in the aftermath of a provocative 1995 opinion by Judge Richard Posner for the United States Court of Appeals for the Seventh Circuit: In re *Rhone-Poulenc Rorer, Inc.*[73] Subsequent appellate decisions have sounded similar concerns about the settlement pressure exerted by class certification.[74] The settlement pressure debate traces its judicial roots to an earlier call for caution from famed Second Circuit Judge Henry Friendly.[75] This is not to suggest that these judicial accounts of the settlement pressure exerted by class certification are entirely consistent with one another. To the contrary, important differences — arguably, inconsistencies — exist.[76] One nonetheless may group together the various accounts, for all of them proceed on the premise that the settlement pressure exerted by class certification is somehow illegitimate.

For its part, the scholarly literature on settlement pressure remains sharply divided between two sets of commentators. One set recognizes the potential for class actions to exert pressure on defendants to settle low-probability litigation, regards that pressure as illegitimate, and accordingly urges some form of judicial inquiry into the merits of the litigation as part of the class certification decision.[77] A second set of scholars recognizes the same potential for settlement pressure to arise from class certification but doubts that it is illegitimate.[78]

My contribution here is to reframe the debate over the legitimacy of class settlement pressure by highlighting its kinship to the preceding discussion of *Daubert*. What one makes of both debates turns, at bottom, on the normative implications one should draw from the cognitive psychology of civil litigation. As I now explain, the approach to class certification in *Rhone-Poulenc*—like the *Daubert* admissibility standard for expert testimony — operates to constrain the amplification in mass tort litigation of preexisting imperfections in civil adjudication. And, interestingly enough, *Rhone-Poulenc* presents similar problems of information and institutional suitability.

Rhone-Poulenc involved appellate review of a federal trial-court decision to certify a nationwide class action in litigation over HIV-contaminated blood products used by tens of thousands of hemophiliacs across the country. Many had become HIV-positive as a result. Unlike in the Bendectin or the breast implant litigation, the central issue in the blood products litigation did not concern the existence of general causation. No one doubted either the injurious capacity of HIV or its presence in some blood products. The crux of the dispute centered, instead, on whether the defendant industry had failed to act with reasonable care in its gathering and treatment of blood during the early phases of the HIV epidemic.[79] This question raised a substantial potential for hindsight bias. The question inherently called for difficult determinations of what was, or should have been, known about the risk posed by HIV to the blood supply at times when scientific knowledge about the disease and its modes of transmission was in a fast-changing state. Moreover, one hardly could imagine a more sympathetic group of plaintiffs than hemophiliacs, who used the defendants' blood products out of medical necessity, not for reasons of cosmetics or personal preference.

In decertifying the blood products class, the Seventh Circuit pointed to a variety of concerns, of which settlement pressure is only one.[80] In perhaps the most famous passage of the opinion, Judge Posner pointed to the "great likelihood that the plaintiffs' claims, despite their human appeal, lack legal merit." Defendants had lost roughly 8 percent of the individual cases—one of thirteen, to be exact—that had previously proceeded to judgment at trial. Given this purportedly low probability of success, Judge Posner saw class certification as exerting inappropriate pressure on defendants to settle as compared to a different procedural route: what he described as "a decentralized process of multiple trials, involving different juries," that held the promise of generating results that "will reflect a consensus, or at least a pooling of judgment, of many different tribunals."[81]

There are formidable reasons to doubt Judge Posner's premise that lawsuits over HIV-contaminated blood products constituted low-probability litigation. At the outset, an obvious question is: Were the thirteen cases litigated to trial representative of the overall run of blood product claims, or were they a skewed sample? In fact, Judge Posner himself acknowledged this question.[82] Concerns of representativeness aside, the focus on outcomes at trial overlooked the phenomenon of settlements, some 100 to 150 of which had occurred.[83] Recognition of the seemingly thriving market for settlement in the blood products litigation pre-*Rhone-Poulenc* raises plaintiffs' win rate to a figure more along the lines of 89 to 92 percent,[84] a far cry from low-probability litigation.

If anything, subsequent developments bear out defendants' own recognition of plaintiffs' capability to precipitate judgments of liability. The Seventh Circuit's initial decertification of the blood products class did not mark the decline of the litigation. Rather, counsel soon thereafter entered into a comprehensive settlement agreement to pay each HIV-positive hemophiliac the sum of $100,000, exclusive of attorneys' fees.[85] Adding to the irony of this result, this comprehensive settlement occurred through the vehicle of a second class action, certified by the same trial judge who had certified the original class overturned by Judge Posner in *Rhone-Poulenc*. Appeals concerning the validity of the class settlement were voluntarily dismissed.[86]

Although inapt in the particular context of the blood products litigation, Judge Posner's discussion of the settlement pressure exerted by class certification nonetheless remains of value. One can figure out what to make of settlement pressure—whether to see it as problem or not—by taking as accurate, for the sake of argument, the 8 percent figure for the probability of loss on the defense side. Concern over settlement pressure rests on the existence of risk aversion on defendants' part.[87] A simple numerical example illustrates the point. Suppose that in the no-class-action world, the defendant would face 1,000 cases with an estimated 8 percent chance of being found negligent in any given case and with each finding of negligence resulting in $1 million in damages to the individual plaintiff, due to the severity of the injury suffered.[88] Given the large number of individual cases, one can be relatively confident that the defendant's loss rate over all 1,000 cases will closely approximate the 8 percent estimated probability of being found negligent in any given case. The result is that the defendant would expect to lose a total of approximately eighty individual cases, resulting in a total payout of $80 million.

In the world of a class action, the risks for the defendant are dramatically different. The defendant faces an 8 percent chance of having to pay $1 billion (based on a classwide finding of a lack of reasonable care that then supports $1 million payouts to each of 1,000 class members) and a 92 percent chance of having to pay nothing (due to a classwide finding for the defense on the care question). The expected value of the classwide proceeding is the same as that for the no-class-action world ($80 million), but the variance in outcomes is much greater. Indeed, as a practical matter, there is no realistic possibility of an outcome in the class action world — aside from one generated by a class settlement short of trial — that would replicate the $80 million expected total payout in individual litigation of the 1,000 claims.

A risk-neutral defendant would not care about the greater variance in the class action world and, accordingly, would settle simply for the expected value of the litigation: $80 million. A risk-averse defendant, by contrast, cares about variance, for that concern is the defining feature of risk aversion. Such a defendant accordingly would be willing to pay more than the expected value of the litigation in order to settle the class action and thereby rid itself of the greater uncertainty of outcome associated with it.

The settlement pressure phenomenon, however, is not one that merely affects the price of settlement. To be sure, the additional increment of money that the risk-averse defendant would be willing to pay in a settlement on top of the expected value of class action litigation exists to some degree throughout the spectrum of litigation, from very low to very high probabilities of plaintiff success. The important point is that settlement pressure operates where a risk-neutral defendant would not settle the class action but a risk-averse defendant would.

As J. B. Heaton demonstrates in an important contribution to the scholarly debate, the settlement pressure exerted by the class action operates where plaintiffs' probability of success on the merits, as perceived by the defendant, is only moderately low, *not* where that probability is extremely low. In extremely low-probability litigation, both a risk-neutral defendant and a risk-averse defendant would take the class action to trial. And, for litigation with a moderate to high probability of success, both a risk-neutral and a risk-averse defendant would settle. Settlement pressure—the situation where risk aversion makes the difference between settlement and trial—arises in the area between these two categories, as the following graph adapted from Heaton's analysis depicts for the eye to see:[89]

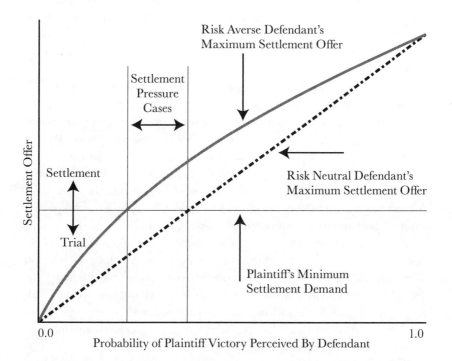

Heaton assumes that the minimum settlement demand of the plaintiff class remains constant, regardless of the probability of victory for the plaintiff class, as perceived by the defendant—hence, the flat horizontal line on the graph. This assumption actually understates the range of cases in which class settlement pressure operates. An upwardly sloping line, on the plausible assumption that the minimum settlement demand of the plaintiff class rises with the probability of victory, would only increase the range of settlement pressure cases.

To observe that class settlement pressure stems from risk aversion on the defense side is not to determine its normative significance. The kinds of business enterprises characteristically sued as defendants in mass tort litigation have access to sophisticated insurance arrangements.[90] And the ability of insurers to pool together risks of various sorts enables them to act — and to influence their insureds to behave — in a more risk-neutral fashion. In fact, Heaton notes the seeming underdevelopment of a vibrant insurance market that would enable defendants to hedge against "the small but positive risk of a catastrophic loss" in a classwide trial.[91] Recognition that insurance arrangements might reduce risk aversion, however, says nothing about the normative significance of the underlying risk in the first place. It simply involves a reallocation of money — specifically, whether plaintiffs (in the price of class settlements) or insurers (in the price they charge for coverage) should reap the gains from defendants' inclination to rid themselves of risk.

With the nature of settlement pressure in mind, one may turn squarely to the debate over its legitimacy. Even those commentators most skeptical of the concern expressed over class settlement pressure recognize that its legitimacy turns on normative considerations, not descriptive ones. Warren Schwartz declares: "There is no normative theory of which I am aware that provides a basis for preferring either the (more favorable to plaintiffs) settlement environment of the class action or the (more favorable to defendants) settlement environment of the individual action."[92] Upon a careful parsing of the debate over class settlement pressure, Charles Silver ends on a similar note: "Even if one knows that the balance of risk aversion differs from one litigation context to another, one may not know which balance is best. The normative point depends on how different bargaining environments connect up with a larger account of the goals of civil justice systems."[93] My suggestion is that linkage of the settlement pressure debate to the *Daubert* gatekeeping function can help us to develop a more precise treatment of the normative question lurking here.

The debate over the legitimacy of class settlement pressure, at bottom, is a debate over a seemingly simple observation: the 8 percent probability of loss for the defendant, to continue the illustration used earlier. The hard question on which normative implications depend is: Why does that 8 percent exist? To see the significance of this question, recall the way Judge Posner frames the procedural alternatives in *Rhone-Poulenc*. The choice, he observes, lies between a nationwide class action and "a decentralized process of multiple trials" that generate "a pooling of judgment" on the factual questions in the litigation across "multiple juries constituting in the aggregate a much larger and more diverse sample of decision-makers."[94] To be sure, this description of procedural alternatives identifies the extreme points but omits options in the middle — say, consolidated trials in multiple cases. If well founded, concern over the settlement pressure exerted by class certification undoubtedly has the potential to extend to other modes of aggregation — to consolidations and even informal modes of aggregation achieved through the representation of multiple claimants by the same law firm.[95]

Middle options aside, Judge Posner's notion of multiple individual trials — the most obvious alternative to class certification — helps to pinpoint the normative questions lurking within the 8 percent figure. Judge Posner's call for a decentralized series of trials before multiple decision makers speaks in terms that resemble those used in what the scholarly literature has dubbed the Condorcet Jury Theorem. Here, I must note emphatically that I do not advance a new theory of class settlement pressure based on an application of the Cordorcet Jury Theorem. I simply suggest that one strand of writing on the Theorem in the context of legal decision making sheds light, by analogy, upon the normative implications of class settlement pressure in a way that the existing literature has not yet grasped.

Named for the Marquis de Condorcet, the Condorcet Jury Theorem speaks to the optimal size of decision-making bodies and their use of majority rule to make decisions. Not surprisingly, given its subject matter, the Theorem has garnered interest from scholars writing on many legal topics: voting in elections, decision making by multimember courts, and the valuation of claims in bankruptcy, to name just a few applications.[96] Briefly summarized, the Theorem holds that, where a group of decision makers must choose "between two alternatives, one of which is correct and the other incorrect" and where the probability of any given decision maker selecting the correct alternative is greater than $1/2$, "the probability that a majority vote will select the correct alternative approaches 1 as the number of [decision makers] gets large."[97] In this sense, more heads are a lot better than one, even if each is only slightly more likely than not to be correct.

The premise of the Theorem is easy enough to identify: the probability of a given decision maker selecting the correct alternative is greater than $1/2$. As Paul Edelman has shown, however, this seemingly clear premise contains within it a variety of possible explanations for why the probability is greater than $1/2$. And the choice among those explanations, in turn, determines the normative implications that one should draw about multimember bodies and the rules they should follow in making decisions. The $1/2$ probability could be the result of pure random variation, in the sense of each decision maker reaching her decision based simply upon a coin flip. Or it could be the result of the selection of decision makers from some larger pool, within which just over $1/2$ of the potential decision makers are sufficiently insightful that they decide correctly all of time. Or it could be that each individual decision maker is apt to be correct in slightly more than 1/2 of the instances for decision.[98] Scholars, in short, must unpack the probability models behind proposed applications of the Condorcet Jury Theorem in order to draw sound normative conclusions. So, too, by analogy, must the law unpack the probability models behind the class settlement pressure debate.

Recall that a moderately low probability of loss for the defendant is what gives rise to the variance in potential outcomes in a classwide trial. This, in turn, gives rise to the interim range of situations graphed by Heaton, in which the variance in outcomes makes the difference between settlement and trial. Whether 8 percent or some other figure stands within the magical Heatonian area of moderately low probability litigation is not of concern. The same question — why some moderately low probability exists — arises with regard to any percentage that one might choose for illustrative purposes. In fact, there are a variety of explanations that one might offer. Consider two, with radically different implications for the settlement pressure debate.

A moderately low probability of loss for the defendant might reflect genuine disagreement about the conclusions that a careful, unbiased fact finder should draw from conflicting evidence — say, on what should have been known by blood product firms at a given time in the fast-developing world of scientific research about HIV. That class certification would give rise to settlement pressure due to such a genuine disagreement about the facts would not be a ground for normative concern.

But the same probability — the same 8 percent — might reflect the influence of the systematic cognitive biases discussed earlier in this chapter: for example, the possibility of hindsight bias, perhaps accentuated by the sympathetic nature of the plaintiffs' plight. Here, the resulting class settlement pressure would be grounds for normative qualms — indeed, much the same normative qualms underlying the gatekeeping role for judges announced in *Daubert*. Once again, the concern is over the amplification of preexisting imperfections in tort adjudication. Where the 8 percent probability arises from cognitive biases, fears of class settlement pressure sound a kind of Hippocratic oath for courts faced with whether to aggregate litigation: First, do no harm. For class actions specifically, the terms of Rule 23 write into procedural law a Hippocratic oath of sorts, conditioning class certification on a judicial determination that class treatment would be "superior to other available [procedural] methods for the fair and efficient adjudication of the controversy."[99]

In sketching these two possible explanations for the 8 percent probability, one quickly must add two caveats. The first concerns the relationship between the class certification decision and judicial assessment of the substantive merits. The second speaks to the very real prospect that a moderately low probability of loss for the defendant, in practice, might well entail a mixture of the two explanations described here. The existing literature contains competing arguments about class certification and merits scrutiny. One camp of commentators dismisses fears of settlement pressure by reference to the possibility of summary judgment. Specifically, this first camp contends that a judicial ruling on a defense motion for summary judgment prior to a decision on the class certification question will effectively cull out low-probability litigation.[100] Only the situations not worthy of summary judgment for the defense would remain; and, there, any remaining probability of loss for the defendant would reflect genuine disagreement over conflicting evidence. A competing camp of commentators embraces fears of settlement pressure and calls for judicial inquiry into the substantive merits as part of the class certification decision[101]—seemingly on top of any earlier opportunity for summary judgment motions from the defense. This second approach would entail the rejection or, at least, substantial clarification of language from the Supreme Court disallowing consideration of the plaintiffs' probability of success on the merits as part of the class certification inquiry.[102]

For present purposes, the key point is that the differing prescriptions offered by these two camps flow from an underlying disagreement over the reason for the low probability of loss that gives rise to settlement pressure in the first place. Each camp has a competing—albeit largely implicit and unarticulated—account of what explains the 8 percent. Not surprisingly, each camp proceeds to draw different normative implications for how the law should think about class settlement pressure.

One observation not raised by commentators on either side is that, if Heaton is correct that settlement pressure operates in moderately low-probability litigation rather than very-low-probability litigation, then summary judgment—even preclass certification—is unlikely to form a robust response to the phenomenon of settlement pressure. To put this point in visual terms, summary judgment operates at the leftward edge of Heaton's graph, whereas settlement pressure—as he shows—operates further to the right. A second observation speaks to the very real possibility that both legitimate and illegitimate reasons might lie behind the 8 percent probability.

The literature on litigation and cognitive psychology offers no reason to believe that cognitive biases operate only within a particular probability range. To the contrary, the literature speaks of predictable, systematic biases that pervade human decision making under uncertainty, whatever the magnitude of that uncertainty. Nor can one casually dismiss the significance of cognitive biases for the class settlement pressure debate by noting that different biases point in different directions as between plaintiffs and defendants.[103] Again, as noted earlier, plaintiffs' law firms have every incentive to select for investment those scenarios in which cognitive biases will tend to operate in their favor, on the whole, rather than against them. These observations underscore the plausibility of the view that any given moderately low, Heatonian probability of loss for the defendant is likely to stem from a mixture of legitimate and illegitimate reasons, both of which class certification stands to amplify.

Courts at least stand a fighting chance of being able, over time, to determine the kinds of research that should comprise the bare minimum for the formulation of expert opinions on the existence of general causation. The process of building on case-by-case decisions is one familiar to the judicial realm. By contrast, the prospect of courts distinguishing in the class certification context between legitimate and illegitimate components of a given probability of loss for the defendant appears far dimmer. At the very least, the analysis here suggests that any such differentiation stands to be highly context-specific.

The pitfalls of *Rhone-Poulenc* and its ilk are not just ones of practicality, however. Judicial inquiry into the mix of legitimate and illegitimate components of a given probability of loss for the defendant would entail looking behind legal outcomes — verdicts at trial and settlements — that courts, for good reason, have long regarded as insulated from second-guessing. Many long-standing principles — that jurors conduct their deliberations in secrecy and need not explain their verdicts, that jurors generally may not be called as witnesses to discuss their deliberations,[104] and that courts do not review at all the settlement terms for nonclass lawsuits[105] — stem from a sense that, for the most part, after-the-fact inquiries into verdicts and settlements are illegitimate.

There are, in short, serious barriers to efforts by courts to untangle the legitimate and illegitimate components of a given probability of loss. Those barriers help to explain why, in the end, an assessment of *Rhone-Poulenc* must be one of ambivalence. Indeed, the ambivalence here recalls the reservations voiced earlier about *Daubert* as an implicit regulatory regime for the development of mass tort litigation. Both *Daubert* and *Rhone-Poulenc* regulate the transition from a litigation stage focused on the exploration of claim merit to one directed predominantly toward comprehensive settlement.

Cast in their best light, the two decisions highlight genuine problems arising from the amplification of defects in tort adjudication. But both decisions seek to implement their respective regulatory regimes in ways that raise institutional concerns of their own.

In regulatory terms, both *Daubert* and *Rhone-Poulenc* involve top-down, third-party regulation of the transition from immature to mature mass tort litigation. The usual difficulty with regimes of top-down, third-party regulation — say, rate-making commissions for a given industry — is that the regulators may well lack sound information on which to make enlightened decisions. To administer the *Daubert* admissibility standard, judges must immerse themselves in subjects far removed from their training in law. To make sense of *Rhone-Poulenc,* judges would have to look behind verdicts and settlements in an effort somehow to discern the degree to which they rest on cognitive psychological biases. But, now, consider the regulatory problem in a different light.

If the real concern is to temper efforts to push the litigation cycle precipitously into the mature stage — if the problem is too little exploration of the merits and too much of a rush to induce comprehensive peace negotiations — then it is far from clear that top-down regulation by courts is the only option available. This is not to say that courts should abandon the scrutiny of expert scientific testimony or that they should take lightly the decision whether to certify a class. Rather, it is to suggest that the law may use additional tools to take some of the pressure off of courts.

Chapter 11 in this book ultimately will argue that much of the difficulty in mass tort litigation today stems from a lack of alignment between the incentives of plaintiffs' lawyers engaged in comprehensive peace negotiations and the interests of those whose rights they stand to affect. Efforts to precipitate comprehensive peace negotiations come with the possibility of considerable gain and relatively little risk for plaintiffs' lawyers. This contrasts with the all-too-real risks that a comprehensive peace poses for mass tort claimants themselves — most significantly, the prospect of inequitable treatment for future claimants relative to those in the present day who are otherwise similarly situated. As for any opportunity that promises the possibility of big gains with little risk to those who pursue it, one should not be surprised that the opportunity will tend to be over-consumed. What I am suggesting, in other words, is that we think of the transition from immature to mature litigation not in isolation but, rather, as one of the opening moves that leads to the real endgame of mass tort litigation: comprehensive settlement. Improvement in the alignment of incentives for those settlement negotiations promises to constrain efforts to press precipitously to the mature stage in the first place. It promises a kind of bottom-up, first-party regulation that might complement top-down, third-party regulation by courts under the auspices of admissibility and class certification decisions.

Linking together the subject matter of this chapter with the challenges of settlement design makes for a natural bridge to the discussion that follows. When mass tort litigation reaches the mature stage, the game changes from the resolution of cases to the crafting of a comprehensive peace. The next chapter traces the shift from ad hoc settlement of pending tort claims to the development of more permanent devices to institutionalize, regularize, and administer the resolution of claims in the future. The familiar distinction in administrative law between adjudication and rulemaking provides a framework with which to understand this move — what one might describe in terms of a transition from retrospective resolution of pending claims to prospective planning for claim resolution in the future. Making peace means making and enforcing in the future a compensation grid much like those already used in public administrative processes. The makings of such a grid are the subject to which the next chapter turns.

PART II

FROM LITIGATION TO ADMINISTRATION

CHAPTER IV

MAKING AND
ENFORCING A GRID

The transition to the mature stage of mass tort litigation makes for a change in strategic outlook for plaintiffs' lawyers and for defendants. Both will tend to regard ongoing lawsuits in the tort system not as a way to explore the merits of the litigation but, instead, as a prelude to its resolution on a comprehensive basis. This chapter and the next analyze the tentative, ad hoc emergence of vehicles for the comprehensive resolution of mass torts. The basic thrust of the shift is from litigation of individual claims in the tort system to creation of private administrative systems for the compensation of claimants in the future.

Three points bear mention at the outset. First, private administrative systems for compensation are not created out of whole cloth. They expose and regularize the process of aggregate settlement in mass tort litigation. Administration of claims may proceed either on a piecemeal basis (through aggregate settlements of claims filed in the tort system over time) or on a comprehensive basis (through the setting of compensation terms as much for future claims as for present ones). This prospective dimension—the power to set the legal rules that shall govern the future and to make those rules binding—is what sets apart private administration in the sense used here from aggregate settlements in ongoing litigation.

Second, this chapter draws on principles of administrative law to frame the transition from litigation to administration as a problem of institutional authority. The contrast between the settlement of pending tort claims and the binding of future claims to a private administrative system recalls the familiar distinction in administrative law between adjudication and rule-making. To see the transition from litigation to administration as a shift from adjudication to rulemaking, in turn, is to raise questions surrounding the authority of the would-be rule makers and the process for the making of the rules.

Third, I use a series of examples to highlight how problems of governing authority and institutional legitimacy arise when the law seeks to make the transition from tort to administration. Two of the examples consist of well-accepted developments in the world of administration: workers' compensation programs and the promulgation by public administrative agencies of gridlike rules for public benefit programs. The other two examples come from the world of mass tort litigation. Both consist of failed experiments from an institutional standpoint. The present chapter concludes with an account of one prominent lower court's attempt to generate a grid for pending asbestos cases by way of judicially supervised statistical sampling. The next chapter analyzes even bolder efforts: attempts by mass tort lawyers to resolve the future liabilities of various asbestos defendants through the vehicle of class action settlements. Both workers' compensation and gridlike rules for public benefits have achieved a high degree of institutional legitimacy. By contrast, court-administered statistical sampling and mass tort class settlements have not. The difference, I suggest, lies in a difference in governing authority.

Adjudication versus Rulemaking, Litigation versus Administration

In discussing the dynamics of the mature litigation stage, chapter 2 pointed briefly to the phenomenon of aggregate settlements. In one common permutation, the defendant pays a lump sum to settle multiple pending lawsuits brought on behalf of plaintiffs represented by a single, common law firm. The plaintiffs' law firm, in turn, allocates the lump sum among the individual clients whose lawsuits the aggregate settlement resolves.[1] Aggregate settlements form a useful starting point for the treatment here of the transition from tort litigation to private administration. By first pinpointing the source of legitimacy for aggregate settlements, one may frame the terms for debate over more ambitious settlement vehicles such as class actions.

The legitimacy of aggregate settlements rests on notions of property and contract. For purposes of the Due Process Clause, the Supreme Court has characterized the right to sue as a form of property.[2] The usual rule for sales of either personal or real property is that the power of sale resides with the property owner or someone to whom the owner herself has delegated that power. Civil litigation stands as the vehicle to sell the plaintiff's right to sue, whether by private contract (a settlement on an individual or an aggregate basis) or by legal compulsion (a judgment rendered at trial). Representation of a particular client by a lawyer amounts to a contractual delegation of the power to sell the client's property, much like an individual homeowner might contract for the services of a real estate broker to sell her home.[3]

Given the economics of mass tort litigation discussed earlier, it comes as no surprise that plaintiffs' law firms should aspire to represent large numbers of clients whose tort claims exhibit varying degrees of similarity. From the standpoint of plaintiffs' lawyers, aggregate settlements are the natural outgrowth of the high fixed costs and low marginal costs associated with the development of mass tort litigation in the first place. The drive for legal representation on a mass-production basis predictably leads to settlement on a mass-production basis.

From the standpoint of the individual plaintiff, an agreement to be represented by a given law firm along with other similar clients stands as a tacit recognition of the potential for joint gains on the part of all such plaintiffs from legal representation on a collective basis. As Charles Silver and Lynn Baker have underscored, the potential for joint gains explains why clients in civil litigation routinely consent to representation by lawyers along with others who have broadly similar claims, even though such arrangements also present a potential for conflicts of interest across the various clients.[4] Here, too, legal representation resembles other kinds of contractual relationships by which people hire agents to assist them. Multiple homeowners, each acting alone, often end up hiring the same real estate broker.

The contractual arrangements whereby would-be plaintiffs delegate to a given law firm the power to sell their rights to sue are not the products of extensive, point-by-point negotiation. The same is also true of the contractual arrangements between homeowners and real estate brokers. In both tort litigation on the plaintiffs' side and real estate sales, one observes the use of standard terms for the sales agent — the contingency fee percentage for the plaintiffs' lawyer or the sales commission for the real estate broker.[5]

Its financial terms aside, delegation of the power to sell the client's right to sue takes place along with limitations upon the power of the sales agent. Most notably for present purposes, the law of professional responsibility writes into the contract for legal representation of multiple clients a constraint commonly dubbed the "aggregate settlement rule." Specifically, Rule 1.8(g) of the Model Rules of Professional Conduct recognizes the possibility of aggregate settlement by a single lawyer on behalf of multiple clients. But the rule requires the lawyer to inform each client of what all other clients are to receive under the settlement and, then, to obtain each client's

consent to the deal.[6] The aggregate settlement rule is not waivable, moreover, though some commentators have argued that it should be.[7]

The individual client consent demanded by the aggregate settlement
rule does considerable work as a conceptual matter. The existence of client
consent—ultimately, an outgrowth of the contractual nature of the lawyer-
client relationship—both legitimizes aggregate settlements and explains
the lack of external scrutiny over the lawyer's choice of which claims to
aggregate in the first place. Apart from the demand for consent from all
clients, the aggregate settlement rule sets no parameters on the degree of
dissimilarity that the settled claims may exhibit—a stark contrast to non-
consensual vehicles for aggregation like the class action, as the next chapter
shall discuss.

Recognition of aggregate settlements as vehicles for the resolution of
claims on a mass basis means that one cannot draw a sharp, black-and-
white line in the mass tort context between litigation and administration.
Rather, administration of a sort inheres in mature mass tort litigation. With
regard to aggregate settlements, the administrator is simply the plaintiffs'
lawyer, who operates under the legitimating device—perhaps, just the fig
leaf—of individual client consent. The existence of aggregate settlements
nonetheless helps to sharpen the terms for discussion of the shift to more
elaborate forms of administration.

When speaking of the autonomy that an individual client has over the
disposition of her right to sue, courts often invoke the ideal that each litigant is entitled to her own "day in court."[8] If only by taking this rhetoric
a bit too literally, some observers rightly criticize the day-in-court ideal as
wildly inapt for a civil litigation system geared toward settlement rather
than courtroom trials.[9] In the mass tort area, an administrative approach to
claims does not intrude upon a literal day in court. But it does have the potential to intrude upon something else that is important: the authority that
each client retains over the disposition of her right to sue. That authority
stems from notions of property—the premise that the client's right to sue is
her right. Apart from situations of client consent, the administration of mass
tort claims stands to act upon an individual's right to sue not in the manner
of a real estate agent retained by contract but, rather, like a local government condemning real property and providing "just compensation" to the
property owner.[10] The thing that makes administration of the latter sort
legitimate is the existence of governing authority, *not* a private contract.

True enough, aggregate settlements entail governance of a sort. The
lawyer exercises discretion on behalf of multiple clients with whom she has
individual contractual relationships. As vehicles for peace in mass tort litigation, however, aggregate settlements are mere stopgaps. They have the

capacity to act only on cases already on file in the tort system, not on future cases. Although they certainly bind the parties to the particular lawsuits that are settled, aggregate settlements are merely predictive with regard to the disposition of future cases. In a given area of mass tort litigation, both plaintiffs' lawyers and their defense counterparts tend to be repeat players in the aggregate settlement process. But both remain perfectly free to treat future cases differently, even to refuse to settle future cases at all.

An analogy to principles of administrative law helps to crystallize the characterization of aggregate settlements as stopgaps. Administrative law is an appropriate template for consideration of governing processes, for that body of law arose as a distinct subject area in the twentieth century to address the new forms of power wielded by modern administrative agencies within the scheme of American government. A commonplace observation in the standard course on the subject holds that administrative agencies may act in ways akin to the rendering of decisions in specific cases by a court (adjudication) or that resemble lawmaking by the legislature (rulemaking).

Adjudication characteristically deals with the legal consequences of past conduct for particular persons. A classic example would consist of a trial-like hearing by the National Labor Relations Board (NLRB) to determine whether a particular employer has engaged in an unfair labor practice. Rulemaking, by contrast, characteristically involves the setting of legal standards for the future that bind the public at large.[11] Thus, for instance, the Environmental Protection Agency might promulgate rules that limit the release of a particular air pollutant and that have the force of law henceforth.

Agency orders in adjudication are highly predictive of what the agency will do in subsequent adjudications involving similar matters.[12] An employer, for example, would not be well advised to replicate in its workplace a labor practice that the NLRB previously found to be illegal in an adjudication involving other parties. But the soundness of that legal advice stems simply from a prediction — usually correct — that the agency will treat later cases like earlier cases. In a subsequent adjudication, the agency instead may choose to take a different approach, at least if that alternative is also within its legal authority and if the agency offers a reasoned explanation for its change of view.[13] Orders in adjudication are not rules, for they lack binding prospective effect on nonparties. The outcome of an adjudication does not bind the agency in a subsequent adjudication, whereas a rule does bind the agency in subsequent adjudication until such time as the rule itself is rescinded or amended through a second rulemaking proceeding.[14]

The crucial observation for present purposes is that the nature of mass torts—their defining feature of latent disease—means that efforts to resolve a given area of litigation on a comprehensive basis must take a prospective form. One must move beyond stopgaps in the present to governance of the future for the sheer practical reason that all impaired persons are unlikely to be identified—or even identifiable—at the point when a given area of mass tort litigation has matured. The content of aggregate settlements in the past may well inform the setting of rules for the handling of cases in the future. But one still must shift from retrospective adjudication to prospective rulemaking.

A vision of the processes for comprehensive peace in mass tort litigation grounded in agency rulemaking raises questions of governing authority. One conceivable vehicle that offers something more comprehensive and prospective in orientation than aggregate settlements is public legislation. There is little doubt that Congress could enact legislation establishing an administrative framework to handle a given area of mass tort litigation. Mass torts, after all, arise from quintessentially commercial activity—the buying and selling of products—that is plainly interstate in scope and, hence, subject to regulation under the Commerce Clause of the Constitution.[15] The most prominent effort by legislatures to switch a category of recurring claims out of the tort system and into a streamlined administrative process consists of workers' compensation statutes.[16] There, too, legislation acted within the backdrop of contractual arrangements, such as private cooperative insurance associations, that had arisen earlier to address the problem of work-related injuries.[17]

To recognize the possibility of legislation is not to suggest that Congress necessarily must make all the microlevel determinations for future mass tort claims. Congress might set the payouts for the various types of implicated claims, as in proposed legislation to address litigation over asbestos.[18] Alternatively, Congress might delegate to an Executive Branch official the power to set the grid in light of various overarching considerations, as in the delegation to the Attorney General and, ultimately, to Special Master Kenneth Feinberg with respect to the compensation fund established for victims of the September 11, 2001, terrorist attacks (the 9/11 Fund).[19]

Like the legitimacy of aggregate settlements, the legitimacy of public legislation is beyond serious question, even though it entails a risk of dereliction by agents—whether the members of Congress themselves or their delegates. The delegation of power from client to lawyer finds its rough analogue in the world of legislation in the delegation of power from "the People" as a whole to Congress in Article I of the Constitution. For legislation, there is no outer limit on the divergent interests that the common agent—the government—might represent. If anything, the very notion of government celebrates the representation of the polity as a composite whole, with "no thought that every separate interest within the polity must receive specific and equivalent representation."[20] Legislation nonetheless comes with constraints of its own, consisting not only of the procedural requirements for the enactment of laws and the substantive limits on legislative power in Article I but also a regularized process for removal of the rule makers from power: electoral accountability, whether of the Members of Congress or of the President, as chief executive. Indeed, in later chapters, I shall argue that notions of governance can help to point the law of mass torts in some fruitful new directions.

For now, the important point about legislation goes to its availability in practical terms, not to its legitimacy. Absent the kind of cataclysmic, galvanizing events that led to the creation of the 9/11 Fund, Congress has shown little willingness to act on mass tort litigation, once it is afoot. Notwithstanding repeated invitations from the Supreme Court,[21] Congress has yet to enact legislation to address asbestos litigation—a subject discussed further in chapter 6. If anything, the emergence of mature mass tort litigation in itself tends to harden political interests on all sides of any proposed reform measures, so as to make deadlock especially likely within Congress.[22] The unavailability of legislation nonetheless has not impeded efforts at peacemaking through other means.

The analogy to agency rulemaking helps to frame the two challenges that any peacemaking effort short of legislation will face: how to set the content of the rules for future claims and how to legitimize the institutional arrangements that generate those rules, such that the law may accord them binding force in the absence of individualized consent. On both fronts, the transition from litigation to administration has not been smooth but, rather, has consisted of tentative, ad hoc experimentation.

Pragmatics and Compromise in the Design of Compensation Grids

In speaking of rules to govern future claims, this chapter thus far has left open the content of those rules. In fact, the nature of mass torts has lent a common, recurring structure to any viable set of rules for the future. This is not to say that there exists a magical, one-size-fits-all solution for every mass tort. My suggestion simply is that any viable set of rules will both categorize and generalize in order to form a compensation grid. Rules will draw distinctions designed to account for significant differences among claims. At the same time, rules will forego the drawing of other distinctions that might have formed the subject of dispute in the event of litigation.

The particular distinctions that a grid draws or foregoes may be nothing more than the result of the diminishing marginal returns to design efforts. A given distinction may be so unlikely to make enough of a difference in enough situations to warrant the efforts of rule makers to account for it in the compensation grid. Rule designers, however, may forego other distinctions for other reasons. A grid might forego a given line of distinction precisely because doing so is part of the grand compromise that facilitates the creation and implementation of a grid in the first place. The foregoing of a distinction, in other words, may serve as the price that one side or another effectively pays in order to enjoy the gains that a grid promises — chiefly, efficiency and reduction of the variance in outcomes across similar cases. The key point is that the need for the rule designers to strike a grand compromise is a function of the institutional vehicle chosen to implement the grid — specifically, its authority to displace the preexisting process for claims.

Two examples — one from the annals of administrative law, the other from historical developments in tort law — illustrate the interplay between grid design and institutional authority. As commentary on administrative law has long recognized, modern public benefit programs have no analogue at common law; rather, they entail the creation of "new property."[23] In their administration of public benefit programs, agencies have used rulemaking to address recurring factual questions concerning eligibility for benefits. In so doing, agencies have curtailed sharply the need for extended exploration of eligibility questions in individual adjudications.

In its 1983 decision in *Heckler v. Campbell*, the Supreme Court upheld the efforts of the Social Security Administration (SSA) along these lines with regard to the federal program for Social Security disability benefits. By statute, the disability determination for any given claimant turns, in part, upon whether jobs exist in the national economy for persons of the claimant's physical ability, age, education, and work experience.[24] The SSA previously had relied on "vocational experts" versed in labor market conditions to address the job availability question in individualized hearings, an approach the agency perceived to have fostered both inefficiency and inconsistency in the treatment of claims.[25]

The SSA rules at issue in *Heckler* take "the form of four tables — one for each classification of work — sedentary, light, medium, and heavy work." Each table is subdivided by categories of age, education, and skill. "Having found that a [given] claimant . . . can do light work, is between 50–54, has a limited education, and has previously done unskilled work, the [agency] can go to the line in the 'light work' table presenting these characteristics and read out the appropriate conclusion—'not disabled.'"[26] The conclusion stated in any given cell of the grid rests on the SSA's analysis of information on the national labor market, as compiled in the rulemaking proceeding that generated the grid. Upholding the SSA's reliance on the grid, the Supreme Court noted that, "even where an agency's enabling statute requires it to hold a hearing [for each individual benefit claimant], the agency may rely on its rulemaking authority to determine issues that do not require case-by-case adjudication."[27]

The SSA in *Heckler* enjoyed the flexibility to choose between dealing with the job-availability question through testimony in individual adjudications or addressing that question in advance through rulemaking. This flexibility flowed from an underlying delegation of governing power from Congress to the agency. By the time of *Heckler*, the Court had long established that agencies with the power to set policy by way of either adjudication or rulemaking may choose freely between those two procedural avenues. As the Court had put it in a famous 1947 case—*Securities and Exchange Commission v. Chenery Corp.*—"the choice made between proceeding by general rule or by individual, ad hoc litigation is one that lies primarily in the informed discretion of the administrative agency."[28] Absent specification otherwise by Congress, an agency may choose between rulemaking and adjudication on purely pragmatic grounds.

Existing commentary recognizes the kinship between the claimant categories in the SSA's grid and the recurring patterns of disease that define a mass tort.[29] A further observation, however, is not part of the literature: When agency rulemaking generates a grid for a public benefit program with no common-law precursor, the design of the grid will turn principally upon pragmatic considerations. By contrast, when a gridlike system stands to operate within the backdrop of a preexisting, common-law regime for compensation, the design of the grid will turn not just on pragmatics but also on the compromises needed to bring about the adoption of the grid in the first place.

The SSA rules upheld in *Heckler* present a clear-cut case. Congress had delegated rulemaking authority to the agency; the Social Security disability benefits program was the creation of the government itself, with no common-law analogue; and the grid faithfully applied the statutory criteria for disability. The *Heckler* Court added that the SSA rules afforded any given claimant the opportunity to present evidence that the grid categories "fail to describe [her] particular limitations."[30] Still, it bears note that the grid in *Heckler* transplanted to the public benefits context an earlier effort at grid implementation — one that operates not in the absence of common law but, instead, as its replacement.

The administration of workers' compensation programs has long centered on the use of grids that match injuries with payouts.[31] In the workers' compensation context, grids recognize broad-brush categories of injury while also removing from consideration matters that would arise in tort litigation over a given workplace injury — most importantly, an inquiry into the existence of fault on the part of the defendant employer, the injured worker, or a fellow worker. The touchstone is not the faithful replication of the previous tort regime for workplace injuries but, rather, the replacement of that regime with one different in substance — an exchange of fault-based principles of tort for no-fault compensation under the grid.[32] The features that made *Heckler* an easy case for grid implementation still remain, however.

The legal authority of legislatures to replace fault-based regimes of liability with a no-fault compensation system is no longer in serious doubt. That question was litigated tenaciously in the early twentieth century, however, as states across the country enacted fledgling versions of workers' compensation legislation.[33] To recognize today that legislatures have the power to replace the tort system for workplace injuries is not to suggest that such legislation came about easily as a political matter. To the contrary, workers' compensation statutes emerged in the early twentieth century from a heated political environment involving interest groups for both workers and industrial employers. The setting was such that any move away from the status quo ante — the tort system — would have to involve joint gains, simply as a matter of political practicality.[34] The larger point remains: Grids that administer compensation systems with no common-law precursor must concern themselves only with pragmatics. Grids that aspire to replace common-law regimes must concern themselves, in addition, with the implementation of the compromises necessary for adoption of the grid.

For workers' compensation laws, the lines of compromise involved countervailing concessions. The move to no-fault compensation for workplace-related injuries came in tandem with a reduction in the variance of payouts for employers.[35] The use of grids as a means of variance reduction brings the discussion here full circle with the treatment in the preceding chapter of efforts to use variance to push mass tort litigation to the mature stage. Once mass tort litigation matures, the question is what concessions are needed to adopt the grid as a substitute for tort litigation, not whether to embrace a grid in order to reduce variance. One notable judicial attempt at grid formulation at the mature stage of the asbestos litigation highlights the limitations of the courts alone as institutions to implement the grid. Workers' compensation statutes arose from the deployment of lawmaking power by state legislatures to implement a compromise struck among contending interest groups. By contrast, court-centered efforts at grid implementation have proven unavailing due to a lack of both lawmaking power and workable terms of compromise.

Judicially Administered Statistical Sampling

Conventional trials in individual cases serve a useful role at the immature stage by generating information on the value of mass tort claims. Once plaintiffs have established a credible threat to prevail at trial, however, full-blown trials in individual cases amount to procedural overkill. The recurring factual patterns exhibited by the cases virtually invite gridlike treatment in the manner of the SSA's treatment of the job-availability question for disability benefit claimants. In the early 1990s, Judge Robert Parker advanced a similar observation in *Cimino v. Raymark Industries, Inc.*[36] when dealing with more than three thousand asbestos cases then pending in the United States District Court for the Eastern District of Texas.

In keeping with the strategic incentives for defendants at the mature stage, the asbestos defendants in *Cimino* had adopted a strategy of contesting every contestable issue, not only in the Eastern District of Texas but also nationwide. Defendants were acting within their rights, but the practical consequences of their chosen strategy were considerable. Judge Parker lamented that even if he "could somehow close thirty cases a month, it would take six and one-half years to try [the existing] cases." Even then, "there would be pending over 5,000 [additional] untouched cases at the present rate of filing."[37] Here, again, one must take care to recognize the uniqueness of the asbestos litigation in terms of the absolute number of cases involved. But differences in number, even to an order of magnitude, do not alter the conceptual challenge identified by Judge Parker. The question of how a court should handle multiple cases that exhibit recurring factual patterns is inherent to the mature stage of mass tort litigation.

With his trial plan in *Cimino,* Judge Parker sought to generate by way of judicial proceedings the kind of compensation grid that experienced asbestos lawyers might have reached — if not explicitly, then as an implicit guide — had defendants been willing to negotiate rather than to delay. Spe-

cifically, Judge Parker posited a multiphase trial that, in effect, would define
the cells of a compensation grid and then supply the dollar amounts for
payouts in each cell. To define the cells, the jury would make findings concerning various factual matters: the work sites involved in the cases pending
before the court, the job categories of workers with exposure to asbestos
sufficient to have caused asbestos-related disease, the time periods of exposure, and the relative presence at each site of products manufactured by
the various asbestos defendants. A later phase of the trial would set payout
amounts. The jury would make actual damage awards in a random sample
of individual cases within each of five categories of asbestos-related disease.
The court then would deem the average award within each disease category to constitute the damage award for the remaining cases.[38]

Judge Parker's attempt at judicial generation of a compensation grid
met with reversal by the United States Court of Appeals for the Fifth Circuit. The contrast in rhetoric between Judge Parker's defense of his trial
plan and the Fifth Circuit's reversal on appeal is revealing. Judge Parker's
opinion offers a pragmatic defense of his trial plan, especially the use of
statistical sampling techniques for the damage calculation. The bulk of his
discussion consists of a paean to the intellectual pedigree and rigor of statistical methods.[39]

By contrast, the Fifth Circuit's opinion speaks of legitimacy, not of statistical methodology. The Fifth Circuit notes that Texas tort law—the
body of substantive law applicable in *Cimino*—affords defendants certain
protections as preconditions to the imposition of liability. Defendants can
insist upon individualized proof not only of a causal link between their particular products and the injury suffered by a particular plaintiff but also of
the damages to which each particular plaintiff is entitled.[40] In emphasizing these features of Texas law—by no means anomalous within tort doctrine—the Fifth Circuit draws on its own earlier decision, invalidating on
similar grounds a predecessor version of the trial plan advanced by Judge
Parker.[41]

The Fifth Circuit's rejection of the *Cimino* trial plan reflects an appropriate skepticism about the power of law reform that courts, acting alone, may
wield by way of procedural techniques. The reason why the *Cimino* trial
plan rightfully foundered on appeal is not because it envisioned the mass
processing of tort claims according to a compensation grid. Such a grid—if
only in a rough, impressionistic form in the minds of lawyers—is needed
to allocate the funds provided by many forms of aggregate settlements.
Had defendants been willing to settle the thousands of cases pending in
the Eastern District of Texas rather than to pursue a strategy of delay, one

easily could imagine plaintiffs' counsel doling out funds received from defendants in an aggregate settlement according to a grid much like the one Judge Parker sought to generate. Damage averaging simply would take place implicitly rather than explicitly, through statistical sampling. The trial plan in *Cimino* did not so much present an innovation in trial structure as it simply laid bare, in a published judicial opinion, the inner workings of practices that usually operate below the judicial radar screen in mass tort litigation.[42]

The real innovation of *Cimino* does not lie in its use of statistical sampling but, more problematically, in its aspiration to impose by way of a trial plan the kind of administrative regime for claim processing that experienced asbestos lawyers might have formulated and operated themselves. The outcome in *Cimino* ultimately stems from the court's lack of power to do what legislatures across the country did, decades earlier, in their enactment of workers' compensation statutes: compel the exchange of defendants' pre-existing rights under tort law for an alternative bundle of rights within an administrative scheme. By attempting to turn trials into more above-board versions of the aggregate settlement process, the *Cimino* trial plan recreated the shortcomings of aggregate settlements as a mechanism for the resolution of mass tort litigation. One may explain the intransigence of the *Cimino* defendants in the same terms that the preceding chapter described the skepticism of defendants generally toward aggregate settlements at the mature stage. Aggregate settlements operate as stopgaps that tend toward the resolution of claims for unimpaired persons on terms out of line with the skepticism of current tort law.

If anything, the average damages determined at trial in *Cimino* reinforce the foregoing concern. Approximately one-third of the individual cases in *Cimino* consisted of those in the category designated "pleural disease," as distinct from the categories for cases of asbestosis or various forms of asbestos-related cancer.[43] The term "pleural disease" is highly amorphous, however, and capable of embracing both impaired and unimpaired persons. The average damages determined through statistical sampling in *Cimino* nonetheless valued pleural disease cases at $558,900, a figure on par with cases of asbestosis and asbestos-related lung cancer, respectively.[44] Asbestos defendants had no reason to embrace such a grid, for the same reason that they had no reason to do so through expeditious aggregate settlements on an ongoing basis.

If a court cannot compel defendants to undertake aggregate settlements through a trial plan that would generate the necessary grid, then what might induce defendants to settle? The answer to this question turns out to have two components. One might describe the first as Judge Parker's solution without Judge Parker: the formulation of the compensation grid through lawyer negotiation, not through court-run statistical sampling. Lawyers on both the plaintiffs' and defendants' sides simply might construct the grid themselves, by reference to their own collective experience in the litigation.

The second component speaks to matters of temporal perspective. From the standpoint of defendants, the problem with the *Cimino* trial plan is that it was not ambitious enough. *Cimino* dealt only with pending cases, leaving open the compensation terms that would apply to the large numbers of additional cases expected in the future due to the nature of latent disease. Indeed, defendants justifiably might have feared that the average damages set in *Cimino* would serve simply to invite a further onslaught of cases on behalf of unimpaired persons. For defendants, the attraction of settlement lies not simply in the resolution of pending cases but, more broadly, in the achievement of a grand, all-encompassing peace in the litigation as a whole. The search for peace soon would lead asbestos lawyers to an innovation that would dwarf the boldness of *Cimino*. As the next chapter shall reveal, the rise of the class settlement would expose even more glaringly the shift from litigation to administration in the world of mature mass torts.

CHAPTER V

THE RISE AND FALL OF THE MASS TORT CLASS SETTLEMENT

In terms of timing, the emergence of mass tort litigation roughly parallels the development of the modern class action in procedural law. Forerunners of the modern class action include proceedings in which a medieval town or a nineteenth-century fraternal organization sought to bind its members collectively through litigation on their behalf.[1] The modern class action, in other words, traces its origins to litigation brought on an aggregate basis by entities with some manner of governing authority over their members. This chapter argues that a conception of the modern class action as an arrangement for governance sheds considerable light on the use of that device in the mass tort context.

Before turning to the specifics of class actions involving mass torts, a brief introduction is in order—first, about the basics of the class action device and, second, about the organization of the discussion thereafter. The class action stands as an exception to the bedrock principle of civil procedure that a person's legal rights cannot be altered by a judgment rendered "in litigation in which he is not designated as a party or to which he has not been made a party by service of process."[2] The class action raises the prospect of one or more persons—the class representatives named in the complaint—suing on behalf of other, similarly situated persons. Those persons then stand to be bound by the judgment in the class action, even though they are not otherwise parties to that proceeding.[3]

In economic terms, the class action confers a monopoly on class counsel with regard to the legal representation of class members. The class action enables class counsel to obtain as their clients the absent members of the class—those other than the class representatives—through the operation of a procedural rule rather than the usual, more cumbersome way: identifying potential clients, meeting them in the flesh, and securing their agreement to legal representation. The class action thus differs in nature from the representation of multiple, similar clients, each with her own separate contractual arrangement with a single, common lawyer. The class action procedure offers a cheaper substitute for privity, the formal term used by the law to describe contractual relationships.

Because it does not spring from a contract between client and lawyer, the class action device remains subject to judicial oversight in two respects pertinent here. The law of civil procedure insists on judicial certification of a lawsuit to proceed on a classwide basis and, further, requires that the court approve any settlement of a class action.[4] The class certification decision and the class settlement approval decision comprise the major chokepoints for judicial regulation of the class action device.[5] Class certification turns on compliance with the conditions for the maintenance of a class action described by procedural rule.[6] Those conditions distinguish between situations in which the court must afford class members the opportunity to opt out of the class proceedings (and, in so doing, to escape the effect of any judgment therein) and comparatively rare situations in which membership in the class is mandatory.[7] Class settlement approval turns on a judicial finding that the settlement agreement is a "fair, reasonable, and adequate" compromise in light of the nature and strength of class members' claims.[8]

The rise of the mass tort class settlement stems from a transformation in defendants' attitudes toward the use of the class action device. As embodied in Rule 23 of the Federal Rules of Civil Procedure in 1966, the modern class action seemed on its face a device with little applicability to mass torts. The drafters of the rule voiced their expectation that courts would certify class actions only rarely for multiple, similar tort claims due to the likely presence of individual questions concerning damages, liability, and applicable defenses.[9] Plaintiffs' lawyers nonetheless began to seek class certification as a means to litigate tort claims on an aggregate basis in the 1980s. These efforts met with steadfast resistance from defendants and mixed reactions, at best, from the courts.[10]

By the early 1990s, however, defendants came to recognize the potential for class actions to serve a very different function. Class actions might operate less as procedures for litigation in court and more as enforcement devices for deals designed out of court by lawyers. Specifically, class actions might put into place comprehensive settlements that would bring peace to entire areas of mass tort litigation. These deals would amount to business transactions whereby defendants would purchase class members' rights to sue. Peace for defendants would come through the preclusive effect of a court-issued judgment approving the class settlement. Such a judgment then would foreclose class members' opportunity to sue again in the tort system at a later time.

Not surprisingly, the peace terms would involve switching claims from the tort system to some form of private regime designed to implement a compensation grid. Peace, in short, would entail a shift from tort to administration. The content of the grid—its dollar limits, if any, and the types of claims that it pays—would be no accident. The terms of the grid would supply what Judge Robert Parker could not in *Cimino*: the inducement for defendants to surrender their own rights to insist upon particularized showings of each tort element in case after case as a precondition to the imposition of liability.

As the previous chapter observes, the *Cimino* trial plan for pending cases attempted to recreate the workings of a well-oiled aggregate settlement process. The ambitions of mass tort class settlements were even bolder. In effect, they would seek to nail down for the future the terms for the resolution of tort claims—to bring about what one might describe as a grand, all-encompassing, super-aggregate settlement, all in one fell swoop.

This chapter tells the story of the most ambitious efforts along these lines: the class settlements in *Amchem Products, Inc. v. Windsor*[11] and *Ortiz v. Fibreboard Corp.*[12] These two class settlements met with rejection by the Supreme Court for lack of compliance with the federal procedural rule for class actions. *Amchem* and *Ortiz*, however, are not ultimately decisions about the technicalities of class action procedure. The real lessons of the two cases concern the institutional position of the class action as a vehicle for governance—specifically, the degree to which the class action may serve as a means for law reform to rival public legislation. As decisions about governance, *Amchem* and *Ortiz* convey a well-founded skepticism about the authority of the class action to replace people's preexisting rights in tort with an alternative bundle of rights described in a class settlement agreement. Seen in this light, the Court's decisions police the boundary between litigation and legislation more so than between class actions and individual litigation.

I start by tracing the developments behind the realization by lawyers that class settlements might function as peacemaking vehicles. I then turn to the structure of the deals in *Amchem* and *Ortiz*, connecting their terms to the preceding discussion of the developmental process of mass tort litigation. The remainder of the chapter focuses on the Court's analysis and its institutional implications.

The Class Action as the Keeper of the Peace

By the 1990s, several developments pointed lawyers in the direction of the class action as a way to make peace and, at the same time, spotlighted the asbestos litigation as an attractive context for experimentation. Prior to *Amchem* and *Ortiz,* the most prominent experiment with class treatment of a mass tort took place in litigation over the defoliant Agent Orange. Military personnel exposed to Agent Orange in the course of their service during the Vietnam War sued the private contractors that had supplied that substance to the Pentagon. By the time of the class settlement negotiations in *Amchem* and *Ortiz,* the Agent Orange class settlement had formed the subject of approving opinions from the United States Court of Appeals for the Second Circuit and an acclaimed book by Peter Schuck.[13]

As Schuck and others have observed, the class settlement in the Agent Orange litigation was largely the product of the tenacity, legal acumen, and sheer will of United States District Judge Jack Weinstein.[14] Taking over the Agent Orange litigation after the elevation to the appellate bench of the judge previously assigned to the matter, Judge Weinstein set the litigation on a swift schedule for trial with the objective of precipitating serious settlement negotiations.[15] Judge Weinstein was openly skeptical of the scientific basis for the alleged causal link between Agent Orange and latent disease. He nonetheless orchestrated a form of shuttle diplomacy, literally on the eve of trial, whereby special masters acting at his behest convinced the defendants to settle the entire litigation for $180 million. The judge himself had suggested this dollar figure, even in the face of remarks by defendants implying their willingness to pay more for the sake of securing peace.[16]

The role of Judge Weinstein did not stop with the overall dollar sum for the class settlement. His impact also extended to construction of the grid for distribution of that sum. Acting on the recommendations of a special master,[17] Judge Weinstein ultimately approved a class settlement that effectively created a private administrative agency.[18] The $180 million would not be paid out immediately in the manner of a conventional damage verdict but, rather, would be distributed over time. In pertinent part, the class settlement would provide cash benefits to the plaintiff Vietnam veterans through what amounted to a ten-year term insurance policy. Class members could seek cash from the overall settlement pot in the event that they developed disease at any time during the ten-year period following class settlement approval in 1984.[19]

On appeal, the Second Circuit upheld both Judge Weinstein's certification of the Agent Orange class and his approval of the class settlement.[20] As the discussion of *Amchem* and *Ortiz* will suggest shortly, there is ample reason to doubt, in retrospect, the propriety of the class certification in the Agent Orange litigation. In pointing to that example here, I speak not so much to its procedural propriety but, rather, to its effect on the imagination of mass tort lawyers by the 1990s, in combination with *Cimino*.

In the *Cimino* trial plan, Judge Parker sought to fashion a compensation grid as a surrogate for an aggregate settlement process for pending asbestos cases. The Agent Orange litigation, by contrast, marked an experiment with the class action as a vehicle to resolve future claims. It would be only a matter of time before sophisticated lawyers would meld the two examples together, all while reducing the need for creativity on the part of judges. Mass tort lawyers would fashion a compensation grid through their own negotiations and then seek to make it binding upon future claimants by way of a judgment approving a class settlement. Defendants in search of a way to resolve their mass tort liabilities, in short, would learn to stop worrying and love the class action. In the past, defendants had objected to broadly defined plaintiff classes for purposes of litigation. But they came to embrace broadly defined classes as a means to expand the peace that they could garner from class settlements.[21]

Two additional developments pointed to the asbestos litigation as the most likely setting for experimentation along the foregoing lines. By the early 1990s, an ad hoc judicial panel for the federal courts had called for exploration of innovative solutions for the expanding numbers of asbestos claims.[22] To the same end, the Judicial Panel on Multidistrict Litigation (MDL Panel) consolidated in the United States District Court for the Eastern District of Pennsylvania the asbestos lawsuits pending within the federal courts as a way to facilitate some manner of resolution.[23] The negotiations that produced the class settlement in *Amchem* arose from this consolidation of federal asbestos litigation.

A second development lent special urgency to the efforts to harness the class action as a vehicle for peacemaking. In 1982, the leading firm in the asbestos industry, Johns-Manville Corporation, filed for protection under Chapter 11 of the Bankruptcy Code, triggering a process of corporate reorganization. Six long years later, Manville garnered final court approval for a reorganization plan that would create a separate legal entity — a trust fund — to handle asbestos claims against the firm.[24] The Manville trust proved to be a perilous institution, however, with large numbers of claims quickly overwhelming its initial capitalization. This depletion precipitated dramatic markdowns in the payout levels originally described in the reorganization plan and repeated judicial interventions to prop up the finances of the trust.[25]

The Manville bankruptcy also raised questions about the authority of bankruptcy courts to discharge future mass tort claims—in practical terms, to bind future claimants to the trust fund created under the auspices of Chapter 11.[26] The legal uncertainty surrounding the Manville proceedings led Congress, in 1994, to add to the Bankruptcy Code a special provision—popularly known by its code section, 524(g)[27]—to bless the Manville trust and to facilitate the pursuit of similar arrangements by other asbestos firms.[28] Chapter 9 shall explore in greater depth the working of § 524(g). The point, for now, is that the Manville bankruptcy lent credibility to fears that continued litigation in the tort system would portend a similar end for other asbestos defendants—all to the delay of compensation for injured persons.

The time period that produced the class settlement negotiations in *Amchem* and *Ortiz* was a fluid one. Lawyers for both asbestos plaintiffs and defendants remained unsure whether the endgame of the litigation as a whole would occur under the newly created § 524(g) or some other alternative. The possibility of mass tort class settlements held particular attraction for defendants, for it had the potential to preserve corporate equity to a greater extent than bankruptcy. By its terms, the Bankruptcy Code prioritizes debt over equity, insisting that a reorganization plan pay debt holders (a category that includes tort claimants against the debtor firm) before equity holders (such as corporate shareholders).[29] The magnitude of the tort claims against most asbestos defendants was such that the prioritization of debt over equity would leave precious little, if anything, for shareholders of those firms.

To identify fears of bankruptcy as part of the context for the class settlements in *Amchem* and *Ortiz* is not to suggest that avoidance of bankruptcy is necessarily a sinister objective. All settlements in civil litigation occur in the shadow of the consequences for one side or the other in the absence of settlement. For asbestos defendants, avoidance of bankruptcy would turn on setting more definite parameters on their future liabilities. And that, in turn, would call for the replacement of tort litigation with a compensation grid. The challenge would come in lending the grid binding force over future asbestos claimants.

Class Settlements as Privatized Administration

The class settlements in *Amchem* and *Ortiz* stand as latter-day elaborations on workers' compensation. Both class settlements contemplated the replacement of the tort system with a private administrative regime. The plaintiff classes in both cases had a workplace nexus, primarily encompassing industrial employees exposed on the job to the asbestos-containing products of the settling defendants.[30] To be sure, the compensation schemes of both settlements ran between workers and manufacturers of asbestos-containing products rather than workers and their employers, as in workers' compensation legislation. But, in broad-brush terms, the basic compromise reached in workers' compensation and in the asbestos class settlements remains strikingly similar. Both traded the delay and uncertainty of tort litigation for a more streamlined administrative approach.

The *Amchem* settlement sought to resolve future claims against twenty manufacturers of asbestos-containing products, whereas the *Ortiz* settlement dealt with future claims against one firm, Fibreboard Corporation. In both cases, the definition of the plaintiff class — encompassing only persons "without already pending lawsuits" — underscored the purely prospective reach of the settlements.[31] To borrow the language of administrative law, the class settlements in *Amchem* and *Ortiz* amounted to rulemaking for future claims. But the settlement designers sought to make those rules binding through a process that literally involved adjudication: through court-issued judgments in class action lawsuits.

The replacement of the tort system contemplated in the *Amchem* settlement was less than complete. There, the settling parties sought certification of an opt-out class under Rule 23(b)(3), such that individual class members would have had the opportunity to avoid the sale of their rights to sue. But class members could do so only by affirmatively opting out of the class shortly after receiving official notice of the settlement terms.[32]

The settlement in *Ortiz* contemplated a complete replacement of the tort system for class members, with the settling parties seeking certification of a mandatory class under Rule 23(b)(1)(B). Although ultimately rejected by the Court for reasons that I shall discuss shortly, the ostensible premise for the mandatory class in *Ortiz* consisted of the contention that claims against Fibreboard amounted to litigation against a limited fund. According to the settling parties, the limited fund consisted of the money made available through the settlement of a separate lawsuit concerning the obligation of Fibreboard's insurers to provide coverage for the asbestos liabilities of the firm.[33] Resolution of the insurance coverage dispute proved simple enough, requiring nothing more than an ordinary settlement agreement between Fibreboard and its insurers as conventional named parties to a civil lawsuit. The trick lay in confining future tort claimants to the proceeds of that insurance coverage settlement. The settling parties in *Ortiz* looked to the mandatory class action to achieve that goal, a strategy that would have had the far-from-incidental consequence of leaving Fibreboard's net worth essentially unscathed.[34]

In terms of their payouts for class members, the class settlements in both

Amchem and *Ortiz* sought to address the dysfunctional features of mature mass tort litigation identified in chapter 2. The grid in *Amchem* set forth a range of compensation payments for each of the various asbestos-related diseases[35] based on the "historical settlement averages" paid by the twenty settling companies in the tort system.[36] The crucial feature of the *Amchem* class settlement lay in its medical criteria, which were consciously drawn to deny immediate cash payment to exposed but unimpaired persons — precisely those whom aggregate settlements tended to overpay from the standpoint of existing tort doctrine. Class members not entitled to immediate cash under the *Amchem* settlement would have received the functional equivalent of an insurance policy — a right to receive compensation later, should they ever meet the medical criteria for asbestos-related impairment.[37] This insurance policy contrasted sharply with the arrangements for unimpaired persons prevalent in aggregate settlements. There, defendants had obtained full waivers of all claims that such persons might bring in the event that impairment emerged at a later time.[38]

Although the *Ortiz* settlement terms were less detailed, their content reflected similar concerns. The *Ortiz* settlement would have established a trust fund for the payment of class members' claims, with the money provided by Fibreboard's insurers forming the overwhelming proportion of the fund.[39] The *Ortiz* settlement itself would not have limited recoveries against the trust based on the type of claim presented. That question remained for the trust administration. The fixed nature of the trust fund nevertheless would have solved for Fibreboard the problems of mature litigation in the tort system. Whatever claims might be presented for payment, the cost to Fibreboard would be limited to the funds provided to the trust. As such, Fibreboard no longer would have had any financial reason to care which sorts of claims were paid.[40]

By encompassing only future claims, the class settlements in *Amchem* and *Ortiz* left untouched large numbers of individual cases already pending in the tort system. Courts describe these as "inventory" cases,[41] a term that underscores their tendency to be represented in bulk by asbestos plaintiffs' law firms. At times proximate to the class settlements, the defendants in *Amchem* and *Ortiz* entered into aggregate settlements to resolve these inventory cases — not only those represented by the law firms that served as class counsel but also those represented by competing firms within the plaintiffs' bar.[42] It comes as no surprise, moreover, that these aggregate settlements gave plaintiffs more in lump-sum dollar terms than those persons would have received immediately, had they come under the class settlements.[43] The whole point of the class settlements from the defendants' perspective was to avoid immediate cash payment to unimpaired persons by providing them with the functional equivalent of an insurance policy. Inventory cases without present-day impairments did not receive this insurance policy and thus had to be paid more cash up front.[44] The resolution of inventory cases in tandem with the class settlements in *Amchem* and *Ortiz* would have implications for the validity of the two class actions for reasons that shall emerge shortly.

Inventory cases aside, both *Amchem* and *Ortiz* involved the use of the class action device to switch future claimants from the tort system to a private administrative regime. The capacity of the class settlements to achieve this goal turned on the ability of the settling parties to obtain favorable judgments in the class proceedings — specifically, court decisions under Rule 23 to certify the proposed classes and bless the terms for the defendants' purchase of class members' rights to sue. These decisions then would form binding judgments that would preclude tort litigation by class members in the future.

The class settlements in *Amchem* and *Ortiz* garnered initial judicial approval at the district court level,[45] but both settlements foundered on appeal to the Supreme Court two years apart. The content of the Court's analysis and its resonance in principles of administrative law form the subjects of the discussion that follows. The hard question in both cases asks whether class settlements may operate as institutional rivals to the conventional process of law reform that produced workers' compensation legislation decades earlier. Buried within *Amchem* and *Ortiz* — in some instances, within passages that seem merely preliminary — rests a conception of the class action as a vehicle for governance. As the remainder of this chapter shall discuss, this conception has three components.

First, *Amchem* and *Ortiz* situate class settlements as institutional rivals to the legislative process. Simply put, the conceptual starting point in both cases is that class actions enjoy no general authority to alter the preexisting rights of class members. As such, class settlements must remain on a rung below legislation in terms of their capacity to replace class members' preexisting rights with an alternative bundle of rights described in a class settlement agreement.

Second, the Court's skepticism about the law reform power that may be wielded by class settlements rests most plausibly upon an underlying vision of the class action as a problematic delegation of power to class counsel. The power that stands to be delegated here consists of the power to offer for sale class members' rights to sue — a power that class members otherwise might have delegated to a lawyer by way of a conventional contract for legal representation. Seen in these terms, the controversy over the class settlements in *Amchem* and *Ortiz* recalls the debate in administrative law over delegations to private persons in New Deal legislation.

Third, the Court seeks to deploy the Rule 23 requirements for class certification to constrain the delegation to class counsel. The Court does so, however, in ways that misconceive the relationship between class certification and class settlement structure. In *Amchem* and *Ortiz,* the Rule 23 requirements for class certification were not what shed doubt on the content of the class settlements; rather, the content of the class settlements — their aspiration to put into place the equivalent of workers' compensation legislation, but without legislation itself — is what shed doubt on the certification of the classes. The discussion that follows treats these three components of the Court's analysis in turn.

Situating Class Settlements within the Scheme of Government

The settling parties in both *Amchem* and *Ortiz* did not disguise their ambitions. For them, the class action would serve as the means to lend binding force to a business transaction rather than as a procedure for actual adversarial litigation. The settling parties literally filed the class action complaints in both cases after having already agreed out of court on the proposed class settlement terms.[46]

In *Amchem,* the Court initially addressed the significance that a settlement should have for the decision whether to certify the class. At first glance, this question concerns simply the technical relationship between questions of class certification (addressed in subsections (a) and (b) of Rule 23) and class settlement approval (required by subsection (e)).[47] By its terms, Rule 23 conditions the certification of an opt-out class upon a judicial finding that "the questions of law or fact common to the members of the class predominate over any questions affecting only individual members."[48]

Writing for the Court, Justice Ruth Bader Ginsburg concluded that the existence of a settlement "is relevant to class certification"[49] but that the settlement itself cannot supply the predominant common issue needed for class certification. So to hold, she said, would "substitute for Rule 23's certification criteria a standard never adopted — that if a settlement is 'fair,' then certification is proper."[50] The Court noted that "[t]he benefits asbestos-exposed persons might gain from the establishment of a grand-scale compensation scheme is a matter fit for *legislative* consideration."[51] The predominance inquiry for class certification, by contrast, "trains on the legal or factual questions" underlying each class member's claim — "questions that *preexist* any settlement."[52]

Although seemingly confined to the relationship between different subsections of Rule 23, the Court's discussion embodies an underlying conception of the class action in institutional terms. If the advancement of laudable policy ends were all that mattered, then the settlement in *Amchem* quite possibly would have passed muster. A good deal cannot make for a permissible class, however, because the permissibility of the class is what legitimizes the deal-making power of class counsel in the first place. That power cannot stem from all the good that the deal ultimately might do but, instead, must arise from matters that preexist the deal. To suggest otherwise, as the district court had in *Amchem*, would be to enable class counsel to engage in a form of self-dealing — to seize by self-appointment a power to sell class members' rights and then to justify that appointment by reference to the exercise of that power. In class actions, no less than in the sphere of government, power grasped solely through self-appointment is power not legitimately held.

Administrative law principles help to nail down the foregoing point about the institutional position of the class action. Even prior to *Amchem*, the Supreme Court had spoken, in passing, of how a class action "resembles a 'quasi-administrative proceeding.'"[53] The modern administrative state is all about delegations of power from Congress to administrative agencies. As chapter 4 observed, agencies frequently promulgate rules that have the force of law upon the citizenry and that alter preexisting rights. Yet the legitimacy of a given rule does not depend simply upon whether it is well supported by information in the rulemaking record or whether the rule advances the regulatory program administered by the agency. Those questions do not speak to whether Congress delegated to the agency a form of rulemaking power in the first place but, rather, to whether the content of the rule chosen is arbitrary. Administrative law has long distinguished these two questions. The first goes to the existence of delegated authority to the agency; the second to whether the agency has exercised its delegated power in an "arbitrary" or "capricious" manner, to borrow the terminology used in the Administrative Procedure Act.[54] To take a simple illustration: Whether Congress has delegated to the Environmental Protection Agency the power to promulgate rules to regulate emissions of a particular pollutant is a question distinct from the maximum emission level the agency should set in its rule.

The question of class certification is the counterpart to the delegation question in administrative law. The class certification question asks whether an implied delegation of power to class counsel exists in the first place, apart from whether that power has been exercised in a permissible fashion in the class settlement at hand. The question of class settlement approval is the analogue to review of agency action for arbitrariness. The settlement approval question asks whether class counsel, having the power to offer for sale class members' rights, have exercised that power to strike a "fair, reasonable, and adequate" deal. If anything, the "fairness hearings" typically convened by courts to consider a proposed settlement resemble the process of public comment used by administrative agencies to guard against arbitrariness in a proposed rule. The upshot for both class counsel and administrative agencies is the same: Those who purport to be the recipients of a delegation—whether an express delegation in regulatory legislation or an implied delegation in Rule 23—must justify their power by something antecedent to all the good that its exercise might do.

If anything, the Court's decision two years later in *Ortiz* points even more strongly toward a distinction between class actions and legislation. As noted earlier, *Ortiz* concerned the certification of a mandatory class under Rule 23(b)(1)(B). The ostensible basis for class certification consisted of the settling parties' assertion that the money gained by Fibreboard through the settlement of the coverage dispute with its insurers constituted a limited fund.

The *Ortiz* Court's analysis of the limited-fund concept is a natural outgrowth of the stricture in *Amchem* against self-dealing by class counsel. Writing for the Court in *Ortiz,* Justice David Souter traced the origins of the limited-fund concept to early equity cases. One case involved investors who alleged the misuse of their money by a company with "nothing . . . left but a pool of secret profits on a fraction of the original investment."[55] Another early case dealt with purchasers of steamship tickets from a seller who "converted to personal use" the funds he had received. The seller "was then adjudged bankrupt, and absconded."[56] Still another case involved a collection of legatees and creditors suing an estate too small to "satisfy the aggregate claims against it."[57] The Court noted that the drafters of Rule 23(b)(1)(B) sought simply "to capture the 'standard' class actions recognized in pre-Rule practice"—in effect, to keep the limited fund class action "close to the historical model" reflected in the early equity precedents.[58] The purported limited fund in *Ortiz* ran afoul of this stricture, said the Court, for that fund was limited by nothing more than the say-so of the class settlement negotiators.[59]

Given the Court's lengthy historical exegesis and the consciously "backward look[ing]" perspective of the rule drafters,[60] it would be easy to dismiss the result in *Ortiz* as the product of a cramped, myopic view of what the modern class action might achieve. There is, however, a deeper theme within the historical trivia. In each of the examples parsed by the Court, the limits on the disputed funds existed wholly apart from the determination to afford class treatment to competing claims. Those limited funds, in short, preexisted class treatment. The purported limited fund in *Ortiz* did not justify mandatory class treatment for the same reason that the class settlement in *Amchem* could not supply the predominant common issue needed for opt-out class treatment: Class counsel must justify their bargaining power by reference to matters that preexist the settlement, not in terms of what the settlement itself does. And what the settlement itself did in *Ortiz*—indeed, its raison d'être—was to constitute the sum obtained by Fibreboard in its insurance coverage settlement as the sole source of recourse for future tort claimants. In so doing, the class settlement would have preserved the remaining equity of Fibreboard—the wealth of the firm's shareholders—that continued tort litigation or a reorganization in bankruptcy could have tapped.

The notion of capping tort liability at insurance coverage as a way to avoid bankruptcy is well known in the annals of public law. In fact, the class settlement struck down in *Ortiz* parallels measures that Congress would write into law a few years later in the 9/11 Fund legislation. The faux limited fund in *Ortiz* sought to achieve for Fibreboard what Congress actually provided for the airlines that operated the ill-fated September 11 flights: a restriction of tort liability to the limits of corporate insurance coverage, notwithstanding the existence of additional corporate assets.

Unlike the mandatory class settlement in *Ortiz*, the 9/11 Fund legislation does not restrict victims to litigation against a pot of money capped at insurance limits. The legislation additionally provides an administrative alternative backed by the United States Treasury.[61] The next chapter shall have more to say about the 9/11 Fund. The key point for present purposes is that the airline liability cap in the 9/11 Fund legislation operates regardless of whether victims exercise their prerogative to seek compensation from the administrative process. The cap alters victims' preexisting rights to sue the airlines, regardless of whether they choose to avail themselves of the alternative bundle of rights created by the legislation.

Within the wide berth afforded by Article I of the Constitution, Congress has the power unilaterally to alter preexisting rights. The class action, by contrast, enjoys no such roving mandate; and the reasons why speak to the private nature of the delegation made by class actions and the one-shot nature of those proceedings. The sections that follow speak to these two features in turn.

The Class Action as a Delegation to Private Persons

Like all of the Federal Rules of Civil Procedure, Rule 23 finds its source in the delegation of rulemaking power to the Supreme Court from Congress in the Rules Enabling Act. There, Congress granted the Court "the power to prescribe general rules of practice and procedure" for cases in the federal courts but notably withheld the power to "abridge, enlarge or modify any substantive right."[62] The full implications of these words have occupied both the Court itself and scholars of civil procedure in a long-running series of commentaries.[63] I do not seek to add to that outpouring here. To the contrary, the constraints on the modern class action as a rival institution for governance flow readily from some very familiar observations about the Rules Enabling Act.

Whatever its outer limits, the delegation made in the Act must stop short of the legislative power that Congress might wield to alter preexisting rights. One may not do everything through a judgment rendered under Rule 23 that Congress might choose to do through reform legislation. Hence, the contrast drawn earlier between the liability cap that the *Ortiz* class settlement could not impose but that the 9/11 Fund legislation could. One must take care, nonetheless, to frame precisely the constraint imparted by the Rules Enabling Act for the class action as a settlement vehicle.

The point is not that the Act somehow forbids all exchanges involving class members' preexisting rights. If that were true, then there would be precious little left to the modern class action, given its prevalent use as a means for settlement rather than trial. The significance of the Act, instead, lies in the boundaries that it implies for the delegation of bargaining power made by Rule 23 to class counsel. If that delegation really were to encompass a general power to alter unilaterally the rights of class members, then there would remain no distinction between what could be done by a class action and what could be achieved by the legislative power of Congress.

These observations about the position of the modern class action relative to reform legislation should not sound new. They actually are quite familiar when considered from the standpoint of administrative law. The recognition of a practical need for some institution (the administrative state in the early twentieth century or class settlements in the late 1990s) to supplement a theoretically preferable but practically constrained avenue for policy-making (legislation) is an observation common to the enduring debate over delegations. Like the modern class action in civil litigation, the modern administrative state in the scheme of government arose from frustration with the inability of previous institutions to address the problems of industrial society.[64] It thus should come as little surprise that the debate over delegation in administrative law should bear upon the institutional basis for the class action. I hasten to emphasize at the outset that one need not embrace a gung-ho revival of the nondelegation doctrine in its defunct New Deal form in order to discern the position of the class action as a vehicle for governance.[65] To the contrary, one strength of the institutional argument I offer here lies in its consonance with even the highly circumscribed version of the nondelegation doctrine embraced today.

A conception of the class action as a vehicle for a mass sale of class members' rights highlights the nature of the delegation made by that device. The recipients of the delegation here consist of private persons in the form of class counsel as the self-appointed agents for the class, not of politically accountable government agencies. The prospect that the law might delegate to private persons a power to alter the rights of others is familiar to the debate about delegations. That, in fact, was the gist of the New Deal legislation struck down in 1936 by the Supreme Court in *Carter v. Carter Coal Co.*

The statute in *Carter Coal* gave the force of law to maximum work hours negotiated as a matter of contract between a specified proportion of coal producers in the nation and a specified proportion of unionized mine workers.[66] As Louis Jaffe pointed out at the time in the article *Law Making by Private Groups*: "The contract itself is a binding regulation, though only among the parties, of the very subject matter of wages and hours. The Act gives to this expression of economic power a universal effect, an effect desired and intended by the parties to the agreement but not previously attainable."[67] One might say much the same thing about the private contracts—the class settlement agreements—that the settling parties in *Amchem* and *Ortiz* sought to give binding effect over class members.

In a revealing choice of words, Jaffe remarked that, under the statute struck down in *Carter Coal*, "the majority [of coal producers and unions] secure the power to negotiate a contract which will be binding on all members of the class." Jaffe nevertheless did not see the delegation in the *Carter Coal* statute as "stand[ing] in absolute contradiction to the traditional processes and conditions of law-making." Rather, he said, the statute "exposes and brings into the open, it institutionalizes a factor in law-making that we have, eagerly in fact, attempted to obscure."[68] One might say the same about how the class settlements in *Amchem* and *Ortiz* expose the gridlike approaches used in aggregate settlements.

The last seven decades have not treated kindly *Carter Coal* or, for that matter, the aggressive enforcement of the nondelegation doctrine characteristic of the New Deal–era Supreme Court. Since then, the federal courts "have consistently allowed delegations of federal power to private actors," to the point that the matter "is no longer a federal constitutional issue."[69] Yet, even those who accept that turn as a matter of constitutional interpretation — or, at least, see no realistic way to go back now — recognize the need to control the pitfalls of lawmaking delegations to private persons. Three examples from recent commentary coalesce around this point.

Writing on administrative law, Lisa Schultz Bressman cautions that "private lawmaking has a tendency to produce regulation that both interferes with individual liberty for suspect public purposes and inadequately reflects a broad public purpose to justify such interference."[70] With only minimal transposition, one could turn this observation into the usual criticism of class settlements: They may serve the interests of the negotiating lawyers but disserve those of class members. For delegations, Bressman argues, the answer lies not in resurrection of the New Deal–era nondelegation doctrine but, rather, in the development of legal principles to discipline the exercise of delegated powers.[71]

Commentary on the phenomenon of privatization reflects a similar insight. Like Bressman, Jody Freeman recoils from the objective of "[r]esurrecting the nondelegation doctrine to invalidate private delegations."[72] The focus, she contends, should be "on how to structure these arrangements effectively and milk their positive potential."[73] Likewise, in an article aptly titled *Privatization as Delegation,* Gillian Metzger declines to revive the nondelegation doctrine along the lines of *Carter Coal.*[74] For Metzger, "the key issue" raised by the privatization of traditional governmental functions is "not whether private entities wield government power, but rather whether grants of government power to private entities are adequately structured to preserve constitutional accountability."[75]

One may translate these discussions of delegations to private persons into the context of class actions. Rule 23 is what structures the settlement arrangements into which class counsel may enter. To be sure, class settlements do not alter preexisting rights solely at the instigation of class counsel. Class settlements do so only on the issuance of an approving judgment that then has preclusive effect. Judicial review for settlement fairness nonetheless cannot legitimize the delegation of power made by the modern class action any more than judicial review for compliance with the statute in *Carter Coal*—say, to ensure that the requisite percentage of unionized workers really did approve a given set of work hours — could legitimize the delegation there. Even in its modern delegation decisions, the Supreme Court has never said that the existence of judicial review to guard against arbitrary agency action somehow relieves Congress of the minimal obligation to supply an "intelligible principle" in the statute that empowers the agency in the first place.[76] Likewise, the existence of judicial review to determine the fairness of a class settlement does not relieve class counsel of the obligation to demonstrate the legitimacy of their power to act upon the preexisting rights of class members.

If the class certification inquiry operates, in effect, as a check upon a delegation of rulemaking power to class counsel, then we must ask: What is the nature of that check, and what is its relationship to judicial review of a proposed class settlement for fairness? The answers shed further light on the relationship of the class settlements in *Amchem* and *Ortiz* to workers' compensation legislation. To anticipate the argument that shall follow: *Amchem* and *Ortiz* seek to constrain the delegation of governing power to class counsel by focusing on two related matters. The first concerns the cohesiveness of the proposed class; the second looks to the existence of conflicts of interest on the part of class counsel. As I shall explain, the Court's approach amounts to an insistence on standards for class actions substantially more stringent than those found on either subject in private contracts for legal representation or arrangements for political representation. The justification for stringency with regard to class actions, however, does not rest on the grounds suggested by the Court: that the representational arrangements for the class are what drive the content of class settlements (rather than vice versa) and that courts are poorly positioned to scrutinize directly the content of those settlements (a reluctance belied by the setting of *Amchem* and *Ortiz*). The real reason to constrain the delegation to class counsel in Rule 23 rests on the nature of class settlements as one-shot transactions. Class settlements jettison the contractual nexus found in conventional lawyer-client relationships without substituting the kind of long-term political accountability found in the legislative sphere.

The Class Action as a Form of Representation

In *Amchem*, the Court noted that the requirements for class certification in Rule 23 "focus court attention on whether a proposed class has sufficient unity so that absent members can fairly be bound by [the] decisions of class representatives." Notions of unity and cohesiveness speak to the similarity of the class members as compared to one another. The inquiry sketched in *Amchem* asks whether the court should certify the class as proposed — there, as a single, all-encompassing class for future claimants represented by a single group of law firms as class counsel — or should insist upon subdivision into multiple subclasses, each with its own separate lawyer.[77]

The *Amchem* Court chided the district judge for concluding that the proposed class was cohesive in the broad sense that all of its members, of course, would prefer to maximize the overall settlement pot.[78] The fundamental dispute in asbestos litigation at the time of *Amchem* involved not just the overall price for any comprehensive settlement but also its allocation. Questions of allocation were especially acute due to the small volume of tort claims expected over time from impaired workers and the comparatively huge volume of claims anticipated on behalf of those merely at risk of future disease. The single class in *Amchem* exhibited a contradiction: It paid no heed to the differences between impaired and unimpaired workers in its structure, but it simultaneously sought to effectuate a compromise across those very same lines. The *Amchem* class settlement made different allocations to different categories of claims within the plaintiff class, prioritizing for immediate cash payment those workers who had not yet sued in tort but who were presently impaired over workers who merely might become impaired in the future.[79]

All of this is not to suggest that the trade-offs made in the *Amchem* class settlement were necessarily bad ones. The Court's consternation at the allocation of cash in the *Amchem* class settlement is ironic, to say the least. Just two days earlier, the same Court had issued its decision in *Metro-North Commuter Railroad Co. v. Buckley*.[80] As discussed in chapter 3, *Metro-North* concludes that persons who lack a present-day impairment have no "injury" compensable under the Federal Employers' Liability Act (FELA). For its part, the *Amchem* Court expressed no view on whether unimpaired workers in the class would have made out poorly with the insurance policies they would have received in lieu of immediate cash. The Court simply insisted as a precondition to approval of the class settlement that unimpaired workers must be represented separately from the presently impaired. As one commentator observes, the Court in *Ortiz* went a significant step further by applying the requirement of class cohesiveness "not simply to gross differences in the nature of the plaintiffs' injuries but also to differences in the legal and negotiating positions of the class members" based on what the Court perceived as variations in the strength of their respective claims.[81]

For the Court, the demand for class cohesiveness as a precondition for class certification is intertwined with the further requirement that the class must be adequately represented.[82] By insisting on division of the single proposed class into discrete subclasses, the *Amchem* Court sought to ensure that the named class representatives would protect the interests of absent class members by advancing their own self-interest. The Court extended this point in *Ortiz,* shifting its focus away from the class representatives per se and toward the economic interests of class counsel.[83] This move expands the class certification inquiry to encompass not only conflicts arising from divergent interests within the class itself but also conflicts arising from the interests of counsel in matters external to the class. The latter inquiry makes pertinent the aggregate settlements of inventory cases represented by class counsel in the tort system.

Inventory cases consisted of those not encompassed by the class defini-tion but represented separately by class counsel. For the Court, such cases created a potential for the economic interests of class counsel to diverge from the interests of the class members they purported to represent. The Court's fear was that class counsel's stake in securing aggregate settlements for their inventory cases — namely, their interest in obtaining contingent fees — might distort their incentives in class settlement negotiations. As Justice Souter noted for the *Ortiz* Court, class counsel "had great incen-tive to reach any agreement in the [class] settlement negotiations that they thought might survive a Rule 23(e) [inquiry by a court into settlement fair-ness], rather than *the best possible arrangement* for the substantially unidenti-fied global settlement class."[84] The italicized language is not a casual or incidental choice on the Court's part. Similar rhetoric appears throughout the opinion. Criticizing the district court's finding of a limited fund, for ex-ample, the *Ortiz* Court noted the absence of "assurance that claimants are receiving the maximum fund, not a potentially significant fraction less."[85]

The Court's approach to class certification in *Amchem* and *Ortiz* casts class settlements into sharp contrast with the representational arrange-ments in both aggregate settlements and the legislative process. In both of those settings, far less cohesiveness and far more conflicts of interest remain the norm. The notion lurking in the background of *Amchem* and *Ortiz* is that the courts may use the class certification requirements of Rule 23 to form highly cohesive classes with unconflicted representatives and then, for the most part, let settlement negotiations proceed as they may. The fairness of a class settlement may not supply the predominant common issue needed to support class certification. But the Court seems to suggest that a rigor-ous inquiry into class certification may function as a rough proxy for class settlement fairness by enhancing judicial confidence in any resulting deal. Good class certification procedure, so the argument goes, will yield the best possible arrangement for settlement.

This approach to class settlements amounts to an inverted version of judicial review in administrative law. At least after the New Deal, review under the nondelegation doctrine involves only the lightest touch. It calls simply for congressional articulation of an "intelligible principle" to guide agency action. By contrast, review of agency action for arbitrariness takes a comparatively demanding form, often summarized as "hard look" review. If anything, one strand of academic commentary questions the stringency of hard look review, suggesting that it produces in agencies a kind of "ossification" that inhibits them from acting boldly to carry out the statutes delegated to them by Congress.[86] For class actions after *Amchem* and *Ortiz*, the counterpart to review of the delegation (the class certification inquiry) carries most of the weight. The counterpart to review for arbitrariness (the class settlement fairness inquiry) is thought to flow largely from confidence in the parameters of the delegation.

There are two untested premises in the Court's approach. The first is that class certification drives class settlement structure. The second is that judicial review into class settlement fairness must—perhaps, out of practical necessity—assume a relatively modest form. The setting of both *Amchem* and *Ortiz* calls into question these premises. When the *Ortiz* Court expressed doubt that the class settlement was the "best possible arrangement" for class members, the Court implied that there must have been a better deal out there, hovering within reach of the class negotiations. The reason class members did not get that deal—so the argument goes—was because class counsel represented a single, undifferentiated class and labored under their own conflicting incentives in settlement negotiations.

To be sure, the deal in *Ortiz* might not have been structured as a mandatory, limited fund class. In this regard, the Court rightly rejected the assertion that that Fibreboard's coverage settlement with its insurers gave rise to a bona fide limited fund. At the same time, defendants would have had no reason to entertain seriously any settlement that would have replicated with greater efficiency the outcomes of aggregate settlements in the tort system. The reason is the same one that explains the resistance of defendants to Judge Parker's stab at statistical sampling in *Cimino*. Absent the ability to limit liability to a fixed settlement amount, the logical move for defendants would have been to pursue an opt-out class akin to that in *Amchem*, no court having opined on that deal at the time of the *Ortiz* negotiations. And their negotiating partners—whether counsel for one big class or a bevy of counsel for multiple subclasses—would have consisted, in all likelihood, of experienced asbestos plaintiffs' lawyers with large numbers of inventory cases.[87]

Dissenting in *Ortiz*, Justice Stephen Breyer retorted: "Of course, class counsel consisted of individual attorneys who represented other asbestos claimants. . . . [A]ny attorney who had been involved in previous litigation against Fibreboard was likely to suffer from a similar 'conflict.' . . . Should [the district court] have appointed attorneys unfamiliar with Fibreboard and the history of its asbestos litigation? Where was the District Court to find those competent, knowledgeable, conflict-free attorneys?" According to the majority in *Ortiz*, however, the existence of inventory cases is exactly what gives rise to the kind of conflicting allegiance that should derail class certification.

In chapter 11 of this book, I ultimately shall argue that the preoccupation with conflicts of interest in *Amchem* and *Ortiz* has pointed the law in precisely the wrong direction. Rather than attempt scrupulously to avoid conflicts of interest, the law actually should deploy those conflicts as a source of constraint upon self-dealing by the lawyers who design any comprehensive peace. To be sure, such an approach cuts sharply against the grain of existing suppositions about mass torts. I shall argue, nevertheless, that a different approach to conflicts of interest flows from deeply embedded ideas that lend legitimacy to the modern administrative state. For now, my focus remains on *Amchem* and *Ortiz* on their own terms.

Problems of class certification ultimately were not what cast doubt on the structure of the settlements in *Amchem* and *Ortiz*. Rather, the structure of the settlements—their aspiration to do for asbestos litigation roughly what Progressive Era legislatures did for workplace injuries—is what cast doubt on the cohesiveness of the proposed classes and the adequacy of class representation. Settlement structure drives class certification, not vice versa, as the Court's analysis would suggest. The upshot of *Amchem* and *Ortiz*, in practical terms, is that class settlements involving a purely prospective replacement of the tort system simply are not viable—not just at the behest of the particular class counsel who happened before the Court in those cases but, more broadly, at the invitation of any law firm realistically positioned to serve as class counsel at any stage beyond the immature one.

Nor was stringency in the class certification inquiry necessary due to the infeasibility of judicial review into the fairness of the class settlements in *Amchem* and *Ortiz*. Rigor in the class certification inquiry would be attractive if judicial review of class settlement fairness really would amount to an amorphous inquiry. Sounding a similar concern, one commentator goes so far as to describe class settlements as a "black box."[88] On this account, any observer would have difficulty saying, after the fact, whether any of the contending forces in a complex negotiation might have fared better than they actually did. The posture of the settling parties undoubtedly compli-

cates judicial review of class settlements. By definition, the settling parties
are no longer adversaries but, instead, have reason to cooperate—in
Amchem and *Ortiz*, to join hands from the outset of the class proceedings—so
as to "put one over on the [reviewing] court, in a staged performance."[89]

The situation in *Amchem* and *Ortiz*, however, diverged dramatically from
a world of informational barriers and nonadversarial presentation, precisely because those cases involved a mass tort advanced well into the mature stage. As the Court recognized at the outset of its opinion in *Amchem*,
class actions in the mass tort context diverge from the situations thought
to comprise the core justification for class treatment—namely, civil claims
too small in value to justify litigation on an individual basis.[90] The Court
saw the divergence of the mass tort class action from this familiar pattern
as a source of consternation. For the Court, that divergence reinforced the
need for probing inquiry into the propriety of class certification. The same
divergence, however, also has implications for the feasibility of review into
class settlement fairness.

Class settlements at the mature litigation stage do not operate in the
absence of a preexisting market for the representation of class members.
Instead, they operate to displace that market—to substitute representation
by class counsel for the representation that class members would have garnered in the tort system from the very same law firms or their competitors.
As a result, a court reviewing a class settlement in the mass tort context may
demand information on recoveries in ordinary litigation—not just actual
damage awards but also settlements previously reached by the class action
defendants—in a way that a court cannot when a class action offers the
only realistic procedure for litigation of the underlying claims.

In fact, developments in the law of class actions prior to *Amchem* and
Ortiz reinforce the notion that data on recoveries in ordinary tort litigation
can ground judicial review into class settlement fairness. Here, recall the
discussion in chapter 3 of judicial efforts to regulate—however problematically—the use of class certification to make the transition from immature to
mature litigation. By the time that *Amchem* and *Ortiz* reached the Supreme
Court, the lower federal courts in decisions like *Rhone-Poulenc* already had
begun to clamp down on the use of class certification to leapfrog litigation
into the mature stage. The implication—unrecognized by the Supreme
Court—is that class settlements in the mass tort area will tend to arise *only*
after development of a market for claims in the tort system through the
kind of "decentralized process of multiple trials" that Judge Richard Posner envisioned as the alternative to early class certification.[91] As the *Ortiz*
Court observed: "In the 1970's and 1980's, plaintiffs' lawyers throughout

the country . . . honed the litigation of asbestos claims to the point of almost mechanical regularity" in the ordinary tort system.[92]

There is even more to the connection between regulation of class actions as a means to jump to the mature litigation stage and regulation of class actions as the means for comprehensive settlement. A "decentralized process of multiple trials" is likely both to generate real-world data on the value of claims and to elicit the involvement of multiple law firms on the plaintiffs' side, as the litigation moves from one stage to the next. The nonadversarial posture of the parties to any class settlement may be offset where there are other plaintiffs' law firms that stand to be affected—perhaps, adversely—by the terms that class settlement would lock into place for the future. Here, too, observed behavior belies the suppositions of the Court. The prime mover behind the legal challenges to the class settlements in both *Amchem* and *Ortiz* consisted of none other than a law firm within the plaintiffs' bar that was a major competitor of those that served as class counsel.[93] The real adversaries in the two cases consisted of different firms *within* the asbestos plaintiffs' bar.

One speculative explanation offered for the foregoing rift focuses on possible differences in the two camps' respective long-range business plans. Class counsel in *Amchem*, for example, may have sought a more dynamic, changing mix of subject matter for their litigation portfolio in the future by comparison to the course of business envisioned by the objecting firm. In essence, class counsel might have viewed the class settlement as a way to conclude their years of success in the asbestos litigation in such a manner that they could reap a big *and quick* financial gain—there, from a fee award for the class representation and from the contingency fees gained from aggregate settlements for their inventory cases. The firms serving as class counsel then could deploy those resources in an effort to secure dominant positions in new subject areas of litigation for the future. They could, in short, use class settlements to advance their competitive position vis-à-vis other plaintiffs' law firms.[94] Whatever the explanation for the rift, however, one thing is clear: If ever there were cases where a thoroughgoing judicial inquiry into the fairness of class settlements was feasible from the standpoint of available information and adversarial presentation, then *Amchem* and *Ortiz* were such cases.

The rigor in the class certification inquiry prescribed by the Court in *Amchem* and *Ortiz* cannot rest on the availability of some dramatically better deal for class members. Nor can it plausibly rest on the impracticality of judicial review there into class settlement fairness. At bottom, the Court's stance instead rests on a largely unarticulated conception of the governing arrangements needed to legitimize the kinds of compromises necessary to switch a recurring category of claims—whether for asbestos-related disease or for workplace-related injuries—out of the tort system and into a streamlined administrative framework. Viewed in this light, the problem with class settlements as institutions for governance—oddly enough—is not that they are too broad and encompassing their scope but, instead, that they are not encompassing enough.

In contrast to the legislative process, a class settlement is not a vehicle for an ongoing series of transactions. It is literally a one-shot deal from the standpoint of class members. The essence of any class settlement is to bring about a grand compromise—to call upon class members to sacrifice some of their individual latitude for the sake of joint gains, with those gains coming largely through countervailing sacrifices by defendants of their own latitude to delay. The compromise consists of making the kind of deal that Judge Parker sought to impose by judicial fiat through the trial plan in *Cimino*. In the legislative process, such a compromise is subject to ongoing negotiation—to modification and, conceivably, to outright repeal—through the sorts of repeated interactions made possible by the existence of a standing legislature. For legislation, one can see how things actually turn out and then tweak arrangements accordingly. The class settlement, by contrast, is a problematic vehicle for governance precisely because of the finality—the peace—to which the settling parties aspire. That finality is what eliminates the possibility of a long run for the contending forces.[95]

In chapter 11, I shall argue that arrangements for peacemaking should seek to create for the deal-making lawyers the rough equivalent of the long run found in the legislative process. How the law might do so is a subject that warrants detailed discussion. For now, it is enough to observe that the peace plans in *Amchem* and *Ortiz* aspired to substitute administrative regimes for the preexisting tort system. But they sought to accomplish that substitution through a vehicle that lacks the accountability over time that is among the hallmarks of administration in its public guise. The class settlements in the two cases would have lent permanence to the gridlike approaches that had long operated outside of judicial scrutiny in the aggregate settlement process. But that permanence itself is what doomed the imposition of the grid through the class action device.

PART III

THE
SEARCH
FOR PEACE

CHAPTER VI

PUBLIC LEGISLATION AND PRIVATE CONTRACTS

The fall of the class settlements in *Amchem* and *Ortiz* did not mark the end of efforts to make peace in mass tort litigation. To the contrary, in the period since the Court's decisions, a rough consensus has emerged about the desirability of moving toward some manner of grid-based solution once mass tort litigation has matured. This sentiment coexists, however, with a striking lack of consensus on the appropriate institutional vehicle to lend binding force to the grid.

The five chapters that comprise this part trace the search for a suitable vehicle to make peace in the aftermath of *Amchem*. The present chapter begins with a brief taxonomy of the various peacemaking vehicles that have emerged. It then explains how the long-standing debate among tort scholars over risk-based claims helps to organize our thinking about developments in the post-*Amchem* world. The remainder of the chapter starts in earnest on the story of mass torts since *Amchem*, discussing the two most straightforward of the many vehicles for peace.

A Taxonomy of Peacemaking Post-*Amchem*

The peace vehicles to emerge in recent years have come in several forms: renewed efforts at public legislation, private contractual agreements, continued experimentation with class actions, and use of the corporate reorganization process in bankruptcy. This is not to say that all of these vehicles were completely unknown at earlier times, only that rejection of the *Amchem* and *Ortiz* class settlements has lent urgency to their pursuit.

The principal developments within Congress have been twofold: enactment of the federal statute establishing the 9/11 Fund and ongoing efforts to secure the passage of asbestos reform legislation. The private contract approach consists of an important but too-little-discussed attempt by Owens Corning Corporation in its National Settlement Program (NSP) to place ascertainable bounds on its future liabilities in the asbestos litigation.[1] The NSP centered on a series of contractual agreements between the defendant corporation and the major asbestos plaintiffs' law firms across the country with regard to the handling of future claims.

Efforts to craft class settlements have pointed in multiple directions, some at odds with others. *Ortiz* notwithstanding, one important strand of academic commentary has continued to tout the use of mandatory class actions across mass tort litigation as a whole.[2] In fact, in litigation against the tobacco industry, one lower court experimented with mandatory class treatment confined to punitive damage claims, but that effort met with reversal on appeal.[3] Mandatory classes, however, have not been the only ones attempted. The most prominent mass tort class settlement to garner appellate affirmance in the post-*Amchem* period — that of Wyeth Corporation in the fen-phen litigation — sought to expand, rather than curtail, the opportunities of class members to opt out.[4] A third approach to class settlements involves amalgamation of the first two. This third approach seeks to straddle the line between mandatory and opt-out classes, aspiring to achieve the closure of a mandatory class in practical effect upon satisfaction of the less demanding strictures for an opt-out class.

Bankruptcy, too, has taken on greater prominence as a vehicle for peace. The demise of the class settlements in *Amchem* and *Ortiz* precipitated a wave of additional asbestos-related reorganizations under the auspices of the Bankruptcy Code.[5] The most innovative of these arrangements involve what have come to be known as "prepackaged" reorganizations under §524(g) of the Code. Here, the debtor corporation seeks to minimize its time in the bankruptcy process by lining up in advance — prepackaging — the requisite votes in favor of its desired reorganization plan. As I shall discuss, the asbestos-related "prepacks," if anything, magnify the problems of representation that plagued the class settlements in *Amchem* and *Ortiz*.

Each of the foregoing arrangements for peacemaking has both promising and problematic elements. Before one may analyze their specifics, however, a thematic overview is in order. A long-running debate over the status of risk-based claims in tort doctrine can help us to organize the discussion of peacemaking in the aftermath of *Amchem*.

The Debate over Risk-Based Claims
as an Organizing Template

Both courts and scholars have long debated whether the substantive law of torts should expand its concept of cognizable injury to embrace the wrongful imposition of risk. As chapter 2 observed, the judicial reception for risk-based claims has been lukewarm, at best. Upon canvassing the prevailing common law across the various states, the Supreme Court declined to recognize claims predicated on the mere imposition of risk for purposes of the federal compensation program for workers in the railroad industry.[6]

The resistance of courts notwithstanding, risk-based claims continue to enjoy attention in segments of the tort literature. Several commentators urge the recognition of risk-based claims in tort law as a whole on justice-based grounds.[7] The same prescription appears in writing on mass torts specifically. In a detailed argument set forth in articles over the past two decades, David Rosenberg does not forego justice-based arguments.[8] Rosenberg, however, advances his affirmative case for the recognition of risk-based claims on primarily instrumental grounds. Indeed, in recent iterations of his position, Rosenberg essentially equates his instrumental arguments with what he regards as the correct account of justice in law.[9]

In Rosenberg's view, the resistance of current law to both risk-based claims and class action treatment of mass tort litigation makes for an undesirable combination, one that undermines the deterrence of risk-taking on the part of product manufacturers. The details of Rosenberg's argument bear close scrutiny, and I shall give them that in chapter 7 as a way to introduce developments in the class action area after *Amchem*. The point, for now, is simply that Rosenberg links his case for risk-based claims to a larger account of the institutions that the law should use to resolve those claims.

All of this is not to suggest that scholarly arguments for risk-based claims stand unopposed in the tort literature. To the contrary, the literature also contains an array of commentary critical of such claims, in whole or in substantial part.[10] One may trace much of the scholarly schism over risk-based claims to the competing accounts of tort law as a whole that have emerged at times contemporaneous with the mass tort phenomenon — chiefly, the rift identified in chapter 1 between theories that see torts largely as occasions for regulatory policymaking by common-law courts and theories that regard tort law as a way to achieve corrective justice between particular private parties. Adherents of the former view, like Rosenberg, tend toward enthusiasm for risk-based claims, whereas adherents of the latter tend toward a more skeptical assessment.

My suggestion here is that the idea of risk-based claims can help to organize our thinking about the attempts at peacemaking in the real world of mass tort litigation after *Amchem*. The scholarly debate aside, risk-based claims exhibit a common feature as a descriptive matter: They seek to compress the future into the present. Some risk-based claims do so by turning what otherwise would be future claims into present ones — say, by treating as a cognizable injury the increased risk today of impairing disease in the future. Others focus on the implications that a future contingency has for persons in the present day — for instance, the fear today that one might manifest disease in the future or the services thought medically appropriate today to mitigate future disease.

Seen in the foregoing light, the sequence for the discussion that follows is no accident. The present chapter starts with public legislation. Within the array of potential peace arrangements, public legislation stands alone in its capacity to act on the future *regardless* of the existence of any right of action in tort for persons exposed to a risky product. Congress, in short, may act upon all exposed persons' rights — creating, modifying, or eliminating them — not based on the existence today of tort claims for such persons but, instead, due to the existence of governing power under Article I of the Constitution. To be sure, Congress often delegates its own power of law reform to some manner of public administrative body. But the important point remains that the recognition or nonrecognition of risk-based claims is of no consequence to the authority of Congress to switch a given area of mass tort litigation out of the tort system and into an administrative compensation grid. Congress may act as if the future were compressed into the present for the simple reason that this is what all manner of rulemaking on the legislative model does. It acts today to set the rules for how the future shall be governed.

The designers of other peace arrangements for mass torts, whatever their chosen mode, also aspire to compress the future into the present. In this sense, they actually have had little difficulty acting as if risk-based claims were recognized under substantive law. As a practical matter, the innovations in peacemaking for mass torts have largely bypassed the simmering debate among tort scholars about risk-based claims. By behaving as if risk-based claims were recognized at substantive law, the various nonlegislative vehicles — private contractual arrangements, class actions, and reorganizations in bankruptcy — act *as if* they are themselves legislatures.

To see the various nonlegislative vehicles for peace as a kind of legislation in disguise is not necessarily to resolve whether the law should alter the substantive law of torts to bring prevailing doctrine into line. To be sure, full-fledged recognition of risk-based claims would smooth the path for nonlegislative vehicles to formulate and implement rules for future mass tort claims. But such a development would only highlight the questions that *Amchem* exposed. Whatever the ultimate outcome of the tort debate over risk-based claims, the most pressing questions for the resolution of mass torts today concern not the content of tort doctrine but the design of institutions—what sorts of arrangements the law should borrow, modify, or invent to govern the future with both legitimacy and practicality.

The central claim advanced in this part is easily stated: What calls into doubt the legitimacy of peacemaking efforts outside the legislative sphere is also what has hampered their success in practical terms. The impediment to both legitimacy and practical success lies in the persistent tendency to separate law reform through public institutions and settlement by way of private negotiation. This tendency runs against the trend of emerging practice. The post-*Amchem* period, in fact, has witnessed a convergence of public and private approaches to the resolution of mass tort claims. That observation naturally raises the question whether the law would benefit from a similar convergence in the ways that it thinks about peacemaking. Resolving mass torts fairly requires us to reconcile public institutions and private arrangements rather than to see them as hermetically sealed spheres. It requires us to conceive the involvement of public institutions as *both* empowering and disciplining private negotiations. In casting the developments since *Amchem* in these terms, the chapters of this part set the agenda for the concluding chapters of the book. There, I shall elaborate how the law may use insights from the world of governance to improve the process of peacemaking for mass torts.

Public Legislation

Before one may proceed to the more exotic arrangements for peace since *Amchem,* developments in Congress during the same period bear mention. In fact, public legislation forms a useful starting point for a discussion of peacemaking. In institutional terms, public legislation is relatively straightforward as a vehicle for peace. One may set aside, in large part, the question whether the peacemaking institution possesses the authority to switch a given subject area out of the tort system and into some manner of administrative scheme. There appears little doubt that Congress had the authority to enact the 9/11 Fund legislation, whatever observers ultimately might make of that legislation as public policy. Matters of authority aside, however, the practical challenges faced by the 9/11 Fund and, later, by proposed asbestos reform legislation help to foreshadow themes that shall recur in the discussion of nonlegislative vehicles for peace. The surmounting of those practical challenges entails the making of contestable value choices and trade-offs — what public legislation does with relative legitimacy but what nonlegislative institutions might not.

The 9/11 Fund

The 9/11 Fund legislation is the subject of an emerging scholarly literature likely to grow in the coming years.[11] Details of the legislation and its implementation will continue to elicit attention from commentators. My goal here is a much more modest and circumscribed one — namely, to use the basic parameters of the legislation to frame the discussion to follow of the various nonlegislative vehicles for peacemaking in the mass tort area.

The 9/11 Fund legislation did what the mandatory class settlement in *Ortiz* could not do. The legislation altered the legal landscape for tort suits by capping the liability of the would-be defendant airlines at the limits of their insurance coverage, estimated to be $1.5 billion per plane.[12] The effect was to remove from play in any ensuing litigation all other components of the airlines' net worth. As two commentators observe, "Congress entered the arena in a desire to provide financial security for the airline industry and backed into the victim compensation scheme as a result of the perceived unseemliness of providing compensation to companies, but not individuals."[13] Almost as an afterthought in the legislation, Congress established a public administrative compensation scheme, backed by the United States Treasury, as an alternative that victims could select in lieu of tort.

Several features simplified considerably the creation and administration of the 9/11 Fund. These features bear acknowledgment in any effort to extract lessons for mass torts generally. First, the events that led to the creation of the 9/11 Fund consisted of what I have distinguished as "mass accidents" rather than mass torts. The 9/11 Fund focused on present-day deaths and injuries, not on latent disease. As such, the attacks gave rise to a pool of potential claimants who could be identified in the present and who suffered the kinds of injuries long considered within the ambit of tort law, whether for the death of a relative on one of the ill-fated flights or for the plaintiff's own physical injuries.[14] As I shall elaborate, this is not to say that plaintiffs ultimately would have had winning tort claims against the airlines, only that the nature of their injuries sounded in long-accepted tort principles, not in any expanded recognition for risk-based claims. Tort law aside, moreover, the immediate nature of the injuries enabled Congress to provide a relatively short lifespan for the 9/11 Fund, which concluded its business in mid-2004.

Second, two features lent extraordinary urgency to the 9/11 Fund legislation: the sheer shock from the underlying attacks and the fear that the financial exposure associated with tort litigation might compromise airline operations. Congress created the 9/11 Fund a mere eleven days after the underlying attacks, before the filing of tort claims.[15] The legislation amounted to less of a peace imposed in the midst of a litigation war and more of an anticipatory or preemptive measure. Swift enactment, moreover, put the 9/11 Fund into place before plaintiffs' law firms could assemble large inventories of claimants or otherwise develop long-term business interests in the litigation. If anything, national organizations of plaintiffs' lawyers displayed admirable public spiritedness, downplaying the idea of tort suits and supplying free legal services to victims.[16]

Third, the involvement of the federal treasury served to reduce concerns over resource constraints, in contrast to the usual circumstances for peacemaking in mass tort litigation. The effect of public funding was to remove from the picture one concern that often dominates the design of a workable peace in mass tort litigation: the ability of the settling defendant to fund the deal. The backing of the United States Government additionally served as a sotto voce acknowledgment of its own responsibility for security, both with respect to air travel specifically and for the nation generally.

Fourth, the use of public rather than private dollars lent plausibility to the creation of a public rather than a private administrative regime. The public nature of the Fund dovetailed conveniently with the perceived need for expeditious action on the part of Congress. Rather than spell out the details of the administrative regime, Congress delegated broadly to a special master, affording him sweeping discretion to determine the compensation for any given claimant "based on the harm to the claimant, the facts of the claim, and the individual circumstances of the claimant."[17] Exercising his rulemaking power under the legislation, Special Master Kenneth Feinberg proceeded to issue — what else — a series of grids for presumptive awards from the Fund.[18] Special Master Feinberg's broad discretionary power over the disposition of the Fund is reminiscent of the role played by Judge Jack Weinstein with regard to the allocation of the Agent Orange class settlement — a fitting similarity, given the involvement of Feinberg himself as one of the special masters appointed by Judge Weinstein in that earlier matter.[19]

The terrorist attacks of September 11, 2001, in short, diverged considerably from the circumstances that define the landscape for peacemaking with regard to most mass torts. Differences aside, however, the 9/11 Fund highlights two features that have bearing on the other arrangements for peacemaking that I shall discuss shortly. First, the 9/11 Fund reinforces the consequences of a move from the tort system to some manner of administrative grid. Workers' compensation legislation in the century prior to the 9/11 Fund did not merely replicate with greater efficiency the outcomes in preexisting tort litigation for workplace injuries. It embodied changes to the principles governing such litigation — changes needed on political grounds in order to fashion the requisite coalition of interested forces in support of the legislation. For the 9/11 Fund, too, the substitution of an administrative compensation regime for tort litigation did not entail the replication of expected claim values in the tort system.

For one thing, it is doubtful that all of the persons whom Congress deemed eligible to seek compensation from the 9/11 Fund would have had viable tort claims against the airlines, much less equally viable ones. At the very least, if tort law were the baseline, then a grid probably would have distinguished between plaintiffs suing for the deaths of passengers on the fatal flights and other plaintiffs suing for the deaths of persons on the ground. A careful analysis of New York tort doctrine by Anthony Sebok suggests that the former would have had substantially stronger claims than the latter.[20] The 9/11 Fund drew no such lines, effectively treating all covered fatalities alike, regardless of their circumstances.

The 9/11 Fund also deviated from tort principles in its payout amounts. Tort law embraces the collateral source rule, which "allows for the recovery in tort of out-of-pocket expenses even if they have been reimbursed by 'collateral' sources such as health and disability insurance."[21] As administered by Special Master Feinberg, by contrast, the 9/11 Fund offset its compensation awards, at least to the extent of payments from collateral sources based on victims' own self-contributions — for instance, insurance coverage they previously had purchased. Compensation awards were not offset, however, based on "private sources of charity received by claimants."[22]

The 9/11 Fund deviated from tort principles in an additional respect. In percentage terms, the grid developed by Special Master Feinberg posited far steeper reductions in the presumptive payouts for high-income decedents relative to their projected lifetime earnings than for payouts to low-income decedents relative to theirs.[23] Persons dissatisfied with the presumptive payout described in the grid could request individualized treatment, upon the presentation of additional claim information. But, even then, the survivors of Cantor Fitzgerald financial brokers took more of a haircut under the Fund than the survivors of World Trade Center janitors. Special Master

Feinberg understandably recoiled from making payouts for high-income decedents that truly would have tracked their projected lifetime earnings, describing such payouts as politically untenable for a fund financed by tax-payers.[24] In his final report on the 9/11 Fund, Special Master Feinberg goes even further, suggesting that Congress might have done better to specify a flat dollar amount for all compensation awards.[25]

My point here is to underscore that any shift from tort to administration creates a need to deviate from the tort baseline in order to fashion — or, for Special Master Feinberg, to preserve — the consensus needed to support such a shift in the first place. At the same time, shifting from the tort base-line opens a wide vista for discretion in the choice of alternative compensa-tion principles. The workings of the 9/11 Fund undoubtedly will remain the subject of considerable debate. But one may daresay, at this early juncture, that the Fund appears to have concluded its business with a fair degree of legitimacy precisely because it was designed and implemented through overtly political means.

A second observation about the 9/11 Fund also has significance for other peace arrangements. In contrast to the workers' compensation laws en-acted decades earlier, the 9/11 Fund legislation did not mark a complete replacement of the tort system with a public administrative scheme. The legislation nominally retained the tort system, but with modifications to dissuade the vast majority of would-be claimants from actually using it in preference to Special Master Feinberg's grid. The 9/11 Fund proved suc-cessful in this regard as well. An estimated 97 percent of the survivors of persons killed in the attacks ultimately opted for administration over tort.[26] This result, however, may well have resulted from the atypical features of the 9/11 Fund legislation mentioned earlier: the perceived obstacles to successful tort suits and the use of public funds to allay fears that payouts somehow would need to be ratcheted down to account for a shortfall in available money. Neither feature is likely to recur in mass tort litigation, where serious efforts at comprehensive settlement occur only upon the demonstration of a credible threat from plaintiffs to prevail in court and where the United States Treasury does not stand to fund the peace. In such circumstances, as we shall see in the class action area, peace plans that leave open the possibility of continued tort litigation but try to deter its use in practice are prone to instability, both in their legal authority and in their actual delivery of peace.

In any event, the confluence of events that lent urgency to the enactment of the 9/11 Fund legislation is unlikely to be replicated in mass tort litiga-tion. If anything, experience with proposed asbestos legislation reinforces the difficulty of obtaining congressional action outside the setting of politically galvanizing events on the scale of the September 11 attacks.

Proposed Asbestos Legislation

Notwithstanding not-so-subtle hints from the Supreme Court in *Amchem* and *Ortiz*, proposed asbestos reform legislation thus far has failed to become a reality. The main proposal to garner attention in Congress — a bill backed by Senator Arlen Specter, chairman of the Senate Committee on the Judiciary — builds upon aspects of the class settlement in *Amchem*, casting them to reach the entire asbestos litigation, not just particular defendants.[27] The creation of an administrative regime to streamline compensation for claimants would come in tandem with medical criteria to withhold immediate cash payment for exposed persons without present disease. Such persons, however, would receive reimbursement for the costs of medical monitoring not otherwise covered by their health insurers.[28] The administrative scheme envisioned in the asbestos bill would be funded by defendants in the first instance — a major complication, as I shall explain, when one moves from the voluntary coalition of defendants who would have funded the *Amchem* class settlement to the full gamut of entities implicated in the asbestos litigation as a whole.

The asbestos bill differs from the opt-out class settlement in *Amchem*, however, in other regards. The bill would displace tort litigation in favor of administration, but with the prospect of resort to the tort system in the event of a shortfall in funding. The bill, moreover, would entrust the administration of claims to a new Office of Asbestos Disease Compensation within the Department of Labor rather than to a private body overseen by asbestos defendants, as in the *Amchem* deal.

The interesting question is why sustained efforts at a legislative solution for the asbestos litigation have failed to bear fruit. One may point, initially, to the absence of the features that smoothed the path for the 9/11 Fund. The contrast with the 9/11 Fund helps one to pinpoint the crucial areas for compromise with regard to asbestos reform legislation. To account for why those compromises have not been forthcoming, however, one ultimately must look outside the four corners of the bill.

The use of public funding greatly simplified the design of the 9/11 Fund. By contrast, as a political matter, public funding for an asbestos compensation plan has remained out of the question as matter of first recourse, notwithstanding the role played by the United States Government in demanding industrial usage of asbestos as part of wartime production.[29] The possibility of public funding arose as a backup source, in the event of short-falls in financing from private sources in the first instance.

The practical necessity to rely predominantly on private funding calls for the development of some means to allocate responsibility for payment among the players on the defense side. Within the context of *Amchem*, nego-tiations on the defense side over allocation questions proved manageable. The settling defendants were jointly represented by the Center for Claims Resolution (CCR).[30] In embracing the *Amchem* deal, those defendants, along with their insurers, built on the rough-hewn but mutually acceptable arrangements that the CCR previously had used to allocate settlement and defense costs among its members in earlier asbestos litigation. By contrast, the aspiration of the asbestos bill to encompass the full gamut of asbestos defendants complicates matters considerably. It increases the sheer number of affected companies on the defense side (plus their respective insurers) and, in so doing, increases the difficulty of reaching a consensus on allocation. A further complication stems from changes in the defendants now being sued in the asbestos litigation. The years after *Amchem* witnessed the demise of the last hangers-on from the asbestos industry. The asbestos plaintiffs' bar then proceeded to target additional companies with increasingly remote connections to the use of asbestos.[31] As a result, past experience in litigation is now only a shaky proxy for the incidence of future liability.

Allocation issues aside, the support of the defense camp as a whole turns on the overall price tag that any bill would carry. But that overall price tag will be a function of design decisions made elsewhere in the bill — for instance, the medical criteria and the dollar amounts used in the compen-sation grid. Every moving part stands to affect every other moving part. Sweetening the deal for asbestos claimants, moreover, stands to make the bill more attractive to Democratic skeptics but, at the same time, endangers support from Republicans concerned about the prospect of runaway costs and their potential to trigger the backup of public funding. In fact, efforts to bring the asbestos bill to a vote in the Senate in early 2006 were derailed when fiscal conservatives interposed a parliamentary objection on budget-ary grounds.[32]

As a matter of design, the obstacles to asbestos reform legislation are accentuated versions of the difficulties that attend any effort to set a price today for the payment of claims in the future. The problem of multiple moving parts calls for a degree of risk taking — a leap of faith — on the part of all contending forces. Risk taking will appear more or less worthwhile, however, based on perceptions of the available alternatives. Perhaps the biggest barrier to the kinds of compromises necessary for the enactment of asbestos legislation does not lie primarily in the design of the legislation itself but, rather, in the perceived viability—both legally and in the eyes of the contending forces—of the peacemaking vehicles available in the asbestos litigation in the absence of legislation. Put less formally, hard compromises and leaps of faith become possible only if the available alternatives would be even worse for the relevant players.

In the asbestos litigation post-*Amchem,* the realistic long-term alternative to congressional action is the use of §524(g) of the Bankruptcy Code, the special provision for asbestos-related reorganizations, not ongoing litigation in the tort system. As chapter 9 shall detail, the problem with §524(g) reorganizations is not that they disserve defendants or the asbestos plaintiffs' bar. The problem, instead, is that they serve those forces all too well, to the detriment of future claimants, in ways that make the qualms about the *Amchem* and *Ortiz* class settlements seem mild by comparison. Ironically, then, congressional intervention to add §524(g) to the Bankruptcy Code in 1994 to facilitate asbestos-related reorganizations may well have had the effect of undermining the prospects for superior solutions from Congress in more recent times.

Private Contracts with Plaintiffs' Law Firms

The barriers to public legislation as a peacemaking vehicle for mass torts are primarily practical and political, not legal. Public legislation has the authority to alter the terms for future claims, even to the point of removing them entirely from the tort system. The only question is whether proponents within the legislature can cobble together the requisite coalition to wield that power. That question holds interest as a matter of political prognostication, but not as one of institutional authority, which is my primary focus here.

Another vehicle for peacemaking draws its authority from notions of private contract, not from a delegation of lawmaking power. In their usual form, aggregate settlements act on pending tort claims represented by a common law firm. At bottom, aggregate settlements are simply contracts, just like ordinary one-on-one settlements in civil litigation generally. In the aftermath of *Amchem,* however, peacemaking efforts have sought to break down the conceptual line between public legislation and aggregate settlements. One effort—Owens Corning's National Settlement Program (NSP)—actually involved the use of private contracts to generalize and project into the future the aggregate settlement process.

The private nature of the Owens Corning NSP has formed an impediment to extensive scholarly exploration of its workings.[33] The information available through public sources nevertheless enables one to sketch its origins and dynamics with enough specificity to situate it within the gamut of arrangements for peacemaking. Named as a defendant in the asbestos litigation since the early 1980s, Owens Corning decided to manage its liabilities outside the auspices of the CCR, declining demands to fund 35 to 40 percent of the CCR's costs.[34] By the early 1990s, however, Owens Corning's strategy of litigating on its own began to appear tenuous. Lower-court approval for the class settlements in both *Amchem* and *Ortiz* resulted in the issuance of injunctions to forestall future litigation against the CCR defendants and Fibreboard, respectively, as the settling parties in those cases. These injunctions, combined with the earlier bankruptcies of leading asbestos firms such as Johns-Manville, increased the attention of the plaintiffs' bar on Owens Corning as one of the remaining defendants in the tort system.[35] The need to manage this ongoing litigation provided the impetus for the Owens Corning NSP.

A familiar adage in corporate acquisitions holds that one should not "buy a lawsuit." In other words, one should not acquire a company with significant, unresolved liability exposure. This, however, is precisely what Owens Corning did in order to increase its negotiating leverage in ongoing asbestos litigation—in effect, to replicate within its own corporate fold the kind of large block of liability that the CCR represented by way of joint defense agreements among twenty other autonomous companies.[36] Specifically, Owens Corning acquired Fibreboard—the settling defendant in *Ortiz*—while the legal challenges to the mandatory class settlement there were winding their way through the federal appellate courts. The insight of the Owens Corning NSP lies in its use of this large block of asbestos liability as a bargaining lever vis-à-vis the asbestos plaintiffs' bar.

As the holder of the largest remaining block of liability on the defense side outside of bankruptcy, Owens Corning was now positioned to induce plaintiffs' law firms to project into the future the aggregate settlement process. The centerpiece of the Owens Corning NSP consisted of contractual agreements between Owens Corning and some fifty asbestos plaintiffs' law firms—a total that later would extend to over one hundred such firms.[37] These plaintiffs' law firms effectively agreed to resolve future claims through an administrative regime run by Owens Corning rather than through tort litigation. The principal features of this administrative regime by now should look familiar. As in *Amchem*, the trade embodied in the Owens Corning NSP consisted of prompt payment of claims according to a negotiated grid in exchange for application of medical criteria that would withhold immediate cash for unimpaired persons.[38]

Two additional features of the Owens Corning NSP invite exploration. They highlight its innovative nature and, at the same time, help to explain why the plan ultimately collapsed. First, the NSP sought to align the incentives of the signatory plaintiffs' law firms with the interest of Owens Corning itself in achieving greater predictability in its asbestos liabilities over time. By acquiring Fibreboard, Owens Corning attempted to accumulate a sufficiently large chunk of the remaining liability in the asbestos litigation as to induce a kind of self-restraint on the part of the plaintiffs' bar. No plaintiffs' law firm would wish to break the bank consisting of the combined resources of Owens Corning and Fibreboard, for fear of endangering the law firm's own cash flow in the asbestos litigation. No one — so Owens Corning believed — would want the largest remaining chunk of asbestos liability to go into bankruptcy.[39]

Second, the NSP used asbestos plaintiffs' law firms as a proxy for legislative authority to set the compensation terms for future claimants. Rather than act directly on the rights of future claimants, the NSP acted indirectly on the lawyers positioned to represent them. Specifically, the NSP sought to capitalize on two features of legal representation on the plaintiffs' side: the dominance of asbestos plaintiffs' lawyers over their clients in the determination of settlement terms, and the relative concentration of asbestos plaintiffs' law firms themselves, at least at the outset of the plan.

As a formal matter, any settlement negotiated with a given claimant within a larger aggregate group has no binding force on any future claimant. In practical terms, however, aggregate settlements are not negotiated between the defendant and actual claimants but, rather, between the defendant and repeat players within the asbestos plaintiffs' bar. The trick behind the Owens Corning NSP lay in cutting deals with these repeat players and, thereby, getting the stability of prospective legislation without the political hassle.

The use of plaintiffs' law firms to regulate, in practical effect, the terms for future claims was not without its own difficulties. The law of professional responsibility places squarely in the hands of the client the ultimate decision whether to settle and under what terms.[40] The same body of law also prohibits lawyers from entering into agreements to restrict their future practice.[41] As a result, the signatory law firms within the asbestos bar cast their agreements with Owens Corning simply in terms of promises to advise any future clients to seek compensation under the terms of the Owens Corning administrative process rather than through tort litigation. The dominance of plaintiffs' lawyers over their clients nevertheless was expected to make this arrangement sufficiently likely to produce the desired result—namely, adherence by future clients to the grid previously negotiated by their lawyers with Owens Corning. It remains at least an open question whether the agreements at the heart of the NSP truly stand outside the ethical stricture against restriction of future law practice. The ethical dimensions of the NSP are of less concern, for present purposes, than the dynamics behind the plan. The possible antitrust implications of the NSP, moreover, went unlitigated—in all likelihood, for reasons that shall soon become apparent.[42]

For nearly two years, the Owens Corning NSP seemed a workable solution—indeed, a prescient one. Shortly after Owens Corning's announcement of the plan in December 1998, the Supreme Court handed down its decision in *Ortiz*, invalidating the mandatory class settlement negotiated by Fibreboard prior to its acquisition by Owens Corning. The result in *Ortiz* was hardly unexpected, given the Court's decision earlier in *Amchem*. The return of Fibreboard to the tort system simply added to the leverage that its new parent, Owens Corning, could wield to induce participation in the NSP. Within one month of the decision in *Ortiz*, the general counsel of Owens Corning testified before Congress, touting the NSP as evidence of the lack of need for federal asbestos reform legislation.[43] This stance, perhaps more than anything, highlights the aspiration of the plan to operate as an institutional rival to public legislation. That, however, ultimately was not to be.

Although it aspired to regulate the compensation terms for future claims, the NSP could do so only by proxy. The ability of the plan to bring order to Owens Corning's future asbestos liabilities was only as good as its scope—namely, the proportion of asbestos plaintiffs' law firms that agreed to participate and the proportion of still-solvent liability exposure held by Owens Corning. The NSP, however, lacked the power to keep either proportion static over time. Empirical research documents substantial entry of new firms into the market for asbestos litigation on the plaintiffs' side in the period since *Amchem*.[44] Commenting on the difficulties faced by the NSP, one long-standing member of the asbestos plaintiffs' bar points to the creation of new plaintiffs' law firms spun off from NSP signatories.[45] The NSP, in short, could not lock in the entire plaintiffs' bar, for new entrants and spin-offs could evade the constraints of firm-specific contracts. Nor could the NSP regulate the expansion of the asbestos litigation in the post-*Amchem* period to encompass increasingly remote defendants. That development had the effect of reducing the proportion of liability held by Owens Corning and, hence, its leverage vis-à-vis the plaintiffs' bar. The viability of the NSP, after all, turned on recognition on the part of plaintiffs' lawyers that Owens Corning was simply too big to fail — that it would be better left as a viable business than nudged into bankruptcy. With the NSP unable to keep pace with claims and its cash flow further dampened by a general downturn in the U.S. economy, Owens Corning ultimately succumbed. The company filed for bankruptcy in 2000.[46]

In the demise of the Owens Corning NSP lurk larger lessons. What Owens Corning lacked was the power to bind future claimants directly, rather than to do so porously by contracts with asbestos plaintiffs' law firms. The shortfall in the binding power of the NSP sets the stage for the discussion in the chapters that follow of class actions and bankruptcy since *Amchem*. In institutional terms, both of those vehicles aspire to the kind of direct regulatory force on future claimants that the NSP lacked. The Owens Corning NSP nonetheless marks a step forward in its aspiration to align, however imperfectly, the incentives of the plaintiffs' bar with the goal of a sustainable compensation regime. That alignment, however, turned on continued expectations on the part of plaintiffs' lawyers that the alternative to the NSP would make for financial peril to their own business interests. Entry of new plaintiffs' law firms and expansion of the litigation to reach new defendants are, on the surface, what undid the NSP. But those changes could occur only on a dampening of the disincentive for the plaintiffs' bar to exceed Owens Corning's capacity to fund its ongoing obligations in the asbestos litigation. That disincentive declined with the emergence of prepackaged reorganizations under §524(g) in the post-*Amchem* period.

The peculiar dynamics fostered by §524(g) and the reorganization process in bankruptcy more generally form the subject of extended discussion in chapter 9. The point, for the moment, is that the perceived desirability or undesirability of bankruptcy, once again, casts a shadow on the viability of other arrangements for peace. The prospect of bankrupting even the biggest player among the remaining solvent asbestos defendants simply became less of a bogeyman for plaintiffs' lawyers. With the rise of prepackaged reorganizations, plaintiffs' lawyers would come to see bankruptcy as something that would not necessarily make for protracted delays in payment for their inventories of cases. If anything, bankruptcy would enhance the leverage of plaintiffs' lawyers to demand generous payouts for their inventory cases — to the detriment of future claimants — in exchange for their assembly of votes for confirmation of the debtor's desired reorganization plan.

Seen in the foregoing light, the Owens Corning NSP displayed a laudable aspiration to align the incentives of plaintiffs' lawyers with the goal of a workable peace that would enhance the available resources for future claimants. The NSP simply lacked the means to maintain the strength of those incentives. To put the point differently, a viable peace arrangement must be just that: an assurance of peace that shuts off, or otherwise renders so undesirable, all alternatives such that affected persons then have a stake in the continued vitality of the peace arrangement itself. But even this lesson is not without complications. As the next chapter reveals, the understandable desire to make any peace the exclusive path for future claimants is at odds with a competing desire — namely, to leave open other paths for compensation as a way to discipline the exercise of bargaining power by the peace designers themselves.

CHAPTER VII

MANDATORY CLASS ACTIONS REVISITED

With public legislation unlikely as a practical matter and with private contracts limited in their capacity to deliver peace, mass tort lawyers would continue to experiment with class settlements. As chapter 5 has observed, the Supreme Court's decisions in *Amchem* and *Ortiz* cast the important questions about peacemaking as questions of governance and representation — of who should design the grids to govern future claims and under what institutional constraints. Developments in the class action area since the Court's decisions highlight the tension between two competing answers — the subjects of this chapter and the next.

One strand of developments springs from the need to avoid the porousness of the Owens Corning National Settlement Program (NSP). The idea is to make any solution reached by way of a class action the exclusive, mandatory avenue for future claimants. The case for mandatory class treatment as "the only option" for mass torts as a whole comes in a series of important articles by David Rosenberg that build on his endorsement of risk-based claims.[1] Rosenberg's writings represent the most detailed effort to build a case for mandatory class actions in the mass tort area. As such, they provide a useful point of departure for discussion of mass tort class actions after *Amchem*.

Attention to mandatory classes, however, has not been confined to scholarly writings. Developments in actual litigation have pushed in the same direction — albeit while stopping short of an across-the-board endorsement of the kind advanced by Rosenberg. One of the boldest experiments in recent years consists of an effort to obtain mandatory class treatment, if not for all claims involved in a given area of mass tort litigation then, at least, for punitive damage claims.

The present chapter starts with a critical analysis of Rosenberg's case for mandatory class treatment. I then turn to the difficulties posed even by mandatory class treatment confined to punitive damage claims. Against these renewed efforts to support some manner of mandatory classes stand efforts to craft viable opt-out class settlements for mass torts. The most intriguing development along these lines consists of efforts to craft an ostensible opt-out class settlement to operate, in practical effect, like a mandatory class settlement. I take up this new kind of opt-out class settlement in the next chapter.

Mandatory Class Actions Generally

The Court's decisions in *Amchem* and *Ortiz* have foreclosed the use of mandatory class actions as peacemaking vehicles for mass torts. But, insofar as the law has witnessed more modest moves — demands for mandatory treatment of punitive damage claims and attempts to achieve the closure of mandatory treatment in practical effect — one is left to wonder how the law should regard those developments. Are they attempts to nip at the edges of an undue restrictiveness that dampens the worthwhile pursuit of mandatory classes for mass torts generally? Or are they just the latest iterations of efforts to push the class action beyond its appropriate institutional bounds? To answer these questions, we must ask what a general application of mandatory class actions would look like.

David Rosenberg's thoughtful case for mandatory class treatment of mass torts rests on two central claims. His first claim starts from the notion of choice on the part of would-be mass tort claimants from an *ex ante* perspective — that is, with each person ignorant of the ultimate value of her particular tort claim. Rosenberg contends that if would-be class members were to consider their collective situation from this *ex ante* perspective, then they readily would consent to mandatory class treatment in order to maximize their collective welfare.[2] Preservation of an opportunity to opt out undermines collective welfare, Rosenberg contends, because it enables each class member to approach the litigation from an *ex post* perspective. Knowing the ultimate value of her particular claim, each person has every incentive to maximize merely her own individual gain, to the detriment of the collective good. The upshot of Rosenberg's first claim is that would-be class members — like the Odysseus of myth — would agree in advance to bind themselves to the mast of the mandatory class action in order to avoid giving in later to the sirens' call to maximize their own individual self-interest. The law therefore should embrace as fair the imposition of mandatory procedures *ex post*. Rosenberg's second claim goes to the conduct of this mandatory class action by class counsel. Here, Rosenberg contends that appropriate regulation of fee awards in the mandatory class action can align the incentives of class counsel with those of the class as a whole.[3]

The first of these claims is open to serious doubt, and the second misconceives the central problem of peacemaking in the mass tort area. If anything, scrutiny of Rosenberg's case for mandatory class treatment actually reveals the inevitability of analyzing the class action in institutional terms. What Rosenberg misses — but what the Supreme Court did not — is that the legitimacy of any governing arrangement must derive from something antecedent to all the good that arrangement would do as an instrumental matter.

Rosenberg's initial claim about choice from an *ex ante* perspective embraces two subsidiary points that bear attention, in turn. The first speaks to the relationship of defendants and plaintiffs' law firms; the second concerns the relationship of would-be class members to one another. Rosenberg's first subsidiary point holds that would-be class members would embrace mandatory classes on the ground that only a mandatory litigation process ensures the optimal deterrence of risk-taking by product manufacturers. This deterrence argument rests on a vision of the litigation process in investment-like terms.

On Rosenberg's account, only mandatory treatment equalizes the incentive of plaintiffs' lawyers to invest in the development of mass tort litigation with the incentive of defendants to do the same for their own self-protection.[4] Defendants, he argues, will invest in the development of information to undercut the merits of mass tort claims based on the possibility that they might be found liable to the entire group of exposed persons. Defendants, in short, will calibrate their investment in the litigation as if all exposed persons were embraced in a single class action. By contrast, plaintiffs' law firms lack comparably robust incentives to invest in the development of information to support mass tort claims. Any given firm stands to obtain as its clients only a portion of the persons exposed and, then, only when they develop some present-day impairment that enables them to sue under current tort doctrine. The equalization of investment incentives brought about by mandatory class treatment — combined with a general recognition of risk-based claims — would end what Rosenberg sees as the systematic underdeterrence of risk-taking today. Rosenberg describes this as the "regulatory advantage" of mandatory class treatment.[5]

Upon examination, however, the contention that asymmetric investment incentives have a dramatic effect on deterrence — enough to weigh heavily on the hypothetical preferences of claimants *ex ante*—appears over-stated. At the outset, it bears emphasis that the point of controversy here centers on the *magnitude* of the effect on deterrence. The deterrent effect of mass tort litigation plainly is a significant consideration in the design of a desirable legal regime in the area; and optimal deterrence involves threatening the defendant with full internalization of the social costs from its wrongful activities. Even under a system that permitted no aggregate treatment of claims whatsoever, the defendant would internalize all social costs of its misdeeds if all meritorious claims are ultimately paid—whether in the settlement of individual cases or under a comprehensive peace plan. There is no disagreement, moreover, that defendants and plaintiffs' lawyers who stand to represent only some subset of exposed persons will have differing incentives to invest in the development of the litigation.

By comparing the potential overall liability exposure of the defendant and the potential overall recovery for a given plaintiffs' law firm, Rosenberg obscures the real question about incentives to invest. The real question is whether a plaintiffs' law firm that stands to obtain only a proportion of exposed persons as its clients nonetheless has a sufficient incentive to make the initial investments needed to break open the litigation. Rosenberg's deterrence argument rests on an unduly static conception of the litigation investment process and an unduly linear conception of the relationship between investment and the probability of success for plaintiffs.

Any investment decision, of course, involves consideration of the expected outcome. The nature of investment in litigation is incremental, however. Plaintiffs' lawyers test the waters. They decide whether to invest further based on the results of an initial investment that ultimately may form only a small part of a larger whole. Each increment of investment brings forth new information that enables the lawyer to revise earlier estimates of the expected outcome. In fact, recent writing on civil litigation from an investment standpoint explicitly frames that process as a series of financial options, to be exercised or not based on earlier results.[6] What determines the pursuit of initial investment stages is the comparison of the expected returns from that stage with the expected costs of undertaking it. The difference in the potential overall liability for defendants and the potential overall recovery for a plaintiffs' law firm—the observation that drives Rosenberg's argument—undoubtedly exists. The point of the litigation options perspective is that overall differences may well exist beyond the point that makes a difference to the pursuit of initial investment stages. The difference between the potential overall liability for the defendant and the potential overall recovery for a plaintiffs' law firm is unlikely to matter, in other words, if the latter is still enough to induce investment at the initial stages.

An additional observation points in the same direction by speaking to the relationship between investment and success on the merits. Deterrence does not stem simply from investment in a given area of mass tort litigation. It is not something that a plaintiffs' lawyer can buy, as long as she comes up with enough money. Deterrence stems, more specifically, from the information and consequent success on the merits that investment yields. Disparities in investment incentives might bear substantially on the development of such information if the quality of that information—its capacity to bolster the investor's case—were a function primarily of how much money is expended to obtain it. But the matters most likely to break open a given area of mass tort litigation—say, evidence suggesting a causal relationship between a given product and latent disease or evidence of punitive-damage-worthy conduct—tend to be related to investment levels only in the sense that some minimal level of investment is needed to bring them to light. True enough, one can always search for more evidence of causation or more evidence of a cover-up. But speaking in those terms is rather like talking about the number of warheads that one can affix to what is already a nuclear missile. What matters most to deterrence is the incentive to make the initial investments that call forth information that first suggests a likelihood of success on the merits. And that is something capable of being induced by the ability of the plaintiffs' lawyer to capture only part of the resulting rewards.

One may rephrase the point more formally: What matters most to the success of mass tort litigation and, hence, to its deterrent effect is the incentive to get to the point of diminishing marginal returns to further investment, not so much the incentive to capture every last increment of gain from investment. Rosenberg points to a theoretical disparity in the latter by focusing simply on the potential overall liability for the defendant and the potential overall recovery for a given plaintiffs' law firm. But that disparity stands to have a less dramatic effect on deterrence once one takes a more nuanced view of the investment process and the way it reveals information progressively.

The disparity in investment incentives is not merely a technical matter. Rosenberg's case for mandatory class actions rests on the consent he believes class members would supply, if only they could view their collective situation from an *ex ante* perspective. But if the gains to collective welfare in terms of deterrence are ambiguous, at best, then more pressure falls on Rosenberg's further contention about *ex ante* choice.

Rosenberg's second subsidiary point holds that would-be claimants choosing *ex ante* would prefer mandatory class treatment for an additional reason. It would, according to Rosenberg, prevent a kind of cross-subsidization among claimants. Specifically, he contends that any opportunity to opt out of the class would enable those who turn out to have high-value claims to maximize their own individual recoveries. That, in turn, will lead to a dampening of the overall recovery for the class, as the defendant withholds resources for its use in the resolution of opt-out cases. According to Rosenberg, would-be claimants viewing their collective situation from an *ex ante* perspective would prefer to maximize the aggregate recovery for the class by binding everyone to a grid that would reflect an averaging of damages.[7] No one, in other words, would want the law to safeguard opt-out rights, for they simply would enable a few persons to play a kind of litigation "lottery" to the detriment of the many in the class.[8] A settlement grid reflecting averaged damages, he reasons, would recreate the kind of insurance policy that class members would have negotiated with the defendant, had they been in a position to do so before the occurrence of the mass tort. Such an insurance policy, on his account, would not provide the sort of individualized treatment accorded in the tort system. It instead would take a more broad-brush approach.[9]

To see mandatory classes as preventing cross-subsidization, however, is to proceed based on a misleading account of what class actions do and where their source of authority lies. One of the challenges in the design of any civil settlement lies in how to divide the gains from the avoidance of continued litigation. These are gains generated by the settlement itself. This is not necessarily to say that these gains must manifest themselves strictly in dollar terms. Any settlement also operates as a technique to reduce the risk associated with continued litigation. Class actions accentuate the difficulty of the negotiation, however, for the gains to be divided are greater and the resulting range for bargaining wider than in ordinary civil litigation.[10] The difficulty stems from the lack of any preexisting entitlement to these gains on the part of any participant in the litigation. Average-value claimants within the class have no more of a basis to benefit from these gains than high-value claimants or, for that matter, the settling defendant. Characterization of opt-out classes as giving rise to cross-subsidization implies the existence of such an entitlement where there is none.

The error runs even deeper, however, to the implication that litigants somehow do not have a preexisting right to maximize their own individual gains. Tort law generally regards damage recoveries as being independent from one another. The remedy of punitive damages complicates this point, as I shall discuss later in this chapter. But Rosenberg's case for mandatory class treatment for mass torts across the board admits of no distinction between compensatory and punitive damages. The basic doctrinal point remains that, absent a bona fide limited fund, the ability of any given claimant to obtain a higher-than-average recovery in individual tort litigation is not thought to trample on the legal rights of other claimants. That ability may be objectionable on instrumental grounds. It may be unwise policy. It may "preserve individualism," yet "foster inequality" of a sort.[11] But it is not thought to abridge the rights of other claimants. Insofar as there is any preexisting entitlement, it is — for better or worse — in the nature of every person for herself.

In effect, Rosenberg's cross-subsidization argument seeks to generalize for class actions as a whole the justification for mandatory class treatment in a conventional limited fund situation. In so doing, Rosenberg makes the same misstep as the class settlement designers in *Ortiz*. The faux limited fund in *Ortiz* was limited only by the settlement designers' own designation of Fibreboard's insurance coverage as the exclusive source of recourse for class members. The limited nature of the fund was the product of class treatment, not its antecedent. Rosenberg's cross-subsidization argument represents a subtler permutation of the same error. The cross-subsidization of which he complains occurs only once there is some demarcation of class members from nonclass members expected to defect from the collective group to maximize their own individual claims. Yet, that demarcation would be the product of class treatment, albeit of a less binding sort than Rosenberg would prefer. The interdependence of claims that leads to cross-subsidization comes from treating claimants as a class rather than as individuals whose recoveries have no bearing on one other. In *Ortiz,* the Court properly rejected such reasoning, for it amounts to the justification of the governing power wielded by a class action based on the assertion of that power in the first place.

Rosenberg's cross-subsidization argument also is objectionable on a further ground: its jarring dissonance with actual behavior in insurance markets. Rosenberg defends the use of damage averaging in class settlement grids as the equivalent of an insurance policy. This comparison is problematic, even on its own terms. Insurance policies — say, for one's car or home — use averaging within a pool of insureds to set the premium for coverage. But payout amounts — the counterpart to the compensation afforded to class members under a settlement grid — are not averaged. A fire at your home does not entitle you to the average of all covered homeowners' losses. It entitles you to the value of your home, on the safe assumption that you purchased such coverage.

Further exploration of the insurance analogy shows how Rosenberg misses a fundamental respect in which the existence of insurance markets, in itself, undercuts his assertions about what class members would choose *ex ante*. The right to opt out of the class—the very thing Rosenberg disparages—operates as a kind of insurance policy against the law reform power to be wielded by class counsel. This is not to say that it is the only insurance policy that one might construct, much less the best one. Chapter 11 in this book shall argue that more direct constraints on class counsel would be preferable. The point, for now, is that opt-out rights constrain what class counsel can do in any deal. For those persons who turn out to have anomalously high-value claims, the opportunity to opt out ensures that, if need be, they can assert their preexisting right to a recovery unconstrained by any settlement grid.

Rosenberg's observation that the right to opt out reduces the size of the overall settlement pie is simply a reformulation of the observation that the right operates in the manner of an insurance policy. One commonplace form of insurance consists of policies that protect people against the kinds of low-probability but high-value losses that are like the bad fortune of having a high-value claim in mass tort litigation. Specifically, "term" life insurance has long enabled people to hedge the loss of future income from premature death. Millions of ordinary people pay for such policies—and, of course, pay before knowing their specific fate—even though only an unfortunate few beneficiaries will ever collect on the coverage provided. The insurance industry is all about effectuating the kind of cross-subsidization—if one can call it that—of which Rosenberg complains. To say that class members would recoil from similar arrangements is to ignore observed behavior in the real world.

To his credit, Rosenberg is right when he posits that peacemaking cannot take place through consent in a contractual sense. The model cannot be homeowners' sales of their property by way of a real estate agent. The power of sale, instead, must be the subject of a noncontractual delegation. The difficult question is what institutional arrangement can legitimize the sale, such that the law properly may regard it as binding for the future.

To see the class action as a regime for governance—as something on a continuum with public legislation—helps one to pinpoint the reductionism of Rosenberg's analysis. Even when viewing their situation from an *ex ante* perspective, people care not just about their aggregate welfare but also about questions of allocation within the collective group. People designing a good government would want it to "promote the general welfare," of course.[12] But they also would want to include brakes upon government action that would seek, instead, simply to advance factional interests. People choosing *ex ante*, in other words, would want to afford those in power ample authority to advance the collective good, but they would grant that authority subject to constraints to ensure that some people are not advantaged arbitrarily over others. Interestingly enough, both objectives — not just the first — animate the notion of *ex ante* choice advanced by the political philosopher John Rawls, whom Rosenberg credits as the source for his analytical framework.[13]

In an article coauthored with Bruce Hay, Rosenberg readily acknowledges that class actions carry a risk of dereliction on the part of class counsel. But the kind of dereliction that concerns Rosenberg involves the possibility that class counsel will fail to maximize the aggregate recovery for the class, not that they will misallocate it. If anything, Rosenberg's proposed solution to the settlement maximization problem actually accentuates the conditions for the kind of misallocations feared in *Amchem* and *Ortiz* — namely, to present claimants from futures ones who are otherwise similarly situated.

For Rosenberg, the solution to the maximization problem lies in how the law sets the fee to be gained by class counsel from the settlement of a mandatory class action. He would direct courts to "eliminate any inventive to settle for too little by regulating the attorney's fee in such a way as to ensure that the attorney's fractional share of a settlement is no greater than his fractional share would have been of the recovery had the case gone to trial."[14] The technical term "fractional share" refers to the fee award, as a percentage of the overall class recovery, that class counsel would have garnered from the court in the event of an actual, classwide trial. The court in a mandatory litigation class action, in other words, would set class counsel's fee in the event of a settlement according to the fee that the court would have awarded class counsel in the event of trial. Rosenberg defends the workability of this approach by pointing out that a court could do his suggested fee calculation without knowing the value of class members' claims.[15] The predicate for all of this, nevertheless, is that the mandatory class action is the sole litigation mechanism for a given mass tort. In Rosenberg's suggested world of mandatory class actions, there would be no separate, individual litigation of claims.

This vision of the fee calculation misconceives the nature of peacemaking for mass torts. The job involves not just maximization of the overall settlement pot but also allocation of the joint gains from settlement itself — the value created by the avoidance of the risks associated with trial. A world without previous litigation of claims would be a world that would run an even greater risk than today of misallocations in the design of the peace due simply to lack of good information. As chapter 3 observes, the kind of individual litigation that Rosenberg rejects has the benefit of facilitating what Judge Richard Posner in *Rhone-Poulenc* described as a "pooling of judgment" through a "decentralized process of multiple trials" that will tend toward greater accuracy in the evaluation of claims.[16] By contrast, a world in which the mandatory class action would be the only ballgame for mass torts would be a world profoundly at odds with observed practices. Whether in workers' compensation legislation or in mass tort litigation, grids evolve from the ground up. And that ground consists of the information about the mix of claims and their respective settlement values brought to light through actual tort litigation. By eliminating individual litigation as a way to empower class counsel to pursue aggregate welfare, Rosenberg would eliminate a central informational constraint on the allocation decisions of class counsel.

In the concluding chapters of this book, I shall return to the idea of good governance as a combination of empowerment and constraint. Rosenberg is on to something important when he speaks of the need to constrain self-dealing by the lawyers who design the peace. The problem, however, is not so much that current law lacks incentives for the peacemaking plaintiffs' lawyers to maximize the overall value of the peace. Rather, as chapter 11 elaborates, the real problem is that the dealmakers may fail to maximize the overall value of the peace *because* they can misallocate — specifically, because they can benefit themselves by benefiting present claimants over future ones. Misallocation is the engine that drives the failure to maximize, not merely its afterthought or indirect consequence, as Rosenberg's analysis implies. The challenge for the law lies not in eliminating the market for preexisting litigation of mass tort claims. The objective, instead, should be to deploy the deal-making lawyers' representation of present claims in large numbers as a source of constraint on their design of the peace terms for future claims. For now, the important point is that Rosenberg's account of the coercive power needed to make a lasting peace rests on an unduly narrow conception of the constraints that should operate on the peacemakers.

Punitive Damage Class Actions

Arguments for mandatory class treatment for all mass torts have remained confined to the academic literature. The Supreme Court's decision in *Ortiz* makes that state of affairs likely to prevail for the foreseeable future. The difficulties in Rosenberg's general argument for mandatory classes nonetheless bear attention, for they help to frame the developments in actual litigation since the Court's decision. The most significant experiment with mandatory classes in recent years has focused not on the treatment of all claims involved in a given area of mass tort litigation but, more narrowly, on claims for punitive damages. The setting for this experiment has consisted of mass tort litigation against the tobacco industry.

A wealth of evidence has emerged that the leading firms of the tobacco industry engaged in a long-running conspiracy to suppress information about the health risks of smoking, to confuse consumers about those risks, and to impede the development of safer tobacco products.[17] Such a cover-up provides the makings for punitive damage awards–potentially, multiple punitive damage awards against the industry in lawsuits spread across the country. Pointing to this possibility, class counsel in In re *Simon II Litigation* sought the certification of a mandatory class under Rule 23(b)(1)(B), comprised of presently diseased smokers nationwide.[18] The limited fund said to justify mandatory class treatment did not consist of the resources available to the tobacco industry to pay in full the claims against it, as in a conventional limited-fund scenario. Rather, class counsel in *Simon II* invoked a limit of constitutional due process upon the aggregate amount of punitive damages that may be awarded based on a single course of tortious misconduct. This argument has become known, in shorthand, as the "limited punishment" theory.[19]

Like Rosenberg's more sweeping proposal, however, even mandatory class treatment confined to punitive damage claims is problematic. Judge Jack Weinstein initially certified the proposed mandatory class on the limited punishment theory, but the United States Court of Appeals for the Second Circuit reversed. The Second Circuit's decision is correct in its result, but the court's reasoning is opaque, at best. The Second Circuit took an unusually long time to issue its opinion, nearly eighteen months from the date of oral argument.[20] Notwithstanding the time available for reflection, the court generated an opinion that one can describe most charitably as undertheorized.

The problem with the limited punishment theory is one that bears a close connection to an idea at the core of *Amchem* and *Ortiz*. The limited punishment theory contravenes the principle that a class action may not legitimize its power over the legal rights of its members by reference to matters that are the creation of the class action itself. To understand why a mandatory punitive damage class runs afoul of this stricture, one first must become acquainted with the constitutional principles that govern punitive damages. Also important are the strategic reasons why plaintiffs' lawyers might wish to focus on punitive damage claims as a way to drive the resolution of mass tort disputes in their entirety.

Constitutional Background and Settlement Strategy

The late 1990s were not just a period of newfound attention from the Supreme Court to the law of class actions. At roughly the same time as its decisions in *Amchem* and *Ortiz*, the Court also began to strike down punitive damage awards in conventional individual lawsuits on grounds of constitutional due process.[21] The Court's interpretation of the Due Process Clause in this regard remains the subject of disagreement among its members. At least two Justices believe that the Clause, properly read, imposes no substantive constraint that punitive damages must be reasonable in amount, only procedural constraints on the imposition of such relief.[22] I do not resolve here the dispute over the proper reading of the Due Process Clause. I instead proceed descriptively, showing how the emerging constitutional jurisprudence of punitive damages created the occasion for experimentation with mandatory class treatment for those types of claims.

Even before the involvement of the Supreme Court, both lower courts and commentators had voiced the fear that a widespread course of tortious misconduct might result in multiple punitive damage awards and that those awards, in the aggregate, would amount to excessive punishment. In an oft-quoted opinion from the late 1960s, the prominent Second Circuit Judge Henry Friendly expressed "the gravest difficulty in perceiving how claims for punitive damages in such a multiplicity of actions throughout the nation can be so administered as to avoid overkill."[23] Pleas along similar lines from defendants in the asbestos litigation garnered expressions of concern from other lower-court judges.[24] But those same courts nonetheless concluded that the problem lay beyond their capacity to solve, for any solution would entail the coordination of tort litigation nationwide.[25] The stark but simple fact remains that no mass tort defendant has succeeded in reducing a punitive damage award based on what Judge Friendly described as the risk of "overkill" meted out over "a multiplicity of actions"—a revealing observation, for reasons that shall become apparent shortly.

The Supreme Court has yet to rule directly on the application of due process constraints to punitive damage awards in mass tort litigation. A fair reading of its decisions, however, points to the existence of an outer constitutional limit upon the aggregate amount of punitive damages that may be awarded based on a single course of misconduct. After referring in earlier decisions to the existence of substantive due process constraints on punitive damages, the Court in 1996 finally struck down an actual punitive damage award as unconstitutional in *BMW of North America, Inc. v. Gore*. The case involved a consumer fraud action centered on the defendant manufacturer's undisclosed repainting of a new BMW automobile prior to its delivery from the factory to the plaintiff consumer. An Alabama jury had returned a punitive damage award five hundred times more than the modest diminution in car value suffered by the plaintiff, as reflected in the jury's compensatory damage award. The *Gore* Court held that the Due Process Clause prohibits a state from advancing its legitimate ends of punishment and deterrence by way of a punitive damage award so excessive in amount that the defendant would not have had "fair notice" that its misconduct would meet with such severity.[26]

The Court elaborated on this due process constraint in its 2003 decision in *State Farm Mutual Automobile Insurance Co. v. Campbell.* There, the defendant automobile insurer had failed to settle an earlier lawsuit against its insureds, the Campbells, for an amount within their insurance policy limits. When the lawsuit resulted in a damage award against the Campbells far in excess of their auto insurance coverage, they sued State Farm for bad-faith failure to settle, fraud, and intentional infliction of emotional distress. A Utah jury returned a punitive damage award that was 145 times the Campbells' actual losses. Overturning the award, the Supreme Court declined to set any "rigid benchmarks" or "bright-line ratio" for the relationship between punitive and compensatory damages. The Court nonetheless stated that, "in practice, few awards exceeding a single-digit ratio between punitive and compensatory damages, to a significant degree, will satisfy due process."[27] The 145 to 1 ratio in *Campbell* dramatically exceeded this rough rule of thumb. Simply as a mathematical matter, then, the existence of a constitutional outer limit on the amount of punitive damages that a jury may award an individual plaintiff based on a particular course of misconduct implies the existence of a limit on the aggregate amount of punitive damages that multiple actions may impose for those same misdeeds.[28]

In terms of timing, the emergence of a constitutional limit on aggregate punitive damages corresponded with efforts to identify an institutional vehicle to facilitate the resolution of mass tort disputes. In any area in which individual tort suits are dispersed over time and across multiple jurisdictions, credible fear of punitive damages on defendants' part will form a major impediment to the resolution of the litigation as a whole. As chapter 3 has noted, punitive damages are a substantial source of variance in the tort system—something that, in turn, increases the uncertainty over the ultimate parameters of the defendant's liability. Defendants have little reason to make concessions for the compensation of individual claimants—say, to agree to the creation of a streamlined administrative regime—unless defendants also can put to rest the question of punitive damages. Mandatory class treatment for punitive damages thus serves the strategic goal of smoothing the path for resolution of the litigation as a whole.

Matters specific to the tobacco litigation by the time of *Simon II* added to the attention on punitive damages. A mandatory class does not simply empower class counsel as the bargaining agents of class members. It also gives class counsel a kind of power over competitors within the plaintiffs' bar. When designed to resolve once and for all the issue of punitive damages, a mandatory class gives class counsel a power of disposition over the one thing with the greatest potential to boost the upside from ongoing individual litigation. A mandatory class action effectively gives class counsel the power to strike a deal for matters that are the lifeblood of trial lawyers. As a result, a mandatory class will be especially desirable from the standpoint of class counsel when there is disagreement over litigation strategy in a given area—specifically, over whether some form of comprehensive national resolution or ongoing litigation on a more conventional scale represents the right approach on the plaintiffs' side. In such an environment, a mandatory class enables class counsel to reap the reward in attorneys' fees from resolution of the entire punitive damage question and, simultaneously, to undercut the potential profitability of competitors inclined toward a different strategy.

Even before *Simon II,* a divergence in strategy along the foregoing lines had emerged in the tobacco litigation. One camp of plaintiffs' lawyers pointed in the direction of comprehensive resolution, seeking initially to bring a nationwide opt-out class action to resolve all tort claims of nicotine-addicted persons against the tobacco industry. This effort foundered in 1996, with appellate decertification of the proposed nationwide class of smokers.[29] Several of the same lawyers went on to represent state governments nationwide that sought reimbursement for the additional outlays from their respective Medicaid programs said to stem from the tobacco industry's misdeeds.[30] Chapter 10 discusses these state reimbursement suits in greater depth. The point, for now, is that the endgame in the state suits was a multibillion-dollar nationwide settlement, not piecemeal trials.

During the same period, however, a second camp of plaintiffs' lawyers pursued a strategy of actual trials and began to garner multibillion-dollar punitive damage awards for individual clients.[31] The roster of class counsel in *Simon II* conspicuously did not include anyone from this second group of more trial-oriented plaintiffs' lawyers. In certifying the mandatory class in *Simon II* under Rule 23(b)(1)(B), Judge Weinstein described the threat that case-by-case trials presented. Absent mandatory class treatment for the punitive damage claims of all diseased smokers, said Judge Weinstein, "the first plaintiffs may recover vast sums while others who arrive later are left with a depleted fund against which they cannot recover."[32]

Within Judge Weinstein's statement lies the structure of the analysis to follow. His statement contains two premises. The first speaks to the limited nature of the "fund" created by the Supreme Court's due process constraints. On appeal, the Second Circuit rested its reversal of the class certification in *Simon II* on concerns regarding this first premise. Writing for the Second Circuit, Judge James Oakes emphasized the words of the Supreme Court in *Ortiz*, which had cautioned against recognition of mandatory, limited-fund classes "in circumstances markedly different from the traditional paradigm" of the early equity cases.[33] The Second Circuit stated that the limited nature of the fund thought to justify mandatory class treatment was simply a "theoretical" limit — one that is merely "postulated, and for that reason . . . not easily susceptible to proof, definition, or even estimation, by any precise figure." The court framed the problem as an evidentiary one. For the Second Circuit, "there was no 'evidence on which [Judge Weinstein] may ascertain the limit and the insufficiency of the fund.'"[34]

It is far from clear that the problem with the limited punishment theory consists of a lack of "evidence" in the sense seemingly intended by the Second Circuit. Evidence is needed, of course, when the purported limit on the fund consists of the resources on hand for the defendant. The "evidence" for the limited nature of the fund in *Simon II*, however, consists not of financial information but, rather, of implications from Supreme Court precedents. Ascertaining the limited nature of the fund is an exercise in legal analysis, not number crunching. Continuing with its evidentiary emphasis, the Second Circuit added that "the record in this case does not evince a likelihood that any given number of punitive damage awards to individual claimants would be constitutionally excessive, either individually or in the aggregate, and thus overwhelm the available fund."[35] As I shall explain shortly, this statement comes somewhat closer to the mark. But, here, too, framing the problem as an evidentiary one — as a deficiency in the "record" compiled in support of class certification — misdirects attention.

The limits of the fund aside, Judge Weinstein's second premise pertains to the allocation of that fund among the members of the plaintiff class. The implication of his remark on this score is that disproportionate punitive damage recoveries for early plaintiffs by comparison to those for later ones are something that warrants mandatory treatment of all plaintiffs from the outset. For its part, the Second Circuit understandably declined to resolve questions about the allocation of the proposed fund, noting that its qualms about the limited nature of that fund were sufficient to warrant reversal.[36]

I seek to supply here the logic that remains buried underneath the surface of the Second Circuit's analysis. The fatal defect of the proposed limited fund in *Simon II* has little to do with evidence or the content of the record that class counsel might muster. The real problem with both the limited nature of the fund and its allocation among class members springs from a common source. Both replicate the self-referential justification for mandatory class treatment that *Ortiz* correctly rejects as a basis for the assertion of governing power.

The Limits of the Limited Fund

As a justification for mandatory class treatment, the limited-fund concept makes sense only for funds that truly would be limited in the context of actual litigation absent the existence of the class action. This is not to say that the limited-fund concept precludes the making of informed predictions. The point of a mandatory, limited-fund class action, after all, is to avoid a rush on the defendant that would deplete the fund in a haphazard manner. The point is not to provide class treatment only after chaos has ensued. But the limited fund concept does mean a fund with limits that exist apart from the class action itself, not a fund limited in a way that has bite only upon certification of the class.

In the equitable forerunners to Rule 23(b)(1)(B) parsed by the *Ortiz* Court, the limited nature of the funds was readily apparent. Company officials had misused funds limited to a particular amount. A now-absconded seller had left only so much against which his defrauded buyers could seek to recover. And a decedent's estate was only so large.[37] The insight of *Ortiz* is that the legitimacy of a mandatory class action turns on preexisting circumstances that already have imposed a degree of interdependence upon the members of the plaintiff class. The text of Rule 23(b)(1)(B) captures this preexisting interdependence when it speaks of "adjudications with respect to individual members of the class which would as a practical matter be dispositive of the interests of the other members not parties to the adjudications or [which would] substantially impair or impede their ability to protect their interests." The "adjudications" referenced in Rule 23(b)(1)(B) clearly consist of the ones expected to be produced by the litigation dynamics already at work among class members, not the adjudication of the class action itself. Under the circumstances described in the rule, a mandatory class does not so much impose its mandate as it, instead, affords recognition to a preexisting interdependence in class members' claims. Put in the parlance of government, the class action does not create the unit of governance so much as it acknowledges its existence "as a practical matter."

A conception of the mandatory class as a response to preexisting conditions helps one to pinpoint the objection to a mandatory class predicated on the limited punishment theory. The Second Circuit comes close to putting its finger on the problem when the court describes the constitutional limit on punitive damages as "theoretical" in nature. But the court quickly muddies the point by casting it in terms of the evidence mustered by class counsel. The problem—what makes the limit merely a "theoretical" one—is not an evidentiary matter but, instead, one of institutional structure. Here, too, the court comes close to the mark when it expresses doubt that "punitive awards to individual claimants would . . . overwhelm the available fund."[38] But, again, the court goes on to mischaracterize the problem as a deficiency in the record.

Notwithstanding decades of mass tort litigation, not a single defendant has succeeded in constraining punitive damages based on the invocation of a constitutional limit on aggregate punishment. And that failure is not for lack of trying. The constitutional limit to which advocates of mandatory class treatment point amounts to the kind of judicially underenforced— probably, unenforceable—norm that commentators have identified in other areas of constitutional law.[39] Here, even if a constitutional limit does exist for aggregate punishment by way of punitive damages, other institutional commitments—principally, the decentralized judicial scheme of the tort system—restrict the capacity of any particular court to give that limit practical effect in actual litigation. The problem is structural, not informational.[40]

Absent any preexisting means to enforce the limit on aggregate punishment, the mandatory class itself is what would have made class members' claims interdependent. To permit class certification on this basis—certainly, to mandate membership in the class—would contravene the stricture that class counsel may not legitimize their power by reference to the class action itself. In this respect, the limited punishment theory ultimately is no different from the assertion of a limited fund in *Ortiz* or the supposed unity of interest among class members created by the class settlement negotiations in *Amchem*. To be sure, the actual enforcement of punitive damage awards over time might lead the tobacco industry to seek protection under the Bankruptcy Code, a development that would make for interdependence in the remaining smokers' claims for punitive damages. But that interdependence would not be in the nature of the limited punishment theory; instead, it would sound in terms of a conventional limited fund. And the existence of such a fund is precisely the assertion that the limited punishment theory seeks to avoid.

Allocation According to Substantive Law

Now, consider the allocation of punitive damages among the class members—what Judge Weinstein feared would amount to a disproportionate windfall for early plaintiffs in the absence of mandatory class treatment. Here, the operation of the mandatory class as a freestanding vehicle for law reform becomes even more apparent. A variety of suggestions exist for how one might allocate a punitive damage fund, whether set by judgment in a class trial or, more likely, negotiated as part of a settlement in the mandatory class action. In *Simon II*, Judge Weinstein stated his expectation to "distribute the funds in accordance with equitable principles, after consultation with class members and, as needed, experts in the medical, legal, and other fields who can assist in devising an appropriate equitable distribution scheme."[41] There is much to be said as a policy matter in favor of a regime that would allocate equitably any overall punitive damage pot among those persons whose tort claims form the predicates for creation of that pot in the first place. One commentator goes even further, suggesting that the punitive damage pot might "be applied exclusively to public health and social welfare purposes, without any distribution to individual claimants," though this source hastens to add that such an approach would raise "unexplored issues."[42] I speak to the subject of allocation not in order to specify how one should divide the pot. The open-ended nature of the allocation decision in itself undercuts the legitimacy of mandatory class treatment.

As conceived in *Ortiz,* the limited-fund concept carries its own principle of allocation—one that constrains both the deal-making power of class counsel and the discretion of the court. Here, too, the analysis of early equity cases in *Ortiz* is telling, not as an exercise in historical trivia but, rather, as an insight about the source of governing power for the mandatory class action. As the Court observed, the "antecedents of the mandatory class action presented straightforward models of equitable treatment, with the simple equity of a pro rata distribution providing the required fairness."[43] Quoting one of the early treatises on equity, the Court explained that the principle of pro rata distribution derives from the underlying inclination of equity "to regard all the demands [on a limited fund] as standing upon an equal footing."[44]

The image of class members "standing upon an equal footing" is not an invention of equity or the modern mandatory class. Nor does it stem from some free-floating conception of what would make for a better, fairer world. It flows from the nature of class members' claims under the body of substantive law that gives them life.

The reason why chaotic individual litigation against a limited fund presents a compelling justification for a mandatory class is that there exists an underlying principle that tort claimants—like civil claimants generally—are equally entitled to recover compensation according to the merits of their particular claims. A person with a meritorious compensatory damage

claim for $100 is no less worthy of being paid $100 by the defendant because some other person has an equally meritorious compensatory damage
claim for $1 million. Absent a limited fund, each should take according to
the merits of her claim. The law takes offense at the prospect that some
tort claimants — or investors or defrauded ticket purchasers or legatees, for
that matter — might get more for their claims due simply to their success
in hunting down the defendant before other, equally worthy claimants can
show up on the scene. Being first in line should not matter with regard to
compensatory damages; and, in practical terms, it does not matter, absent
a bona fide limited fund. Outside of the limited-fund scenario, in other
words, no properly proven claim for compensation in tort is any more or
less entitled to payment than any other based simply on matters of sequencing. If there is to be a ratcheting down of recoveries due to the existence of a
limited fund, then all would-be claimants should share alike in the shortfall,
with each taking some reduced number of cents for every dollar of compensation to which she otherwise would be entitled.

To recognize the origins of the mandatory class action in equity, as the
Ortiz Court does, is not to recognize a roving power to mandate whatever allocation might conceivably make for the betterment of public policy.
Preexisting tort principles of compensation are what situate tort claimants
"upon an equal footing" and, in turn, dictate a pro rata distribution in a
Rule 23(b)(1)(B) class. A mandatory class simply enables the law to bring
the allocation of the limited fund more closely into line with the preexisting
notion that all meritorious claims for compensatory damages are equally
worthy of payment.

The seeming flexibility involved in the allocation of a fund for punitive damages under the limited punishment theory arises precisely because
tort law is so thin on principles of allocation for that form of relief. As the
Supreme Court has noted, the current law of punitive damages focuses on
the "moral condemnation" warranted by the defendants' misdeeds, not
any "concrete loss that the plaintiff has suffered."[45] As a result, the prospect
of some tort plaintiffs obtaining lottery-like windfalls of punitive damages
works no offense to tort principles. This state of affairs might not be a desirable way to run a civil justice system. The point nonetheless remains that
tort law takes no offense at such an allocation.

One conceivably might argue that matters of allocation should have
no bearing on the legitimacy of a mandatory class on the limited punishment theory. The important thing, so the argument would go, is that the
defendants' extreme misdeeds should meet with appropriate punishment.
Because tort law is indifferent to the allocation of punitive damages, there

is no basis upon which to say that any allocation chosen for a mandatory class like the one in *Simon II* is any more or less desirable as a tort matter as compared to what individual lawsuits would produce in the absence of the class. From a broader policy standpoint, there is undoubted appeal to the notion of all diseased smokers sharing in a single punitive damage award, as that would tend to avoid the discrepancies of sequencing described by Judge Weinstein.

But notice the move that has been made here: The allocation to be achieved by the mandatory class action is superior not by reference to the yardstick supplied by tort law but only from a broader policy standpoint — from something outside the body of law that defines class members' claims. By viewing the class action as a delegation of governing power, one may pinpoint what is problematic about this move. The law sensibly infers a delegation to class counsel to act on class members' rights on a mandatory basis in a conventional, limited-fund scenario. There, preexisting circumstances portend an allocation that is offensive to the principles of applicable substantive law. The mandatory class, in turn, would serve to improve that allocation not under some yardstick invented by those in charge of the class litigation but, rather, under the criteria supplied by applicable substantive law itself. To borrow the categories invoked earlier in this chapter, empowerment comes only with constraint. The source of the constraint is preexisting substantive law — something embedded within the claims that comprise the class — not faith in those conducting the class litigation to pursue enlightened policy aims, defined from without. Confidence in the ability of a mandatory class action to secure an allocation superior under applicable substantive law to what would occur otherwise — not merely an allocation that is equally good or bad from that vantage point — is what justifies a mandatory, limited-fund class.

What Judge Weinstein finds disturbing about the sequencing of punitive damage awards in the tobacco litigation springs not from the substantive law of torts. The thing that is jarring about that sequencing stems from something external: the sense that a thoroughly modern law of torts really should not be indifferent about the allocation of punitive damages but, instead, should treat them more like compensatory damages. This sentiment arguably is an enlightened one as a matter of desirable law reform. But it contradicts the very source of law that underlies the limited punishment theory: the Supreme Court's due process decisions on punitive damages. There, the premise is that punitive damages under the current law of torts are not compensatory and, for that reason, do not "redress the concrete loss that [a particular] plaintiff has suffered by reason of the defendant's wrongful conduct."[46] Here, again, one might well take issue with this characterization as a matter of what the law ought to be, and several scholars have done so.[47] My point remains precisely that the class action — especially a mandatory class — is not a freestanding vehicle for law reform. The law should not infer a delegation of governing power when the thing that makes the allocation of punitive damages seem superior is not anything antecedent to the mandatory class but, instead, is a measure of law reform made possible only upon the constitution of the class in the first place.

Mandatory class treatment would not mark the only direction of experiments with the class action device in the aftermath of *Amchem* and *Ortiz*. A second approach takes the Supreme Court at its word, expanding rather than contracting the individual autonomy of class members to escape the peace prescribed by a class settlement. Here, interestingly enough, the attempt to enhance the legitimacy of class settlements as vehicles for peace has operated in tension with the objective of peacemaking. The next chapter speaks to the conflict between the legitimacy of the mass tort class settlement and its capacity actually to deliver peace in practical terms.

CHAPTER VIII

MAXIMIZING OR MINIMIZING OPT-OUTS

Efforts at mandatory class treatment push hard at the legitimacy of the class action as a way to secure the peace. This chapter analyzes two significant moves in the opposite direction. The subject here consists of attempts to enhance the legitimacy of class settlements, either by dramatically expanding the opportunity of class members to opt out of the deal or by preserving that opportunity in nominal terms while, at the same time, deterring its exercise in practice.

In litigation over the diet drug combination fen-phen, a class settlement expanded opt-out rights. Specifically, the fen-phen deal created additional opportunities for class members to return to the tort system in the future — what have come to be known as "back-end" opt-out rights, beyond those required by Rule 23. Although they enhanced the legitimacy of the class settlement, these back-end opt-out rights endangered the security of the peace — and, not incidentally, the capacity of the settlement grid actually to deliver streamlined compensation for fen-phen users.

A separate development presses at the line between mandatory and opt-out classes. Here, the game is to craft a class settlement that ostensibly preserves class members' opportunity to opt out but that structures its terms so as to discourage class members from actually doing so. The aspiration, in short, is for the peace of a mandatory class settlement in practical effect through an opt-out class in outward appearance. An early version of a class settlement in litigation over hip implants manufactured by Sulzer Orthopedics, Inc. illustrates the problems associated with this strategy of opt-out deterrence.

This chapter uses the fen-phen and Sulzer hip implant examples to highlight the fundamental tension in mass tort class settlements between legitimacy and peace. The well-taken concerns of the Supreme Court in *Amchem* and *Ortiz* about the legitimacy of mass tort class settlements have pushed peacemakers toward measures that undermine their capacity to achieve peace. The respect demanded by *Amchem* and *Ortiz* for the individual autonomy of mass tort claimants is what endangers the security of the peace. In procedural terms, that respect manifests itself in the preservation of the opportunity for class members to opt out of any overall deal. Opt-out rights are best understood, however, not as advancing individual autonomy for its own sake but, rather, as means to an end—as ways to constrain class counsel in the design of any peace. Opt-out rights create an avenue by which rivals within the plaintiffs' bar may guard against self-dealing by class counsel in a class settlement. It is far from obvious, however, that opt-out rights are the best means to discipline the power of deal-making lawyers. The discussion in the present chapter thus sets the scene for the treatment in later chapters of other kinds of constraints on the governing power wielded by mass tort lawyers that would have less of a tendency to undermine the peace.

Back-End Opt-Out Rights

The treatment here of the fen-phen class settlements begins with background on the underlying litigation, followed by an overview of the class settlement structure. I then analyze the back-end opt-out rights that comprise the signature feature of that deal. Specifically, I use a description of those rights as "options," akin to those purchased by investors in financial markets, to help pinpoint the legitimacy of the fen-phen class settlement. Turning from legitimacy to practicality, I then trace the obstacles confronted by the class settlement in the securing of peace. Those obstacles stem, at bottom, from tensions in the institutional position of the class action device.

Litigation Background and Class Settlement Overview

The vast majority of fen-phen users were women between twenty-five and forty-four years old who knowingly took the diet drug combination to lose weight.[1] In light of mounting safety concerns, the manufacturer of the two drugs withdrew them from the market in 1997.[2] For simplicity, I refer to the manufacturer of fen-phen under its current name, Wyeth Corporation, rather than its name at the time of the initial proceedings concerning the class settlement, American Home Products.

As a scientific matter, concern over fen-phen focused on the existence of a causal relationship between extended use of that drug combination and the development of valvular regurgitation in the heart. In simplified terms, valvular regurgitation is a condition that can lead blood to flow in the wrong direction within the heart. Some minimal forms of heart valve regurgitation are "common in the general population and are not generally considered abnormal."[3] Indeed, this medical fact would go on to assume considerable importance for the ability of the class settlement actually to deliver peace. The point, for now, is that other forms of valvular regurgitation go beyond the parameters of normal heart functions. At least at the time of the class settlement, science had left open the possibility that heart valve regurgitation might have the potential to progress to severe valvular heart disease, although subsequent research has tended to undercut that possibility.[4]

Concern over the relationship between fen-phen and heart valve regurgitation contributed to the influx of eighteen thousand claims in the tort system by the time of the class settlement. The sheer number of claims was not the only point of concern for Wyeth. Evidence presented in the small number of individual fen-phen cases litigated prior to the class settlement lent credibility to demands for punitive damages. The evidence implied that Wyeth had inadequately monitored — perhaps even affirmatively suppressed — consumer complaints that suggested a possibility of heart valve problems.[5] Months before the class settlement, a Texas jury had returned a $20 million punitive damage award in an individual lawsuit that featured much of the foregoing evidence.[6] Along similar lines, the federal government had initiated a criminal investigation to assess whether the company had withheld risk information in regulatory proceedings convened to determine the content of product warning labels.[7] In short, the legal environment leading up to the class settlement raised the possibility of multiple punitive damage awards over a larger run of cases.

Unlike in *Amchem* and *Ortiz,* the class definition for the fen-phen settlement was not purely prospective in the sense of reaching only claims yet to be filed. The fen-phen class also included pending cases, encompassing all persons in the United States who took fen-phen and whose claims against Wyeth had not already been resolved. This Rule 23(b)(3) opt-out class consisted, in turn, of several subclasses defined by reference to class members' duration of fen-phen use and their then-existing medical condition.[8] One portion of the class settlement funded a screening program for former fen-phen users, whereby they could receive an echocardiogram to assess their current heart functions. For present purposes, however, the more significant parts of the deal consist of those designed to address punitive damages and the possibility of progression to severe valvular heart disease.

Like its predecessors in *Amchem* and *Ortiz*, the fen-phen class settlement established a private administrative compensation system, with the payout levels of its grid calibrated by the severity of disease. Payment under this administrative system did not turn on proof of causation as a tort matter or compliance with statutes of limitation that restrict the time period within which a tort suit must be brought. The class settlement nonetheless did not aspire to a complete replacement of tort litigation. Fen-phen users instead could choose between the tort system and the benefits provided by the class settlement at any one of three points: during an initial 120-day period following official notice of the class settlement terms; upon diagnosis of a mild heart valve abnormality, as revealed by an echocardiogram under the settlement screening program; or, even later, upon diagnosis of severe heart valve disease. The last two of these opportunities to opt out came at the back end, after the initial opportunity required by Rule 23. And these back-end opt-out rights came with an important caveat: Class members who opted out at either of the last two points would be limited to compensatory damages in tort litigation. They could not seek punitive damages from Wyeth.[9]

When discussing David Rosenberg's general case for mandatory classes, I referred to the development of mass tort litigation as a series of investment options for plaintiffs' lawyers. Option concepts also shed light on the structure of the fen-phen class settlement. Here, the people who stand to exercise options consist of the plaintiff class members themselves rather than the lawyers representing them.

At the outset, I hasten to underscore that the back-end opt-out rights in the fen-phen deal do not track completely the features of options in financial markets. In fact, I ultimately shall highlight some significant respects in which back-end opt-out rights diverge from financial options. The starting point nonetheless remains that concepts about options in the world of finance give us a useful vocabulary to analyze the fen-phen class settlement. As I shall explain, both the similarities and the differences between the fen-phen deal and options in the financial world have important implications for peacemaking.

One common kind of option in financial markets is a "put." The essential structural feature of a put option is that it gives the option holder the right to compel the purchase of some asset under specified terms.[10] For example, an investor who owns stock in General Motors might purchase a put option entitling her to sell her shares at the price of $50 per share before the end of the calendar year. As its name suggests, the put option need not be exercised. The option holder would exercise the option in this example only if the exercise price were higher than the price at which General Motors shares were trading on the New York Stock Exchange. The put option effectively empowers the holder to force the option seller to buy her shares at the exercise price when it exceeds their price on the stock market. In this way, the put option insulates its holder against the downside risk that the stock market price for General Motors shares might fall.

The back-end opt-out rights in the fen-phen class settlement functioned as the rough equivalent of a put option in the sense that they provided class members with the right to compel Wyeth to purchase their tort claims. The class settlement grid served as the analogue to the $50 exercise price of the put option for General Motors stock. Like the holders of put options in financial markets, moreover, fen-phen users were not obligated by the class settlement to exercise their put options. Rather, the put option enabled them, over time, to compare the compensation available under the class settlement and that available in tort litigation.

The fen-phen settlement also insulated class members against risk in the tort system in the same way that put options insulate investors against risk on the New York Stock Exchange. Many fen-phen users might have encountered barriers to recovery in tort based on the expiration of applicable statutes of limitations. Wyeth had withdrawn the underlying drugs in 1997, and applicable statutes of limitations for tort claims typically extend to two years at most. As a result, Wyeth would have had a substantial argument that those statutes had run on the bulk of fen-phen users.[11] This is not to say that statutes of limitations necessarily would have formed an airtight defense for Wyeth. It is merely to point out that the existence of that defense stood as a source of risk for fen-phen users in the tort system. The put option protected fen-phen users against the possibility that their claims would be deemed time-barred and thus worthless in tort.

The framing of back-end opt-out rights as put options is not simply of interest from the vantage point of finance. The comparison highlights two features that facilitate analysis of the fen-phen class settlement in institutional terms. First, the description of back-end opt-out rights as the rough equivalent of put options draws attention to the idea that the option holders must pay some premium in order to obtain such rights. This observation naturally raises the question whether punitive damages stand as the appropriate premium for the put option. The remainder of this section addresses this question, contrasting the fen-phen class settlement with the more problematic, mandatory treatment sought for punitive damage claims in *Simon II*.

Second, the comparison to put options also underscores that they restrict the latitude of the option seller—here, the settling defendant. Back-end opt-out rights effectively project into the future the process of aggregate settlement in the tort system. In so doing, they diverge from put options in financial markets in ways that have troubling implications for the security of the peace. Those points of divergence reveal the kinship between the fen-phen class settlement and the Owens Corning National Settlement Program (NSP) discussed in chapter 6. That kinship, in turn, will help us to understand the huge practical difficulties encountered by the fen-phen deal in the actual delivery of peace.

Punitive Damages as Put Option Premium

Consider, first, the appropriate premium for the put option. Upon judicial review in the shadow of *Amchem* and *Ortiz*, the fen-phen class settlement garnered approval at the district court level, and the United States Court of Appeals for the Third Circuit affirmed without issuing an opinion.[12] Writing for the district court, Judge Louis Bechtle observed that, unlike in *Amchem* and *Ortiz*, the fen-phen settlement did not exclude pending claims from its class definition. The class itself included various subclasses, with separate representation, to account for salient differences among the class members. In the parlance of *Amchem*, the various subclasses formed relatively cohesive litigation groups whose parameters preceded the formation of the class.

The district court went on to assert that the fen-phen class settlement posed no "futures problem," because all fen-phen users who might develop severe valvular heart disease could be identified as having some milder heart valve abnormality through the settlement screening program.[13] The district court's statement notwithstanding, the fen-phen deal did pose the same "futures problem" inherent in any prospective resolution of tort claims involving latent disease. The class settlement purported to change in advance the terms under which class members without severe valvular heart disease today might seek redress for the manifestation of that disease in the future. Those terms consisted of a trade: punitive damage claims for back-end opt-out rights. Oddly enough, the district court devoted scant attention to the appropriateness of this trade, mentioning in a mere footnote that the treatment of punitive damages "represent[ed] a fair and wholly appropriate trade-off" for the benefits provided to class members.[14] To form a richer understanding of this trade, one must start with an account of the settlement strategy behind it.

Given the existence of evidence from which juries might infer some manner of corporate cover-up, it comes as no surprise that Wyeth focused on punitive damages as its desired option premium. Wyeth's objectives, however, went beyond the obvious one of minimizing its ultimate payout. By limiting punitive damage claims to those fen-phen users who opted out of the class settlement at the outset — in the initial opt-out process required for all Rule 23(b)(3) classes — Wyeth sought to confine within a modest time period the uncertainty surrounding its ultimate liability for such relief. In practical terms, the period would consist of the time needed for Wyeth to enter into aggregate settlements that would resolve the claims of the initial opt-outs from the class in the tort system. In so doing, Wyeth could put to rest quickly the prospect of multiple punitive damage awards in individual lawsuits spread over time and, with it, the uncertainty that would hamper its financial position. Wyeth, in fact, had an especially urgent reason to create at least the appearance of manageable limits on its liability for fen-phen. At times proximate to the class settlement, the company was negotiating a $70 billion merger with another pharmaceutical firm, Warner-Lambert, though the merger ultimately was not completed.[15]

In effect, Wyeth sought to purchase protections that resemble those conferred by the Constitution on defendants in the criminal justice system — specifically, the protection against double jeopardy and the right to a speedy trial. One of the recurring themes in the Supreme Court's double jeopardy decisions is the notion of preventing the prosecution from keeping a criminal defendant in a perpetual state of flux and peril through repeated prosecutions for the same crime.[16] The Court has emphasized that the Double Jeopardy Clause has no application, of its own force, to damage claims between private parties[17] — hence, Wyeth's need to purchase such protection by way of the fen-phen class settlement. The Speedy Trial Clause offers complementary protection, enabling criminal defendants, if they wish, to insist that the prosecution take its shot at imposing punishment without massive delay.[18] In drawing these comparisons, I do not mean to suggest that the fen-phen class settlement somehow imported the whole corpus of double jeopardy and speedy trial doctrine. I mean simply that Wyeth's objectives sounded in credible constraints upon punishment that go beyond mere tightfistedness.

Wyeth's situation explains why a trade of punitive damages for put options would tend to emerge from the fen-phen class settlement negotiations as a strategic matter. For those fen-phen users still in the class after the initial opt-out period, however, there remains an important normative question: whether punitive damages comprised the appropriate premium for the put option they received. Within the panoply of available tort damages, the punitive damage remedy is unique. As the previous chapter suggested, only a thin doctrinal thread ties that remedy today to individual plaintiffs.

Punitive damages relate to the plaintiff only in the limited sense that they depend on the existence of some nominal damages.[19] The goal of punitive damages, as presently framed in tort law, is not to compensate the person wronged by the defendant but, rather, for that person to serve as the vehicle for punishing and deterring extreme misconduct—hence, the common description of punitive damage plaintiffs as private attorneys general. This vision of the plaintiff as the incidental vehicle to advance broader goals accounts for the windfall nature of punitive damages for those who happen to receive them—the point that later would trouble Judge Weinstein in *Simon II*. Plaintiffs are entitled to compensatory damages when a tort has been committed upon them, but they have no entitlement to an award of punitive damages.[20] At most, one may say that tort law affords the plaintiff a right to seek such additional relief as one aspect of her larger right to sue in tort.

These observations, together, help to frame a defense of punitive damages as the appropriate premium for back-end opt-out rights. When punitive damages are in play, individual control over the course and nature of litigation has a distinctive drawback not present for other forms of damages. Compensatory damages awarded to individual plaintiffs pose no risk of overkill, for they relate inextricably to the particular plaintiff alone. Total liability that exceeds a defendant's net worth would give rise to a conventional limited fund of the sort that would warrant mandatory class treatment. But massive liability for compensatory damages, properly proven, raises no normative qualms. It simply means that the defendant caused much harm to many people.

Punitive damages, by contrast, raise not only a practical concern (that individual lawsuits might deplete defendants' resources) but also a normative concern that rises to a constitutional level (that defendants will lack fair notice of the punishment that their misconduct may elicit). Recall, here, the implication from the Supreme Court's due process decisions of an outer limit, as a constitutional matter, upon the punitive damages that may be awarded in the aggregate based on a single course of extreme misconduct.[21] A trade of punitive damages for put options enhances defendants' peace of mind—it gives practical bite to the due process limit—without reducing the autonomy of class members in a manner that the law should regard as normatively significant. In this respect, punitive damages as the put option premium stand in contrast to other conceivable premiums—say, the right to jury trial—that would involve matters to which tort claimants enjoy a preexisting entitlement.

In effect, the fen-phen class settlement aspired to achieve by other means what the mandatory class action in *Simon II* could not. The fen-phen deal sought to prevent the chaos of multiple punitive damage awards not by curtailing the autonomy of class members in a mandatory class but, instead, by enhancing their autonomy—by creating additional, back-end opt-out rights and conditioning their exercise upon the relinquishing of punitive damage claims. By preserving the autonomy of class members, the fen-phen class settlement played out the seeming implications of *Amchem* and *Ortiz*. It created relatively cohesive subclasses and, even then, curtailed the opportunity to sue in tort only to a minimal extent. The operation of the settlement in practice, however, would not go smoothly. Precisely by enhancing the legitimacy of the class settlement through the provision of back-end opt-out rights, the fen-phen deal undermined its ability actually to deliver peace.

Peace and the *Field of Dreams* Problem

Buoyed by the legitimacy of the fen-phen class settlement in procedural terms, both other scholars and I underestimated its difficulties in operation.[22] The problems encountered by the fen-phen settlement highlight the crossroads where the law of mass torts finds itself after *Amchem*. The constraints articulated by the Supreme Court upon the class action as a rival regime of law reform have tended to push settlement designers in directions that undercut the very peace they seek. To illustrate this larger point, I detail here how a conception of the fen-phen deal in option-based terms reveals its kinship with the difficulties that undermined the Owens Corning NSP.

Put options involve payment of a premium by the option purchaser and constraint of the option seller. The practical effect of the put option in the fen-phen class settlement was to specify the grid that Wyeth would apply to future claims, if fen-phen users were to call upon Wyeth to do so. In this respect, the position of Wyeth was analogous to that of the seller of the hypothetical put option for General Motors stock that I described earlier. By creating the put option, the seller effectively makes a standing offer to purchase the underlying shares. The option purchaser will accept this standing offer if the share price in the stock market falls below the exercise price of the put.

As discussed in chapter 6, the Owens Corning NSP also amounted to a standing offer. It attempted to project into the future the process of aggregate settlements in the asbestos litigation by using contractual agreements with plaintiffs' law firms to set in advance the compensation terms for those firms' prospective clients. In so doing, the Owens Corning NSP attempted to use the signatory law firms as a proxy for the power to regulate directly the compensation terms for future asbestos claimants in the manner of public legislation. That proxy contained the makings of its own demise, however, for it left the NSP vulnerable to new entrants among asbestos plaintiffs' law firms and to spin-offs from the signatory firms. The incentives of asbestos plaintiffs' bar lawyers ran toward availing themselves of the streamlined claims processing of the NSP in the short term and then simply returning to the tort system upon its demise — indeed, precipitating that demise through their own actions.

In shying from a complete replacement of the tort system, the put options created by the fen-phen settlement sought to keep faith with the lessons of *Amchem*. But, in doing so, those same put options gave rise to a dynamic that undermined the peace. The put options created by the fen-phen deal were peculiar ones by comparison to those sold in financial markets. The seller of a put option for shares of General Motors stands to be called upon to purchase those shares only in the event that their price in the stock market falls below the exercise price of the option. The seller otherwise pockets the premium obtained for the creation of the put option, and the General Motors shareholder may sell her shares, if at all, to some other investor in the stock market. The put option in the fen-phen settlement, by contrast, placed Wyeth in the position of being compelled to purchase the tort claims of fen-phen users in the event that they exercised their put options (by seeking compensation under the settlement grid) *and* if they did not (by suing in the tort system instead, if only for compensatory damages).[23]

The capacity of such an arrangement to deliver peace turned on the stability of both the option exercise price (the payouts described in the settlement grid) and the premium paid to obtain the option (the prohibition against claims for punitive damages). The exercise price determines whether the option seller will be forced to make good on its standing offer to purchase fen-phen claims. The premium determines what the option seller stands to gain, regardless of whether the option is exercised.

In an ordinary put option in financial markets, both the exercise price and the option premium are set in terms of specific dollar amounts. The one thing that fluctuates — the one moving part, if you will — is the value of the underlying shares in the stock market. The put options in the fen-phen settlement lacked a comparable stability in both their exercise price and their premium. For the fen-phen settlement, the option exercise price, the option premium, and the value of fen-phen claims in the tort system *all* were subject to change.

Any class settlement that affords class members the opportunity to opt out raises a potential for the class to unravel to some degree when class members hold claims of differing value.[24] Those with atypically high-value claims stand to lose the most from a settlement grid that constrains the variance of payouts. As a result, high-value claimants will tend to depart, leaving mid- to low-value claims in the class. The one-time opportunity to opt out required by Rule 23(b)(3) constrains this process by confining it to a relatively short time period. Those class members who opt out at the outset cannot precipitate an ongoing process of defections that would leave the class comprised only of atypically low-value claims. By conferring additional, back-end opt-out rights on class members, the fen-phen settlement accentuated the risk that the class would unravel. More precisely, the class settlement design increased the pressure on the exercise price represented by the settlement grid, for the exercise price would determine whether fen-phen users would wield their back-end opt-out rights.

Although seemingly specified in dollar amounts, the fen-phen settlement grid nevertheless was not stable in the manner of a $50-per-share exercise price. The ability of the class settlement actually to deliver the specified dollar amounts in its grid turned on the accuracy of the claim projections used to calculate Wyeth's commitment of $3.75 billion to the deal. Those projections were far from seat-of-the-pants guesses. In approving the class settlement as fair, the district court emphasized that the projections used by the peacemaking lawyers stemmed from uncontradicted scientific research on the incidence of heart valve abnormalities associated with diet drug use.[25] In operation, however, the accuracy of claim projections turns not simply on science but also on the ability of the settlement administrators quickly to distinguish genuine abnormalities from trumped-up ones. But, in order for any settlement to operate in a more streamlined manner than the tort system, one cannot realistically insist on the detail and rigor needed to prove the presence of heart valve abnormalities in tort litigation. The whole point is to avoid full-scale trials, not simply to transfer them into the administration of the settlement.

The instability in exercise price gave rise to a dynamic similar to that exhibited by the Owens Corning NSP. The major practical problem with the fen-phen settlement has consisted of an influx of claims in numbers wildly in excess of projections. The unanticipated number of claims ground the administrative regime to a halt, with an independent audit revealing that only about 12.5 percent of claims were payable under the settlement criteria and, further, that high percentages of unfounded medical diagnoses correlated with particular physicians and particular plaintiffs' law firms.[26] At its extreme, the claim filing process included contingency-fee-like arrangements, whereby some plaintiffs' law firms boosted the sums paid to physicians based on the severity of the heart valve problems they diagnosed.[27] The presence of back-end opt-out rights meant that the unanticipated numbers of claims under the settlement raised both a problem of administration and a threat to the peace that Wyeth stood to gain.

The unanticipated number of claims effectively reduced the exercise price of the put option, increasing the likelihood that tort litigation, over time, would seem a more promising route for fen-phen users. In a series of amendments over several years, the peacemaking lawyers desperately sought to shore up the credibility of the class settlement. The seventh and most recent amendment, approved by the district court in early 2005, created a new administrative regime funded by an additional $1.275 billion from Wyeth. The new regime continued to pay the sums to high-value claims promised in the original class settlement. But it reduced dramatically the sums for persons with the least severe valvular problems, albeit while preserving their existing right to seek additional compensation under the settlement should their condition worsen. Most significantly, this seventh amendment eliminated the back-end opt-out rights that were the signature feature of the original deal. In their place, the seventh amendment provided for class members either to accept the new compensation terms or to opt out within a confined time period and thereby to preserve their opportunity to seek compensatory damages in the tort system.[28] In effect, the seventh amendment converted the structure of the fen-phen class settlement into that of a conventional opt-out class, whereby class members must make a one-time, front-end choice between private administration and the tort system.

The option exercise price was not the only thing in flux. The option premium for Wyeth also proved unstable. True enough, only class members who opted out at the front end could seek punitive damages as such. For back-end opt-outs, however, the prohibition on punitive damage claims proved to be porous. After the Supreme Court decisions tightening judicial review of punitive damage awards, observers on the defense side began to warn of efforts by tort plaintiffs to seek such awards under the rubric of compensatory damages for pain and suffering.[29] In the fen-phen litigation, the district court attempted to enforce the terms of the class settlement by enjoining back-end opt-outs not only from seeking punitive damages but also from presenting in support of their permitted claims for compensatory damages any evidence "related directly or indirectly" to punitive damages or extreme misconduct on Wyeth's part.[30] On appeal, the Third Circuit acknowledged the "justifiable fear . . . that plaintiffs were seeking to obtain through the back door what they were barred from receiving through the front."[31] But the Third Circuit still lifted the injunction, correctly noting that the class settlement barred back-end opt-outs from seeking punitive damages but contained no restrictions on the evidence they might seek to admit at trial in support of demands for compensatory damages. At most, Wyeth could call on trial courts to exercise their existing discretion under the law of evidence to exclude particular items of evidence as tangential or unduly prejudicial.[32]

All together, the difficulties encountered by the fen-phen class settlement made for an estimated 60,000 back-end opt-outs and an overall cost to Wyeth of $21 billion as of September 2006.[33] To put these numbers into perspective: The 60,000 back-end opt-outs *by themselves* exceed the projected total of just over 35,500 fen-phen users that scientific experts had estimated would develop compensable heart valve problems based on the application of "conservative assumptions likely to overstate [claimant] demands."[34] And scientific research since the original class settlement hardly has developed in a direction more favorable to plaintiffs.

There is a larger lesson lurking within the unraveling of the fen-phen deal. Any private administrative regime that does not foreclose resort to the tort system in relatively short order — either by its own mandatory nature or through the operation of the single, front-end opt-out process required by procedural rule — carries a serious potential for instability. To put the point less formally, any class settlement that does not displace the tort system has the potential to prompt the same response as the fictional baseball diamond constructed amid the Iowa cornfields in the film *Field of Dreams*: "If you build it, they will come."[35] The game will be to overwhelm the settlement regime as a way to grind it to a halt, shed doubt on the credibility of the settlement grid, and thereby precipitate an unraveling of the class through the operation of the back-end opt-out process.

The important point is that the unanticipated numbers of claims that undermined the fen-phen settlement are not the product of matters unique to that litigation. They have the potential to arise across many areas of mass tort litigation due to two recurring features of the landscape: what toxicologists describe as the "background" incidence of disease and the ever-increasing sophistication of medical technology. I discuss these two features in turn.

The latent diseases implicated in mass tort litigation typically are not "signature" diseases in the sense of arising exclusively or overwhelmingly from the underlying product in question. Mesothelioma, a devastating form of cancer in the lining of the lung caused by long-term asbestos exposure, is widely considered to be such a signature disease.[36] But mesothelioma is the rare exception that proves the general rule. Mass tort litigation more commonly calls for identification of the additional increment of disease cases attributable to a given product, as distinct from those cases of disease that would have arisen anyway—what scientists dub the background incidence of the disease. Valvular heart disease existed long before the fen-phen fad and will remain part of our world after it. So, too, for connective tissue disease and silicone gel breast implants, for impairments in lung functions and occupational asbestos exposure, and for limb deformities and the morning sickness drug Bendectin. The existence of a background incidence of disease is what creates the possibility that persons exposed to a given product may suffer from that disease by sheer coincidence. If anything, litigation over a drug combination used for purposes of dieting is especially prone to this phenomenon. Fen-phen proved to be a popular drug combination, after all, because users wanted to lose weight. But that meant that they already tended to be overweight, a condition well understood to pose a broad range of risks to the heart.

Advances in science, moreover, have facilitated the detection of minute changes in the body, some of which do not impair bodily functions yet are relatively close in their characteristics or appearance to those that do. Advanced medical technology—say, the sophisticated echocardiograms now used to analyze the heart—tends not to give rise to black-and-white distinctions between disease and normalcy. Rather, it tends toward gradations of gray that call for the exercise of judgment on the part of medical professionals evaluating the outputs of the technology. The unexpected influx of fen-phen claims played on this gray area. The class settlement designers had expected that class members would be diagnosed by their own doctors or, at least, those made available to them via the settlement screening program. Reality did not match these expectations. In the words of the district court, "many plaintiffs' attorneys set up 'echocardiogram mills,' or facilities in hotels or other non-medical facilities to conduct large numbers of echocardiograms." Seemingly choosing its words with delicacy, the district court observed that "a major controversy" existed as to whether the personnel conducting these echocardiograms were "properly supervised."[37]

One can see a similar phenomenon at work in the asbestos litigation, where the distinction between diagnosis of disease and detection of non-impairing changes in the lung turns quite literally on interpretation of the gray areas of an X-ray. Scientific research from Europe suggests that many middle-aged adults in an industrialized nation like the United States might well meet the most minimal standard for an abnormal X-ray, simply due to aging and other non-tort-related reductions in lung functions over time.[38] When combined with the prevalence of asbestos exposure, the ability to detect minute changes in the lung adds to the potential for streams of claims. Here, too, there are suggestions of abuse.

A 1995 audit of asbestos claims filed with the Manville bankruptcy trust revealed that roughly 50 percent of them failed independent review, even when the medical professionals who evaluated the submitted X-rays "were selected in consultation with the plaintiffs' bar" and the review process itself was "designed to give the benefit of any doubt to the claimant."[39] Even more stark are the results of an academic study from 2004 that compared the evaluation of X-rays by experts retained by asbestos plaintiffs' lawyers with the evaluation of the same X-rays by independent consultants. The plaintiffs' experts diagnosed abnormality in over 95 percent of the X-rays in the sample, whereas the independent consultants did so for less than 5 percent. For the study authors, the magnitude of the difference in diagnoses was too pronounced to be the result simply of "variability" across the two sets of experts.[40]

Perhaps the most prominent cataloguing of problems in medical diagnoses came in a 2005 opinion by United States District Judge Janis Jack in consolidated individual lawsuits concerning workplace exposure to silica dust. The litigation centered on activities such as sandblasting, mining, and quarrying that involve the generation of silica dust from the drilling or grinding of rocks. For centuries, workers in such industries have been understood to stand at risk of silicosis, a potentially debilitating disease of the lung. Although the United States as a whole "has enjoyed a steady 30-year decline in silicosis rates and mortality" due to improved workplace precautions, Mississippi — a state "ranked 43rd in the U.S. in silicosis mortality" — suddenly experienced "a crush of new silicosis lawsuits" in the early years of the twenty-first century.[41] Thousands of these silicosis cases were brought on behalf of workers who previously had made claims of asbestosis, even though "a dual diagnosis of silicosis and asbestosis is extremely rare" as a medical matter.[42]

Although the silicosis plaintiffs identified some eight thousand different doctors as their treating physicians, the doctors who actually had diagnosed them with silicosis consisted of only twelve. In Judge Jack's words, "[t]his small cadre of non-treating physicians, financially beholden to lawyers and screening companies rather than to patients, managed to notice a disease missed by approximately 8,000 other physicians — most of whom had the significant advantage of speaking to, examining, and treating the Plaintiffs."[43] The twelve doctors, by contrast, worked as part of an "assembly line" process in which a different person performed each of the many steps in the process of diagnosis—from the taking of the worker's occupational history, to the reading of the X-ray, to the analysis of lung function tests, to the taking of the worker's medical history, to the diagnosis itself.[44] The diagnosing physicians stated that they had proceeded on "blind faith" that other doctors "had taken the necessary steps to legitimize their diagnoses" when, in fact, "most" of those involved in this multiperson process "had no medical training."[45] As Judge Jack concluded: "[T]hese diagnoses were driven by neither health nor justice; they were manufactured for money."[46]

It is all too easy to say that a private administrative regime should ferret out dubious claims. The problem of overclaiming inheres in any move from a tort system predicated on individualized proof toward a streamlined administrative regime. Efficient application of a compensation grid necessarily involves cutting corners by comparison to the detailed proof that might be demanded in tort litigation. Even public administrative regimes for workers' compensation have struggled with this trade-off between no-hassle efficiency and scrutiny of claims. The key point, for present purposes, is that the trade-off poses a question of sound administration when the compensation grid stands as the only game in town. When a private administrative scheme operates in extended competition with the tort system—as when class members retain back-end opt-out rights—the same matters of administration are the kindling for destruction of the administrative scheme itself.

The continued existence of the tort system provides a safety valve that circumscribes the law reform power of the class settlement. This, to be sure, is the direction in which *Amchem* points. But settlements that do not shut off the tort system give rise to dynamics of their own. The continued existence of the tort system invites efforts to undermine the class settlement regime, essentially as a way to reopen the deal. Even if class counsel do not wish to go that route, their competitors within the plaintiffs' bar might. Such a strategy proved to be a powerful one in the fen-phen litigation, effectively precipitating the commitment of additional resources from Wyeth through the settlement amendment process. But there were considerable human costs in terms of the allocation of resources. The undermining of the fen-phen class settlement took place through the securing of millions of dollars in compensation by early claimants, "85 percent of [whom] were being paid without any real check on their legitimacy" prior to a court-imposed audit in mid-2002. In the words of the district court, the audit did help to address "the problem of potential payment . . . of claims unsupported by any reasonable medical basis."[47] But that description only underscores the depletion of the settlement pot through the payment of unsupported claims before then—money that might have gone to fen-phen users with real heart valve problems.

As chapter 2 observed, the consumption of available resources by unimpaired claimants, to the detriment of the impaired, is a feature endemic to the mature stage of mass tort litigation. It is part of the dysfunctions that can emerge if the litigation is permitted to continue. Because it did not displace the tort system, the fen-phen class settlement did not stop the progress of the litigation toward those dysfunctions. In effect, the peace plan simply transplanted those dysfunctions into its own private administrative regime.

Deterring Opt-Outs through Settlement Design

A third variation in mass tort class settlements since *Amchem* flows predictably from the first two. Mandatory classes, whether across the board or confined to punitive damage claims, avoid the practical difficulties associated with a private compensation regime that operates in ongoing competition with the tort system. But mandatory class treatment remains subject to constraints that go beyond those that apply to opt-out classes—chiefly, an insistence on a fund that really is limited by something other than the mandatory class action. Pursuit of an opt-out class settlement—certainly, any supplementation of opt-out rights at the back end—bolsters the legitimacy of the deal as a procedural matter. But it raises a considerable potential for problems in the actual delivery of peace.

It comes as little surprise that attorneys in the mass tort area eventually would aspire to the best of both worlds. To resolve mass tort litigation over hip implants defectively manufactured by Sulzer Orthopedics, Inc., class counsel and their defense counterparts sought to craft an ostensible opt-out class settlement that would operate in the manner of a mandatory class settlement. This effort ultimately did not meet with success, and a modified class settlement came to supplant the original design.[48] The workings and ultimate fate of the original Sulzer class settlement nonetheless bear close attention. They form a fitting denouement to the treatment here of class settlements in the aftermath of *Amchem,* and they serve to introduce techniques that resurface in the next chapter, which addresses developments in bankruptcy during the same period.

Litigation Background and Settlement Structure

The Sulzer hip implant litigation arose from the discovery in the late 1990s of a manufacturing defect in one component within a larger medical device designed to replace the ball and socket of the hip joint. The defect had the potential to prevent the system from bonding properly with the thigh bone of the implant recipient. For its part, Sulzer voluntarily recalled the defective units, but not until after tens of thousands of them already had been implanted in patients across the country.[49] The ensuing litigation not only threatened Sulzer itself but also carried the remote potential to rope in its Swiss parent corporation. The amenability of the Swiss parent to lawsuits in this country nonetheless remained uncertain. In fact, that uncertainty contributed to the eventual modification of the original class settlement terms.[50]

The plaintiff class consisted of hip implant recipients with claims of varying value. The substantial majority of class members consisted of patients with claims that would not have been marketable on an individual basis. At most, their situation called for modest medical examinations to confirm their lack of need for "revision" surgery to replace the defective component in their hip implants. Other class members had claims of considerable value, however, as they already had undergone revision surgery, needed it in the future, or suffered from impairments under medical circumstances that made them ineligible for surgery.[51] For settlement negotiators, the challenge lay in ensuring that this minority of high-value claimants would not opt out and thereby precipitate the unraveling of the class.

Sulzer pursued the foregoing goal not only through the terms of the class settlement itself—about which I shall have more to say momentarily—but also in its choice of bargaining agent. Sulzer retained as its class settlement negotiator Richard "Dickie" Scruggs, a prominent plaintiffs' lawyer from Mississippi who previously had taken a leading role in lawsuits against the asbestos and tobacco industries, among other areas of mass tort litigation. By retaining Scruggs, Sulzer sought to use his stature in the eyes of his fellow plaintiffs' lawyers as a selling point for a class settlement that would bring closure to the hip implant litigation. For these services, Sulzer reportedly agreed to pay Scruggs "a 'low seven-figure number,' plus a 'success fee' of about $20 million should the settlement be approved."[52]

Sulzer had good reason to ingratiate itself with the mass tort plaintiffs' bar, even at the cost of paying $20 million to Scruggs. That reason stemmed from the deal that Sulzer sought to strike in a class settlement designed to deter the high-value claimants in need of revision surgery from opting out. One way to achieve that goal would have been for the class settlement to provide generous benefits for high-value claims and, for that matter, for the rest of the class too. The original version of the Sulzer hip implant settlement did so to a degree, though it structured much of the benefits for those in need of revision surgery in terms of stock in a corporate affiliate, as distinct from cash.[53] In practical terms, the predominant use of stock over cash for high-value claimants would have given them — or, perhaps more accurately, the would-be rivals to class counsel who might represent such persons — reason to stay in the class settlement. Doing so would enhance the peace that the class settlement would bring to Sulzer and, as a consequence, would boost the value of the shares in the hands of the high-value claimants. There was even more to the deal envisioned by Sulzer, however.

In its original form, the class settlement agreement did not leave peace to chance. It called for the creation of a lien on all of Sulzer's assets in favor of a trust created by the settlement itself to fund the benefits promised to class members. This trust fund notably would have consisted of less than Sulzer's entire net worth. Specifically, the trust fund would have included Sulzer's available insurance proceeds, available cash (but for one month of working capital), a specified number of shares, plus one-half of its net annual income until the time when all benefits promised in the settlement had been distributed.[54] Sulzer's Swiss parent corporation would have received a release from liability, without any contribution of its own resources to the deal.

The lien on Sulzer's assets in favor of this trust fund included a revealing loophole. The class settlement agreement would have permitted Sulzer to sell its assets "for business purposes" free and clear of the lien, as long as the proceeds from those sales were not used to pay opt-out claimants.[55] Liens are common features of commercial credit transactions in the business world. The loophole in the lien for the settlement trust fund, however, was broader in its terms than the counterpart provision of the Uniform Commercial Code (UCC). Under the UCC, a creditor may retain a security interest in an asset of the debtor — basically, as a source of recourse for the creditor if the debt goes unpaid. The debtor may sell that asset free and clear of the security interest — indeed, may do so without the creditor's consent — but only if the sale occurs "in the *ordinary* course of business."[56]

The effect of the lien in favor of the Sulzer settlement trust would have been simple enough in practical terms. In order to obtain actual payment on any judgment or settlement in conventional tort litigation, an opt-out claimant would have to wait roughly six years — the time period anticipated for distribution of benefits under the class settlement to the entire plaintiff class. Even then, an opt-out claimant could not count on finding much left.

As Scruggs summarized the deal in an interview with the *Wall Street Journal*: "[I]f anybody opts out, they still have to try their case, win their case, win their appeal, and then there would be no assets to satisfy their judgment, because they are all pledged to the class."[57]

The Settlement Trust and Lien as a Restructuring of Rights

The class settlement did not merely portend delay for opt-out claimants, however. Its effect on the preexisting rights of all would-be class members is subtle — consciously so on the part of the class settlement designers. Absent the lien in favor of the trust fund created for their benefit, class members as a collective group would not have been entitled to priority vis-à-vis anyone who had obtained a damage judgment against Sulzer. Nor, in particular, could they collectively have blocked payment to any other person pursuant to a settlement of a conventional individual lawsuit. Rather, absent the class action, those injured by Sulzer would have stood in a race against one another. Their ability to reach the finish line — actual receipt of payment — would have depended simply on the unencumbered assets left in the defendant's hands at the time that payment either was made or obtained through the coercive process of law. For that matter, the same is true of the relationship between persons tortiously injured by Sulzer and, say, any persons whose ordinary business contracts the corporation had breached. All would have the right to race one another to obtain payment, with the winners of the race consisting of those whom one might describe as the more wily runners.

Here, too, as in the earlier discussion of punitive damages, the recognition that claimants stand in a race against one another is not necessarily an endorsement of that race. One might imagine a variety of alternative ways that the law might deal with the possibility of multiple claims against a common defendant. The point simply is that the legal world in existence prior to the class settlement gave would-be tort claimants the opportunity to race one another to obtain payment from the assets of the defendant.

There is room in this race for the creation of security interests. It is common for a corporation, for example, to grant a security interest in some portion of its assets in favor of a particular "person" — the term used in the definition of a "secured party" under the UCC.[58] Article 9 of the UCC is all about secured transactions, whereby creditors gain an advantage in the race to get at the debtor's assets in the event that their deal goes sour. All those upon whom a corporation has committed torts stand at risk that the corporation might convey security interests in corporate assets to other creditors, before tort litigation can make successful demands on those assets.

The original class settlement in the Sulzer hip implant litigation would have altered the rules of the race. In so doing, it would have changed the preexisting rights not just of those who might remain in the class but also of any opt-outs. To this end, the lien and the trust fund would have worked in tandem. In effect, the lien would have placed opt-out claimants behind class members in line for ultimate payment and would have prohibited them from leapfrogging those class members — all of this, even though they previously were free to attempt to leapfrog any other would-be claimants in the race. The loophole in the lien spotlights this effect. The security interest enshrined in the lien would have been a security interest only in the sense of restructuring hip implant recipients' rights vis-à-vis one another, not as against any other creditors. Sulzer might choose to satisfy other creditors' demands — indeed, apparently, to enter into new contracts for any "business purposes," outside the ordinary course of its operations — in ways that might involve the sale of assets free and clear of the lien.

The crucial point is that the indispensable vehicle for this change — what would have made possible the change in the rules of the race — was none other than the class settlement itself. Here, one must take care to frame clearly the effect of that settlement. Any class settlement does not bind class members unless it garners judicial approval; and a court-issued judgment serves as the manifestation of that approval. But a judgment approving the Sulzer class settlement would not have entitled any person within the class to immediate payment of a specific sum in the manner of a damage judgment in a conventional, individual tort suit. Class members could not have filed a judgment lien on Sulzer's assets upon the issuance of the judgment approving the class settlement. A judgment lien turns on the reduction of one's claim to "a definite amount" that is "not dependent on any contingency."[59] The judgment approving the Sulzer class settlement, by contrast, would not have fixed the amount of any class member's claim or even the amount for the class as a whole. Rather, the class settlement simply would have been a contractual promise to pay the claims ultimately presented according to the settlement terms. The role of the class judgment — the reason for using a class settlement at all — was simply to make the members of the class parties to the private contract consisting of the class settlement agreement.

Absent the binding effect of the class judgment, the deal-makers behind the Sulzer class settlement could have attempted to create security interests only in the conventional manner: by actually entering into contracts with individual members of the class. That process, however, still would have consisted of an individualized race. The various security interests would

stand vis-à-vis one another in the usual manner of multiple security interests in the same asset under commercial law: The first filed would have
priority over the second filed, and so on.[60] In particular, the wily runners
able to extract security interests from Sulzer as part of their individual settlements would have priority over all other tort claimants. The race would
still be on; it simply would be a race to obtain and file one's own security
interest. The class judgment was essential precisely because it would bypass
and restructure this individualized process of securitization. And the way
that the class judgment would have done so is by bringing into being a
new legal entity—the trust fund—to serve as the juridical person through
which Sulzer then could provide a security interest to all members of the
class *in one fell swoop*.

In short, prior to the class settlement, the rules of the race were such that
persons with legal claims against Sulzer would have remained vulnerable to
the granting of security interests in corporate assets to other specific persons.
And those who ran a better race stood to gain priority over others. But the
one kind of "person" not in existence—the one entity to whom all claimants were not vulnerable in any race—was exactly the juridical person that
the Sulzer class settlement would have brought into being: a trust created
as the payout vehicle for the class on a collective basis and constituted by
the class judgment itself. Seen in this light, the class settlement attempted
in the Sulzer hip implant litigation exhibited the same fatal circularity as
the faux limited funds in *Ortiz* and *Simon II*. It would have restructured the
legal rights of hip implant recipients—even those who might opt out of
the class—through the vehicle of something that would have existed only
by the say-so of the class settlement designers. This kind of self-referential
legitimacy the class action cannot properly sustain.

The justification for leaving undisturbed the ability of any given claimant
to leapfrog others in the race for Sulzer's assets undoubtedly would have
withered in the event of a bona fide limited fund. The existence of such
a fund, however, was the one assertion that the designers of the original
Sulzer class settlement had to avoid. Reliance on the existence of a bona
fide limited fund would have cast the original class settlement on a collision
course with *Ortiz*—specifically, the Supreme Court's insistence there that
the fund must be "set definitely at [its] maximum" and that the "whole" of
it must be devoted to the class.[61] These demands the Sulzer class settlement
could not possibly have satisfied. There was no reason to believe that the
trust fund, sizeable though it was, constituted Sulzer's entire net worth. The
apparent objective, instead, was to create by way of an opt-out class settlement something decidedly less than the "maximum" available fund and

then to make that settlement operate in the manner of a mandatory class by deterring class members from opting out. Had the original class settlement succeeded in its ambition to deter opt-outs, the practical effect would have been to cap the liability of Sulzer at the pot of cash it obligated to the trust fund. The $20 million "success fee" for Scruggs then would have been a mere pittance for Sulzer to pay for all-encompassing peace.

Judicial Review and Settlement Revision

For its part, the federal district court tasked with review of the original Sulzer class settlement recognized it as an "inventive" arrangement "on the 'growing edge' of Rule 23(b)(3)'s provisions for an opt-out class action."[62] But the court blessed the deal nonetheless. Writing for the court, Judge Kathleen O'Malley stated that rejection of the original settlement based on the fear that little or nothing would remain for opt-out claimants "would place an impossible and inherently irreconcilable obligation upon class counsel — to negotiate a class-wide settlement which is fair, adequate, and beneficial to its participants, while leaving *completely unaffected* the interests of those who would choose not to participate in it."[63] The district court's italics notwithstanding, the telling word here is "interests."

What must remain "completely unaffected" are not the economic "interests" of opt-out claimants but, rather, their preexisting rights. One may encapsulate the distinction in terms of measures that merely affect the economic value of the right to sue and those that change the content of that right. The district court was correct in the narrow sense that a good opt-out class settlement need not undertake to ensure that conventional litigation by opt-out claimants will be comparably lucrative. A good opt-out class settlement always affects the "interests" of would-be opt-out claimants in a strictly economic sense. It dangles in front of them a superior alternative to what they already have. In so doing, a good opt-out class settlement necessarily increases the opportunity costs associated with adherence by class members to their preexisting rights to sue. What should have doomed the original Sulzer class settlement in legal terms was not the pragmatic concern that opt-out claimants ultimately might obtain only "minuscule" recoveries upon the lifting of the lien but, instead, the taking away of their preexisting right to attempt to leapfrog over other tort claimants in the race to obtain Sulzer's assets. To continue the race analogy: There is a difference between assuring someone a desirable outcome in the race and subjecting her, in her effort to win the race, to a barrier created only by the class action itself.

The district court's approval aside, the original class settlement came

undone in practical terms due to the presence of objectors within the plaintiffs' bar — specifically, firms that already had obtained as their individual
clients substantial numbers of hip implant recipients in need of revision
surgery.[64] Seen in this light, the original class settlement was especially suspect, for it would have installed class counsel as the representatives of such
persons in lieu of the lawyers that they actually had retained by contract. A
strategy on the objectors' part to opt out these individual clients would have
been to no avail, for opt-outs still would have faced the alteration of their
preexisting rights in the manner described above. The objectors, instead,
appealed the district court's settlement approval decision to the United
States Court of Appeals for the Sixth Circuit, which expressed "serious
doubts as to the legitimacy of the proposed class settlement" in the course
of granting a preliminary motion to lift a stay on related litigation imposed
by the district court.[65] The efforts of the objectors ultimately led class counsel and their defense counterparts to fashion a substantially different deal
before the Sixth Circuit could rule on the original one.

Given the district court's approval of the original Sulzer class settlement,
the same court's blessing of the final version is hardly surprising.[66] This
time, however, the court was right. The final class settlement eliminated
the controversial lien and trust fund at the heart of the original deal. Absent
the ability to induce class members to forego the opportunity to opt out
by altering their preexisting rights, the final settlement predictably boosted
the benefits to be gained by class members for remaining in the class —
most tellingly, the benefits for persons who must undergo revision surgery
and, hence, who would stand to have high-value tort claims. Not only did
the final settlement boost the overall value of the benefits for high-value
claims — and, to a lesser extent, for low-value claims as well — it also restructured those benefits by providing them virtually entirely in cash rather
than stock.[67] The boost in the value of the final class settlement stemmed
largely from the willingness of Sulzer's Swiss parent corporation to help
fund the peace in order to put to rest the objections to the original deal.[68]
The release of the Swiss parent, of course, would have been a major benefit
to the defense side from the original class settlement, confined as it was to
funds committed by Sulzer alone.

The point is not that one should applaud the final version of the Sulzer
class settlement simply because it gave class members more money. The
point is to highlight the practical consequences that flow from constraining
the law reform power that a class action may wield over class members'
preexisting rights. Absent the ability to alter unilaterally class members'
preexisting rights to sue in tort — as the combination of the lien and trust

fund in the original deal would have done — settlement designers must purchase those rights by way of the benefits promised to class members for remaining in the settlement. Class members' preexisting rights to sue truly must be purchased rather than simply appropriated, in keeping with their status as a form of property.

One may see the same effect in product liability litigation over wire leads used in pacemakers manufactured by Telectronics Pacing Systems. There, the settling parties originally had pursued a mandatory, limited-fund class settlement. That effort foundered upon appellate review in light of the Supreme Court's intervening decision in *Ortiz*.[69] The settling parties thereafter crafted a similar deal but, this time, as an opt-out class settlement. The principal change consisted of higher benefit levels for class members.[70]

It is not surprising, moreover, that the opt-out class settlements ultimately reached for the Sulzer hip implant and the Telectronics pacemaker should have avoided serious problems of overclaiming. The line separating high-value and low-value claims in both instances was more readily suited to policing in an efficient manner, for that line turned, respectively, on physical separation of the Sulzer hip implant from the thigh bone of the recipient or actual breakage of the wiring of the Telectronics pacemaker. The line between high- and low-value claims, in short, did not entail the exercise of significant discretion on the part of an expert examiner, such as might carry a potential for fakery. In situations of this sort, the stability of the class settlement — its ability actually to deliver peace — will turn principally on its allocation of the gains from settlement more to the members of the class and less to the settling defendant.

The Dilemma of the Mass Tort Class Action

The specifics of the Sulzer example aside, a larger point remains: Efforts to craft ostensible opt-out class settlements to operate in the manner of mandatory class settlements typify the dilemma faced by the class action device in the aftermath of *Amchem*. Here, legitimacy and practicality, due process and the actual delivery of peace, remain in conflict. The enterprise of replacing tort litigation with a private administrative compensation regime inherently entails reduction in the variance of outcomes in litigation. To describe the operation of private administration in terms of a reduction in variance is to maintain a certain agnostic attitude about the features of the tort system that give rise to variance in the first place. For better or worse, the pursuit of punitive damage awards through uncoordinated individual lawsuits is part of the bundle of rights that existing law affords tort plaintiffs.

Yet it is also what creates the potential for multiple awards that might excessively punish the defendant. Even outside the punitive damage context, pursuit of tort recoveries for high-value claims free from the compression in claim values inherent in any grid is an opportunity that existing law affords to claimants. But it is also what carries the potential to unravel the process of collectivization necessary to implement the grid.

The conception of the right to sue as an individual right — as some particular person's property for purposes of due process analysis — commits the tort system to the prospect that some individuals may seek anomalously high recoveries. In order to replace that variance with a grid on the model of workers' compensation, one effectively must redistribute those windfalls and anomalies by averaging them across all would-be claimants. But to redistribute — however laudably as a policy matter — one must undertake a kind of tort reform in microcosm. The lesson of *Amchem* and *Ortiz*, reinforced by what has followed in their stead, is that the modern class action is an institution ill-suited for such a redistributive program.

No less than the Constitution distinguishes between the judicial process (governed by Article III) and the legislative process (governed by Article I). In the mass tort area, what is needed is a vehicle that grounds its authority in Article I, the source of power to engage in law reform, not an Article III judicial proceeding that must take as given the content of existing rights. Aside from the limited efforts at public legislation canvassed earlier, the major development under Article I since the Court's decision in *Amchem* has consisted of innovations in bankruptcy — specifically, the rise of pre-packaged corporate reorganizations in the asbestos litigation. As the next chapter shall discuss, however, the move from Article III to Article I — without more — has actually amplified the most troubling features of class settlements as institutions for law reform. Close analysis of those problems, nonetheless, helps to point the way toward a different kind of law reform under the auspices of Article I.

CHAPTER IX

BANKRUPTCY
TRANSFORMED

The period prior to *Amchem* saw a transformation in the attitude of defendants toward mass tort class actions. The period since that decision has seen a similar transformation in outlook toward bankruptcy. The threat of bankruptcy provided much of the impetus behind efforts to make peace through class settlements. With the viability of class settlements thrown into doubt by *Amchem* and *Ortiz,* renewed attention focused on bankruptcy as a way to make the peace terms binding on present and future claimants. Once again, the asbestos litigation would prompt the stretching of institutional boundaries.

For bankruptcy to become an attractive vehicle from the standpoint of both asbestos defendants and plaintiffs' lawyers, the bankruptcy process itself would have to be transformed. The major downside of bankruptcy was all too familiar from the Johns-Manville proceedings that had prompted experimentation with class settlements in the first place. Bankruptcy holds out the tantalizing promise of a binding peace. It brooks no opt-outs, for example. But peace in asbestos-related bankruptcies previously had come only after years of wrangling—six years, on average, for the bankruptcies of eleven major asbestos defendants.[1] These delays resulted in dissipation of the debtor corporation's resources and delay in payouts to the clients of the asbestos plaintiffs' bar. For lawyers on both sides, the challenge lay in somehow streamlining the bankruptcy process, such that it could impose the desired peace terms much more swiftly. The present chapter analyzes the changes that would bring this goal within the sights of peacemakers.

The story begins where we left off with the Manville bankruptcy in chapter 5. Efforts to reform the foundering Manville trust led to an array of judicial innovations that Congress ultimately wrote into law in 1994, with

the addition of § 524(g) to the Bankruptcy Code. By its terms, § 524(g) applies only to asbestos-related reorganizations. It does not extend to mass
tort-related bankruptcies generally. As I shall explain, however, the transformation of § 524(g) in recent years forms a useful perspective from which
to assess how the law might design institutional arrangements for peacemaking, whether styled as bankruptcy proceedings or otherwise.

The chapter starts with an overview of the innovations in the Manville
reorganization and their impact on the content of § 524(g). I then proceed
to the heart of the discussion, showing how § 524(g) came to dominate
peacemaking in the asbestos litigation in the aftermath of *Amchem*. The trick
consisted of turning § 524(g) — a provision based on the negotiations that
had emerged, ad hoc, in a reorganization already underway — into a means
to lend binding force to private deals reached *prior* to the initiation of the
bankruptcy process. These "prepackaged" reorganization plans — "prepacks," as they are known by bankruptcy lawyers — stirred much well de-
served controversy in the asbestos context. I illustrate the parameters of the
controversy through close examination of the prepack struck down by the
United States Court of Appeals for the Third Circuit in a significant 2004
case, In re *Combustion Engineering*.[2] The lessons from the controversy surrounding prepacks nonetheless resonate well beyond the asbestos context.

Just as the class settlement in *Amchem* made explicit the use of gridlike compensation schemes, the story of the *Combustion Engineering* prepack
brings to light the underlying strategic dynamics of peacemaking. Prepackaged reorganization plans expose where the real bargaining power lies in
the peacemaking process for mass torts — namely, with plaintiffs' law firms
representing large blocks of present claimants. As I shall explain, clear perception of this dynamic sheds doubt on the core prescription common to
both *Amchem* and § 524(g) — namely, insistence that future claimants have
their own, separate representative, unburdened by the conflicts of interest
thought to stem from an inventory of present-day claims. Prepacks reveal
the untenable nature of such a prescription, for the source of the perceived
conflict of interest is also the major source of bargaining leverage in peace
negotiations. Prepacks, in short, highlight that lawyers representing present
claimants form the nub of the governance problem in mass torts. They —
not the elaboration of separate representation for future claimants — are
the proper focus of meaningful reform.

From Manville to § 524(g)

The Manville proceedings took place under Chapter 11 of the Bankruptcy
Code,[3] which provides for reorganization of the debtor corporation rather

than liquidation under Chapter 7. Broadly stated, the idea behind Chapter 11 is that creditors sometimes will be better off with the debtor able to continue in business rather than having its assets sold off in pieces. This justification for Chapter 11 has long been contested in the bankruptcy literature, with some scholars arguing that the case for reorganizations over liquidations is overstated.[4] Chapter 11 nonetheless remains a well-entrenched part of bankruptcy law. The thinking behind it dovetails with the underlying theme that mass tort settlements — whatever their procedural vehicle — have a tremendous potential to be value-generating transactions for both plaintiffs and defendants.

The potential for the reorganization process to enhance the resources available for distribution to creditors helps to explain why the law does not insist on a showing of insolvency as a precondition to the invocation of Chapter 11.[5] Nor does the use of Chapter 11 depend on the kind of showing regarding the debtor's assets and liabilities that the *Ortiz* Court thought essential for certification of a mandatory, limited-fund class action. The idea, instead, is that the debtor corporation may seek protection in bankruptcy at times before its situation has become so dire as to undermine the potential for substantial gains through reorganization. The relative strictness of the *Ortiz* opinion actually has the effect of protecting the terrain of Chapter 11 and the procedural strictures specified therein from intrusion by the class action device.

The central innovation of the Manville reorganization lay in measures designed, at least in theory, to enable asbestos claimants to benefit from the improvement that the reorganization would bring for Manville's business prospects. The centerpiece of the reorganization plan was its creation of a trust fund separate in the eyes of the law from Manville Corporation. A "channeling injunction" issued under the general equitable powers of the bankruptcy court under § 105(a) of the Code was supposed to confine both present and future asbestos claimants to seek compensation exclusively from the trust and thereby to remove the cloud of mass tort liability from the reorganized Manville.[6] The consequent improvement in Manville's business prospects, in turn, would enable the firm to continue as a "going concern" and, in so doing, to provide an "evergreen" source of funding for future claimants. In addition to Manville's insurance proceeds, the principal sources of funding for the trust consisted of stock in the reorganized corporation and a right to receive up to 20 percent of its profits for as long as needed to compensate asbestos claimants. In effect, the funding package for the trust would make asbestos claimants the largest block of shareholders in the reorganized corporation.[7]

As chapter 5 observed, the Manville reorganization quickly encountered huge obstacles, with an unexpected number of claims overwhelming the resources of the trust. These formidable difficulties aside, the Manville reorganization plan involved several innovations that would shape developments in the post-*Amchem* period. The possibility of bankruptcy previously had served as the bogeyman driving efforts to make peace through class settlements. With class settlements now a perilous vehicle for peacemaking, lawyers in the asbestos litigation turned anew to bankruptcy — specifically, to the amendments to the Bankruptcy Code spawned by the Manville proceedings. To understand the dynamics unleashed by those amendments, one must grasp the major structural features of the Manville reorganization.

The viability of the Manville trust turned crucially on the willingness of financial markets to back the business ventures of the reorganized Manville Corporation. Open questions remained, however, concerning the legal basis for each of the matters central to the reorganization. That uncertainty stemmed, at bottom, from the design of the Bankruptcy Code with conventional business creditors in mind. Mass tort claimants, by contrast, stand to make demands on the debtor that will extend years into the future and, at the same time, that are less readily amenable to valuation in the manner of conventional business debts.

The credibility of the Manville reorganization depended on the existence of authority to confine future asbestos claimants to the resources in the trust. Yet, as the bankruptcy court itself acknowledged, considerable uncertainty remained over whether the category of "claims" dischargeable under the Bankruptcy Code encompasses future demands for compensation in tort. In the Manville proceedings, the bankruptcy court sought to finesse this issue, asserting that future tort claims were not actually being discharged but simply would be subject to the court's channeling injunction that would prevent them from suing the reorganized Manville.[8] The scope of the channeling injunction — designed to shield not only the reorganized corporation but also those doing business with it — represented an expansive reading of the general equitable powers provided to the bankruptcy court by § 105(a).

The process for confirmation of the Manville reorganization plan also was unusual. By its terms, Chapter 11 provides for the confirmation of a reorganization plan in the face of objection from particular creditors "if such plan . . . has been accepted by creditors . . . that hold at least two-thirds in amount and more than one-half in number of the allowed claims" within each creditor class impaired by the plan.[9] The bankruptcy court for Manville, nonetheless, sought to avoid the need to value each pending asbestos claim as a prelude to reorganization. For purposes of voting, the court simply fixed at one dollar the value of each pending asbestos claim against Manville and deemed acceptance by those claimants to consist of an affirmative vote by two-thirds in number.[10] On appeal, the Second Circuit sidestepped the validity of this procedure, holding that any alleged violation of the Code specifications constituted "harmless error"—something that would not have changed the outcome of the voting process.[11] The specifics of the voting process aside, the hard negotiations that produced the reorganization plan took place at the behest of a creditors' committee that included plaintiffs' lawyers representing the largest blocks of pending claims against Manville. To add to the innovations of the proceeding, the court also had appointed a separate representative for future asbestos claimants—commonly dubbed a "futures representative"—who did not himself have an inventory of pending claims.[12]

The lingering uncertainty over each of the foregoing features—the treatment of future claims, the channeling injunction under § 105(a), the voting procedure, and the appointment of a futures representative—made for considerable drag on the ability of Manville to garner the backing of investors after its reorganization. In the meantime, a second asbestos defendant, UNR Industries, had pursued a similar reorganization plan. Responding to repeated pleas to set the legality of these reorganizations on a more secure footing,[13] Congress added § 524(g) to the Bankruptcy Code in 1994. In substance, § 524(g) blessed retrospectively the major features of the Manville reorganization and, more importantly, set them as a model for future asbestos-related reorganizations.

Even § 524(g) does not lump future asbestos claims into the general category of "claims" dischargeable in bankruptcy. Congress instead created a separate category of "demands" that are not dischargeable claims at the time of the reorganization but that nonetheless arise "out of the same or similar conduct or events" that give rise to the reorganization.[14] Section 524(g) goes on to authorize the use of a trust, separate from the reorganized debtor, to pay both present claims and future "demands." In turn, the trust must treat those demands "in substantially the same manner," insofar as they are "similar" in nature, apart from their timing.[15] As a precondition for confirmation of such a trust arrangement, the bankruptcy court must appoint a separate futures representative[16]—the counterpart in § 524(g) to what *Amchem* later would prescribe for representation in mass tort class actions.

Most significantly, § 524(g) also specifies the voting procedure for confirmation of an asbestos-related reorganization plan and the scope of the channeling injunction that gives it force. Indeed, the voting process remains intertwined with the channeling injunction. Confirmation of a reorganization plan under §524(g) calls for satisfaction of the normal voting specifications under Chapter 11 plus — as a condition for the further protection of a channeling injunction — a favorable vote by at least 75 percent of "the claimants whose claims are to be addressed" by the trust to which the injunction channels claims.[17] Having carved out future claimants into the separate category of "demands," §524(g) thus effectively affords bargaining power in its voting process to present claimants — a move admittedly in keeping with the goal of writing the Manville negotiations into law. As to the channeling injunction, §524(g) sweeps broadly, authorizing the injunction to encompass the debtor corporation, many kinds of third parties that form financial relationships with the debtor — through loans, insurance, or ownership of a financial interest, for example — and any "past or present affiliate" corporation.[18]

For present purposes, the specifics of §524(g) are less significant than the overarching premise behind them. In writing the Manville example into law, Congress proceeded from a fundamentally static conception of the reorganization process. Section 524(g) enshrines a process that had evolved, ad hoc, from negotiations concerning a debtor already in bankruptcy. The Manville bankruptcy petition had taken asbestos plaintiffs' lawyers by surprise,[19] at which point all of the key players — Manville, its business creditors, asbestos plaintiffs' lawyers, and the bankruptcy court — faced the task of working out a reorganization plan. At the time of §524(g), no one seems to have foreseen its effect on the dynamics of peacemaking in the asbestos litigation. Section 524(g) would become not so much a framework for years of negotiation in bankruptcy — as in the Manville example — but, instead, a blueprint for how private negotiations might largely bypass the conventional reorganization process. The story of this transformation of bankruptcy is the story of prepackaged reorganization plans for asbestos defendants in the aftermath of *Amchem*.

Prepackaged Reorganizations

It is far from unusual in the business world for creditors to work out their competing demands on the resources of a debtor wholly outside of bankruptcy. In fact, when a corporation borrows heavily to finance the acquisition of another firm through what is known as a "leveraged buyout," creditors routinely put into place, in advance, financial arrangements designed to smooth the path for reorganization of the corporation in the event that it later encounters financial distress.[20] In many business settings, bankruptcy law stands simply as an off-the-rack set of procedures where the relevant players have not contracted in advance for some other arrangement.

Prepackaged reorganization plans stand as an intermediate solution by comparison to arrangements that aspire to bypass bankruptcy entirely. Outside the mass tort context, conventional business creditors have used prepackaged reorganizations since the mid-1980s.[21] Prepacks entail invocation of the Bankruptcy Code, but they hold out the promise of a quicker, easier trip through its rigors based on the working-out in advance of a reorganization plan. Invocation of the Bankruptcy Code nonetheless remains essential, for it is what makes binding upon mass tort claimants the terms of the plan.

The bankruptcy of Manville and several other leading players in the asbestos industry added to the financial strain on the remaining asbestos defendants. One economic analysis concludes that early asbestos-related bankruptcies had a domino effect. They shifted liability to the remaining solvent defendants in such as way as to increase the chances that those firms, too, eventually would seek protection in bankruptcy.[22] The Manville proceedings thus spawned the legal framework for later asbestos-related reorganizations and, at the same time, increased the likelihood that such reorganizations would need to occur.

Of the seventy-three asbestos-related bankruptcy filings from 1976 to 2004, more than half occurred after 1997—that is, in the period since *Amchem*.[23] By the mid-2000s, prepackaged reorganization plans under §524(g) emerged as the most innovative technique for the resolution of asbestos claims in bankruptcy.[24] I focus here on the prepack that led to the Third Circuit's decision in In re *Combustion Engineering*, for it illustrates most dramatically both the innovations and the perils of the format. The important point to bear in mind, at the outset, is that the challenge to which the Combustion Engineering prepack responded—the need to fashion a binding peace for both pending claims and future ones—is not unique to that particular example or, for that matter, to the asbestos setting. Rather, the making of such a peace represents the central challenge in mass tort litigation generally.

The Combustion Engineering prepack involved a constellation of corporations known collectively as the ABB Group. Combustion Engineering itself is a wholly owned subsidiary of a domestic corporation, Asea Brown Boveri, Inc. ("U.S. ABB"). A Swiss holding company, ABB Limited, is the parent of both Combustion Engineering and U.S. ABB. Since the mid-1990s, asbestos plaintiffs in the United States had sued Combustion Engineering as a defendant, necessitating infusions of funds by U.S. ABB in order for Combustion Engineering to meet its financial obligations. With no end to the asbestos litigation in sight, the liability exposure of Combustion Engineering added to the precarious financial position of both U.S. ABB and ABB Limited.

During the 1990s, ABB Limited had grown rapidly through the acquisition of other firms in the power technology business. By the end of the decade, however, those acquisitions had left ABB Limited with a huge debt burden, including $1.5 billion in obligations set to come due in late 2002 and another $2.1 billion in 2003. Creditors of ABB Limited voiced their unwillingness to refinance these debts absent a better idea of what the asbestos litigation would hold for Combustion Engineering. Along similar lines, creditors of U.S. ABB threatened to institute an involuntary bankruptcy proceeding for that firm unless it could provide greater certainty about the demands on its resources that might arise from its relationship with Combustion Engineering. A collapse in the financing for U.S. ABB, in turn, stood to endanger a $402 million note by which that firm earlier had obligated itself to contribute to Combustion Engineering's asbestos liabilities. In short, by late 2002, the fate of Combustion Engineering turned on funding from the ABB Group; and the ABB Group's own financial position turned on resolution of Combustion Engineering's asbestos liabilities.[25]

The challenges for the ABB Group took three forms: placing more definite parameters on Combustion Engineering's future liabilities, defining the extent to which both ABB Limited and U.S. ABB would need to fund those liabilities, and ensuring that related corporations within the ABB Group would gain the protection of a §524(g) channeling injunction. Achievement of these ends would enable ABB Limited to service its debt obligations by selling a corporate affiliate—ABB Lummus Global, Inc.—free and clear from asbestos-related liabilities. But, to do that, the ABB Group needed the channeling injunction to extend to Lummus.

Like the contractual agreements used by Owens Corning in its National Settlement Program, the Combustion Engineering prepack played on the concentration of the asbestos plaintiffs' bar. In testimony summarized by the bankruptcy court, the general counsel of the ABB Group conveyed "his understanding that the asbestos litigation was controlled by several plaintiffs' lawyers and that it was necessary to find someone who could coordinate negotiations with representatives of the asbestos plaintiffs' bar."[26] For Combustion Engineering, reorganization under §524(g) offered a solution superior to firm-specific contracts on the Owens Corning model, for confirmation of a reorganization plan would regulate all future asbestos claims, regardless of the law firm that might represent them. The voting provisions of §524(g) underscored the need to persuade the key players within the asbestos plaintiffs' bar to supply the requisite votes for the reorganization plan.

Given the precariousness of its own financial position, the ABB Group did not leave to chance the voting process needed for plan confirmation. Rather, the ABB Group contacted prominent asbestos plaintiffs' attorney Joseph Rice—a lawyer who had served earlier as one of the class counsel in *Amchem*—to negotiate a prepackaged reorganization plan that he then would persuade other asbestos plaintiffs' law firms to support in numbers that would satisfy the 75 percent threshold in §524(g). The strategy used by the ABB Group—a mass tort defendant calling upon a prominent plaintiffs' lawyer to craft a peace agreement and then to sell his cohorts on its virtues—recalls the path taken earlier by Sulzer in its retention of Richard Scruggs to craft a class settlement in the hip implant litigation. For his efforts in the design of the Combustion Engineering prepack, Rice stood to gain a "success fee" in the same amount—$20 million—as Sulzer had offered Scruggs to garner support for the hip implant class settlement.[27] The sum of $20 million seemed the going rate for such services. As in the Sulzer example, that sum stood to be pittance for the gains that would flow to the ABB Group from a quick trip in and out of bankruptcy on the part of Combustion Engineering.

As an ethical matter, Rice's situation was more complicated than that of Scruggs. Rice's status as a prominent asbestos plaintiffs' lawyer meant that he represented large numbers of pending asbestos claims—that is, creditors of Combustion Engineering—but also stood to be paid by the debtor for his work on the reorganization plan. The apparent conflict of interest involved in the simultaneous representation of creditors and the debtor corporation garnered much critical commentary.[28] One asbestos claimant went so far as to sue Rice for breach of fiduciary duty. A federal district court dismissed the lawsuit, however. The court concluded that Rice owed no fiduciary duty to claimants, like the plaintiff, who had not retained him as their lawyer and who remained represented by other members of the asbestos plaintiffs' bar—this even though all claimants against Combustion Engineering stood to be governed by the reorganization plan that Rice had crafted.[29]

Rice's apparent conflict of interest is not my primary concern here. Its ethical propriety aside, the ABB Group's selection of Rice as deal-maker stands as a tacit recognition of the power that bankruptcy law places in the hands of those positioned to gather up the necessary votes in favor of a reorganization plan. The 75 percent vote demanded by §524(g) accentuates this power, but much the same tendency already arises under the ordinary voting process of Chapter 11. That process, too, contemplates plan confirmation at the behest of a favorable vote from a supermajority of creditors. The ABB Group's decision to turn to one of the most powerful lawyers for its tort creditors simply exposes to the light of day the dynamics involved in peacemaking for mass tort litigation. Even if the ABB Group had not actually hired Rice, the ABB Group eventually would have had to garner the support of enough asbestos plaintiffs' lawyers like him in order to ensure the assent of sufficient pending claimants to its desired reorganization plan. Insofar as the ABB Group's hiring of Rice is discomforting, that discomfort is much the same as the unease that the *Amchem* class settlement elicited from the Supreme Court. The actions of the ABB Group and Rice reveal, in a stark and above-board way, matters that otherwise would proceed below-board.

The features of the reorganization plan crafted by Rice reveal the importance of vote gathering. Rather than resolve both pending and future asbestos claims against the debtor corporation through a single trust fund constituted in bankruptcy, the reorganization plan for Combustion Engineering involved the creation of two distinct trusts: a "settlement trust" created prior to the bankruptcy proceeding in order to address pending claims and a separate §524(g) trust established in bankruptcy for the payment of future claims. This two-trust structure, in fact, represents a recurring feature of many prepacks in the asbestos litigation. Combustion Engineering devoted roughly one-half of its value to the settlement trust, which, in turn, was to pay pending claims based on specified percentages of their historical settlement values. These percentages ranged from a high of 95 percent to a low of 37.5 percent, depending on how long a given claim had been pending in the tort system and on whether the claim was the subject of a settlement that remained unpaid, not depending on severity of injury. Persons with pending claims then would look to the §524(g) trust established in bankruptcy to satisfy the remaining percentage—the "stub"—of their respective claims.[30]

It was no accident that the separate settlement trust would make immediate payments to pending claims but leave them with a stub for purposes of the bankruptcy proceeding. Resolution of pending claims in their entirety prior to bankruptcy would have rendered them unable to do the one thing crucial from the standpoint of the ABB Group: to vote in favor of the proposed reorganization plan. As a formal matter, participation in the settlement trust did not legally obligate pending claimants—or, more accurately, their lawyers — to vote their remaining stub claims in favor of the reorganization plan. Those lawyers did promise, however, to "recommend" such a favorable vote on the part of their clients.[31] As the Third Circuit observed, participation in the settlement trust was "conditioned, at least implicitly, on a subsequent vote in favor" of the reorganization plan.[32] In fact, the result was a lopsided vote in favor of the plan, with over 85 percent of the favorable votes — and over 82 percent of all valid votes cast — coming from stub claims.[33] In practical effect, stub claims alone surpassed the 75 percent threshold needed for confirmation under §524(g).

The bankruptcy court confirmed the Combustion Engineering prepack, and the district court largely upheld that decision. On appeal, however, the Third Circuit reversed. Portions of the Third Circuit's opinion speak to the extension of the channeling injunction to "non-derivative" claims against Lummus — that is, tort claims against a third party that are "wholly separate" from claims against the debtor, Combustion Engineering.[34] Writing for the court, Judge Anthony Scirica observed that the relationship between Lummus and Combustion Engineering — two entities connected merely by their presence within the larger tent of the ABB Group — did not fit within any of the categories in §524(g) for extension of a channeling injunction to third parties. That being so, the bankruptcy court could not use its general equitable powers under §105(a) to issue a channeling injunction that would "achieve a result not contemplated by the more specific provisions of §524(g)."[35]

Given the importance of the channeling injunction for the ABB Group's plans to sell Lummus, the Third Circuit's ruling on the scope of that injunction effectively doomed the reorganization plan as originally crafted. A modified reorganization plan for Combustion Engineering fashioned in the aftermath of the court's decision would contemplate an entirely separate reorganization proceeding for Lummus. The eventual sale of Lummus still was expected to provide the ABB Group with resources to fund the reorganization plan for Combustion Engineering, but the ABB Group's financial commitment to that end was no longer contingent, at least formally, on its sale of Lummus.[36]

The most significant portions of the Third Circuit's decision speak to the two-trust structure of the original plan. The Third Circuit ultimately remanded the case for further factual findings. The opinion, nonetheless, fairly bristles with concern over the effect that the separate, prebankruptcy settlement trust had on the reorganization plan for future claimants.

Neither the bankruptcy court nor the district court had made findings concerning the payouts for present claimants under the settlement trust by comparison to those that future claimants stood to receive under the §524(g) trust. This omission was especially troubling, said the Third Circuit, because future claimants "appear to receive a demonstrably unequal share of the limited Combustion Engineering fund"—that is, the resources made available under the settlement trust and the §524(g) trust, understood as an integrated whole. The settlement trust paid, on average, 59 percent of the value of present claims, a percentage unlikely to be duplicated by the §524(g) trust for future claimants.[37]

Even the ABB Group stopped conspicuously short of a full-fledged argument that the settlement trust and the original §524(g) trust, viewed as an integrated whole, would have made for equitable treatment of present and future claims otherwise similar in nature. In its brief to the Third Circuit, the best that the ABB Group could muster came in a passage of startling circumlocution. The ABB Group simply remarked that the Bankruptcy Code "nowhere assures that the aggregate amount of payments made to claimants before and during bankruptcy must be equal."[38] This statement, at best, sidesteps whether a prepack may engineer unequal payments as a means to induce the necessary votes for plan confirmation.

Concern over the separate settlement trust, however, was not confined to the treatment of similar claims over time. An additional strand of concern centers on the allocation of resources across different types of claims. The legal challenge to the confirmation of the Combustion Engineering reorganization plan came at the behest of persons suffering from asbestos-related cancers who stood to have especially high-value tort claims against the debtor. Cancer claimants stood to suffer from the allocation of resources to lower-value claimants, as necessary to secure the numbers of votes needed for confirmation. Here, recall from chapter 2 the greater absolute number of lower-value claims in the asbestos litigation by comparison to cancer cases.[39]

The Third Circuit ultimately found the record before it insufficient to pin down the treatment of the various types of asbestos claimants. Even while shying from definitive conclusions, however, the court included language that lent credence to the concerns of cancer claimants. Judge Scirica emphasized that the "manipulation" of the confirmation vote through the creation of stub claims "is especially problematic in the asbestos context, where a voting majority can be made to consist of non-malignant claimants whose interests may be adverse to those of claimants with more severe injuries."[40] In the words of one commentator quoted by the court, "[a] distinct minority—for example, those tort claimants with especially serious injuries and strong cases—might get outvoted by a large number of holders of small claims who favor a quick pay-out of relatively small amounts with little proof required."[41]

For the Third Circuit, the problem at the heart of the Combustion Engineering prepack was not just one of payouts, whether across time or across different disease categories. The payouts were a manifestation of a deeper structural deficiency. Invoking *Amchem*, Judge Scirica noted that "the first phase of the integrated, global settlement—the establishment of the [settlement trust]—included neither representation nor funding for" future claimants. The separate § 524(g) trust for future claimants then "was ratified by a majority of 'stub votes' cast by the very claimants who obtained preferential treatment from the debtor" under the settlement trust. The role of stub claims in the confirmation process revealed the "structural inadequacy" of the Combustion Engineering prepack.[42] Put differently, the concerns surrounding the payouts under the prepack ultimately stemmed from a deficient regime of governance—one whose structural features did not lend legitimacy to its results. The payouts, in short, were symptoms of a deeper problem of legitimacy.

Developments in the aftermath of the Third Circuit's reversal have largely papered over with money the structural deficiency that troubled the court. In 2005, Combustion Engineering negotiated a modified reorganization plan with those who had challenged the original plan. The centerpiece of the modified plan consisted of an additional infusion of $204 million from the ABB Group to fund the § 524(g) trust for future claimants.[43] The availability of these additional resources was itself a product of the time that the ABB Group effectively bought with the original reorganization plan and the period of wrangling over its validity. By 2005, the ABB Group stood "in a far more financially secure position in comparison to its status in 2003," having staved off the distress that had precipitated the Combustion Engineering prepack in the first place.[44]

The $204 million infusion from the ABB Group enabled plan proponents to persuade the bankruptcy court that future claimants and pending ones would be treated equitably under the modified plan, with each group of claims now expected to be paid 45 to 48 percent of their value.[45] The modified plan included beefed-up medical criteria to guard against payment by the § 524(g) trust for the sorts of medically dubious asbestos claims discussed in chapter 8.[46] For cancer claimants specifically, the modified plan adjusted its payment ratios so that those claimants would receive a dramatically higher percentage of their value than nonmalignant cases.[47]

Still, the central structural problem of the original plan—the two-trust format—remained in place. The modified plan deemed the settlement trust to be the sole source of compensation for pending claimants with stubs, such that they now would be ineligible for additional payment from the §524(g) trust. In effect, the modified plan wiped out the value of the stubs. But that move, in itself, "change[d] the expectations" of claimants who had participated in the settlement trust, thereby "entitling them to vote"—just like before—on the confirmation of the modified reorganization plan for future claimants.[48] That vote, like the first, went overwhelmingly in favor of the modified plan. The bankruptcy court and district court that had blessed the original plan not surprisingly confirmed the modified one. And, this time, no one appealed.

In the end, one may see the $204 million added to the pie by the ABB Group as tangible evidence for the value-creating potential of settlement. Its considerable flaws notwithstanding, the original reorganization plan had the far-from-trivial benefit of saving the ABB Group and enabling it to expand the resources potentially available to compensate future claimants. The modified plan undoubtedly allocated more of these gains from peace to future claimants by comparison to the original plan. But it did so by throwing money at the problem—quite literally—rather than addressing the deeper structural concern identified by Judge Scirica. One wonders whether, had a second appeal to the Third Circuit been taken, the modified plan would have passed muster. *Amchem*, after all, counsels skepticism for eminently practical deals spawned by structurally deficient means.

For present purposes, perhaps the most notable aspect of the Combustion Engineering story lies in its implicit challenge to the notion that separate representation of future claimants can drive an equitable allocation of resources. The existence of a futures representative in Combustion Engineering was not what elicited the $204 million boost from the ABB Group. And the reasons why can help us to discern a more productive direction for future reform.

The Future of the Futures Representative

That the Third Circuit should have looked to *Amchem*—a nonbankruptcy case—when addressing the structure for representation in a §524(g) reorganization is not surprising. The two-trust structure in Combustion Engineering largely replicates the deal struck down in *Amchem*, where the class settlement for future claimants took place in tandem with aggregate settlements for claimants with pending tort cases. The one cosmetic difference in the original reorganization plan struck down in *Combustion Engineering* consists of its creation of stub claims that nominally would straddle the two trusts but would be paid primarily through a trust separate from the one established in bankruptcy for future claimants. At first glance, then, the story of the Combustion Engineering prepack seemingly reinforces the wisdom of *Amchem*. A structurally flawed regime of governance should fare no better when labeled as a reorganization plan in bankruptcy than when framed as a class settlement.

At a deeper level, however, the rise of prepacks in the asbestos litigation sheds doubt on the core prescription advanced in both *Amchem* for class actions and §524(g) for asbestos-related reorganizations. Both *Amchem* and §524(g) celebrate the idea that future claimants are appropriately protected in peace negotiations by having separate legal representation — in particular, a representative who does not have his own inventory of pending claims. Indeed, even without any specific command in the Code, bankruptcy practice in mass tort-related reorganizations under the general Chapter 11 routinely entails the appointment of a futures representative.[49]

The futures representative in *Combustion Engineering*, David Austern, was a widely respected figure in the asbestos litigation by virtue of his service in the administration of the Manville trust. Upon the retention of several financial experts, Austern did manage to wring from the ABB Group some relatively modest enhancements to the resources of the original §524(g) trust for future claimants.[50] The structure of the original prepack, nevertheless, turned the futures representative — even one with integrity, experience, and expert financial advice — into largely an afterthought.

The command of §524(g) to appoint a separate futures representative arises only after the commencement of the bankruptcy proceeding.[51] By then, the real deal-makers — Rice, the other leading players within the asbestos plaintiffs' bar, and their negotiating counterparts for the ABB Group — already had removed from the table one-half of Combustion Engineering's value for distribution by the settlement trust. The Bankruptcy Code does contemplate the possibility of litigation to recover transfers made from the assets of the debtor where those transfers prefer particular creditors over others. But the Code makes possible such litigation only as to preferential transfers made within ninety days of the bankruptcy petition,[52] a window of time that prepack designers easily may avoid in their implementation of a separate settlement trust.

The two-trust structure, nonetheless, is not the root of the problem for the futures representative. The two-trust structure is simply a manifestation of a deeper truth. The real bargaining leverage in a reorganization proceeding lies with plaintiffs' lawyers who control large inventories of present claims. They, not so much the futures representative, are the people with whom the debtor must negotiate seriously, for they have the power effectively to veto any proposed reorganization plan under the general voting procedures of Chapter 11 and, especially, the 75 percent vote required by §524(g) for the asbestos setting. The modified reorganization plan in Combustion Engineering ultimately did do better by future claimants. But that change reflected not the negotiating savvy of a futures representative but the bringing to bear upon lawyers for present claimants of the need to safeguard the welfare of future ones.

The bargaining power of the futures representative stems simply from the possibility that he might persuade the court that the reorganization plan does not merit confirmation. Yet, both the ability of the futures representative to put up a significant fight and the incentives for him to do so are meager. The lack of flesh-and-blood clients means that the futures representative — unlike lawyers for pending claimants — lacks the ability to threaten the debtor with mass tort litigation as an unpalatable alternative to the debtor's preferred reorganization plan. In particular, the power to initiate an involuntary bankruptcy case against the debtor — say, to liquidate it under Chapter 7 — rests with the holders of claims that are neither "contingent as to liability [n]or the subject of a bona fide dispute."[53] In effect, this category consists of claimants with judgments or settlements that remain unpaid — precisely the kinds of claims that the separate settlement trust in Combustion Engineering would have treated most generously in terms of its payout percentages.

Because the futures representative inherently represents claims that are not now pending in court, there is no conventional client to appoint him. Section 524(g) accordingly calls for the bankruptcy court to appoint the futures representative in asbestos-related reorganizations. In practice, however, this judicial appointment ratifies the debtor's preexisting choice as part of the run-up to its bankruptcy petition. Indeed, "because the person representing future claimants is not a court appointee when the negotiations [prior to the formal filing of the bankruptcy petition] are taking place, the debtor has the ability to terminate him or her if the negotiations get too tough."[54]

Under current law, the futures representative receives compensation on an hourly basis, not compensation contingent on the resources obtained for future claimants.[55] One response suggested by some scholars would be to switch to a regime of contingent compensation,[56] but even that change would not solve the fundamental problem with the futures representative. Contingent compensation would not supply the leverage that the futures representative lacks by virtue of the absence of actual clients. To hold out the prospect that the futures representative might share in the securing of additional resources for future claimants does little good, in other words, without a bolstering of the ability actually to secure those resources in negotiation.

It is far from clear, moreover, that compensation contingent on the resources obtained for future claimants in a given reorganization would capture the relevant contingencies for the futures representative. In addition to the resources obtained for future claimants in the current reorganization, another contingency consists of whether the futures representative will become a "repeat player"—someone whom later bankruptcy courts and debtors would feel comfortable placing in a similar role again. Enhancing one's chances to become a repeat player, however, depends on putting up just enough resistance to secure some nominal concessions in the reorganization plan but not protesting so much as to scuttle the plan entirely. If anything, compensation contingent on the resources made available for future claimants would magnify the incentive for the futures representative to pull his punches. Actual defeat of the reorganization plan would leave no corpus for contingent compensation of the futures representative and, at the same time, would undermine that person's chance of becoming a repeat player. Going on as a futures representative requires going along.[57]

The incentive to become a repeat player operates differently upon a futures representative than upon a conventional plaintiffs' lawyer. Contingency fee arrangements are the dominant method of compensation for mass tort plaintiffs' lawyers. And many such lawyers are repeat players across different areas of mass tort litigation. For a mass tort plaintiffs' lawyer, however, the incentive to become a repeat player operates in consonance with the incentive provided by contingency fee arrangements to maximize the recovery for a given client or group thereof. The larger the recovery for the client, the greater the resources available for the lawyer to redeploy elsewhere and the greater the enhancement of the lawyer's reputation for purposes of subsequent client recruitment. For the futures representative, by contrast, the possibility of becoming a repeat player undercuts the incentive to maximize the resources allocated to future claimants in a reorganization plan, because repeat-player status turns on pulling one's punches.

Experience suggests that the repeat-player phenomenon is quite real. Eight of the eleven prepacks initiated through 2005 involved futures representatives who previously served, or would serve, in the same capacity in other asbestos-related reorganizations—in several instances, other prepacks:[58]

Table 1

Debtor	Petition Year	Court	Futures Representative (repeat players italicized)
Fuller-Austin Insulation Co.	1998	D. Del.	*Eric Green*
Western Asbestos Co.	2002	N.D. Cal.	Charles Renfrew
J. T. Thorpe Co.	2002	S.D. Tex.	*Richard Schiro*
Shook & Fletcher Insulation Co.	2002	N.D. Ala.	*R. Scott Williams*
ACandS, Inc.	2002	D. Del.	*Lawrence Fitzpatrick*
Halliburton Co.	2003	W.D. Pa.	*Eric Green*
Combustion Engineering	2003	D. Del.	*David Austern*
Congoleum Corp.	2003	D. N.J.	*R. Scott Williams*
Utex Industries, Inc.	2004	S.D. Tex.	*Richard Schiro*
Quigley Co.	2004	S.D. N.Y.	Albert Togut
API, Inc.	2005	D. Minn.	Thomas Carey

In an extreme example, the futures representatives for one non-prepack reorganization garnered something well beyond repeat-player status. They were appointed to serve as ostensibly neutral "advisors" by the federal judge handling five other asbestos-related reorganizations that presented "many of the same issues . . . many of the same creditors, and possibly some of the same asbestos claimants."[59] In a decision issued prior to *Combustion Engineering*, the Third Circuit concluded that these advisors operated under a conflict of interest. On the one hand, they were obligated to advance the interest of future claimants in the matter for which they were their representatives. But, on the other hand, they had been appointed to provide "non-partisan" advice to the court with regard to the five similar reorganizations. The Third Circuit found this conflict to be so serious as to warrant the extraordinary step of a compelled recusal from the five similar reorganizations of the federal judge responsible for the advisors' appointment.

Efforts to dampen the incentive to become a repeat player—say, by prohibiting service as a futures representative in multiple reorganizations—would operate only in considerable tension with the competing goal of expertise. The role of the futures representative for a mass tort bankruptcy calls for an unusual combination of characteristics. One wants a person with a sophisticated understanding of the full array of issues—legal, financial, and otherwise—with the potential to affect future claimants under a reorganization plan. But one cannot select the futures representative from among the persons who would have the most detailed knowledge of the particular mass tort at hand from the perspective of claimants — namely, plaintiffs' lawyers who have inventories of claims and, as such, represent existing creditors of the debtor. One wants, in other words, someone well versed in mass tort litigation yet uninvolved in litigation against the particular debtor. As a result, the pool of persons who plausibly might serve as futures representatives in mass tort bankruptcies is not large. Disallowance of repeat players would only narrow the pool even further.

The Gap in the Academic Debate

Not surprisingly, the challenges posed for future claimants in mass tort-related reorganizations have elicited several proposals in academic commentary. These proposals raise difficulties of their own. All of them nonetheless bear attention, less for their prescriptions per se and more for their shared premise about the relationship between present and future claims. The piece missing from existing commentary concerns the implications that the law should draw from that relationship for the representation of future claimants. The dynamics revealed by the Combustion Engineering prepack — troubling though they are — actually help to point the way toward more productive reform.

Two early contributions to the literature on mass tort bankruptcies — a 1984 article by Mark Roe and a 1994 article by Thomas Smith — seek in one way or another to use financial instruments to allocate the resources of the debtor between present and future claimants.[60] Roe draws on the idea of a variable annuity, a common form of investment whereby investors purchase shares in a larger pool comprised of various stocks. Investors then may redeem their shares gradually, over the course of several years. The value of the shares at any given time of redemption depends on the performance of the underlying pool of stocks. For Roe, a variable annuity in the context of mass tort bankruptcies would entail the creation of a trust for tort claimants consisting of the value of the debtor corporation — the analogue to the pool of stocks in a conventional variable annuity. The trust would issue shares to tort claimants based on the dollar value of their claims, one share per dollar. Tort claimants then could redeem those shares over time, as needed for purposes of funding ongoing medical care or income replacement. The value of the shares at any given time would depend on the overall value of the trust, divided by the estimated number of claims against it. Initial underestimates of future claims would result in the issuance of additional shares, such as would reduce the redemption value of the shares already issued. The shares in the trust, in short, would form the mechanism to ratchet down payouts for present claimants based on the emergence of future claimants.[61]

Roe's variable annuity proposal represented an important step forward in its time by recognizing the inevitable connection between the treatment of present claimants and estimates of future claimants. As subsequent commentary has observed, however, the administration of Roe's proposal turns crucially on the ability to estimate future claims against the trust and, thereafter, to adjust the redemption value of trust shares based on new information about future claims.[62] Yet the variable annuity proposal does not alter the structure of representation in mass tort bankruptcies so as to induce the key players to make accurate estimates and adjustments rather than self-serving ones.

Smith seeks to solve the problem of representation by circumscribing even more dramatically the decisions needed for the creation and administration of the bankruptcy trust. For Smith, the trust again would consist of the value of the debtor firm. But the trust would be a "liquidating trust," one that would pay out its value after all future claims have emerged. In the meantime, the trust would issue shares to mass tort claimants that they then could sell on the capital markets in order to obtain needed cash. Unlike courts, lawyers, or futures representatives, investors in the capital markets would have a financial incentive to evaluate in an unbiased manner the magnitude of all future claims expected to emerge in the underlying litigation by the time that the trust is to be liquidated. The magnitude of future claims, in the aggregate, will affect the value of trust shares at the time of liquidation and, hence, the price at which those shares should trade on the capital markets at earlier times. Underestimates of future claims would only hurt investors, as any underestimates would lead them to overpay for trust shares.[63]

Smith's "capital markets" approach builds on Roe's recognition of the need to link the treatment of present claimants to the emergence of future ones. Rather than reform the structure for representation in mass tort bankruptcies, Smith would leave little for the representatives to do. The ability of capital markets to supplant flesh-and-blood representatives, however, turns on the emergence of what economists describe as "thick" markets—ones where large numbers of trades in the underlying shares would collate the available information in the marketplace as to the magnitude of future claims. As Smith acknowledges, shares in mass tort bankruptcy trusts would be "rather exotic securities."[64] Absent the emergence of a thick market for trust shares, prospective investors would have to devote their own resources to the development of estimates concerning future claims.

The result would be that shares would trade — if at all — only at sharply discounted prices to account for the cost of gathering information concerning their value. By linking the payout to mass tort claimants to the marketability of the trust shares, Smith inherently allocates to claimants the risk that a thick market might not develop in a given instance.[65]

The most recent addition to the literature on mass tort bankruptcies — a 2004 article by Yair Listokin and Kenneth Ayotte — builds on the insight that reorganization plans allocate not only resources but also risk.[66] Listokin and Ayotte observe that future claimants under any reorganization plan bear a substantially greater risk of resource misallocation than present ones and, accordingly, should receive higher payouts than present claimants to account for that risk. For Listokin and Ayotte, the means for improving risk allocation consists of the futures representative. By making the compensation for the futures representative contingent on the resources allocated to future claimants, Listokin and Ayotte would provide an incentive for that representative to be attentive to related questions of risk allocation.[67] For the reasons canvassed earlier, however, contingent compensation would address neither the meager bargaining leverage of the futures representative nor the incentive for him to pull his punches in order to become a repeat player.

The picture that emerges from existing commentary nonetheless is not a cause for discouragement. The story of prepackaged reorganizations actually helps one to assemble into a better whole the various components of the existing literature. Listokin and Ayotte are right to emphasize that reorganization plans inherently allocate risk as well as resources. The principal risk concerns the capacity of the plan do what §524(g) prescribes: to pay "in substantially the same manner" present and future claims that are similar in nature. At the same time, Roe and Smith are on to something important in their search for a mechanism to link present claimants with future ones. They simply misdirect the power of their insight, allocating risk to persons not well positioned to bear it (mass tort claimants) rather than to those with real power over the design of the reorganization plan on the claimants' side (the lawyers who control large inventories of claims). The challenge for mass tort bankruptcies consists of bringing to bear upon those lawyers — as distinct from claimants — the reality that resources devoted to their clients stand to reduce the likelihood of equitable treatment for future claimants who are otherwise similar in nature.

Prepackaged reorganizations like the one struck down in *Combustion Engineering* are rightly the focus of consternation, but not primarily for the reasons that observers have emphasized thus far. The real outrage of *Com-*

bustion Engineering is not that Joe Rice stood to gain a $20 million success fee from his representation of present claimants simultaneously with his design of a reorganization plan for future ones at the debtor's behest. The real outrage is that the law has yet to grapple candidly with the dynamic that *Combustion Engineering* exposes. Peacemaking in the mass tort setting involves the use of present claimants by plaintiffs' lawyers to assert a broader kind of power — namely, the power to set prospectively the terms under which future claimants shall have their rights of action in tort replaced with some alternative set of rights.

The two-trust structure in *Combustion Engineering* is problematic as a legal matter, for the reasons identified by the Third Circuit. But it at least exposes the unreality of the premise that a separate futures representative with no inventory of cases can function as a robust protector for future claimants. The idea of a futures representative seeks to paper over the true dynamics of peacemaking through a kind of dogged insistence that future claimants really have their own agent separate from those ostensibly representing only present ones. The idea of a futures representative misdirects our attention, however. Better to bring to bear the concerns of future claimants upon those who, as a functional matter, wield the real power to govern their rights: not primarily the futures representative but, rather, the lawyers for present claimants.

Chapter 11 of this book takes up the challenge that *Combustion Engineering* has brought into focus, casting that challenge as one that is not limited to the bankruptcy context but that forms the fundamental problem posed by any peace arrangement for mass tort litigation. Before one may proceed along that path, however, a further development in the period since *Amchem* bears exposition. If the making of peace in mass tort litigation entails an act of governance — if it involves the fashioning of binding rules for the handling of future claims — then one might think that having the government itself serve as plaintiff might mark an improvement in the peacemaking process. As the next chapter explains, turning the government into another form of mass tort plaintiff gets the direction of productive reform precisely backward.

CHAPTER X

GOVERNMENT AS
PLAINTIFF

T he preceding chapters reveal how the peacemaking process in mass tort litigation has come to operate as a rival regime of governance. If peacemaking involves a kind of governance, then one might think that the law would be better off by having the government undertake the litigation that leads to peace negotiations. The government, after all, is in the business of making difficult trade-offs and distilling competing considerations into public policy. This chapter explains why the idea of the government as plaintiff points the law of mass torts down a blind alley. Walking down blind alleys is not necessarily a pointless activity, but its value lies chiefly in enabling one to discern other, more productive paths to travel. So, too, with the idea of the government as plaintiff, as I shall explain.

The focus here is on a significant innovation that has come to stand side by side with tort suits on behalf of private claimants, whether on an individual or an aggregate basis. The 1990s saw the rise of government re-imbursement litigation — that is, lawsuits brought by the government at the federal, state, or local level to achieve two intertwined goals: (1) to recover the additional increment of expense to the public fisc alleged to stem from some manner of wrongdoing by the defendant industry in the past, and (2) to bring about changes in the ways that industry markets its products, so as to advance public health and safety in the future. The premise of government reimbursement litigation typically is that the underlying product will remain on the market in some form, not disappear entirely.

In 1998, government reimbursement litigation brought by the vast majority of state attorneys general on behalf of their respective governments led to the largest civil settlement in history: the Master Settlement Agreement (MSA), under which the major firms in the tobacco industry shall make annual payments to the states estimated to run in excess of $200 billion for the first twenty-five years and thereafter in perpetuity.[1] The MSA followed earlier settlements in which four states at the forefront of tobacco reimbursement litigation had resolved separately their respective actions against the defendant industry, each for its own multibillion-dollar stream of payments.

The state attorneys general did not work alone. Many retained on a contingency-fee basis several of the mass tort plaintiffs' lawyers already familiar from previous chapters—Ron Motley, Joe Rice, and Dickie Scruggs—as well as other prominent members of the plaintiffs' bar involved in tort litigation against the tobacco industry on behalf of smokers. Motley and Rice's firm ultimately represented a majority of the states in the union.[2] The multibillion-dollar payouts for the states under the MSA, in turn, led to fee awards ranging into the billions of dollars for the plaintiffs' bar, as determined through an arbitration process established in connection with the MSA.[3]

The significance of the MSA goes well beyond dollar figures, however. In operation, the MSA has made for a dramatic restructuring of the tobacco industry. One commentator does not exaggerate in characterizing the MSA as "a legal innovation in cartelization technology."[4] The terms of the MSA effectively have enabled the tobacco industry to do three things: to raise prices for current smokers far beyond the levels needed to fund the industry's payment obligations under the MSA, to split the resulting profits with the states, and to enlist the legislative apparatus of the states themselves to protect the industry cartel from competition that might undercut prices. Here is the image of settlement as a rival regime of law reform writ large.

All of this is not to suggest that boosting cigarette prices and suppressing competition to keep them up bear no connection at all to objectives within the aegis of government. Higher cigarette prices are capable of reducing the incidence of smoking—arguably, to do so especially among underage smokers. And the reduction of smoking bears more than a passing connection to the long-standing governmental interest in the protection of public health, apart from any financial repercussions for the government. Even so, one might very well question whether state-protected cartelization of the tobacco industry represents a credible public health strategy, not just a way to boost the dollar payouts for the states and the lawyers who negotiated on their behalf. The point remains that government reimbursement litigation puts into play two dimensions of government: what one might dub its "regulatory" and "proprietary" dimensions.

Broadly stated, governments do two things. They act to advance the public welfare, with health and safety being the most salient components. In addition, governments have a legal existence in themselves as proprietors.[5] They own property. They enter into contracts. They can sue and be sued in their own name, apart from the natural persons that run them. Governments might provide insurance to their citizens — indeed, sometimes may be better positioned to do so than private firms. In seeking reimbursement for the additional increment of expenditure said to flow from civil wrongdoing, the government invokes this proprietary dimension. The expenditures made under a public program are, on this account, no different from those that a private insurer might make by contract to cover the health expenses of its insureds. In seeking to shift those costs to the person alleged to be responsible for the harm — the tortfeasor said to have caused it — the government acts in the same way as a private proprietor in the business of insurance.

When wearing its proprietary hat, however, the government need not somehow shed its regulatory hat. Describing the objectives of the states in their reimbursement actions against the tobacco industry, one court accurately invokes a mixture of regulatory and proprietary goals: "to reduce teenage smoking, address public health concerns, and recoup state health care expenditures."[6] This mixture is not an anomalous feature of the tobacco litigation or of the particular expenditures for low-income persons under Medicaid that the states sought to recoup. One can see the same combination in government reimbursement litigation against the firearms industry. There, the plaintiffs consisted primarily of localities seeking reimbursement for the additional increment of expenditures by their police, emergency service, and other public programs said to result from wrongful industry marketing practices. The objectives of the litigation nonetheless were not exclusively proprietary. They also embraced the regulatory goal of protecting the public from gun violence.

The enterprise of this chapter is to show how identification of the regulatory and proprietary dimensions of government reimbursement litigation helps to pinpoint what is problematic about it as a framework for peacemaking. The usual pathology in peacemaking involves collusion between mass tort plaintiffs' lawyers and defendants with regard to the peace terms. Making peace involves making difficult trade-offs between present and future claimants, trade-offs that go to the allocation of resources and risk. The law rightly is reluctant to accord binding force to arrangements — whether styled as class settlements, reorganizations in bankruptcy, or otherwise — that generate little confidence that the trade-offs made are likely to reflect a reasoned evaluation of the competing considerations, not simply the self-interest of those crafting the deal. One, for example, does not want the distinction between present and future claimants to form the axis for collusion between the peacemakers on both sides.

The axis for collusion in government reimbursement litigation relates closely to the combination of regulatory and proprietary dimensions, not just in the litigation to be settled but also in government itself. The involvement of the government as plaintiff expands the potential domain for collusion, because the government as regulator is uniquely empowered to lend its imprimatur to measures that could not lawfully be implemented as part of a peace brokered by private parties alone. The cartelization that has arisen from the MSA, for example, would stand no realistic chance of surviving scrutiny under the antitrust laws absent the involvement of the states. The important point, however, is not simply that the MSA fostered cartelization. Boosting cigarette prices by way of a state-protected cartel bears at least some connection to the protection of public health, just as the class settlement in *Amchem* or the original reorganization plan in *Combustion Engineering* would have provided at least some compensation to future claimants. The point, instead, is one that strikes a familiar chord.

The structure of government reimbursement litigation does not yield confidence that peacemaking through the vehicle of settlement will involve reasoned trade-offs between regulatory and proprietary goals, as distinct from trade-offs that simply serve the interests of the peace designers. When making peace, defendants can play on the combination of regulatory and proprietary dimensions in government in the same way that they can play on the combined representation of present and future claimants by mass tort plaintiffs' lawyers. Situating the government as plaintiff, without more, does not solve the governance problem in peacemaking. It replicates — even accentuates — the problem in a new setting.

This chapter traces the rise and operation of government reimbursement litigation as a vehicle for peace. The chapter starts with an explanation of why government reimbursement litigation emerged only in the 1990s as a feature of the legal landscape for mass torts. The chapter then situates government reimbursement litigation in continuity with the preceding discussion of aggregation techniques as vehicles for peacemaking. The capacity of government reimbursement litigation to induce settlement — in the case of the MSA, to do so based on novel legal arguments largely untested in court — sheds additional light on the discussion in chapter 3 of the settlement pressure that flows from aggregation. Here, I offer an explanation of why government reimbursement litigation produced the largest civil settlement in history in the tobacco litigation but made comparatively few inroads against the firearms industry. The answer turns, in substantial part, on the very size and resource advantages that the tobacco industry previously had deployed to fend off tort liability.

The chapter next turns to the confluence of regulatory and proprietary goals in government reimbursement litigation, tracing the path to the MSA and translating the technicalities of that deal into understandable terms. The chapter concludes by fitting the lessons learned about the government as plaintiff within the broader thrust of my argument. The rough analogue here to the *Amchem* Court's notion of separate representation for present and future claimants would be a strict insistence upon separation of the government's regulatory and proprietary dimensions. I argue that such a separation principle is even more unrealistic in the government setting than it is for peacemaking through private negotiations. I then chart a path out of the blind alley created by the idea of the government as plaintiff. The path out involves casting attention away from notions of separation—whether based on types of claimants or dimensions of government—and toward the project of aligning the interests of the peace designers with the making of reasoned trade-offs between competing goals. One can see faint glimmers of that project in some facets of the tobacco litigation. The project in a fuller form shall occupy the concluding chapters of the book.

Explaining the Emergence of Government Reimbursement Litigation

That government reimbursement litigation should have emerged only in the 1990s initially might seem something of a puzzle. Governments, after all, have been paying for public benefit programs of various sorts for decades. The risks to public health posed by smoking and guns have been part of long-running debates in public policy. In academic writing, the first suggestion of government reimbursement litigation against the tobacco industry appears in a 1977 law review article by Donald Gardner.[7] Why did it take nearly two more decades for the idea to come to fruition in practice? The explanation rests on several developments that would coalesce by the mid-1990s.

The story begins with the prior history of tort litigation against the tobacco industry. Existing scholarship documents that rich history, enabling me to compress the narrative here.[8] One observer neatly summarizes the bottom line for tobacco defendants in litigation through the early 1990s:

"Eight hundred and thirteen claims filed against the industry, twenty-three tried in court, two lost, both overturned on appeal. Not a penny paid in damages."[9] This remarkable track record for defendants stemmed from two related features of early tobacco litigation: the capitalization of the lawyers on the plaintiffs' side and the individual nature of the lawsuits they brought.

An infamous internal memorandum prepared in 1988 by an attorney for R.J. Reynolds Tobacco Company invokes the war rhetoric of General George S. Patton to describe the litigation strategy of the industry: "[T]he way we won these cases was not by spending all of [R.J. Reynolds's] money, but by making that other son of a bitch spend all of his."[10] Put less vividly, the bigness of Big Tobacco — the defendants' position as part of multibillion-dollar corporations — enabled the industry to wear down its opponents. Tobacco defendants could spread the costs of discovery across all claims they faced, whereas plaintiffs' counsel could spread the costs on their side of the litigation only across their particular individual clients. The individual nature of early tobacco cases also enabled the industry to shape its defense on the merits around what remains to this day a powerful obstacle to tobacco liability in tort: the widespread sense that smoking is a matter of individual choice, such as to relieve product manufacturers from responsibility for the ills that result. By the mid-1990s, the critical challenges for plaintiffs' lawyers in tobacco litigation thus consisted of addressing their own undercapitalization and, at the same time, shifting attention away from the individual smoker. Asbestos and aggregation, together, would point the way.

By the mid-1990s, the success of the mass tort plaintiffs' bar in the asbestos litigation had left many of its leaders with formidable financial resources, enough to litigate on something closer to a level playing field with tobacco defendants. One journalistic account of the renewed interest in tobacco litigation during this period quotes asbestos plaintiffs' lawyer Dickie Scruggs as looking specifically for an opportunity to "reinvest" his capital in a new type of client.[11] The sheer amount of money made available by the asbestos litigation is only part of the story, however. Having more money on hand may well have made asbestos plaintiffs' lawyers more willing to take risks in the pursuit of new, uncharted areas. Multiple accounts trace the idea of government reimbursement litigation in the tobacco context to informal brainstorming involving Scruggs, other asbestos plaintiffs' lawyers, and Mississippi Attorney General Michael Moore, with whom those lawyers had long-standing personal and professional connections.[12] Moore later emerged as a first-mover in government reimbursement litigation against the tobacco industry, ultimately persuading his peers in other states to file similar actions.

Aggregation, too, would help to address undercapitalization by raising dramatically the potential payout from a successful tobacco case and thereby supporting additional investment in its development by the plaintiffs' lawyers involved. Aggregation also made for economies of scale in discovery. By the mid-1990s, the tobacco litigation would look very different from its previous incarnations. Its signature features — class action litigation on behalf of smokers and the emergence of government reimbursement litigation by the states — reflect the desire to find a viable path to aggregation.

A consortium of mass tort plaintiffs' lawyers provided both the financing and the strategic thinking for class action litigation. The consortium would come to be known as the "Castano group," after the name of the class action that it filed in federal court on behalf of a proposed plaintiff class comprised of smokers nationwide. This attempt at nationwide class treatment ultimately failed, with the United States Court of Appeals for the Fifth Circuit overturning the class certification in 1996. The proposed plaintiff class in *Castano v. American Tobacco Co.*, the court said, would have lumped together smokers in widely different factual circumstances, persons whose claims against the tobacco industry would be governed by subtly different bodies of state tort law.[13] The decertification of the nationwide class in *Castano* led to efforts to certify classes of smokers on a state-by-state basis. But that, too, proved unavailing, for even a statewide class governed by a single body of tort law would encompass widely divergent smokers. One such class for Florida smokers — *Engle v. R. J. Reynolds Tobacco Co.* — did produce an eye-popping punitive damage award of $144.8 billion at the trial level in 2000. But appellate review overturned the class certification in *Engle* that had provided the predicate for that award.[14]

The class action device was not the only possible route to aggregation, however. Government reimbursement litigation also held the promise of framing the costs of smoking in the aggregate — if not in terms of the diseases suffered by smokers themselves, then based on the additional increment of cost borne by the states under Medicaid. Although the costs at issue differ, both government reimbursement litigation and class actions promised to raise sufficiently the stakes of a given lawsuit and, in so doing, to undercut the defendants' spending advantage. Litigation by the government rather than by an aggregation of private plaintiffs carried a further advantage that was far from incidental. By suing in its own right, the government could position itself as the advocate for its citizens who had never smoked but who, nonetheless, shared in the cost to the public fisc arising from smoking-related disease. The individual diseased smoker whom the industry might depict as having gotten what she bargained for would be replaced by the notion of the "innocent" taxpayers made to pay for the conduct of others.[15]

By the mid-1990s, then, the money provided by the asbestos litigation came together with the recognition of the need for aggregation on the plaintiffs' side of the tobacco litigation. Serendipity also played a supporting role. The same period saw the release of the first trove of what ultimately would come to be reams of internal industry documents.[16] The documents discussed with startling candor the tobacco industry's suppression of information concerning the risks of smoking and, further, its manipulation of nicotine, the addictive substance in cigarettes. The idea of nicotine addiction formed the basis for the assertion by the Food and Drug Administration of regulatory authority over the tobacco industry on the ground that nicotine is a "drug." In 2000, the Supreme Court turned away that effort by a closely divided vote, holding that the federal food and drug laws do not reach tobacco products.[17] The focus on nicotine addiction nonetheless added to the image of product manufacturers as cynical manipulators and, at the same time, undercut their assertions that smokers make a simple individual choice in continuing to smoke.

The damning nature of the words from the defendants' own mouths heightened the sense that a win for a plaintiff—whomever it might be and whatever the theory of liability—could generate a whopping punitive damage award. The implication for aggregate litigation was even more dramatic. The willingness of a jury to find some underlying liability on an aggregate basis might well be the only real firewall standing between tobacco defendants and a punitive damage calculus that could threaten their viability. The possibility of a lucky hit that might push the tobacco defendants into bankruptcy added mightily to the desirability of settlement in the state reimbursement suits, even before the industry confronted the $145 billion punitive damage award at trial in the *Engle* class action.

The emergence of government reimbursement litigation in the tobacco context—especially its capacity to precipitate settlement—formed a template for similar lawsuits by localities against the firearms industry. There, individual plaintiffs did not face quite as steep of a disadvantage in capitalization vis-à-vis the defendant industry, a point of contrast to which I shall return. Individual litigation nonetheless had proven difficult. True, there was little sense that shooting victims somehow bear responsibility for their own injuries. But victims did have great difficulty demonstrating a sufficiently close connection between particular incidents of gun violence and the industry marketing practices said to constitute negligence in tort. As in the tobacco litigation, government reimbursement litigation held the promise of reframing the dispute from an aggregate perspective. The question no longer would be whether the marketing practices of the industry caused a particular shooting but, rather, whether they made for some additional increment of public expense related to gun violence. The workings of this aggregate perspective — its bearings in legal doctrine and its settlement implications — are the topics to which I now turn.

Doctrinal Labels

Strictly speaking, many kinds of government reimbursement actions are not tort suits in the same sense as individual tort claims or an aggregation of many such claims in a class action. The term "government reimbursement litigation" makes for a useful description precisely because it can encompass the mixture of doctrines, from both outside and inside tort law, that might lie behind a given lawsuit. Doctrinal labels ultimately are less important to government reimbursement litigation than its strategic dynamics. A brief word about doctrine nonetheless is helpful at the outset. Different doctrinal labels are invoked in different settings. But, for the most part, they speak to the same basic idea behind the demand for reimbursement. I do not purport to present here an exhaustive map of all the labels invoked in government reimbursement litigation but, rather, use the most prominent ones to illustrate the basic nature of the government's claim.

In the tobacco litigation, government reimbursement suits are more properly described as mass restitution actions than as mass torts per se. The notion of torts committed upon many individuals nonetheless remains close at hand. The most straightforward formulation of the demand for reimbursement in the tobacco litigation invokes a mixture of restitution and tort concepts. The claim is that the tobacco industry would be unjustly enriched were it not to make restitution to the states — to pay them back — for the Medicaid funds they expended for the care of smokers as a result of the industry's own misconduct. The most common formulations of the underlying misconduct speak in terms of misrepresentation and deception of smokers, behavior that might form the basis for tort actions by smokers themselves against the industry. The underlying misconduct on the industry's part might take nontort forms as well: say, violation of a state consumer fraud statute or, in the case of the federal government's reimbursement action filed after the state MSA, violation of the federal racketeering statute.[18] Some special features of the federal reimbursement lawsuit enable one to pinpoint with unusual clarity its regulatory and proprietary dimensions, a matter on which I elaborate later in this chapter.

In the firearms litigation, the doctrinal label most commonly invoked as the basis for government reimbursement litigation is one drawn entirely from tort law itself. Here, many localities sued the firearms industry on the theory that its marketing practices created a public nuisance. Localities typically sued firearms distributors in addition to manufacturers, but I focus here on the latter to underscore the similarity with the state reimbursement actions in the tobacco context.

The concept of a public nuisance remains highly amorphous in tort law. The authors of one prominent treatise go so far as to say that "[t]here is perhaps no more impenetrable jungle in the entire law than that which surrounds the word 'nuisance.'"[19] The concept of a "private nuisance" in tort remains tied to an interference with the plaintiff's use or enjoyment of her land. The notion of a "public nuisance" reaches more broadly, encompassing "an unreasonable inference with a right common to the general public" in the words of the widely cited Restatement (Second) of Torts.[20] Classic situations in this category include public nuisance lawsuits directed against houses of prostitution or properties emitting noxious odors. The Restatement goes on to note that the requisite "public right" is "collective in nature and not like the individual right that everyone has not to be assaulted or defamed or defrauded or negligently injured."[21] Drawing on this language, some courts have plausibly questioned whether any public right implicated by the marketing practices of the firearms industry is, at bottom, anything other than an aggregation of many individuals' rights not to be assaulted or negligently injured.[22]

In short, government reimbursement actions against the firearms industry—like their counterparts in the tobacco setting—focus on the additional cost to the public fisc from some underlying misconduct on the defendants' part vis-à-vis private persons. The underlying misconduct is what makes the interference with a public right unreasonable. The misconduct alleged here takes a variety of forms that sound a general theme of negligent marketing: deficiencies in the oversight of gun retailers by manufacturers; the design and marketing of guns by manufacturers to appeal to persons who intend to use them in criminal activities; and conscious industry "saturation" of markets with less restrictive gun control laws, such that many of the guns sold there find their way illegally into jurisdictions (the plaintiff localities) that have comparatively strict gun laws. Again, some underlying misconduct sounding in tort—though, perhaps, not exclusively so—provides the predicate for the government's demand for reimbursement.[23]

Settlement Pressure Revisited

To lay out the doctrinal labels invoked in government reimbursement litigation is not to suggest that doctrine provides anything like a clear-cut endorsement for such lawsuits. Government reimbursement litigation against
the tobacco industry produced a multibillion-dollar settlement even while
the doctrinal basis for the litigation remained essentially untested. As tort
scholar Gary Schwartz observes, "never has so much money changed
hands on account of lawsuits in which the legal theories have been so uncertain."[24]

The principal point of uncertainty centers on whether a given demand
for reimbursement on the part of the states — however couched — is independent from the commission of some wrong by the defendant industry
with respect to smokers. Recall that one of the major attractions of aggregation by way of the government suits lies in the possibility that it might
cast attention away from the responsibility that smokers might bear for
their ills. But if the states have been harmed financially in a manner that
warrants reimbursement only insofar as smokers have been wronged by
the defendant industry, then a determination of the reimbursement due to
the states seemingly would have to confront questions of responsibility as
between the industry and smokers — exactly what reimbursement actions
seek to avoid. Even where the wrong takes the form of misrepresentation
or fraud, individualized questions might arise about the extent to which
smokers relied upon the industry's dissembling in such a way as to make
their later manifestations of disease something for which the industry bears
at least some responsibility.[25]

Government reimbursement litigation against the firearms industry
produced the opposite result from tobacco: plenty of doctrinal testing and
no settlement. Put bluntly, the litigation was largely unsuccessful, though
one can say that with hindsight only because the defendants — with one
intermittent exception — chose to fight rather than to settle. A large number of judicial decisions dismissed reimbursement actions on legal grounds
prior to trial. The doctrinal cubbyholes for those dismissals were many:
for example, a reluctance to deem as a public nuisance the marketing of a
product in compliance with extant regulatory requirements, whatever their
arguable shortcomings;[26] the lack of a legal duty on the part of firearms
manufacturers to safeguard the public at large against the risk of injury
from criminal misuse of firearms by persons outside the manufacturers'
control;[27] and, on a related note, the absence of a close causal connection
between the disputed marketing practices of the industry and the harms
suffered by the public at the hands of violent criminals.[28]

After litigation costs mounted, two prominent localities—Boston and Cincinnati—voluntary dismissed their actions on the advice of the mass tort plaintiffs' lawyers retained as their counsel.[29] Still other localities found their actions foreclosed by subsequent legislation in thirty states disempowering them from suing the firearms industry.[30] In 2005, Congress sounded a similar note, generally barring civil lawsuits against firearms dealers, manufacturers, or trade associations for any form of relief resulting from the "criminal or unlawful misuse" of a firearm by a third party.[31] Some lingering uncertainty nonetheless remains over the impact of this prohibition. As of late 2006, at least one district court permitted New York City's action against the firearms industry to continue forward under one of the narrowly drawn exceptions in the federal statute.[32]

Even prior to the federal legislation, the one instance of settlement by the firm that was, at the time, the largest manufacturer in the industry—Smith & Wesson Corporation—proved to be short lived. In 2000, Smith & Wesson agreed to a "Code of Conduct" for its marketing of guns, unaccompanied by any dollar payouts. Its counterpart in the deal consisted of the Department of Housing and Urban Development in the Clinton administration, which was coordinating the efforts of local authorities to prepare lawsuits alleging that gun marketing practices had contributed to violence in public housing projects.[33] Upon entering office in 2001, the Bush administration rescinded the deal, deeming it simply a "memorandum of understanding" that did not actually bind either side. And, apart from the change of administrations, a boycott of Smith & Wesson by gun buyers infuriated at its willingness to settle had left the company "in ruins," such that even adherence to the marketing code would have had little impact.[34]

All of this raises a question unexplored in the scholarly literature: Congressional action aside, what explains the starkly divergent results for government reimbursement litigation in the tobacco and firearms settings? The explanation is multifaceted and entails a degree of speculation due to limitations of information that I shall describe. Doctrine is part of the story. The connection between the misrepresentations of the tobacco industry and some additional increment of smoking-related disease is more straightforward—at least by comparison—than the connection between the disputed marketing practices of the firearms industry and some additional increment of gun violence. The latter situation involves an intermediate actor engaged in the highest grade of misconduct known to the law: a crime. Tort law has long been reluctant to obligate one set of persons to take steps to prevent another set of persons from committing crimes against a broad class of potential victims. The situations in which tort law has done so have tended to involve special relationships — say, between apartment owners and their tenants — that go beyond the placement of a risky product in the stream of commerce and that create the conditions for the defendant to serve as a frontline safeguard against criminal misdeeds.[35] There is more to the story than doctrine, however.

As chapter 3 observed, the pressure to settle exerted by the aggregation of litigation — whether by procedural rule in a class action or, indirectly, through the government's status as plaintiff — stems from the greater variance in outcomes posed by the aggregate proceeding. Defendants will be more willing to settle when the aggregate proceeding carries the possibility of a firm-threatening damage award rather than payouts across multiple, individual cases that are more likely to conform to the expected value of the litigation overall. The connection between settlement and variance serves to direct attention to an additional distinguishing feature in the tobacco setting.

Government reimbursement suits against the tobacco industry could rely on scores of internal documents detailing the industry's long-standing campaign to mislead smokers. As noted earlier, the documents raised the possibility of a huge punitive damage award if a given reimbursement action somehow could manage to get over the initial hurdle of liability. There is more to the explanation, however, than the possibility of punitive damages by itself. The prospect that the industry might be able to fend off liability in the vast majority of reimbursement suits would be unavailing if the punitive damages from a few — maybe just one, if the plaintiff state were large enough — would render the industry insolvent. To contest the reimbursement actions seriatim rather than settling them together, the industry effectively would have to bet its future on the prospect that it could beat the rap, not just in most instances but in virtually all instances.

The existing literature on the tobacco litigation recognizes the foregoing points about punitive damages and the multiplicity of fora in which the industry would have to prevail in order to forestall a ruinous award.[36] What remains unexplained is the contrast in result for government reimbursement litigation against the firearms industry, pre-federal legislation. True enough, punitive damages were much less of a threat due to the absence thus far of telltale internal documents. In addition, the status of the plaintiff governments as localities rather than entire states, for the most part, ratcheted down the magnitude of the sums they could seek as reimbursement. The variance in outcomes attributable to aggregate treatment thus was less in the firearms context, even though it too involved litigation in multiple fora.

The magnitude of the variance in potential outcomes is only part of the story, however. Variance contributes to settlement pressure only in combination with aversion to risk on the defendants' part.[37] Much less is known about the finances of the firearms industry as compared to the tobacco industry. But the information that is available suggests a genuine possibility of differences in risk aversion that would translate into a greater willingness on the part of the firearms industry to stand and fight.

The major players of the tobacco industry are part of large, publicly traded corporations with diverse product lines.[38] The consequence is that the uncertainty arising from tobacco litigation—especially, litigation with the potential to threaten the viability of a given firm—makes for a significant drag on the firm's share price. Reduction of that uncertainty through settlement thus holds the promise of considerable gains for shareholders. Industry share prices then would reflect the profitability of the firm's entire product line, with less of a discount for the liability risk arising from its tobacco components. By contrast, virtually all of the major manufacturers of firearms in the United States are privately held companies. In addition, as one leading authority on the industry observes, "[a] number of other major domestic gun-makers are subsidiaries of secretive foreign companies."[39] As a result, "next to nothing is publicly available about the finances of the gun industry."[40]

Litigation of all sorts against the tobacco and firearms industries is not just a matter of money. It also implicates the cultural meaning of smoking and guns.[41] I do not purport to advance objectively verifiable insights on the ideology of those running the major tobacco firms or the major firearms makers. But it stands to reason that, even aside from the obvious financial motivations, those who run firms that make controversial products are likely to have atypically positive views about the broader cultural meaning of their wares—for tobacco executives to believe that the world really is better off with people able to enjoy the pleasures of smoking, its health risks and broader social costs notwithstanding, and for firearms executives to believe that the world is better off with relatively unimpeded availability of guns, even though they can be misused in crime. Persons with such views are likely to regard litigation challenges of all sorts—perhaps, especially when brought by the government—not as being just about money but as part of larger efforts to recast the social meaning of their respective products and, hence, as things to be resisted steadfastly. The notion of gun availability as a bulwark against government tyranny, for example, is a familiar theme sounded in favor of a broadened reading for the Second Amendment to the Constitution.[42]

Ideology and corporate finance are likely to interact differently in the tobacco and firearms settings. Those running publicly held firms must temper any ideology on their own part in light of the wishes of a broad cross-segment of investors who, as such, are much less likely to attach intense cultural significance to the sale of the product. They are more likely, instead, to regard their shares in the firm for what they are: simply as investments, like any other investment. Sophisticated capital markets have less room for ideology as such. For that matter, publicly traded firms tend to be run by professional managers who are less apt to be deeply committed to any particular product line as an ideological matter. One accordingly should not be surprised to find less risk taking in litigation over a controversial product marketed by publicly traded firms. For privately held firms, by contrast, those running the litigation on the defense side are more likely to have both an ideological allegiance to their product and a greater degree of latitude to act on it.

There is more than a hint of irony here. On this account, a major contributing factor to the multibillion-dollar tobacco settlement arises from the very feature that, earlier, had given tobacco defendants the upper hand: the bigness of Big Tobacco itself. To explain the tendency toward settlement in the tobacco situation, nonetheless, is to leave open an even more important aspect of the litigation. For any set of defendants, the attractiveness of settlement depends on the terms they realistically might seek to obtain from the government in a deal. As I now explain, the feature that makes government reimbursement litigation a problematic framework for peacemaking lies in the nature of government itself: its combination of both regulatory and proprietary dimensions that defendants can play off in peace negotiations for their own ends. The MSA precipitated by the state reimbursement actions against the tobacco industry stands as a primer in this regard.

The Regulatory and Proprietary Dimensions of the MSA

Before one may analyze the content of the MSA, a brief account of its genesis is in order. The provisions of the MSA represent a slimmed down version of the peace arrangement originally designed by the states and the tobacco industry in the summer of 1997. The original deal and its demise occupy the first portion of the discussion here. I then turn to the MSA itself, explaining its intricacies in terms of the contrast drawn earlier between the regulatory and proprietary dimensions of government.

From Proposed Federal Legislation to the MSA
As originally framed, the deal between the states and the tobacco industry took the form of an ambitious proposal for federal legislation that prom-

ised a grand peace for the tobacco wars.[43] From the industry, the proposal called for a stream of annual payments to the states estimated to total $368.5 billion, one-third of which would be earmarked for use to combat teen smoking. The proposal contained an array of restrictions on tobacco advertisement and would have ratcheted up the payments required from the industry if specified targets for reductions in teen smoking were not met over time. The proposal also would have conferred statutory authority for the FDA to regulate tobacco products.

In exchange, the proposal would have afforded the industry considerable protection against liability, not only by settling the states' reimbursement suits but also by constraining private litigation. The proposal would have barred class actions or similar consolidated treatment of claims by smokers and would have prohibited punitive damages in the remaining individual actions. The proposal also contained a formula that, in practical effect, would have capped the funds available to pay individual plaintiffs at $5 billion annually and credited 80 percent of any funds actually expended against the industry's obligation to pay the states. In operation, the formula would have reduced the cost of any liability ultimately found in individual cases, such that each dollar paid to plaintiffs — up to the $5 billion annual cap — would cost only 20 cents.[44] Finally, the proposal included a sweeping grant of antitrust immunity for activities that the tobacco companies might undertake in coordination with one another to fulfill their obligations under the deal.

The willingness of the tobacco industry to embrace the foregoing peace package represented a sharp break from its previous stance. An industry that had resisted any manner of payment with remarkable success suddenly agreed to pay hundreds of billions of dollars over time. The sea change on the industry's part would color the politics of the proposal once it reached Congress. Critics of the tobacco industry in the public health community and within Congress itself reportedly took the industry's willingness to support the proposed legislation as evidence of an even greater willingness to pay for peace. If the industry was prepared to pay $368.5 billion to the states, then it seemingly "could be squeezed for much more."[45]

Given the ultimate content of the MSA, one might say with hindsight that antitobacco forces overplayed their hand in Congress. The major changes to the peace arrangement upon congressional consideration consisted of a dramatic increase in its price tag — to $516 billion — and the removal of the liability protections. Not surprisingly, the industry balked at the notion of paying much more money for much less peace. In the end, the industry actively campaigned against the revised federal bill, casting it as "half a trillion [dollars] in new taxes" that would go to support "17 new bureaucracies."[46] The proposed legislation died in Congress in mid-1998.

The demise of federal legislation nevertheless did not spell the end of efforts to settle the state reimbursement actions. Some features of the original proposal — the various liability protections against private litigation and the conferral of regulatory power on the FDA — could be achieved only through legislation. But other features could be repackaged simply as settlements of the state reimbursement suits. In short order, the industry entered into separate settlements with the four states — Mississippi, Florida, Texas, and Minnesota — whose reimbursement actions were moving most rapidly toward trial. The run-up to the proposed federal legislation had induced virtually all of the other states across the country to join the reimbursement litigation, with the only outliers consisting of a few tobacco-producing states. In late 1998, the MSA resolved the remaining state lawsuits.

Cooperation by the plaintiff states in the MSA negotiations did not stem from conscious initial coordination of their lawsuits. Cooperation instead "emerged" from what Thomas Schmeling describes as "a process of interdependent decision-making." The prospects for state reimbursement suits to induce settlement in any given instance turned on presentation of the industry with the disheartening prospect of having to win in virtually all of a large total number of states. Initial filings by states like Mississippi encouraged a few other states to file their own actions. The presence of several plaintiff states then increased the chances of precipitating settlement, thereby inducing still other states more skeptical about the cause to join "until the process 'snowballed.'"[47]

The four early settlements may have formed a modest additional impetus for the remaining states to move together toward a deal. The costs of the settlements for Mississippi, Florida, Texas, and Minnesota were to be funded by price increases for cigarettes sold throughout the country. Absent a deal for the remaining states, consumers in each would have ended up subsidizing the payments to the four initial settlers. Newfound cooperation was not the dominant theme of the MSA only on the plaintiff states' side, however. The enduring impact of the MSA centers on the cooperation it both induces and insulates against attack on the industry side.

Settlement as Cartel

Absent the kinds of liability protections available only through legislation, what exactly did the industry get in the MSA for its agreement to pay the states hundreds of billions of dollars — indeed, to keep doing so in perpetuity? In effect, a nationwide cartel. The major tobacco firms gained the ability to raise dramatically the price of cigarettes while protecting themselves from competition that might beat down that price. In practice, the MSA amounts to the kind of tax hike for present-day smokers that the industry had depicted as undesirable public policy in its campaign against the proposed federal legislation.

Cartels usually are unstable things. The members of any industry, of course, would like to increase prices well beyond competitive levels. But the problem with doing so is that it induces efforts to undercut the cartel price, whether through defection from the cartel by its own members, expansion by smaller fringe players outside the cartel, or entry into the market by new firms.[48] The attraction of the MSA from the standpoint of the major tobacco firms lies in its promise to constrain defection, expansion, and entry, all in one fell swoop.

The obligation of each signatory defendant to maintain a multibillion-dollar stream of payments to the states in perpetuity would induce each to raise its prices and, thereafter, to act as an ongoing source of pressure to keep prices up. One might say that the signature pages for the settling defendants at the end of the MSA literally constituted — they defined and brought into being — the membership of the cartel. The allocation of the payments required from the settling defendants and the resulting price hikes for their cigarettes bear examination, for they reveal the intermingling of regulatory and proprietary themes in the MSA.

Consider initially the nature of the industry payments. One might expect the payment obligations of particular settling defendants to bear some connection to the idea behind the state reimbursement lawsuits in the first place — the notion of an additional increment of smoking-related disease attributable to industry misdeeds over the span of many decades. The payment grid of the MSA, however, bears little connection to even a rough guess about the various defendants' relative responsibility for the past ills of smokers. Payments instead track the settling defendants' *current* market shares, as manifested in units of present-day sales across the country. Philip Morris, for example, leads the industry with roughly a 50 percent market share today. It bears a commensurate share of the MSA payment load, even though it has only a 23 percent market share for all sales since 1950.[49]

The allocation of payments among the various states bears more of a connection to their relative Medicaid expenditures for smokers. But, even here, the connection is only a loose one. A comprehensive analysis of the MSA allocation formula for the states reveals that many received more than their relative share of Medicaid costs — in some instances, over 70 percent more — whereas others received substantially less. But, here, at least, the differences might stem from the relative political bargaining power of the various states in the MSA negotiations.[50] Perhaps the most striking feature of the allocation formula is its inclusion of the tobacco-producing states that had not even filed reimbursement actions. The strategic reason for their inclusion shall become apparent later, after consideration of the conditions imposed on all states' receipt of MSA payouts.

Allocation of the MSA payments is not the only notable feature of the deal. The magnitude of the resulting price hikes is also striking. The industry could have funded its obligations under the MSA with a cigarette price increase in the neighborhood of 19 cents per pack. The major tobacco manufacturers, however, implemented a 45-cents-per-pack increase at the time of their initial implementation of the MSA, a price hike that would rise even further to a total of 76 cents per pack by the mid-2000s.[51] One commentator observes that the magnitude of the implicit cigarette tax resulting from the MSA "bears no reasonable relationship to any of the estimated costs of cigarettes," even if "only medical costs incurred by the states enter the tally, and one excludes any cost savings due to cigarettes."[52]

If the proprietary dimension of the state reimbursement actions were the only benchmark here, then the MSA would seem a curious deal indeed. The inducement of price hikes beyond the levels needed to fund the MSA does bear at least some connection, however, to the regulatory dimension of the litigation. Demand for cigarettes is relatively inelastic. Smokers will tend to keep smoking as prices rise more so than consumers of less addictive products faced with price increases. Still, smoking is not completely impervious to the laws of supply and demand. Reviews of the available empirical studies suggest that a 10 percent increase in cigarette prices reduces overall cigarette consumption by 2.5 to 7 percent.[53] Some research suggests that the dampening effect on demand may be stronger among teenagers, due to their greater financial constraints.[54]

Untangling the effects of the MSA from other possible influences on smoking rates in recent years is a difficult endeavor. But, even without advancing firm conclusions about cause and effect, one may observe that the MSA corresponds in time with the reversal of a previous upward trend in smoking among high school students. Smoking by high school students rose 33 percent from 1991 to 1997—the year before the MSA—but subsequently has dropped by nearly 40 percent.[55] As for smoking by persons of all ages, the Centers for Disease Control document a "sustained decline," though one that started before the MSA.[56]

To observe that cartel-like pricing may have had some beneficial impact on smoking rates nonetheless is not to say that it was the only means to advance the states' regulatory goal. A wholehearted commitment to use price hikes to reduce smoking would have produced a different calculus for industry payments under the MSA. The implicit tax on cigarettes associated with the MSA is a "specific" tax, one based on the units of cigarettes sold. In economics, a specific tax stands in contrast to an "ad valorem" tax that looks not to product units but, instead, to price — say, a tax of 10 cents for every dollar of cigarette prices. An ad valorem tax effectively taxes all costs that go into the product, including advertising costs, whereas a specific tax hones on only one attribute: quantity. The difference is not incidental, given the interests of the major tobacco firms. Economists Jeremy Bulow and Paul Klemperer observe that "specific taxes encourage firms to produce and market high-price and highly promoted premium brands, while ad valorem taxes encourage the sale of low-priced generics."[57] Premium brands are precisely where the major tobacco firms hold a competitive advantage, having already established those brands — Marlboro, Camel, and the like — in the marketplace.

The industry did agree in the MSA to restrictions concerning the advertising of cigarettes through avenues with tendencies to reach teens — albeit, less stringent limits in some respects than those in the proposed federal legislation.[58] But even the MSA restrictions are a double-edged sword, notwithstanding the reduction in teen smoking since the MSA. Absent the advertising restrictions in the MSA, the tobacco industry was spending millions to promote its wares to new smokers who had yet to settle on particular brands of cigarettes. If the major players in the industry instead could agree — even better, could be obligated by the MSA — to eliminate those expenses, then they might increase their profits notwithstanding a decline in the number of new consumers. "The companies would . . . effectively be trading three customers for whom they had competed fiercely for two customers on whom they would earn monopoly profits."[59]

To be sure, any defendant might aspire to pass along the costs of a multibillion-dollar settlement to its consumers in the form of product price increases. Doing so effectively would redistribute the financial burden of the settlement to present-day consumers from the shareholders of the defendant firm. The usual constraint upon this approach, however, consists of the opportunity for other firms outside the deal to compete away the price hike. The most distinctive features of the MSA consist of those that attempt to guard against this possibility — indeed, that could try to do so through means short of legislation *only* because of the state governments' status as plaintiffs.

The MSA did not leave to chance the ability of the settling defendants to boost prices beyond their settlement obligations and to make those price hikes stick. The MSA used both a carrot and a stick to address the possibility of price competition, whether through expansion of existing firms or entry of new ones. The carrot consisted of terms whereby small, fringe firms not named as defendants in the state reimbursement suits — chiefly, the Liggett Group, which had settled previously with the states — could sign on to the MSA nonetheless. Upon doing so, fringe firms could keep their future revenues up to 125 percent of their respective levels immediately prior to the MSA.

As a way to guard against price competition, this carrot proved to be a mixed blessing for the major firms. On the one hand, it did foreclose the possibility that fringe firms might compete with the majors without any MSA-related obligations whatsoever. On the other hand, the carrot provided for participation in the MSA effectively enabled fringe firms to pay the states based only on sales markedly above their preexisting market shares, whereas the major firms had to pay based on all their units sold. Not surprisingly, by 2003, the market share of fringe firms had increased to 7.3 percent from 2.6 percent before the MSA.[60]

The stick consisted of inducements for the enactment of state legislation to require any remaining nonsignatories to the MSA — chiefly, subsequent entrants to the tobacco industry — to make escrow payments to the states. An exhibit appended to the MSA even set forth a model text for the desired state laws.[61] The ostensible public policy justification for the escrow payments would be to address the possibility of state reimbursement litigation in the future against firms not named as defendants by the states. As the term "escrow" suggests, the states would have to return the payments made by nonsignatories if no liability were shown. But the states' obligation to return the payments would arise only after twenty-five years. Cast as escrow payments, moreover, the required sums would not be tax deductible, unlike the settlement payments required under the MSA. The net effect would be to place nonsignatories at a cost disadvantage in any effort to compete with firms covered by the MSA. The escrow payments, moreover, would have to be made on all units sold, not just those above the 125 percent ceiling applicable to fringe firms that took the carrot for signing the MSA.[62]

The multibillion-dollar payment stream promised by the MSA, in turn, provided the leverage to induce the states to enact escrow legislation. Any state that did not do so stood to lose its entire share of the MSA pot. Here, one may discern the practical importance of including within the payment stream even the tobacco-producing states that had not filed reimbursement suits. They too — perhaps, they especially — would need to enact escrow legislation to deter the entry of new firms. The MSA cast its leverage not only at state legislatures but also, indirectly, at state courts. If a state enacted escrow legislation but a state court later invalidated that law, the state would lose up to 65 percent of its MSA share.[63]

Here, too, efforts to impede competition have not proven airtight. By 2003, the market share of all nonsignatories had increased to 8.1 percent from 0.37 percent before the MSA.[64] The consequent reduction of market share for signatories, in turn, triggered a "renegade" clause in the MSA, whereby signatories may reduce their payments to the states. Under the complex formula used by the MSA, the percentage reduction in the payments might, in a given instance, be substantially more than proportionate to the percentage reduction in the signatory's market share.[65] The reduction in MSA payments led to further efforts to bolster the state escrow laws — not only more vigilant enforcement but also additional legislation by forty-three states to reduce the ability of new entrants to evade the original escrow laws through the use of corporate shells based abroad.[66]

For my purposes, the importance of efforts to inhibit competition lies less in their details than in what they say about the core question for this chapter. That question asks whether the law may address the governance problems involved in peacemaking by situating the government as plaintiff. Whatever their ultimate success, efforts to suppress competition in the tobacco industry by way of the MSA could occur only because of government involvement. A peace arrangement for private lawsuits could provide no endorsement for the cartelization of the defendant industry, but peacemaking for government lawsuits might. The involvement of the government *as regulator*—not merely as proprietor, by analogy to a private health insurer—is central to any hope that the MSA and related measures might escape invalidation under the federal antitrust laws.

States as Potential Antitrust Immunizers

The MSA stands not just as an agreement between the various states and the signatory firms in the tobacco industry. It also is an agreement among those signatories themselves. And agreements among competitors to raise prices are illegal per se under the federal antitrust laws.[67] As one court observed in summarizing the MSA: "Had the executives of the major tobacco companies entered into such an arrangement without the involvement of the States and their attorneys general, those executives would long ago have had depressing conversations with their attorneys about the United States Sentencing Guidelines."[68]

As originally cast in the form of proposed federal legislation, the deal reached by the states and the tobacco industry sought to call off the federal antitrust laws through an express statutory exemption. Congress, of course, can turn off the application of an earlier statute through an exemption provided in a later one. In the absence of federal legislation, the industry had to rely on a more complicated route. In a series of decisions, the Supreme Court has made clear that the federal antitrust laws do not displace the power of state governments to authorize anticompetitive arrangements in furtherance of legitimate state policy objectives, such as the promotion of public health and safety. A state regulatory program thus may immunize anticompetitive conduct that otherwise would violate the federal antitrust laws.

One line of cases — stemming from the Supreme Court's 1943 decision in *Parker v. Brown*—affords immunity to anticompetitive acts of the state itself.[69] The concern here is that the federal antitrust laws not tread upon principles of federalism and state sovereignty. In its 1980 decision in *California Retail Liquor Dealers Association v. Midcal Aluminum, Inc.*, the Court extended *Parker* immunity to anticompetitive acts by private parties if undertaken pursuant to "clearly articulated and affirmatively expressed" state policy and if "actively supervised" by the state.[70] Private acts that satisfy these standards are considered acts of the state itself and, as such, are immune from the federal antitrust laws. The Court has construed strictly the demand for active supervision by the state, emphasizing that state officials must "have and exercise power to review particular anticompetitive acts of private parties and disapprove those that fail to accord with state policy."[71]

As of this writing, antitrust challenges to the MSA itself and related state legislation continue to percolate through the lower federal courts. Thus far, federal appellate courts properly have proven reluctant to afford antitrust immunity under the *Parker-Midcal* line of cases. As the United States Court of Appeals for the Third Circuit observed in its 2001 decision in *A. D. Bedell Wholesale Co. v. Philip Morris Inc.*, the MSA does stand as a clear expression of state policy, and the states "are actively involved in the maintenance of the [MSA] scheme." But the states "lack oversight or authority over the tobacco manufacturers' prices and production levels. These decisions are left entirely to private actors."[72] A subsequent Second Circuit decision embraces similar reasoning.[73]

A second line of immunity doctrine also speaks to the intersection of antitrust law and the processes of government, but the focus here is not on the states as states but on the rights of private persons. This second line — known in antitrust law as *Noerr-Pennington* immunity after the two main Supreme Court cases on the subject — does not ask whether the anticompetitive acts in question are acts of the state itself.[74] *Noerr-Pennington* immunity instead protects efforts by private parties to seek the adoption of anticompetitive public policy. Here, the idea is to reconcile the strictures of antitrust law with the right of private parties under the First Amendment "to petition the government for a redress of grievances."

In the leading decision on the question thus far, the Third Circuit in *Bedell* extended *Noerr-Pennington* immunity to the MSA. The court did so even while withholding *Parker-Midcal* immunity in the same case, for the reasons summarized earlier. The Third Circuit observed that the Supreme Court "has yet to speak definitively on extending [*Noerr-Pennington*] immunity to settlement agreements with sovereign states."[75] But the Third Circuit correctly concluded that there is no basis to distinguish petitioning in more conventional forms, such as legislative lobbying, from efforts to settle litigation with the state. The shakier portion of the court's analysis consists of the assertion that *Noerr-Pennington* immunity extends to the harms to competing firms that flow not only "from the petitioning itself" but also from "the government action which results from the petitioning"[76]—here, the success of the tobacco industry in obtaining a settlement on terms that would promote and protect a cartel.

The Third Circuit in *Bedell* confers *Noerr-Pennington* immunity on the product of successful petitioning even while the court withholds *Parker-Midcal* immunity absent active state supervision of industry pricing. These two components of *Bedell* make for a jarring combination. The Third Circuit's reasoning places the *Noerr-Pennington* and the *Parker-Midcal* lines of antitrust immunity doctrine on a collision course. The implication of *Bedell*, read as a whole, is that anticompetitive acts that do not amount to the acts of the state under *Midcal* nonetheless may gain refuge from antitrust strictures based simply on their genesis in private petitioning activity that seeks anticompetitive state policy. The petitioning effectively guts the active supervision requirement of *Midcal*.

In fairness to the Third Circuit, the Supreme Court has yet to delineate the precise interaction of the two lines of antitrust immunity in this regard. But there is no good reason, much less necessity, to read the two lines as *Bedell* implicitly does. A more cohesive reading is possible: Once protected petitioning succeeds in precipitating the adoption of anticompetitive state policy, courts should determine the immunity available for private actions pursuant to that policy by applying the same legal standard as they would to those same actions if undertaken without previous petitioning—namely, the strictures of *Midcal*. So framed, the MSA would not garner antitrust immunity due to the lack of active state supervision.

The potential glitch in the antitrust immunity for the MSA remains a little noticed outgrowth of state reimbursement litigation against the tobacco industry.[77] But even a definitive Supreme Court decision along the lines suggested—one that would withhold antitrust immunity under both lines of doctrine—likely would not spell doom for the MSA in practice. The states' expectation to receive multibillion-dollar MSA payouts in perpetuity and the budgetary chaos that likely would arise from a threatened stoppage of the payout flow would generate formidable pressure on Congress, after the fact, to supply by statute the immunity that existing doctrine might not. My point here, nonetheless, is not dependent upon the ultimate fate of the MSA as an antitrust matter. I draw upon the MSA, instead, to illustrate what is problematic about government reimbursement litigation more generally.

Trade-Offs between the Dimensions of Government

Situating the government as plaintiff in reimbursement litigation does not solve the governance problem in peacemaking. The combination of regulatory and proprietary dimensions in the government actually expands the domain for collusion in the crafting of any peace. The states' governmental status is what enabled them to clothe the MSA with the mantle of a public health initiative. A simple desire to create an industry cartel in order to share in the resulting profits would not, in all likelihood, have amounted to a legitimate state objective with the capacity to beget antitrust immunity.[78]

To be sure, localities as plaintiffs in reimbursement litigation enjoy less latitude to make deals along the precise lines of the MSA. Localities can provide antitrust immunity under the *Parker* line of cases, for example, only insofar as they act pursuant to statewide policy.[79] Localities do not possess antitrust immunization power in their own right. This difference, too, sheds light on the relative unattractiveness of settlement from the firearms industry's standpoint by comparison to the tobacco experience. Even within their more limited spheres, however, localities do possess a degree of autonomous regulatory authority—they can undertake their own ostensible health and safety measures—that they can promise to exercise in particular ways as part of any peace. For a settling industry, the potential gains from playing the settlement game may be less. But the nature of the game still will be to collude with the government as proprietor to obtain things that the industry could not otherwise get from the same government in its capacity as regulator. Defendants still can seek to get themselves into a more attractive regulatory regime for the future by buying off the plaintiff localities in their proprietary guise.

The greater regulatory authority of state and federal governments by comparison to localities does suggest that the problematic nature of reimbursement litigation goes up as one proceeds higher in the hierarchy of governments as plaintiffs. The higher the government plaintiff, the greater the regulatory power potentially in play in any peace negotiation. This is the counterpart for plaintiff governments of the irony identified earlier for the tobacco defendants. The states may well have turned the bigness of Big Tobacco against itself to precipitate settlement negotiations. But Big Tobacco likewise turned the near-nationwide scope of the state reimbursement actions against itself in the design of the settlement terms. The unprecedented dollar figures of the MSA within the annals of civil settlements reflect the gains available to the major players in the tobacco industry from a cartel endorsed and safeguarded by all fifty states.

The analysis here places in a new light the retention of mass tort plaintiffs' lawyers on a contingency-fee basis by the vast majority of the plaintiff states. Their retention is not the main problem with government reimbursement litigation, some popular critiques of the MSA notwithstanding.[80] The crux of the problem lies not with the lawyers but in the combination of regulatory and proprietary dimensions in their government clients themselves. Representation of the states on a contingency-fee basis simply adds to the existing tendency toward the sale of regulatory authority as the inducement for defendants to settle the proprietary dimensions of the litigation.

To speak in terms of problematic trade-offs between the regulatory and proprietary dimensions of government is to sound a familiar theme. The usual axis for trade-offs in mass tort settlements runs between present and future claimants. The fear underlying much of the law today—running through *Amchem* and the rise of futures representatives in bankruptcy, to take two examples—is that peacemaking will systematically shortchange future claimants when the defendant can buy off the lawyers who purport to negotiate on their behalf by skewing the peace terms to favor those lawyer's present clients. The defendant stands to capture more of the gains from settlement, thereby reducing the pot available for all claimants. And the pot itself stands to be allocated inequitably, such that persons with claims otherwise similar in nature receive radically different payouts due to the happenstance of their relative position in time. The winners are defendants, plaintiffs' lawyers, and (if only incidentally) present claimants; the losers are future claimants.

The structure of government reimbursement litigation does not mark an improvement on the structure of representation that has proven problematic for mass torts. It actually replicates that structure. Rather than induce the selling out of future claimants through the payouts provided to present ones, defendants may induce the selling out of regulatory policy through the payouts to the plaintiff governments as proprietors. The point is not that cartelization along the lines of the MSA is capable of generating no gains whatsoever for public health. Even the skewed structure for negotiation of the original reorganization plan in *Combustion Engineering* would have yielded at least some payout for future claimants. The problem, as in the ordinary mass tort setting, is that the structure for peacemaking aligns poorly with the making of reasoned trade-offs between competing goals.

Regulation typically is not a money-making enterprise for government. To the contrary, regulation usually involves substantial expenditures of budgetary resources to run a regulatory regime. And its benefits tend to flow to the citizenry generally in ways that do not all result in revenue back to the government. The combination of regulatory and proprietary dimensions in government reimbursement litigation skews the making of reasoned trade-offs through what one might term the self-referential monetizing of regulatory policy. The combination boosts the attractiveness of approaches, like industry cartelization, with the capacity to yield a high payout for the plaintiff governments themselves from the proprietary dimension of the litigation. And it simultaneously devalues approaches that might stand a better chance of advancing legitimate regulatory goals, albeit without promising a financial jackpot for the government. Efforts to quantify in monetary terms the benefits of regulatory initiatives have become a widespread—if still controversial—feature of the modern administrative state.[81] But no one seriously contends that regulatory policymaking should turn on monetization in the self-referential sense I describe—upon whether the monetized benefits of regulation flow to the government.

Most importantly, one can make the foregoing observation—one can identify a deficient regime for governance *in structural terms*—while also acknowledging that the appropriate regulatory response for a product like tobacco remains contested. The most prominent analysis of the MSA in the existing literature—W. Kip Viscusi's book *Smoke-Filled Rooms: A Postmortem on the Tobacco Deal*—concludes with an outline for a regulatory approach unlike the cartel created by the MSA. For Viscusi, the MSA represents inept regulation that had not "gone through the kind of analytical process of evaluation that is the norm for any other major federal policies."[82] A more reasoned regulatory approach, in his view, would involve a combination of better information for consumers and encouragement of innovation to reduce product risk. As for information, Viscusi envisions "a comprehensive rating system to indicate the hazards associated with different cigarettes to assist consumers in being able to match their cigarettes with their risk preferences." Better information would coexist with government efforts to encourage "technological advancements in cigarette design that reduce either their nicotine content or other health hazards of cigarettes."[83]

The combination of brand-specific risk information and technological innovation to design safer products is familiar. Think of automobile crashworthiness ratings and the development of airbags in tandem with regulation by the National Highway Traffic Safety Administration. In fact, some public health scholars invoke the example of advances in automobile safety to support the idea of tort litigation generally as a kind of public health initiative.[84]

Viscusi's recommendations, of course, are not the only ones available. As Commissioner of the FDA, David Kessler led that agency's unsuccessful effort in the 1990s to regulate tobacco products under the existing federal food and drug laws. In his best-selling account of that effort, Kessler advocates an approach radically different from that of Viscusi. Kessler calls for the reorganization of the tobacco industry to supply cigarettes at cost to those who want them, but with no way to profit from the enterprise in a manner that would perpetuate the industry's existing incentives to boost sales. The model here would be the sort of non-profit, government-chartered entities like those that "stimulate the flow of credit to home buyers, farmers, and students."[85]

There undoubtedly are still other permutations in regulatory policy. The point is that, in making reasoned regulatory choices, the government should not look chiefly to whether one or another approach will benefit the government as proprietor. Their differences notwithstanding, the recommendations of both Kessler and Viscusi are in keeping with the usual pursuit of regulatory goals. Both proposals tend not to rain money on the government. Kessler's prescription actually would cut off the profit-making capacity of the tobacco industry. And the feature that some might well regard as the major benefit of Viscusi's prescriptions—the enhancement of informed consumer choice as a value in itself—may be difficult to monetize. One can, in short, see how government reimbursement litigation stands systematically to shortchange the regulatory dimension of government, even without coming to rest definitively on the ideal policy for a product like tobacco. For that matter, one may translate the same point back to the ordinary context of mass tort settlements. One need not posit the existence of a single, irrefutably "right" settlement design in order to understand the objectionable quality of a structure for representation that is systematically prone to allocate too little money and too much risk to future claimants along any plausible metric.

In pointing to Viscusi and Kessler for purposes of illustration, moreover, I do not mean to suggest that the sole benchmark for evaluation of the MSA consists of some new regulatory regime that one or another person might regard as ideal. Whether the MSA represents an improvement over the status quo ante—no price hike, but also no state protection for an industry cartel—also remains open to question as a matter of regulatory policy. The point is that the answer to that question, too, should not turn on the cash flow to the government.

The Allure of Separate Representation Revisited

If government reimbursement litigation exists in continuity with the problems of peacemaking for mass torts, then further questions arise: Is there an analogue for the government as plaintiff to the prescription conventionally offered for the representation of mass tort claimants by private lawyers? And, if so, how does that prescription fare here? The prescription offered by the law for the representation of mass tort claimants is easy enough to state. As the previous chapters have discussed, both *Amchem* and bankruptcy law, among other sources, call for the separate representation of present and future claimants. The idea is not to prohibit altogether the making of trade-offs between the two camps. Trade-offs are well nigh inevitable in any peace arrangement. The idea, instead, is to regulate the structure of legal representation so that each camp shall have its own advocate—pristine and unconflicted—in any grand peace negotiation.

Government itself is a kind of representative, albeit of a political rather than a contractual sort. One could not, without some sweeping restructuring of federalism principles, create a direct counterpart in government reimbursement litigation to the kind of separate representative prescribed for ordinary mass tort settings. It is not as if certain levels of government are, or realistically could be made, exclusively proprietary or exclusively regulatory in nature as a general matter. As suggested earlier, the combination of the two dimensions is central to the notion of being a government in the first place. One nonetheless might envision something that is, if not a direct counterpart, then at least a sibling with a close resemblance—say, a stricture that the government *as plaintiff* may pursue in reimbursement litigation only proprietary or regulatory goals. In colloquial terms, the government would have to choose which of its hats to wear as plaintiff. The following discussion explains how such a stricture actually would replicate the pitfalls of separate representation for present and future claimants.

Writing about the MSA, David Dana raises the possibility that the use of contingency-fee lawyers by governments might be limited "only to monetary issues" in reimbursement litigation. "A 'cash-only' limitation would address concerns about the 'sale' of unjustified, real nonmonetary benefits to industries as part of settlements." But Dana ultimately shies from a full-fledged endorsement of such a limitation, cautioning that "public interest considerations arguably dictate trade-offs between monetary and nonmonetary" components of the peace.[86] There is wisdom in this hesitancy to import some version of the separate representation prescription from *Amchem* and its ilk, whether for contingency-fee lawyers retained by the government or for the government itself as plaintiff. If anything, further developments in the tobacco litigation provide something of a convenient, real-world experiment on this score.

Shortly after the completion of the MSA, the Clinton administration in 1999 brought a federal reimbursement action against the tobacco industry — this time, for the additional increment of federal expenditures under Medicare said to result from industry wrongdoing. Medicare is the major spending program that supports health care for the elderly. The federal government based its suit on three specific federal statutes, not on general equitable principles. Two statutes provided explicitly for reimbursement-like remedies, but the district court soon dismissed the government's case under both. One simply did not cover Medicare expenditures. The other did, but it authorized reimbursement only where the federal government had paid expenses properly covered by insurers, not other sorts of private entities like the tobacco defendants.[87] The district court's decision left intact the federal government's demand for reimbursement under a third statute, the Racketeer Influenced and Corrupt Organizations Act (RICO). In keeping with the title of that statute, the federal government alleged that the tobacco industry had engaged in a "four-decade long conspiracy" to deceive consumers about the nature and risks of its products.[88]

Even RICO ultimately proved unavailing for purposes of the requested reimbursement. The relevant language of the statute confines the remedial power of the court thereunder to the issuance of equitable orders that "prevent or restrain" RICO violations. Ruling on appeal in 2005, the United States Court of Appeals for the District of Columbia Circuit read this language as "limited to forward-looking remedies that are aimed at future violations."[89] The Medicare reimbursement sought by the federal government amounted to what equity would call "disgorgement" — in common parlance, the giving back of one's ill-gotten gains. Writing for the court, Judge David Sentelle observed that disgorgement "is a quintessentially backward-looking remedy," one "measured by the amount of prior unlawful gains and . . . awarded without respect to whether the defendant will act unlawfully in the future."[90] To permit disgorgement on a theory of preventing or restraining future violations would be at odds, the court noted, with a separate portion of RICO that provides explicitly for the "forfeiture" of past gains from prohibited activities. RICO authorizes forfeiture as a remedy only in the context of criminal prosecutions, not civil actions like the federal lawsuit against the tobacco industry.[91]

The DC Circuit's decision left the federal lawsuit with only the possible hammer of forward-looking injunctive remedies — say, smoking cessation and education programs. On remand, the district court ultimately issued a massive opinion detailing — I daresay, by then, to the surprise of no one — that the tobacco industry had engaged in the kind of decades-long conspiracy of deception that the government had alleged. The forward-looking relief ordered by the district court, however, consisted of no measures that would carry a major financial cost for the industry, not even the modest sorts of antismoking programs that remained on the menu of potential remedies after the DC Circuit's ruling. Wall Street shrugged, with shares of the Altria Group, Inc. — the present-day incarnation of Philip Morris — continuing their 70 percent rise in price over the preceding two years.[92]

I do not seek here to determine the proper reading of RICO as a matter of statutory construction. The federal RICO lawsuit speaks more broadly to the difficulties that would be posed by efforts to craft a counterpart in government reimbursement litigation to the separate representation stricture of *Amchem*. As read by the DC Circuit, RICO effectively embodies something roughly like the stricture described earlier. When bringing a civil action under that statute, the government is confined to prospective remedies. The government may not seek retrospective ones, like disgorgement. The line between prospective and retrospective remedies does not track perfectly the line between the regulatory and proprietary dimensions of government. But the two lines are similar, if only in a rough hewn way. The usual focus of regulation — if not its only one — is to alter conduct on a prospective basis. The usual focus of a lawsuit by a proprietor for money — again, not necessarily its only goal — is to recover for some wrongful loss in the past. The DC Circuit's decision effectively means that the government can use RICO in civil litigation only for regulation in the foregoing sense, not as a way to recoup past expenditures as a proprietor. Yet the threat of regulation, without the hammer of potential disgorgement, has proven a weak instrument.

Stripped of its proprietary hat and made to wear only its regulatory one under RICO, the federal government as plaintiff is the analogue here to a character from the preceding chapter: the separate, pristine, and unconflicted representative for future claimants in bankruptcy. The feature that makes for elimination of the apparent conflict of interest—the absence of present-day clients—is simultaneously what denudes the futures representative in peace negotiations. It is one thing for a particular statute to place the government in a similar posture in a given instance. But it is quite another to think that the law should generalize our RICO thought-experiment into a more thoroughgoing prescription. What makes government reimbursement litigation problematic is also what gives it the potential to induce real change: its combination of regulatory and proprietary dimensions. Put differently, the prospect of peace along *both* dimensions is what gives rise to the possibility of huge mutual gains through settlement. All of this, again, starts to sound familiar. It is the possibility of achieving "global peace"—of setting rules for future claimants, not just muddling through as to present ones—that makes such peace something for which defendants might pay dearly in ordinary mass tort litigation. Making trade-offs is the necessary means to unlock the gains from settlement.

The real challenge in government reimbursement litigation is much the same as the one presented in the asbestos-related reorganizations in bankruptcy discussed in the preceding chapter. Rather than split apart the representation of present and future claimants or, here, the regulatory and proprietary dimensions of government, the law might endeavor to improve the alignment between the interests of the peace designers and the making of reasoned trade-offs, not merely self-serving ones. Looking at the reimbursement litigation against the tobacco industry in this light, one can start to discern some crude, halting, and unconnected features that point in the right direction—albeit, perhaps, only inadvertently.

At the outset, it bears notice that the state attorneys general who signed the MSA were themselves elected officials. The effect of the MSA nonetheless was to increase cigarette prices for a discrete political minority within each state comprised of persons—present-day smokers—who do not exactly elicit great sympathy from the electorate at large. At the same time, the MSA added to the resources available for the states to disperse broadly to the electorate, whether through additional state expenditures or, implicitly, through avoidance of increases in general taxes. If anything, criticism of the MSA often points to its lack of earmarking, such that only a modest fraction of the payments received by the states has gone toward health-related programs. The biggest chunk has gone, instead, to cover state budget shortfalls.[93] Whether this amounts to a fair criticism depends, once again, on how one conceives reimbursement litigation along the dimensions of government.

If the people who paid in the past for the Medicaid expenses of smokers were taxpayers generally—the "innocent" victims whom the states wished to invoke in place of risk-taking smokers—then it is hardly a grave defect of the MSA that the money recouped should be dispersed broadly. Such use is seemingly consistent with the proprietary dimension of reimbursement litigation. It is only from a regulatory perspective that the lack of earmarking starts to look problematic. In any event, the political accountability of the state attorneys general might not have inhibited distortion in the regulatory dimension of government but, rather, might actually have encouraged it. Some go so far as to attribute Mississippi Attorney General Michael Moore's enthusiasm to serve as a first-mover in tobacco reimbursement litigation, in part, to a belief that the litigation actually might burnish his image for higher office.[94]

Identification of the group that stands to pay for the selling out of regulatory goals, coupled with analysis of that group's ability to wield political influence, may be useful beyond the tobacco setting. Specifically, it can help to account for the greater impact of political checks on reimbursement litigation against the firearms industry. There, as mentioned earlier, state and federal legislation had a substantial dampening effect on reimbursement suits by localities. But, of course, there is a well-funded, long-standing, and politically energized National Rifle Association in a way that there is not a National Cigarette Association.

The original deal reached between the state attorneys general and the tobacco industry actually may have stumbled on a somewhat better structure for peacemaking than the one ultimately pursued in the MSA. Congress is arguably a better institution to decide whether to lend the force of law to a deal that would trade government-protected cartelization for a stream of future payments to the states—at least, better than the MSA in relative terms—because Congress itself stood to gain little in the way of additional resources for its use. Although the Clinton administration initially flirted with the idea of claiming for the federal government a share of the funds sought by the states in the proposed federal legislation, the administration ultimately backed off.[95] Reimbursement claims by the federal government would have to await the subsequent litigation under RICO. At the same time, Congress stood to bear at least a share of the political brunt for increasing the price of cigarettes—a point on which the industry played in its successful campaign to defeat the final version of the bill.

One might see the active supervision requirement for antitrust immunity under *Midcal* as a crude way to bring to bear upon the states themselves the costs of lending their imprimatur to industry cartels. As a condition for the conferring of antitrust immunity, *Midcal* effectively requires the states to expend their own resources to undertake the active supervision of industry pricing. A state cannot simply sit back and share in the profits from the cartel-like pricing it has facilitated. A state, in short, cannot act as antitrust immunizer for free — what it could do, in effect, under an expansive reading of *Noerr-Pennington* immunity to swallow up the active supervision constraint of *Midcal*.

There is a larger point lurking here, one that helps to define the agenda for the final chapters of this book. Both the preceding chapter and this one point in a direction markedly different from the thrust of *Amchem* and its ilk. The analysis here of government reimbursement litigation dovetails with the observation made in the preceding chapter concerning the difficulties of separate, unconflicted representation — whether of future claimants or, here, of one particular dimension of government. If the real objective is to align the interests of peace designers with the making of reasoned trade-offs rather than self-serving ones, then the law might proceed in a new direction. Government reimbursement litigation might not have something to learn from the ideal of separate representation in *Amchem*. Rather, the supposed ideal of separate representation might have something to learn from the notion of conflicting dimensions, all encompassed within the same government as representative. The implications of such a perspective and the ways in which it requires us to challenge some of the most deeply ingrained ideas in the law of mass torts today, together, form the subject for what follows. It turns out that there is a meaningful role for government with regard to mass torts — not as the plaintiff or as the dictator of peace terms but, rather, as the vehicle for turning conflicts of interest into their own source of constraint. It is now time to walk out of the blind alley and toward a more productive path for reform.

PART IV

PEACEMAKING AS GOVERNANCE

CHAPTER XI

LEVERAGING CONFLICTS OF INTEREST

In the period since the Supreme Court's *Amchem* decision in 1997, the law of mass torts has meandered. The story of mass torts since *Amchem* is the story of a halting search. The elusive goal remains an arrangement to make comprehensive peace in mass tort litigation. To implement their desired peace arrangements, settling lawyers have sought to use public legislation, contracts with plaintiffs' law firms, revamped forms of class settlements, and reorganization plans in bankruptcy. On occasion, the government has become involved as a litigant and a participant in the peacemaking process. Insofar as learning has occurred in this process of ad hoc experimentation, that learning itself has been ad hoc and episodic in nature. The time has come to synthesize the lessons learned from pursuit of the various paths.

Words like "peace," "settlement," and "resolution" have a certain soothing tone to them. When we hear those words in connection with mass torts, however, we also should hear the word "coercion." Any peace arrangement in the mass tort setting will entail the exercise of coercive power. For the people who stand to sue over a mass tort, peace inherently means the replacement of their individual rights of action in the tort system with a new set of rights to compensation under some manner of administrative grid. Making peace, moreover, means making that replacement stick, such that people no longer enjoy the kind of autonomy over their claims that the tort system provides. Tort claimants, however, do not comprise the only persons, or even necessarily the primary persons, whom the peacemaking process should stand to coerce. This chapter contends that another significant dimension of coercion should concern the peacemaking lawyers themselves. Peace arrangements shift the compensation of claimants from the tort system to an administrative grid. So too, I shall argue, should peace

mark a sharp break in the way we think about the compensation of lawyers. But, to make that break, the law must question some of its most deeply
ingrained suppositions about mass torts. The work of this chapter consists
of exposing these suppositions and thinking about what the world might
look like without them.

To date, the law has approached the problem of mass torts chiefly as
a problem of litigation. That understanding proceeds from a core truth:
Mass tort claims do manifest themselves in lawsuits. To regard mass torts
primarily as a matter of litigation, however, is to proceed based on a set of
suppositions grounded in the relationship between lawyers and clients in
conventional lawsuits. These suppositions are closely intertwined and concern, respectively, the appropriate structure of representation, the parameters for compensation of lawyers, and the autonomy of individual claimants as their clients.

As to the structure of representation, the conventional view today regards with great suspicion the simultaneous representation of persons with
present-day disease and other persons at risk of future disease. The conventional view holds that this structure involves an inherent conflict of interest that the law should assiduously avoid. As to lawyer compensation,
conventional thinking understandably regards legal fees as stemming from
what the lawyer does for the client—whether in the form of an individual
or, perhaps, a group of persons in the aggregate. No one thinks that the
fees garnered by the lawyer from the representation of one client somehow
should turn on what happens to a different client or, even more fancifully,
to persons who never form lawyer-client relationships with that lawyer. Finally, with regard to claimant autonomy, the conventional view is that individuals generally must have the opportunity to opt out from any framework
for claim resolution crafted by their lawyers. Any client, after all, retains the
ultimate power of disposition over her individual claim. A lawyer can no
more sell an individual's tort claim without some manner of consent than a
real estate agent could sell an owner's home.

Simply as a descriptive matter, a conception of mass torts primarily as
a litigation problem obscures the reality that litigation operates as the prelude to administration. Peacemaking efforts for mass torts aspire to a kind
of privatized law reform. They strive to replicate, in microcosm, the process
by which workers' compensation legislation came to replace tort lawsuits
over workplace injuries in the early twentieth century. They involve governance, not litigation.

Once one sees mass torts as a problem of governance, it is far from
obvious that notions of representation grounded in one particular kind of

principal-agent relationship — that between lawyer and client — should supply the touchstone for analysis. The word "governance" resonates in many different segments of the law. For that matter, "governance" cuts across disciplines, comprising a subject of exploration in both political science and business. For scholars of public law, "governance" brings to mind the political representation that constitutes the government itself. For scholars of private law, the same word invokes the array of legal arrangements for "corporate governance."

An exposition of governance in both its public and private forms is far beyond the scope of this book. My point is a more focused one: In seeking to wedge the mass tort problem into the conceptual framework of litigation, current law both skews and unduly narrows the agenda for reform. This chapter proceeds along a different path, seeking not to pound the square peg of mass torts into the round hole of litigation concepts but, instead, to reshape the hole itself. That reshaping consists of measures — unburdened by the suppositions of litigation — to hew more precisely the loyalties of mass tort lawyers to the interests of those whose rights they seek to reform. Improvements in peacemaking call for the law ultimately to draw upon the authority of government in its public form — not to dictate the peace terms but to discipline the exercise of governing power by the peacemaking lawyers.

The chapter begins with a brief overview of the lessons from the post-*Amchem* period about the ways in which peace arrangements can go awry in the mass tort setting. That overview — what one might dub the "pathologies" of peacemaking — compresses the learning from the preceding chapters and provides the springboard for the main argument here, which challenges head-on the suppositions behind the conventional, litigation-based view of mass torts. Contrary to conventional thinking, the simultaneous representation of presently diseased persons and future claimants is not something that the law should avoid. It is a reality of mass tort litigation on which the law should build to improve the design and practical operation of peace arrangements. The crucial move consists not of scrupulously avoiding a conflict of interest between present and future claimants but, actually, in accentuating that conflict — specifically, in the design of the fee arrangement for plaintiffs' lawyers to use their representation of presently diseased persons as a source of constraint upon their crafting of the compensation terms for future claimants.

The foregoing approach — what I encapsulate as "leveraging conflicts of interest" — would move away from the supposition that the lawyer's fee for representation of a given client should turn strictly on what happens to that client. The leveraging proposal instead posits that the fee calculus should build on the strategic dynamics behind any effort at comprehensive settlement in the mass tort area. Those dynamics involve a kind of leveraging—namely, use of the threat posed by large numbers of present clients to bring the defendant to the negotiating table in order to set the compensation terms for future claimants. The disposition of future claims is the strategic end to which present-day claims are used. The fees that lawyers gain from the representation of presently diseased persons accordingly should turn not simply on what happens to those clients but also on what happens to future claimants who are like them in relevant respects, but for the fortuity of when they manifest disease.

The chapter explains how pursuit of the proposed fee arrangement requires the overriding of contingency-fee contracts for the representation of claimants already in the tort system. What is needed, in other words, is coercive law reform as much for mass tort lawyers as for mass tort claimants. Existing institutions for peacemaking—chiefly, class settlements and reorganizations in bankruptcy—are poorly equipped for this enterprise. Coercive law reform, however, is the ordinary business of the administrative state. The chapter shows how implementation of the leveraging proposal for fee design may take place as part of a partial shift of peace negotiations into administrative bodies. All of this, I hasten to add, would not entail a top-down, command-and-control approach to the resolution of mass tort disputes. Rather, in chapter 12, I shall outline ways in which the law may meld private negotiation with public rulemaking. Specifically, agencies may draw on recent experience with negotiated rulemaking, along with competition within the mass tort plaintiffs' bar, to facilitate the design of the peace terms.

The objective of the law, in short, should be to acknowledge, expose, and systematize what already transpires in the peacemaking process. When litigation operates chiefly as a means to make rules to govern the future, it is time to move out of court-centered processes and into institutions overtly charged with rulemaking. That move, in turn, would help to legitimize the coercive power that any peace arrangement must wield. Implementation of peace through agency rules appropriately recasts the source of protection for claimants. That protection consists not of individual autonomy of the sort celebrated in litigation but, rather, of structural constraints that hew the interests of rule makers to those of rule subjects. Good governance, not self-help, is the principal source of protection. The legitimacy of agency rules for mass torts accordingly would stem as much from their implementation of the leveraging proposal for fee design as from the fact of agency involvement per se. Here, as in other regimes for governance in both public and private law, legitimacy turns not on raw power but on its exercise within a structure that extends over time the relationship of those in power with those they govern.

The Pathologies of Peacemaking

Like workers' compensation laws in the early twentieth century, peace arrangements for mass torts use grids to match medical conditions with compensation payouts in a systematic manner. Grids proceed on a straightforward premise. The happenstance of when a particular kind of injury befalls a person should not make for a radical difference in the compensation that she receives by comparison to other persons who suffer the same injury at other times. The use of grids transcends the institutional arrangement used to make peace in the mass tort setting, extending across proposals for public law (as in proposed asbestos legislation), class settlements, reorganization plans in bankruptcy, and private contracts between defendants and mass tort plaintiffs' law firms (as in the Owens Corning National Settlement Program [NSP]). Peacemakers, moreover, are unlikely to invent the grid entirely from whole cloth. Like workers' compensation legislation,[1] the grid for a given mass tort will take as its starting point the existing practices by which experienced lawyers on both sides have come to settle claims. The process of grid design is bottom-up, not top-down.

To recognize that grids build on existing settlement practices, however, is not to say that they simply replicate them. Were prior settlement practices all well and good for all concerned, there would be no need for systematized grids. From the defendant's standpoint, comprehensive peace beats "muddling through" with prior settlement practices only insofar as the defendant gains something from that move. Systematized grids arise because comprehensive resolution of mass tort disputes has the potential to be a value-generating transaction. Reduction of uncertainty through the binding of future claimants to the grid can make available additional resources by enhancing the business prospects for the settling defendant.

Whatever the institutional vehicle, peace arrangements in their ideal form should (1) maximize the overall value of the settlement, (2) allocate that value equitably among claimants, and (3) take place at a time when sufficient information exists with which to evaluate the implicated claims. Matters of maximization, allocation, and timing relate closely to one another. Pathology in the pursuit of one goal often will arise as the outgrowth of pathologies in the pursuit of others. The failure to maximize in the mass tort setting likely will stem from misallocation among claimants or from competing goals of the peacemaking plaintiffs' law firm that stem from its own long-term business strategy. To understand these dynamics, one first must grasp the role that present-day claims play in the peacemaking process.

Even without much work on the part of plaintiffs' lawyers, early successes in individual lawsuits plus the sheer numbers of affected persons that define a mass tort will tend to bring additional claims into the firm's inventory. To have a realistic chance at a leading role in a comprehensive negotiation, however, any given firm cannot leave the accumulation of its inventory to chance. The firm's body count — its claims on file in the tort system or readily available to be so filed — will determine its place at the negotiating table. The structure for approval of reorganization plans in bankruptcy confers voting power based, in significant part, on the raw number of creditors. Numbers mean votes, both under the general Chapter 11 of the Bankruptcy Code for corporate reorganizations and under §524(g) for asbestos-related reorganizations specifically.[2] Even outside of bankruptcy, the firm's body count will tend to enhance its influence within any committee of plaintiffs' lawyers formed to handle pretrial proceedings upon the consolidation of pending federal lawsuits by the Judicial Panel on Multidistrict Litigation (MDL Panel). Consolidation by the MDL Panel often serves as the springboard for negotiations aimed at comprehensive peace. One likewise can see the drive to seek class certification early in the mass tort litigation cycle as an effort to accumulate something akin to an inventory of pending claims, albeit by operation of procedural rule rather than conventional client recruitment.[3]

The accumulation of claims as the prelude to peace negotiations has important implications, both for the bargaining between defendants and plaintiffs' lawyers and for the economics of plaintiffs' law firms. Defendants might seek to exploit the existence of large inventories to influence the overall value of the peace arrangement. In economic terms, defendants care about allocation of the gains from settlement as between themselves and claimants generally, but they do not have reason to care about allocation among those claimants. The mass tort literature has long understood that the gambit for the defense side is to use misallocation in favor of inventory claimants as a way to induce their lawyers to agree to a division of the gains from settlement that favors the defense side over claimants generally.[4] By "misallocation" in favor of inventory claimants, I mean specifically a deviation from the premise of temporal equity that underlies all forms of compensation grids — the notion that fortuitous differences in the timing of disease should not produce radical differences in compensation.

The tendency to favor inventory claimants over future ones, however, is not simply a by-product of bargaining strategy on the defense side. The tendency stems, more fundamentally, from considerations of capitalization on the plaintiffs' side and the relationship of mass tort plaintiffs' lawyers to one another. The organization of plaintiffs' law firms to achieve greater capitalization has characterized civil litigation as a whole in recent decades.[5] Any given area of mass tort litigation is not merely a source of firm revenue in its own right. It is also the source of firm capital for investment in the development of new enterprises. Well-capitalized plaintiffs' law firms need not look to one subject area as their target for investment but, instead, may develop a portfolio of areas. As long as that portfolio produces a sufficient rate of return, the cycle can repeat itself over time in the same manner that corporations might move from their original lines of business to a succession of new ones. As in business generally, there is an advantage in mass tort litigation to being the "first mover" in a given area. One thereby can gain a competitive advantage in the accumulation of claim inventories to precipitate comprehensive settlement negotiations. As a result, even apart from the inducements that defendants might provide in peace negotiations, plaintiffs' lawyers might forego maximization in order to obtain capital today for investment in other areas tomorrow. Put less formally, the lawyers might take the money and run. Ironically, then, what has enabled the mass tort plaintiffs' bar to litigate on something approaching more of a level footing with well-capitalized corporate defendants is also what contributes to problems of settlement design.

Indeed, considerations of capitalization can contribute to a kind of misallocation in the administration of the peace arrangement, even apart from its initial design. Early claimants under the peace arrangement might consume its resources and, thereby, undermine the credibility of the grid to make its specified payouts for future claimants. In this manner, present and future claimants effectively are split apart, not so much by settlement design as by the dynamics unleashed by the creation of the settlement. Misallocation through fund depletion plagued the Manville bankruptcy trust virtually from its inception, with present claimants quickly consuming the resources of the trust.[6] One can see much the same dynamic at work outside of the bankruptcy setting as well. A rush of claimants under the fen-phen class settlement resulted in administrative delays that undermined the operation of the settlement fund for future claimants.[7]

Finally, peace arrangements for mass torts present a question of timing, though it, too, relates closely to misallocation. Any grid allocates not only dollars but also risk—specifically, the risk that the resources behind the grid will not suffice for it to operate as billed.[8] Grids ideally should not be designed when little is known about a given mass tort—about the incidence of disease, its latency period, its range of physical consequences, the likelihood of a causal connection to the defendant, and so on. To put the point more precisely, precipitous imposition of a grid may come with too great of a risk that the peace arrangement will falter for those most dependent on its operation—namely, claimants who happen to manifest disease later rather than sooner.

The Source of the Pathologies

The pathologies of peacemaking in the mass tort setting are manifold, but they stem from a common source: a fundamental mismatch between what mass tort plaintiffs' lawyers actually do when they negotiate a comprehensive peace and the structure of the incentives that apply in that negotiation. Whatever the institutional vehicle, plaintiffs' law firms precipitate peace negotiations through what one might call the leveraging of present claims. By "present claims," I refer to both inventory claims (already on file in the tort system) and claims that the firm readily can bring forth (for compensation in tort or under the peace arrangement). Specifically, plaintiffs' law firms use the threat posed to the defendant by present claims as the basis for assertion of a broader power to bargain over the terms that shall govern future claims. This leveraging notably extends beyond determination of the compensation grid for future claimants. It also effectively encompasses the financial rewards available to the lawyers who might represent them in the making of claims under the grid—lawyers who may be different from the ones who design the peace. The leveraging at the heart of any peace negotiation, in other words, reaches from present to future claimants *and* from the negotiating law firm on the plaintiffs' side to its rivals.

Class certification makes this leveraging especially apparent. As a procedural matter, the point of a class action is for class counsel to use its representation of conventional, individual clients as the basis for assertion of a power to litigate on behalf of a larger collective group. By its terms, the modern class action rule describes when "[o]ne or more members of a class may sue . . . on behalf of all."[9] Class certification enables class counsel to obtain as their nominal clients—at least for purposes of the class proceeding—persons who might otherwise form conventional lawyer-client relationships with rival law firms and, indeed, who might go on to do so for the purpose of obtaining compensation under any class settlement. Leveraging is not confined to mass tort class actions, however. As noted earlier, the voting structure for the confirmation of reorganization plans in bankruptcy effectively empowers the representatives of present claimants to wield formidable influence over the plan design. The private contracts of the Owens Corning NSP likewise sought to use the accumulation of present claims by asbestos plaintiffs' lawyers as the basis to induce restraint on their part with regard to future ones.[10]

The leveraging of present claims into the power to govern both future claims and the rival law firms that might represent them is the cold, hard fact of peacemaking in the mass tort area. Yet conventional wisdom inhibits the law from perceiving the true parameters of peace negotiations and, even worse, from rethinking the incentives that operate therein. This conventional wisdom takes several forms, speaking to the appropriate structure of representation, the basis for the calculation of legal fees, and the autonomy of individual mass tort claimants. Each of these components stems from an underlying misconception of mass torts primarily as a problem of litigation rather than of governance.

Conflicts of Interest and the Structure of Representation

For all the uncertainty since *Amchem* surrounding the choice of vehicles for peacemaking, one bedrock point remains widely shared. If anything, it is so ingrained in conventional thinking that it operates as an unquestioned starting point for discussion today of what to do about mass torts. Whatever arrangements the law might develop, there is one kind of arrangement regarded as off limits: one in which the dealmakers on the plaintiffs' side simultaneously represent both persons with present-day disease and persons at risk of disease in the future.[11]

One form of the stricture against simultaneous representation arises from the inclusiveness of the settlement group — that is, its specification of who must seek compensation under its grid rather than through tort litigation. The touchstone here is no less than *Amchem* itself. There, the Supreme Court pointed to the lack of a "structural assurance of fair and adequate representation" where a single, undifferentiated plaintiff class encompassed both "currently injured and exposure-only categories of plaintiffs." The interests of these two sorts of claimants were "not aligned," said the Court, for the goal of those with present disease to obtain "generous immediate payments" conflicted with "the interest of exposure-only plaintiffs in ensuring an ample, inflation-protected fund for the future."[12] As the Court would summarize later in *Ortiz,* the logic of *Amchem* makes it "obvious" that a class encompassing both present and future claimants in the foregoing sense "requires division into homogeneous subclasses . . . with separate representation to eliminate conflicting interests of counsel."[13]

The same view permeates bankruptcy law and practice in the mass tort setting. Section 524(g) for asbestos-related reorganizations explicitly requires the appointment of a separate futures representative.[14] Even outside of the asbestos context, mass tort-related reorganizations under the general Chapter 11 of the Code routinely entail a similar appointment.[15] Pointing to this practice, the influential 1997 report of the National Bankruptcy Review Commission goes so far as to deem the appointment of a separate futures representative "an absolute necessity and a fundamental prerequisite to the discharge of mass future claims."[16]

A second form of the stricture against simultaneous representation also concerns a conflict of interest on the part of deal-makers on the plaintiffs' side. But, this time, the conflict stems from the exclusiveness of the settlement group — specifically, its exclusion of the firm's inventory claims, such that they must be resolved apart from the larger peace. The class definitions in both *Amchem* and *Ortiz* encompassed only claims that were not already pending in the tort system — claims not in some firm's inventory — on the dates that the respective class settlements were reached.[17] For the Court, the exclusion of class counsel's inventory claims undercut any assumption that those law firms would "be of a mind to do their simple best in bargaining for the benefit of the settlement class." The need for separate resolution of class counsel's inventory claims gave those lawyers a "great incentive to reach any agreement in the global settlement negotiations" in order to obtain generous terms for their inventories.[18] Fear of the same dynamic underlies the controversy surrounding the prepackaged, asbestos-related reorganization plan originally struck down in *Combustion Engineering*. There, a separate trust fund nominally outside of §524(g) provided for compensation of inventory claims but left unpaid a small "stub" of each. The stubs, in turn, enabled inventory claimants to vote in large numbers — via the plaintiffs' law firms that represented them — for confirmation of the §524(g) reorganization plan designed to serve primarily as the source of compensation for future claims.[19]

What makes the separate representation of present and future claims seem so "obvious" as to be "an absolute necessity"? The answer lies in an effort to understand peacemaking as an extension of litigation rather than a problem of governance. Representation in litigation means representation of clients by lawyers. The law of professional responsibility regulates the conflicts of interest that may arise when a lawyer undertakes the representation of multiple clients. The basic conflict-of-interest rule in legal ethics holds that, absent informed consent, the lawyer may not represent a given client if "there is a significant risk that the representation will be materially limited by the lawyer's responsibilities to another client . . . or by the personal interest of the lawyer."[20] The routine providing of individualized client consent is what makes possible the accumulation of large claim inventories by plaintiffs' law firms in the mass tort setting, among others.[21]

Any comprehensive peace, however, must proceed in the absence of individualized client consent of the sort envisioned in legal ethics, for peace inherently involves moving beyond the process of settling individual cases. Peace is coercive, not consensual in an individualized sense. Given the coercive dimension of peacemaking, the reason for the current insistence on separate representation of present and future claimants is not hard to discern. Where individualized consent is not possible, conventional wisdom holds that the law may alter preexisting rights only through arrangements that afford affected claimants a level of protection roughly comparable to the basic conflict-of-interest rule in litigation. Current law does so by insisting on a high degree of similarity among the claims that the deal-making lawyer represents. Client consent is not needed, in short, because substantial conflicts are not allowed to emerge in the first place. Absent the requisite similarity among claimants, conventional wisdom regards the solution to be roughly the same as in litigation generally: The claimants generating the conflict must have separate representation.

Simply as a practical matter, it is hard to conceive of a separate representative for future claimants who would have the requisite background in the underlying litigation and yet somehow not have individual clients of her own.[22] Recent asbestos-related bankruptcies have sought to solve the problem of expertise on the part of the futures representative by drawing on a relatively small cadre of persons with experience in the resolution of mass tort litigation generally. But this approach has led to the effective creation of repeat players whose own interests lie primarily in continuing to be appointed as futures representatives—an objective that tugs against putting up too much of a fight against the confirmation of a reorganization plan.[23]

The problem is not just one of expertise, however. It ultimately is one of leverage—or, more accurately, the lack of leverage that a separate representative for future claimants has in peace negotiations precisely because her body count is zero. If anything, the recent prepackaged, asbestos-related reorganizations lay bare the dynamics of peacemaking. The whole point of prepackaged reorganizations is for the defendant to line up the requisite votes for confirmation of its desired plan through negotiation with the real holders of power — the leveraging plaintiffs' law firms — and only thereafter to present the futures representative with a fait accompli. The futures representative — characteristically, a person of experience and genuine integrity — enters the game only when it is largely over. Try though it might, the cosmetic device of separate representation cannot beat down the leveraging at the heart of peace negotiations.

The law, to be sure, might attempt to buttress the power of a separate representative for future claimants — for example, by tinkering with the priority scheme in bankruptcy to accord "super-priority" to involuntary creditors, such as tort claimants, so as to move them ahead of secured creditors for payment under any reorganization plan.[24] I contend that an even more fundamental break with conventional thinking is needed. Understood as a problem of governance, peacemaking in mass tort litigation does not obviously require the separate representation of present and future claimants. In neither its public form (modern representative democracy) nor its most prominent private form (the corporation) does governance entail — much less require — the pristine separation of discrete interests. Governance, instead, is chiefly a matter of the constraints that hew the interests of those wielding power to the interests of those whom they govern. Governance in its public form does this most obviously through periodic elections designed to tether — if only roughly — the representatives' interest in retaining office to the views of the electorate.[25] Corporate governance does the same through a rich constellation of measures concerning the appointment and removal of corporate managers, the financial incentives under which they function, and the constraints upon their business decisions.[26]

It would be one thing if a litigation-based view could lead to the design of an incentive structure that captures the leveraging in mass tort peace negotiations rather than simply trying to make it go away. That, however, is not so. The incentives that prevail today in peace negotiations bear little connection to underlying dynamics. Those who purport to design the peace terms do not bear the costs to future claimants from the allocation of resources and risk in a manner that favors present ones. In fact, the suppositions of litigation actually inhibit the law from pursuing reform to set right the incentives for mass tort plaintiffs' lawyers.

Fees from the Representation of Clients

Consider initially the fee structure associated with mass tort class settlements. Plaintiffs' lawyers stand to gain fees from three sources: contingency fees from their representation of inventory claimants, a fee award from the court based on the creation of a "common fund" for class members by way of the class settlement, and contingency fees from the representation of claimants under the settlement. Both sources for contingency fees—from inventory claims and from claims made under the settlement—stem from actual, lawyer-client contracts. Indeed, insofar as the class settlement itself encompasses inventory claims, these two categories will converge into one. As to contingency fees, two further points bear mention. First, the class settlement agreement is likely to cap the contingency fee percentage that lawyers may obtain from the representation of claims thereunder.[27] Second, the lawyers who obtain contingency fees—whether from inventory claims or from claims under the settlement—need not be the same lawyers as class counsel.

Fee awards by the court for the creation of a common fund translate conventional contingency fee arrangements into the context of class settlements, setting the award at a percentage of the common fund. The underlying theory for the award is restitutionary. Absent a fee award, class members who benefit from the availability of the common fund without contributing to its creation would be unjustly enriched at the expense of class counsel.[28] The fee award, in effect, taxes the class collectively for the benefits made available to it through class counsel's efforts. The fee award nonetheless depends on the achievement of a settlement that creates some manner of common fund. And the achievement of a settlement turns on the ability of class counsel to secure the defendant's assent. No settlement, no fee award—at least, unless class counsel go to the considerable expense and risk of obtaining a damage verdict by way of a classwide trial. The fee award, moreover, stems from the creation of the common fund, not from how the fund comes to be allocated upon the making of claims against it by class members.[29]

All of the avenues for fees in connection with a class settlement remain beholden to the notion of a lawyer-client relationship, whether in the sense of individual lawyer-client contracts or a conception of the class as a whole as the client. In practical effect, the various avenues for fees create lines of demarcation between different client groups. Those lines, however, bear little connection to the leveraging involved in peacemaking. If anything, they play into the tendency of plaintiffs' lawyers to use the bargaining power gained from the representation of present claimants to create a peace plan for future ones while, at the same time, insulating themselves from the risks that the plan poses. Rather than concentrating the risks and rewards of peacemaking, the tripartite structure for fees in connection with class settlements actually enables plaintiffs' lawyers to separate those risks and rewards—passing off the former, while pocketing the latter.

Class counsel might seek to secure the assent of the defendant to a class settlement that creates at least some manner of common fund. What ultimately happens to claimants under the class settlement may be of little moment to class counsel. Neither the contingency fees for their inventory claims nor the fee award for creation of the common fund turns on the fate of future claimants. To be sure, an inadequate class settlement might reduce the contingency fees to be gained from the representation of claims thereunder. But that is a risk that class counsel might choose not to bear — indeed, that they effectively might impose on rival lawyers who may wish to continue their involvement in the subject matter of the litigation. Any class settlement does remain subject to judicial approval.[30] *Amchem* and *Ortiz,* however, reflect an understandable reluctance on the part of courts to engage in thoroughgoing review of class settlement terms and an inclination to focus instead on the structure of the bargaining process.[31] The major structural prescription of *Amchem* and *Ortiz*—separate representation of present and future claimants—pursues the quixotic goal of eliminating the leveraging in the peacemaking process rather than harnessing it for the protection of future claimants.

The structure for fees in bankruptcy does not fare much better. Chapter 11 of the Bankruptcy Code authorizes fee awards to counsel for creditors whose legal services make a "substantial contribution" to the reorganization proceeding.[32] Courts have understood the phrase "substantial contribution" to encompass services by a lawyer that benefit not just her creditor clients but also all parties involved in the reorganization — that "foster and enhance, rather than retard or interrupt the process of reorganization."[33] A mass tort plaintiffs' law firm that helps to craft a reorganization plan thus may obtain a fee award under Chapter 11.[34] The recognition that a lawyer for a particular group of creditors might make a "substantial contribution" to a reorganization plan points vaguely in the right direction. It at least suggests that the impact of a lawyer's efforts might extend beyond her nominal clients to persons who are not, and may never be, her clients. Current law, however, sets the fee award based on the equivalent of the "lodestar" method for fee awards in class actions, not on the magnitude of benefit to the reorganization.[35] The lodestar method entails a judicial determination of a reasonable hourly fee for the lawyer's services, multiplied by the number of hours reasonably spent in advancing the reorganization.

Its details aside, the bankruptcy fee structure shares much the same deficiencies as its counterpart for class settlements. In neither area does the fee structure capture the leveraging that operates as the fulcrum of peacemaking for mass torts. If anything, prepackaged reorganization plans accentuate leveraging in a manner that replicates in bankruptcy the pathologies of mass tort class settlements. The recurring feature of prepackaged reorganization plans — what enables them to be prepackaged — is the establishment of a separate trust fund prior to the filing of a reorganization petition. The separate trust provides for the payment of inventory claims in substantial part and, in so doing, enables the plaintiffs' law firms representing them to gain contingency fees. The unresolved stubs of inventory claims, in turn, afford voting power to those same lawyers to confirm a second trust fund in bankruptcy for future claimants. Here, again, plaintiffs' lawyers effectively engage in privatized law reform for future claimants. But they may choose not to bear the risks that reform poses for the future by focusing instead on the rewards from their representation of present claimants and any contribution that their legal services make toward the creation of the reorganization plan.

Individual Autonomy as Client Autonomy

The prevailing conception of mass torts as a problem of litigation does not merely influence the structure of representation and the determination of legal fees. It also shapes the ways in which the law attempts to legitimize the coercion that takes place in any peace arrangement. By "coercion," I mean the power of the peace arrangement to bring about law reform — to replace a person's preexisting right to sue in tort with an alternative set of rights to compensation under a grid. As currently understood, this coercive power remains grounded in notions of individual consent that stem from the autonomy of each individual client over the disposition of her legal claims. A bedrock principle of legal ethics holds that the client, not the lawyer, retains the ultimate power to decide whether to settle.

I do not mean to suggest that individual autonomy on the lawyer-client model is required under all peacemaking vehicles for mass torts. Both reorganizations in bankruptcy and limited-fund class settlements are mandatory in nature. The point nonetheless remains that a commitment to individual autonomy is a central feature of the present, litigation-based view of mass torts. That commitment exercises a kind of centripetal force in current thinking, calling for a compelling justification in order to be overridden. Even bankruptcy proceedings and limited-fund classes override individual autonomy not so much by choice but by necessity. In both settings, claims against the defendant are already interdependent in the sense that the treatment of any given claim will necessarily affect all others, regardless of the procedural format chosen. These counterexamples aside, individual autonomy remains the norm and coercion the deviation.

The centripetal force of individual autonomy is most apparent in the current conception of constitutional due process for class actions outside the limited-fund scenario. In its 1985 decision in *Phillips Petroleum Co. v. Shutts*, the Supreme Court held that individual claimants seeking damages generally must be afforded an opportunity to exclude themselves from the binding effect of a class action.[36] Insofar as they do not opt out, they may be bound and their rights to sue replaced. The failure to opt out effectively operates as an indication of consent—albeit, one that turns on an inference drawn by procedural law from inaction on the claimant's part. On this account, the coercive force of a class settlement depends on consent at an individual, retail level, akin to the way that an individual client retains autonomy over the disposition of her claim in the context of a conventional, nonclass lawsuit. Some commentators would push even further the assimilation of class settlements to ordinary lawyer-client relationships by calling for class members to be bound only when they affirmatively opt into a class settlement.[37]

A conception of peacemaking as a problem of governance suggests the possibility of a different agenda for the law. True enough, governance in private law includes something very much like the right to opt out of a class action. Each holder of shares in a corporation remains free to sell her shares. But governance in public law notably does not embrace an individual right to opt out, even though government regulation—like peace arrangements for mass torts—often works significant change in preexisting rights. Insofar as law reform affords anything like a right to opt out, it does so as a matter of policy choice, not constitutional command.[38] Individual autonomy in the sense respected in litigation is the deviation and coercion the norm. The justification for this stance bears exposition, for it too calls into doubt the prevailing understanding of mass torts as a problem of litigation.

Individual autonomy as an attribute of due process is not something confined to litigation. It also arises in connection with the most common manifestation today of governance in its public form: action by administrative agencies. As chapter 4 observed, administrative law divides agency action into the procedural categories of adjudication and rulemaking. The paradigmatic kinds of agency adjudications entail the use of trial-type procedures to apply the law to a particular factual setting, as when the National Labor Relations Board determines whether a given employer engaged in an unfair labor practice. By contrast, the paradigmatic sorts of agency rules regulate conduct prospectively and have the force of law indistinguishable in operation from legislation itself, as when the Environmental Protection Agency promulgates a rule limiting the release of a particular air pollutant.

Comprehensive settlements in many areas of complex civil litigation retain much of the mantle of adjudication. They provide for payouts to claimants that are virtually immediate — at most, that call for a ministerial calculation of the loss suffered from, say, securities fraud or an antitrust conspiracy to fix prices. The peace arrangement cashes out each claim in roughly the same manner as if all investors or consumers had sued individually. The central enterprise of peacemaking in the mass tort setting, by contrast, involves prospective rulemaking to regulate the compensation of claimants years into the future. The peace arrangement does not so much cash out claims as it describes and lends binding force to a set of rules with which to do so, even with regard to persons who may not have been inclined to sue individually at the time the deal is reached. Peacemaking in mass tort litigation thus is analogous to the adoption by statute of a workers' compensation regime, as distinct from its application to a given workplace accident.

In constitutional terms, the contrast between adjudication and rulemaking for administrative agencies traces its lineage to two foundational Supreme Court decisions from the early twentieth century: *Londoner v. City of Denver* and *Bi-Metallic Investment Co. v. State Board of Equalization of Colorado*.[39] The constitutional point drawn from the two cases by administrative law is easy enough to state: Affected persons are entitled as a matter of constitutional due process to an individualized "opportunity to be heard" in adjudication but not in rulemaking.[40] The basis for this distinction is not that agency rules somehow wield no coercive power or somehow do not alter rights. Rather, as Justice Oliver Wendell Holmes bluntly declared for the Court in *Bi-Metallic*, agency rules — like legislation — can "affect the person or property of individuals, sometimes to the point of ruin, without giving them a chance to be heard," let alone any right to opt themselves out of the rule. In agency rulemaking, due process rights "are protected in the only way that they can be in a complex society": by the power, "immediate or remote," that affected persons have "over those who make the rule."[41]

The constitutional analysis of *Bi-Metallic* is undoubtedly terse and presented by way of rhetorical flourish, a style characteristic of Justice Holmes's opinions generally.[42] There nonetheless is a deep truth beneath the terseness. The alternative to individual rights of self-help — whether to be heard or, even more, to opt out — consists of an institutional structure that links the self-interest of the rule makers with the well-being of the rule subjects. The process due is not one that safeguards individual autonomy in a litigation sense but one that *extends over time* the relationship between rule makers and rule subjects. Insofar as rulemaking springs from something that one might regard as consent, that consent does not take an individualized form. Consent takes the guise of a delegation of rulemaking power within an institutional structure designed to constrain the rule makers — specifically, that does so by ensuring that rulemaking is not a one-shot, self-contained affair but, rather, something with the potential to redound to the detriment of those who wield rulemaking power.

It ultimately is no surprise that the subject of individual autonomy in mass tort litigation should be part and parcel of a discussion that also embraces the structure for representation and the determination of legal fees. In order to legitimize the coercive power wielded by any mass tort peace arrangement, the law ultimately must align the interests of rule makers and rule subjects by extending their relationship over time. That enterprise, not efforts to extend individual autonomy, forms the real challenge for the law when peacemaking moves from adjudication to rulemaking. The remainder of this chapter takes up that challenge.

Leveraging Conflicts of Interest through Fee Design

What would the law of mass torts look like, were it to cast aside the narrowing suppositions of litigation and lawyer-client relationships? The law would not regard the simultaneous representation of present and future claimants as a disabling conflict of interest. The law instead would seek to accentuate that conflict for the protection of future claimants and the constraint of plaintiffs' lawyers. Specifically, the law would build on the reality that the dynamics of mass tort litigation push plaintiffs' law firms toward the accumulation of present claims in large numbers as the prelude to comprehensive peace negotiations. As a strategic matter, present claims are what provide plaintiffs' law firms the leverage to induce serious negotiation by the defendant to fashion a comprehensive peace. But present claims are also what tempt plaintiffs' lawyers to provide their assent to peace arrangements that allocate resources, risk, or both to the detriment of future claimants. In addition, present claims drive the tendency toward precipitous depletion of the settlement pot, once peace is made. The mechanism for misallocation, however, is not the fact of simultaneous representation — whether of inventory claims and claims resolved separately by a settlement or both present and future claims under a common settlement regime. Rather, the mechanism depends on separation of the risks that the peace arrangement poses for future claimants from the rewards that plaintiffs' law firms — whether the peacemakers or rival firms — gain from their representation of present claimants. Uninhibited by the suppositions of litigation, the law would focus directly on this separation of risks and rewards.

The crucial insight is that the structure of representation — the simultaneous representation of present and future claimants — does not form the problem for the law to solve. It instead provides the vehicle to *connect* risks and rewards. Making the requisite connection calls for a rethinking, not just of the mechanical details for legal fees but also of the core premise that fees should stem from what plaintiffs' lawyers do for persons whom the law regards as their clients. Fee design should focus on the leveraging of present claimants into the power to set the compensation terms for future ones and, indirectly, for the rival law firms who stand to form conventional lawyer-client relationships with them. The law, in short, should endeavor to turn the leveraging at the heart of peace negotiations into its own source of constraint.

Operational Details

Connecting risks and rewards inherently involves connecting the gains for plaintiffs' lawyers from the representation of present claimants with the fate of future claimants. The fate of all future claimants is not known at the time of peace negotiations and is unlikely to become known for decades. Connecting the present with the future nonetheless need not depend on information about how the peace arrangement will turn out in the end. The key, instead, is to link risks and rewards through means that are capable of straightforward administration and that depend on information available in short order. I sketch here one relatively simple approach to fee design that pursues these objectives. In speaking of specifics, I do not purport to set forth the one true path to enlightenment. My goal here is to initiate a new line of discussion about mass torts as a problem of governance, not to conclude that discussion. The details of one possible path for law reform simply help to frame in a concrete way the benefits of breaking from the narrowing suppositions of litigation.

The basics of my leveraging proposal are easily summarized. The proposal would link the rewards for plaintiffs' lawyers from the representation of present claimants to the viability of the peace arrangement for future ones. Specifically, the contingency fee to be gained by a plaintiffs' lawyer from representation of a present claimant would involve application of the agreed-upon fee percentage to the lesser of what that claimant receives and what similarly situated claimants receive under the peace arrangement as of a specified number of years in the future. By "similarly situated," I mean future claimants who are like present ones but for the fortuity of when they manifest the relevant disease. During the specified period of years, the fees to be garnered from the representation of present claimants under the terms of their contingency fee contracts would be placed in an interest-bearing escrow account. At the end of the specified period, the actual determination of the fee—what the lawyer ultimately gets—would take place, subject to the additional contingency specified in the leveraging proposal.

The period of years during which the fee calculation would remain open need not be especially long—certainly, not as long as the latency periods for the kinds of diseases implicated by mass torts. The period, instead, might consist of only three to five years. In the history of mass torts, significant problems for future claimants have never taken long at all to emerge, as the Manville asbestos trust and the fen-phen class settlement underscore.

The leveraging proposal would leave undisturbed what one might call the "take-home pay" for present claimants—that is, the sums they obtain in settlement of their tort claims, after deduction of the contingency fee percentage that they have agreed by contract to pay their lawyers. The linkage of payouts for present claimants and the financial rewards for their lawyers under conventional contingency fee arrangements is what bedevils the design of comprehensive peace arrangements. The problem does not arise from a desire to benefit present claimants per se. The treatment of present claimants is simply the vehicle through which to benefit the lawyers who represent them. The leveraging proposal alters contingency fee arrangements so as to focus attention on the most problematic contingency involved when lawyers leverage their representation of present claimants into rulemaking power over future ones: the uncertainty over how those future claimants will fare under the chosen rules. The leveraging proposal trains on that contingency rather than the payout to present claimants and, in so doing, connects the rewards to plaintiffs' lawyers with the real risk posed by peacemaking efforts. The desired effect of the leveraging proposal, of course, is to inhibit the misallocation of resources and risk to the detriment of future claimants—something likely to reduce payouts for present ones. But that result would be the consequence of the way that the leveraging proposal restructures the rewards for plaintiffs' lawyers, not its objective as such.

What should happen in the event of a discrepancy between the contingency fee placed in escrow with regard to a given claim and the fee ultimately garnered by the lawyer under the leveraging proposal? The most logical persons to receive that discrepancy would be future claimants, though not because it somehow stands as any measure of "compensation" due to them for a settlement regime gone bad. Future claimants simply have a superior claim to any discrepancy in funds as compared to other potential recipients. The escrowing of fees operates less as a resource for future claimants than as a means to align the interests of plaintiffs' lawyers more closely with those claimants' welfare.

The leveraging proposal speaks in terms of escrow accounts due to their widespread use in many settings where the law wishes to remove from the control of lawyers the funds implicated by a given representation. By placing into escrow the fees that plaintiffs' law firms otherwise would have gained immediately from their representation of present claimants, the leveraging proposal accounts for the time value of money during the period of years in which those fees are held. The proposal nonetheless could accommodate other treatments of those funds. The law, for example, might permit the relevant plaintiffs' law firms to choose the vehicles for investment of the funds. The one obvious caveat would be that the funds not be converted for use in support of the firm's practice until the contingency imposed by the leveraging proposal is resolved.

A more exotic variation would permit the firms to market to investors their right under the proposal to a stream of contingency fees based, in part, on how similarly situated claimants fare in the future. Investors would set the present value of that future payment stream based on independent evaluation of how the peace arrangement is likely to operate in practice, a process that would impart a degree of market discipline to the design of the peace in the first place. The analogy here would be to the way in which some state governments have "securitized" their rights to a stream of future payments from the tobacco industry under the MSA.[43] Securitization involves the sale of those rights to investors in exchange for their present value.

In any event, the gap in time between payouts to present claimants and determination of the contingency fees for their lawyers would operate on a rolling basis. For example, the contingency fee obtained from the payout received by a given claimant at the outset of the peace arrangement would depend on whether similarly situated claimants fare at least as well in, say, the fourth year of that arrangement. Fees from claims during the first year of the peace would depend on the treatment of similarly situated claimants in the fifth year, and so on. Operation of the leveraging proposal on a rolling basis would mean that plaintiffs' lawyers could not evade its strictures simply by holding back claims in their inventory so that they will be presented for payment under the peace arrangement.

The leveraging proposal ultimately would turn off its escrowing of fees on a rolling basis at the end of a specified period of settlement operation—one that, again, need not extend to the full life span of the settlement itself. One approach would be to set the end of the rolling escrow period according to when disease claims are expected to peak in their annual numbers. The one caveat to this approach would be that the escrow period should continue if claims deviate markedly from the pattern predicted at the time that peace is made. Whatever the specifics, the goal would be to apply the escrow feature for a sufficient period to gauge the actual operation of the peace arrangement.

The leveraging proposal, moreover, would regulate the fees from the representation of present claimants regardless of the law firm that represents them. The proposal would inhibit the incentive for plaintiffs' law firms—whether the designers of the peace arrangement or other firms—to undermine the operation of the settlement grid in practice. The goal, in short, would be to guard against the *Field of Dreams* problem, as exemplified by the influx of claims that decimated the Manville asbestos trust and bollixed up the fen-phen class settlement. Undermining the operation of the settlement grid for future claimants would serve only to reduce the fees ultimately obtained from the representation of present ones. By reaching the fees for plaintiffs' law firms in addition to those that design the peace plan, the proposal also would have implications for the timing and negotiating dynamics of any comprehensive peace, subjects that I defer for treatment in connection with other strategic implications of the proposal.

Two further points bear mention now to fill out the description of the proposal, with exposition again deferred to the discussion of strategic implications. The leveraging proposal acts on contingency fee arrangements but not on fee mechanisms designed to induce the peacemaking plaintiffs' law firm to maximize the overall value of the settlement. In particular, the leveraging proposal would not displace a court-made fee award based on the magnitude of the common fund created by the settlement regime. In fact, use of the leveraging proposal to address problems of misallocation would give greater impact to existing features of fee design aimed at the problem of maximization.

Finally, the proposal raises the need for some institutional framework to specify the multiyear period during which contingency fees shall remain contingent as well as the overall time period in which the escrow feature shall remain in force. As I explain in the next chapter, the institutional choice for these operational details flows directly from the answer to a related question: What institution has authority to do what the leveraging proposal necessarily would do with regard to claims pending in the tort system—namely, override the compensation terms of existing lawyer-client contracts? The answer to that question turns out to enable the law to discern, with relative ease, the who and the how for specification of the necessary time parameters.

Strategic Implications

The leveraging proposal speaks most directly to the allocation problems that have plagued peace arrangements for mass torts. The proposal reinforces the principle of temporal equity by inhibiting the generation of significant differences in compensation due simply to the fortuity of when disease manifests. Plaintiffs' lawyers gain contingency fees from the representation of present claimants only to the extent that future claimants who are similarly situated garner similar compensation under the settlement regime. Allocation problems nonetheless are not the only ones that confront the peacemaking process. As noted earlier, peacemaking efforts also should maximize the overall value of the peace arrangement and should take place at a time when sufficient information exists to design a viable peace. The strategic implications of the leveraging proposal for matters of maximization and timing form the subjects for discussion here.

The law does not lack ways to provide mass tort plaintiffs' lawyers with an incentive to maximize the overall value of peace arrangements. Fee awards based on the value of a common fund created by a class settlement provide class counsel with an incentive to maximize that fund. This is not to say that fee awards from common funds—or, for that matter, contingency fee arrangements in nonclass litigation—ever align perfectly the interests of lawyers and class members. It is simply to recognize that those fee awards increase commensurate with boosts in the overall value of the peace.

In making a fee award from a common fund, moreover, a court might adopt a wait-and-see approach, delaying the distribution of the award until more information emerges about the actual performance of the class settlement regime. As chapter 9 observed, the class settlement in the fen-phen litigation encountered significant problems, with an unexpected rush of claims delaying payments under the settlement grid. In his oversight of the class settlement, Judge Harvey Bartle declined to make a fee award based simply on the value of the common fund created for claimants, regardless of how the fund operated in practice. He opted instead to make only an "interim" award of "less than one-fifth" of the amount sought by class counsel, leaving open the timing for distribution of the remainder. Judge Bartle explained that a full-fledged fee award would have been "inequitable when so many Class Members are experiencing prolonged delays in the receipt of their benefits" and when ongoing efforts were afoot to shore up the class settlement through revision of its terms.[44] Delay in the fee award, however, took place only after problems had emerged. The prospect of delay was not made clear in advance, so as to influence the conduct of class settlement negotiations from the outset. The point nonetheless remains that the law has techniques to encourage maximization of the overall value of peace arrangements and can tweak those techniques after the fact, depending on how claimants actually fare.

The real problem is that fee mechanisms directed to matters of maximization coexist with other avenues by which plaintiffs' lawyers might gain from the peace—avenues that turn on the payout received by a particular claimant at a particular time, not on the overall value of the peace arrangement. As a result, peace negotiations are under constant pressure to make implicit tradeoffs across the different fee avenues. Plaintiffs' lawyers can reap rewards quickly by agreeing to arrangements that neither maximize the overall value of the peace nor allocate it equitably between the present and the future. Misallocation in favor of present claimants, in short, is the principal vehicle for avoidance of maximization.

The leveraging proposal envisions a different dynamic. The proposal effectively allocates greater risk to plaintiffs' lawyers in connection with the peacemaking process. The additional risk consists of the contingency that the leveraging proposal adds to what already are contingency fee arrangements for present claimants. In effect, the proposal prevents plaintiffs' lawyers from setting rules for future claimants based on the leverage gained from present claimants while, at the same time, reaping rewards from present claimants as if they were those lawyers' only "clients." The leveraging proposal forces plaintiffs' lawyers to consider the interests of future claimants, even though only present ones may be their clients as conventionally understood.

In order to secure the assent of plaintiffs' lawyers to a peace arrangement, the defendant effectively will need to compensate those lawyers for bearing additional risk. The only way for the defendant to do so under the leveraging proposal, however, is by simultaneously boosting payouts for both present and future claimants. Boosting payouts for present claimants alone would not compensate their lawyers for the additional risk that they bear under the proposal absent credible assurance that future claimants will fare at least as well under the peace arrangement. The structure of the leveraging proposal also places a floor on the extent to which peace negotiations simply might ratchet down payouts to both present and future claimants. A ratcheting down of payouts across the board would reduce the risk to plaintiffs' lawyers arising from the leveraging proposal. But any such ratcheting down stands to hurt plaintiffs' lawyers on all possible fee dimensions — contingency fees from present claimants, contingency fees from any future claimants they represent, and any fee award based on creation of a common fund for claimants as a whole. The leveraging proposal, in short, would restructure negotiation over matters of allocation so as to support, not undermine, existing incentives to maximize overall settlement value.

The scope of the leveraging proposal — reaching all plaintiffs' lawyers on a rolling basis — accentuates the foregoing effects. Making peace under the leveraging proposal increases the risk borne not only by the particular lawyers who negotiate the peace on the plaintiffs' side but also by their rivals. Unlike the designers of the peace arrangement, rival law firms within the plaintiffs' bar stand to reap no fee award from the making of the peace. They gain, if at all, only the contingency fees from their representation of particular claimants — precisely what the leveraging proposal would affect. To forestall objection to a peace arrangement by rival plaintiffs' lawyers, the peace designers could not buy them off — as they might now, in effect — by allocating resources and risk so as to favor present claimants generally. The peace designers could do so only by also providing credible assurance that future claimants will fare at least as well on a rolling basis.

Extension of the leveraging proposal to all plaintiffs' lawyers would have an additional effect. It would inhibit efforts by any given plaintiffs' law firm to evade the leveraging proposal through manipulation of the fee terms for its present clients. Attempts at such manipulation might take a variety of forms. The firm might try to raise the fee percentage that it charges present clients in order to offset the "tax" that would be imposed by the leveraging proposal for the skewing of payouts in favor of such persons. Or the firm might raise the fee percentage indirectly by demanding side payments from present clients as recompense for the tax. In the market for representation of mass tort claimants, however, plaintiffs' law firms are constantly jockeying for market share. As a result, any effort on the part of an individual law firm to move off the usual contingency fee percentage would risk a loss of market share and, with it, credibility for that firm to serve as the leader for the plaintiffs' side in any eventual peace negotiation. Realizing this, plaintiffs' lawyers might seek to agree collectively — to collude, in antitrust parlance — to a form of price fixing with regard to the contingency fee that all of them will charge, whether explicitly or in practical operation. Implementation of the leveraging proposal, however, would take place in tandem with the existing per se prohibition in antitrust law against price fixing by horizontal competitors.[45]

Timing Implications

The leveraging proposal also would have implications for the timing of peace negotiations. At present, the incentives of plaintiffs' lawyers run in the direction of accumulating large numbers of present claimants as a means to gain leverage in the eventual peace negotiations. Any comprehensive peace, however, depends on projections of future claims. Those projections inform negotiations over both the overall value of the peace arrangement and matters of allocation in the settlement grid. Under current law, plaintiffs' lawyers may make rules for future claimants while largely insulating themselves from the risk of error in claim projections. Plaintiffs' lawyers—in particular, those who act as the peace designers—bear the risk of error only insofar as those lawyers choose to represent individual claimants under the settlement regime years into the future. Put differently, risk bearing turns on whether future claimants ultimately become clients, as conventionally understood.

Who bears the risk of error in claim projections should not depend on the choices of plaintiffs' lawyers about long-term business strategy. The leveraging proposal casts aside notions of conventional lawyer-client relationships in order to make the fee structure for peacemaking reflect underlying dynamics. Making peace means allocating not only dollars but also risk. The additional layer of contingency imparted by the leveraging proposal captures this idea, for any uncertainty about whether future claimants will fare at least as well as present ones turns in large part on the accuracy of the claim projections behind the settlement grid. Inhibited by the leveraging proposal from passing off the risk of error in claim projections to future claimants, plaintiffs' lawyers would have to account for that risk in deciding when to pursue comprehensive peace negotiations. The incentive would be to do so only when enough is known about the underlying litigation to make credible claim projections, for only then would plaintiffs' lawyers be positioned to assess the risk that the proposal places on them.

By linking risks and rewards, in other words, the leveraging proposal would make for a more accurate assessment by plaintiffs' lawyers of when the time is right to move from litigation to the design of rules for claim administration. Here, too, application of the leveraging proposal to all plaintiffs' lawyers, not just to the peace designers, would underscore the desired effect on timing. By linking the fees of all plaintiffs' lawyers to how future claimants fare relative to present ones, the proposal gives rival plaintiffs' lawyers a heightened incentive to scrutinize claim projections. The deal-making lawyers accordingly would want to make peace only when their underlying claim projections will bear scrutiny by their rivals.

Improved timing for peacemaking also would ease the administration of the leveraging proposal. Application of the proposal would not entail fine-grained inquiries into the particulars of claims. Rather, the proposal would push comprehensive peace arrangements to the point when both plaintiffs' lawyers and defendants have developed a relatively stable idea of what the relevant disease categories should be within the compensation grid. The grid, developed explicitly in the peace arrangement for the future, would have a secondary benefit. It would facilitate comparison of how present and future claimants with the same basic disease have fared. All disease categories in mass tort grids, of course, make rough, rule-of-thumb distinctions. They account for important differences but suppress unimportant details. That, however, is the same thing that would need to be done for purposes of the comparison for which the proposal calls.

Comparison to Risk-Based Claims

Before I turn in the next chapter to matters of implementation and institutional choice, a comparison of the leveraging proposal with a prominent alternative is in order. The comparison fills out the exposition of the proposal by highlighting the features that make it distinctive. The leveraging proposal capitalizes on the conflicting interests of present and future claimants by building that conflict into the fee design—specifically, by linking the fees for plaintiffs' lawyers to a contingency that looks to actual payouts for future claimants. In so doing, the proposal translates to the mass tort setting the lesson of *Bi-Metallic* about due process and the making of rules by public administrative agencies. Those to be bound by the rules are appropriately protected by structural measures that extend over time the connection between their well-being and the self-interest of the rule makers.

In each of the foregoing respects, the leveraging proposal stands in contrast with another path that remains open to the law. Scholars have long debated whether the law should recognize liability for the tortious imposition of risk. As chapter 6 noted, tort doctrine to date has manifested little receptiveness for risk-based claims, though scholars continue to debate whether that resistance is justified. Much of the debate takes place at the level of high theory, with risk-based claims providing an occasion for commentators to play out larger disagreements over the proper conception of tort law as privatized regulation or corrective justice. I do not purport to settle that debate here. My more modest goal is to consider risk-based claims as the basis for peacemaking, in contrast to the leveraging proposal.

The theoretical debate over risk-based claims has largely overlooked a point apparent only when one considers mass torts as a problem of governance. Whatever else one might say about it, disease manifestation as the touchstone for injury has the capacity to serve an important role as a constraint on peacemaking in the mass tort setting. If anything, to forestall the difficulties raised by risk-based claims in the context of peace negotiations, the law would need to make additional repairs along the lines of the leveraging proposal.

In the form most pertinent here, risk-based claims would enable all persons exposed to a given product to hold liable the defendant manufacturer for the additional increment of disease risk attributable to that exposure. The wrongful imposition of risk on product users generally, not the actual manifestation of disease in particular users, would form the focal point for liability. As elaborated by scholarship in the mass tort context,[46] risk-based claims along these lines would call for a corresponding change in tort remedies. In a world where liability would not turn on disease manifestation, the appropriate remedy for risk-based claims would not take the form of conventional damages. The remedy instead would consist of insurance policies to provide coverage to exposed persons for the increment of disease risk added by the defendant. As envisioned by one commentator, "[t]he premium contribution and the extent of coverage would reflect the probability of [disease] causation and thereby redress only the injury imposed by the long-term excess risk" attributable to the defendant's misdeeds.[47] In effect, all exposed persons would become policyholders under a group insurance plan, with the rewards for their lawyers keyed to its overall value.

Risk-based claims do bear a passing resemblance to the leveraging proposal. In effect, the proposal forces plaintiffs' lawyers who represent present claimants to consider the interests of future claimants as if they too were their clients. Recognition of risk-based claims would imply that plaintiffs' lawyers *literally* could have as their clients the persons whom I have described as future claimants. In the form described here, risk-based claims would eliminate the distinction between present claimants and future claimants by redefining the nature of injury in tort. All exposed persons would have the identical, present-day claim for the increment of risk imposed upon product users as a group. Plaintiffs' lawyers, in turn, would have reason to obtain as many such persons as possible as their present-day clients. Indeed, recognition of risk-based claims as a matter of substantive law would facilitate the use of class actions—potentially, in a mandatory form—where the plaintiff class would consist of all exposed persons.[48]

In short, both the leveraging proposal and risk-based claims contemplate the treatment of future claimants as clients, whether in practical operation (through fee design for the representation of present claimants) or literally (through a change in tort doctrine). This, however, is as far as the resemblance goes. Risk-based claims seemingly eliminate the conflict between present and future claimants by making all exposed persons the same for tort purposes and thereby facilitating their joint representation. In fact, risk-based claims do not eliminate the conflict. They just kick it down the road.

The conflict between present and future claimants stems not from tort doctrine but, instead, from the need for payouts to occur over time from some pool of resources — call it the total premiums collected in order to provide group insurance coverage, call it the common fund created by a class settlement, call it the net worth of the debtor corporation in bankruptcy. Risk-based claims convert all claimants into present claimants and thereby raise the possibility of compressing in time the bringing of claims. But they do not, and cannot, compress the time frame for payouts under insurance-type remedies. The disjunction between the time frame for claiming and the time frame for payouts is what poses the challenge for peacemakers in mass tort disputes.

In order to set the premiums necessary to fund any insurance-type remedy, one must estimate all of the variables that already go into peace negotiations: the magnitude of the additional risk attributable to the defendant, the range of losses associated with the manifestation of disease, the spacing of those losses over time, and so on. Setting the right premium so as to pool the right amount of resources, in other words, remains tied to the expected pattern of payouts in future years. In this regard, insurance-type remedies in tort are no different from more familiar insurance arrangements — say, for automobile or life insurance.

Risk-based claims would provide plaintiffs' lawyers with the upside of increases in the premiums that they initially negotiate for defendants to pay into the insurance scheme. Those increases would boost the fee award to the lawyers associated with the establishment of the insurance arrangement. Designing a viable insurance regime, however, turns not simply on estimation of the premiums to support it but also, more importantly, on the degree of confidence associated with that estimate. By enabling plaintiffs' lawyers to sue immediately on behalf of all exposed persons — certainly, by paving the way for mandatory class actions on their behalf — risk-based claims would add to existing incentives for plaintiffs' lawyers to focus primarily on immediate rewards rather than on the design of a viable insurance regime. The rewards for plaintiffs' lawyers would be sensitive only to the overall value of the insurance arrangement that they fashion, not the uncertainty about whether it ultimately will supply the requisite coverage over time. Only by making the rewards to plaintiffs' lawyers contingent on actual payouts under an insurance-type scheme can the law induce those lawyers to account for this uncertainty.

In addition, one would want to ensure that plaintiffs' lawyers themselves do not have an incentive to deplete available resources as a means to re-open the peace arrangement. This problem can be especially significant in settings, such as the fen-phen litigation, in which the line between disease manifestation and normal bodily functions is not clear-cut. The leveraging proposal addresses this problem by reducing the contingency fees that all plaintiffs' lawyers receive insofar as future claimants do not fare as well as present ones. Some proponents of risk-based claims implicitly acknowledge this *Field of Dreams* problem by suggesting that shortfalls in resources should mark the occasion for renegotiation to boost the premiums that the defendant must contribute.[49] But raising the possibility of renegotiation only fuels the incentive for resource depletion in the first place.

The foregoing difficulties take different forms, yet they are all of one piece. The existing link in tort doctrine between injury and disease manifestation affects not only claimants but also the lawyers who represent them on a contingency-fee basis. The effect of current doctrine—possibly, an inadvertent effect but one that is real nonetheless—is to make the rewards for plaintiffs' lawyers dependent on actual payouts to claimants associated with disease manifestation. By contrast, risk-based claims would move the law in the wrong direction precisely because they would redefine tort injury to consist of risk imposition rather than disease manifestation. Risk-based claims would enhance the governing power of plaintiffs' lawyers by enabling them to negotiate explicitly on behalf of all exposed persons. But, at the same time, risk-based claims would reduce the array of measures that the law might use to constrain the wielding of rulemaking power. Rather than enhance the connection between the rewards for plaintiffs' lawyers and the long-term viability of the insurance regime that they create, risk-based claims would further decouple the two. Everything depends on the upside provided to plaintiffs' lawyers by fee awards keyed to the overall value of the insurance regime, as initially created. Such a reward structure contravenes the fundamental lesson of *Bi-Metallic* by centralizing at one time the relationship between rule subjects and rule makers rather than extending that relationship over time.

All of this is not to say that the law would be unable to combine the recognition of risk-based claims with additional measures to align the rewards for lawyers with the risk that their peacemaking efforts pose. It is simply to highlight an undercurrent of my argument throughout: that the problems of mass torts are not chiefly problems of tort doctrine but, rather, problems of governance. One indication that the leveraging proposal is on to something central to mass torts lies in the need for the law to implement something like it to improve the peacemaking process, wholly apart from whether substantive law chooses to characterize the imposition of risk as a tort in itself.

The question that remains is: How might the law implement the leveraging proposal? As the next chapter explains, the job of implementation entails the playing out of implications from the basic shift to privatized administration from conventional tort litigation. Appropriately enough, there is a role for the administrative state here—not as the dictator of peace terms but, rather, as the means to improve the alignment of risks and rewards for private peacemakers as a condition for lending their handiwork the force of law.

CHAPTER XII

ADMINISTERING
THE LEVERAGING
PROPOSAL

With the exposition of the leveraging proposal in mind, I turn now to its implementation. Making peace for mass torts means supplanting not only tort litigation but also the financial arrangements associated with it on the plaintiffs' side. Specifically, the leveraging proposal turns on the overriding of fee agreements reached by contract between plaintiffs' lawyers and their clients. The effect of the override, moreover, is not simply to alter the fee terms to which the lawyer and the client previously agreed. The override envisioned in the leveraging proposal effectively would bring into being a relationship between the present claimants who are represented by the lawyer and future claimants who are not currently—and, indeed, may never become—clients of that lawyer.

The restructuring of fee agreements along the lines of the leveraging proposal is unlikely to occur simply as a matter of private negotiation, for both plaintiffs' lawyers and settling defendants stand to benefit from collusion within the backdrop of conventional fee designs. The implementation of the leveraging proposal accordingly turns on selection of an institution to impose the needed change as part of the peacemaking process. I initially explain how the job of implementation sits uneasily with the primary institutions used for peacemaking in recent years: class settlements and reorganizations in bankruptcy. There is, to be sure, some room for experimentation by these institutions; and, more broadly, there remains the possibility that they might be the subject of additional legislation along the lines of the leveraging proposal. In this chapter, I set forth a vision of the future that would play out more fully, in institutional terms, the bedrock observation that peacemaking for mass torts means turning from tort to administration.

When litigation operates largely as the vehicle for prospective rule-making, it might well be time to move out of court and into an institution overtly engaged in the making of rules. Peace arrangements might involve administration not just in their end-products — the grids they create for the payment of claims — but also in the process by which they gain binding force. Administration, appropriately enough, might involve the administrative state.

I hasten to emphasize that the involvement of the administrative state would not entail a vast new public bureaucracy whereby agencies would dictate solutions to mass tort disputes. Agencies do not stand to solve mass tort problems by themselves, but they can facilitate the pursuit of solutions within appropriate constraints. Precisely because they are public, administrative agencies have a capacity to do two things: (1) align with greater precision the risks and rewards associated with peacemaking through the overriding of fee agreements; and (2) lend binding authority to the results of private negotiations through the promulgation of the peace arrangement in the form of agency rules. The connection between implementation of the leveraging proposal and promulgation of the peace arrangement through agency rules is not accidental. Under the system that I shall describe, both plaintiffs' lawyers and settling defendants may engage in peacemaking as a rival regime of law reform; but they may do so only as part and parcel of measures to discipline their behavior. Power, in other words, would come only with the enhancement of responsibility.

The Need for Administration

The primary institutions used for peacemaking in recent years have some degree of authority over contingency fees. As chapter 11 in this book noted, mass tort class settlements often cap the contingency-fee percentage for lawyers who represent individual class members who then make claims under the settlement grid. As part of their review of class settlements, courts have authority to scrutinize any provision therein that would cap contingency fees. On occasion, moreover, bankruptcy courts have drawn upon precedents approving contingency fee caps under class settlements to uphold similar caps on the fees associated with at least some forms of payouts from bankruptcy trusts to mass tort claimants.[1]

The authority to cap the fee percentage associated with payouts under a class settlement or a bankruptcy trust nonetheless would mesh awkwardly with the leveraging proposal. Caps on contingency fees do override the fee terms of preexisting lawyer-client contracts, but that is where the similarity to the leveraging proposal ends. In upholding fee caps, courts have grounded their authority in various sources: the judicial obligation to review for reasonableness the fees associated with class actions, the inherent power of courts to regulate the conduct of lawyers practicing before them by setting aside contingency-fee agreements that would yield excessive fees, and the judicial obligation to safeguard the administration of class settlements to ensure that their fruits are not consumed unnecessarily by legal expenses.[2] Whatever the doctrinal pigeonhole, the overarching concern is that adherence to preexisting fee contracts would enable the lawyer to take too large of a cut from the payout to the client, given the reduction in risk that any settlement brings.

The leveraging proposal sits uneasily with judicial authority directed toward fee excessiveness. As a formal matter, the proposal does not purport to affect the "take-home pay" for the client. The concern that animates the proposal is not that application of preexisting fee contracts will leave present claimants with too little. The concern, instead, is that the structure of those contracts will influence the lawyer's actions in the design of the peace arrangement, such that the client might well receive an inequitably high payout by comparison to future claimants who are otherwise similarly situated. It would be ironic, to say the least, were courts to transform the existing authority for the regulation of contingency fees to guard against excessiveness into the basis for unleashing dynamics that ultimately might reduce the payouts to present claimants as clients.

If implementation were simply a question of authority, then new legislation for mass tort-related class settlements or reorganizations might well suffice. The mismatch between the leveraging proposal and existing authority to override fee agreements runs deeper, however. That authority proceeds from the premise that fee caps will alter the terms of the lawyer-client relationship so as to correspond more closely to what the lawyer and the client would have negotiated themselves, had the client recognized the reduction in risk associated with the peace arrangement. There is little reason to believe, however, that the leveraging proposal somehow would push lawyer-client relationships toward what they hypothetically would have been if both lawyer and client had negotiated the fee with full information. The leveraging proposal acts upon contingency fees to protect future claimants from both present clients and their lawyers, acting together, not to protect client from lawyer. The additional layer of contingency in the leveraging proposal effectively brings into existence a relationship between the lawyer and future claimants that neither the lawyer nor her present client is likely to desire.

Attempts to implement the leveraging proposal through the extension of existing authority for fee caps would come close to the assertion of a freestanding law reform power of the sort that the class action device does not possess. Bankruptcy law initially might seem a more promising vehicle for legislative reform, but that path too would be problematic. Bankruptcy law does stem from an explicit grant of authority to Congress in Article I of the Constitution to establish "uniform Laws on the subject of Bankruptcies throughout the United States."[3] This lawmaking power generally remains confined, however, to setting forth principles that "preserve substantive rights determined outside of bankruptcy while providing procedures to solve the collective action problem that arises when many creditors have claims on a limited pool of assets."[4] Put differently, the usual approach is to categorize as "claims" dischargeable in bankruptcy only what substantive law already regards as claims outside of that setting. Bankruptcy law simply provides an orderly process whereby the resolution of competing claims turns on their relative dollar value outside of bankruptcy, not on the happenstance of particular creditors garnering payment in full from the debtor before others can arrive on the scene.

Bankruptcy law countenances deviation from underlying substantive law only very sparingly and, then, only when necessary to preserve respect for the relative value of competing claims against the debtor. Thus, for example, mass tort-related reorganizations routinely discharge the claims of persons expected to manifest disease in the future, regardless of whether underlying substantive law would consider those persons to have tort claims at the time of the reorganization. The justification for this stance nonetheless stems from necessity rather than any freestanding law reform power. A mass tort-related reorganization that did not address future tort claims would work considerable distortion in the relative value of claims against the debtor. That kind of distortion would be well nigh inevitable and systematic in nature — a mass tort-related reorganization would be a pointless exercise — absent the treatment of future tort claims in the reorganization plan.[5] Even here, bankruptcy law acknowledges the deviation from its general resistance to law reform. For asbestos-related reorganizations, §524(g) creates a separate category of dischargeable "demands" for payment at future times that would not constitute "claims" dischargeable in bankruptcy generally.[6]

The fee reform contemplated by the leveraging proposal certainly would bear some connection to the objective of preserving the relative value of tort claims as they exist outside of bankruptcy. The goal, after all, would be to enhance the incentives for plaintiffs' lawyers to treat similarly claimants who are similarly situated but for the timing of disease. The leveraging proposal nonetheless does not rise to the level of something necessary or essential in order for a mass tort-related reorganization to occur at all as a practical matter.

Even if bankruptcy proceedings could implement the leveraging proposal, it is far from clear that they should be the exclusive vehicle to do so. The opportunity to reorganize under Chapter 11 does not turn on a showing of insolvency.[7] But courts have long regarded Chapter 11 as including an implicit requirement of "good faith" for the filing of a reorganization petition under its auspices. Debtors may not visit the strictures of Chapter 11 upon their creditors simply in order to gain respite from bothersome litigation. Rather, a reorganization petition must stem from a "serious threat" to the continued successful operation of the debtor corporation.[8] Only some mass torts pose such a "serious threat" to defendants. In seeking to make the peace process into a value-generating exercise for all concerned, the law should avoid pushing all peace efforts into the bankruptcy category. An implicit declaration of a serious threat to the debtor's operations likely would diminish its capitalization in the short term and thereby reduce the resources available for distribution in peace negotiations.

In sum, the overriding of contingency fee contracts in the manner envisioned by the leveraging proposal is a job not well suited to existing institutions, even with legislative supplementation. What is needed, more broadly, is an institution that routinely overrides private contracts in the pursuit of larger goals: the modern administrative state.

Negotiation as Rulemaking

Both the mass tort plaintiffs' bar and would-be defendants are unlikely to relish implementation of the leveraging proposal absent some benefit that would accompany it. Recognition of the need for the administrative state to implement the leveraging proposal actually helps to identify the quid pro quo that the law might provide. The involvement of the administrative state would raise the possibility of moving beyond the halting search for a suitable peacemaking institution in the post-*Amchem* period. For both plaintiffs' lawyers and defendants, the upside of implementing the leveraging proposal would consist of the opportunity to sweep away questions surrounding the binding force of peace arrangements by embodying them in agency rules.

The notion of peace arrangements promulgated as agency rules would not be as startling of a change as it initially might seem. Just as the leveraging proposal flows from the underlying dynamics of peacemaking, the use of agency rules would drag out into the clear light of day practices that already have come to operate as rival regimes for rulemaking. I discuss here how the law might meld the idea of peace arrangements crafted through private negotiation with the use of agency rules to lend those arrangements binding force.

The observation that agency rulemaking might draw upon private negotiation is hardly unfamiliar to administrative law. The 1990s saw private settlements in mass tort litigation increasingly take on dimensions of public rulemaking. In administrative law, the same decade witnessed a development in the opposite direction: the rise of negotiated rulemaking—"regneg," as the practice is popularly known[9]—to enable public rulemaking to draw on private negotiation. Our thinking about the convergence of private settlement and public rulemaking in the mass tort context stands to benefit from consideration of a corresponding convergence in administrative law.

To understand the features that distinguish negotiated rulemaking, a simplified overview of conventional agency rulemaking is helpful. Under conventional rulemaking procedures, initial responsibility for the development of a proposed rule rests with the rulemaking agency. The agency publishes a Notice of Proposed Rulemaking in the Federal Register, thereby commencing the process for public comment on the proposed rule. The agency then must give reasoned consideration to the comments it receives in the course of determining the content of the final rule.[10] Administrative law refers to this process as "notice and comment rulemaking."

During the 1980s, critics of notice and comment rulemaking suggested that it had become needlessly adversarial, as interested persons engaged in uncooperative posturing during the rulemaking process and then tied up rule implementation with litigation.[11] Drawing on discussions in the scholarly literature and ad hoc experimentation by agencies,[12] Congress enacted the Negotiated Rulemaking Act of 1990.[13] As described in the Act, negotiated rulemaking consists of an alternative path for the formulation of proposed rules but leaves unchanged the subsequent steps in the rulemaking process.

The first step in negotiated rulemaking consists of an agency determination that "there are a limited number of identifiable interests that will be significantly affected" by a rule on a given subject, such that the agency can convene a committee of persons who can "adequately represent the interests identified."[14] The agency publishes a notice in the Federal Register announcing its intention to use a negotiated rulemaking committee to develop a proposed rule, listing the interests "likely to be significantly affected" and identifying the persons proposed to represent those interests on the committee.[15] Negotiation then proceeds within the committee, which includes representatives of the rulemaking agency.[16] The Act calls for "consensus" on any proposed rule, consisting of either "unanimous concurrence among the interests represented" by the committee members or, if they choose, "a general but not unanimous concurrence."[17]

The agency retains the ultimate authority to determine whether to issue the proposed rule for public comment. In deciding to use negotiated rulemaking in the first place, however, the agency already will have considered whether it will use the rule negotiated by the committee "to the maximum extent possible consistent with the legal obligations of the agency."[18] Promulgation of the final rule and any litigation to seek judicial review remain unaffected. The Act specifically provides that a rule generated through negotiated rulemaking "shall not be accorded any greater deference by a court" than one produced by conventional notice and comment rulemaking.[19]

In terms of actual practice, negotiated rulemaking has proven to be that most rare of creatures: an academic idea that has changed the real world. Instances of negotiated rulemaking cut across the administrative state, involving the Environmental Protection Agency (EPA), the Federal Aviation Administration, the Occupational Safety and Health Administration, the Department of Transportation, and the National Park Service.[20] Negotiated rulemaking has attracted particular interest in environmental protection, with the EPA using the procedure to develop proposed rules on such subjects as performance standards for wood-burning stoves, abatement of asbestos-containing materials in school buildings, underground "injection" of hazardous waste, emission standards for coke oven batteries, and "fugitive" emissions of air pollution from leaks in industrial equipment.[21] Encouragement of negotiated rulemaking is a feature common to the divergent regulatory policies of Presidents Bill Clinton and George W. Bush.[22]

All of this is not to say that negotiated rulemaking has proven uncontroversial within administrative law. The criticisms leveled against the practice, however, are unlikely to have traction in the mass tort setting. Early critics of negotiated rulemaking feared that it would produce rules that interested parties regard as acceptable but that bear "scant resemblance" to the objectives of regulatory statutes.[23] Negotiated rulemaking in the mass tort context, by contrast, would not operate as a substitute for existing agency actions to implement statutory objectives. Making rules to compensate tort claimants for their past exposure to a product would remain distinct from the range of regulatory actions that the agency might undertake under existing law with regard to future product sales, for example.

Administrative law scholars disagree, moreover, about the practical benefits touted for negotiated rulemaking, with early research finding only minimal time savings and little difference in litigation rates for negotiated rules but later commentary faulting the methodology behind those conclusions.[24] The case for negotiated rulemaking in mass tort litigation, by contrast, rests less on efficiency in rule promulgation and more on improvement in rule content. Making peace for mass tort disputes already is a time consuming exercise fraught with the potential for litigation. Implementation of the leveraging proposal in tandem with negotiated rulemaking holds the promise that the time spent actually will advance the interests of future claimants, not merely those of plaintiffs' lawyers and the settling defendant.

Other critics have suggested that the resources needed to participate in negotiated rulemaking would push the practical operation of the process in favor of powerful, well-financed interests.[25] Peacemaking for mass tort disputes, however, is already the province of well-financed interests on both plaintiffs' and defendants' sides. If anything, negotiated rulemaking affords an opportunity to integrate other voices more explicitly into the peacemaking process, at least by comparison to existing institutions. Chapter 10 discussed the impact of public health perspectives on the resolution of mass tort disputes and catalogued the difficulties that arise when the government sues to advance public health goals. One overarching conclusion from that discussion is that efforts to turn the government into another form of mass tort plaintiffs' law firm get the direction of law reform precisely backward. My argument here is that a more fruitful course consists of disciplining the rulemaking to be achieved at the behest of plaintiffs' lawyers by bringing that process within the aegis of government. The negotiated rulemaking committee might include representatives of the public health community as well as the lawyers on the contending sides. For that matter, the representatives of the rulemaking agency likely will reflect a regulatory perspective on the issues under negotiation, one informed by public health considerations.

Negotiated Rulemaking for the Mass Tort Setting

As applied to the mass tort setting, negotiated rulemaking is unlikely to raise concerns akin to those voiced about the practice in ordinary agency regulation. The law nevertheless would need to adapt negotiated rulemaking to the particular challenges posed by mass tort disputes. To cast peace arrangements in the form of agency rules is not to say that the rulemaking agency would fund either the payouts to claimants or the administration of the compensation scheme. The agency rule, instead, might require the establishment of a compensation program funded and run by the settling defendants in the same manner that agency rules already mandate a wide range of programs and associated expenditures on the part of regulated industry. The agency would retain authority to monitor compliance with the rule—again, in the same manner as conventional regulation.

With these basic points in mind, I turn to five matters surrounding the use of negotiated rulemaking in the mass tort setting: (1) the source of authority for the agency rule, (2) the timing of negotiated rulemaking, (3) the harnessing of competitive forces within the mass tort plaintiffs' bar to work in tandem with the leveraging proposal, (4) the parameters for judicial review of the agency rule, and (5) constitutional considerations regarding the treatment of pending cases.

Rulemaking Authority

In administrative law, negotiated rulemaking does not supply additional substantive authority for agencies to make rules. It merely adds private negotiation to the menu of procedures available to agencies when they wish to wield their existing authority to make rules on the subject of environmental protection and the like. For mass torts, conversely, the law must add rulemaking authority to private negotiation. Specifically, application of negotiated rulemaking to the mass tort context would entail an initial delegation of power to issue rules that would displace tort litigation.

Any suggestion of federal power to displace tort litigation implicates contentious debates over "tort reform" and the preemption of state authority by federal law. To lessen these concerns here, the law might introduce two kinds of constraints. The first would be procedural in nature—namely, that agency rulemaking to displace mass tort litigation may occur *only* by way of negotiated rulemaking. The objective, in other words, would be to confer not a freestanding power to displace tort litigation but, rather, a more limited power to do so only on the basis of private negotiations.

The second constraint would speak to the scope of rulemaking authority in terms of both time and subject matter. Specifically, the law might look to the development of negotiated rulemaking itself, which started with isolated instances of agency experimentation before Congress set forth those practices in a general statute. Even experimentation confined to a particular agency, however, would require an initial delegation of rulemaking authority. Like the original Negotiated Rulemaking Act, a delegation to a single "test" agency might include a sunset provision, such that the rulemaking power conferred would expire within a period of years unless renewed.[26] Given the prevalence of pharmaceuticals and medical devices in mass tort litigation, the Food and Drug Administration (FDA) would be a logical choice for experimentation.

In the present political climate, the mere mention of the FDA—like the phrase "tort reform"—is enough to stir controversy. Criticism of the FDA in recent years, however, has the potential to induce fresh thinking about how the law might better coordinate litigation with administration. Studies of pharmaceutical regulation have long voiced concern over "postmarketing surveillance" by the FDA—that is, the resources, authority, information, and inclination needed for the agency to monitor the safety of products after the agency has approved them for sale.[27] In recent years, concern over postmarketing surveillance by the FDA has moved considerably beyond academic circles. Much of the impetus for this attention stems from indications in scientific research of a possible causal link between the prescription pain relief medication Vioxx and heart attacks in long-term users.[28]

The controversy surrounding Vioxx predictably has led to a flood of litigation nationwide.[29] Litigation, in turn, has led to the release by manufacturer Merck & Company of internal studies that its critics believe should have alerted the company to an increased risk of heart attacks at times prior to the public controversy surrounding Vioxx.[30] The controversy has spread to the scientific community, with the prestigious *New England Journal of Medicine* publicly questioned for not pressing researchers associated with Merck with concerns regarding the data used in an early published article initially invoked to support the safety of Vioxx.[31] One commentator plausibly faults the same journal on a different ground: that its editors employed "sloppy and rushed" procedures in the course of demanding that the article authors issue a correction to their results.[32] The FDA itself has not emerged unscathed, having approved Vioxx as a prelude to its prescription on a widespread basis. Attention has focused on whether the FDA undertook appropriate postmarketing surveillance to learn of emerging problems associated with the drug and whether the agency acted expeditiously upon information that it received.[33] The controversy surrounding Vioxx has gone on to engulf other prescription drugs for pain—Bextra and Celebrex—within the same chemical class known as "Cox-2 inhibitors."[34]

The design of a regime for FDA postmarketing surveillance is not my project here. In the course of thinking afresh about that subject, however, policymakers should consider the full range of consequences that flow from initial agency approval of a pharmaceutical product. The debate over postmarketing surveillance has centered largely on FDA action to revisit the safety of approved products — action to undo for the future what the agency's own regulatory determination enabled to happen in the past. My suggestion is that the undoing of a previous drug approval appropriately encompasses a role in the resolution of mass tort claims. Those claims, after all, are among the most significant by-products of agency approval. The debate over postmarketing surveillance by the FDA, in other words, should encompass the regime that currently provides surveillance over the safety of drugs once they enter the marketplace — namely, mass tort litigation and the settlements that it produces.

Triggering Negotiated Rulemaking

The need for rulemaking authority aside, other operational details would concern the initiation of the rulemaking process. One would not want efforts to initiate agency action to become just another means to push mass tort litigation precipitously from the immature to the mature stage. One approach to constrain manipulation of the timing for negotiated rulemaking would draw upon the existing framework of the MDL Panel. Recall that current law authorizes the MDL Panel to transfer pending federal lawsuits involving "one or more common questions of fact" to a single federal district court for purposes of "coordinated or consolidated pretrial proceedings."[35] Upon the conclusion of pretrial proceedings — chiefly, consolidated discovery into factual questions common across all claimants — the transferee court must send the cases back to the respective federal courts from whence they came.[36]

As a practical matter, consolidated pretrial proceedings at the behest of the MDL Panel already form a setting ripe for plaintiffs' lawyers and defendants to begin discussions about a comprehensive peace. In fact, the steering committees typically formed on the plaintiffs' side to conduct consolidated pretrial proceedings would provide a natural springboard for selection of representatives for any negotiated rulemaking committee. The law might build on these realities by conditioning the exercise of agency authority to pursue negotiated rulemaking in a given area of mass tort litigation upon the conclusion of pretrial proceedings in consolidated MDL litigation. This approach would require no additional authority for the MDL Panel. It simply would use the byproducts of that authority as an indication that mass tort litigation on a given subject has progressed to an extent sufficient to warrant consideration of a comprehensive resolution.

Linking negotiated rulemaking to the completion of consolidated pretrial proceedings would have two implications. Both speak to the implementation of the leveraging proposal as part of the rulemaking process.

The first implication concerns information and the allocation of power to set the operational details of the leveraging proposal. Negotiated rulemaking, of course, would encompass the terms of the compensation grid. But negotiation would not properly encompass the operational details of the leveraging proposal—that is, the precise number of years that contingency fees from present claimants would remain in escrow and the total number of years that the proposal would operate on a rolling basis. The reason is that one would not want to enable the negotiators to make implicit trade-offs between the terms of the compensation grid and the specific ways in which the leveraging proposal would affect the fees for plaintiffs' lawyers. The latter should comprise the subject for specification by the agency itself, as part of its announcement to pursue negotiated rulemaking in the first place. This would be consistent with the idea of using agency rules to lend binding authority to the negotiated peace, but only with the quid pro quo of submission by the peacemaking lawyers to the leveraging proposal.

Setting the number of years for the escrow period and the overall operation of the leveraging proposal does not call for anything approaching scientific exactitude. The improved alignment of risks and rewards flows primarily from the core notion of linking contingency fees for present claimants to payouts for future claimants, not from the exact number of years selected for either of the necessary parameters. What is needed for both consists simply of rough, ballpark estimates. The important point is that, in specifying the necessary time periods as part of its commencement of negotiated rulemaking, the agency may draw upon the information about the underlying litigation developed in consolidated pretrial proceedings.

In fact, the agency should consider making compliance with the leveraging proposal a precondition for membership on the negotiated rulemaking committee. As a formal matter, the date on which the leveraging proposal would take effect over plaintiffs' lawyers as a whole would be the same as the effective date for the eventual agency rule. Compliance with the proposal in the interim by plaintiffs' representatives on the negotiated rulemaking committee nonetheless would be desirable. Willingness to comply with the proposal would evidence the suitability of plaintiffs' lawyers to participate in negotiated rulemaking. Their pledge of voluntary compliance effectively would signal to the agency that they are willing to stake their financial rewards on the soundness of the rule they craft. As a practical matter, moreover, compliance with the leveraging proposal by plaintiffs' representatives on the committee would inhibit efforts to settle their pending cases prior to the date on which the agency rule would take effect as a means to evade the escrowing of fees.

Linkage of agency rulemaking to the existing MDL Panel has a second implication that goes to the idea of leveraging itself. The constraint imparted by the leveraging proposal turns on the representation of present claimants in substantial numbers. The prospect of profiting from those representations is what the leveraging proposal employs in the service of future claimants. Tying the initiation of negotiated rulemaking to the completion of consolidated pretrial proceedings helps to ensure that mass tort litigation will have progressed sufficiently that large numbers of claims already will be on file. That, after all, is the practical justification for consolidation by the MDL Panel in the first place. Having invested the resources to precipitate MDL Panel consolidation, moreover, many plaintiffs' law firms likely will have an interest in the representation of additional claims in the short term. The link to MDL Panel consolidation, in short, enables one to be confident that the leveraging proposal will have a source of leverage on which to operate.

Competition, Fees, and the Content of the Final Rule

By placing peace negotiations in the hands of a rulemaking committee, I do not mean to suggest that all plaintiffs' lawyers share the same perspective on the appropriate content of the rule. Fissures and rivalries likely will emerge, as they do now. Crafting a workable peace can be as much a process of resolving disagreements within the mass tort plaintiffs' bar as it is a way to hammer out a deal between plaintiffs and defendants. If anything, identification of the rulemaking committee members—literally, who shall have a place at the negotiating table—has the potential to exacerbate tensions within the plaintiffs' bar. The features of the negotiated rulemaking process that I have sketched nonetheless hold the promise of channeling these rivalries in a more productive direction.

As adapted for the mass tort setting, negotiated rulemaking would remain a process for the generation of proposed rules. Later stages of the rulemaking process—in particular, the notice and comment phase—would remain unchanged. In administrative law, the procedures for notice and comment rulemaking do not exist in isolation; rather, they relate closely to constraints on the content of the final rule. The agency, of course, must act within its substantive authority and in accordance with applicable procedural requirements. In addition, the content of its rule must be neither "arbitrary" nor "capricious."[37] Judicial review for arbitrariness—what administrative law dubs "hard look" review—examines the rigor exercised by the agency in its determination of rule content.

Hard look review recognizes that "policymaking in a complex society must account for uncertainty," much like the design of peace arrangements for mass torts. In the words of the leading Supreme Court decision on hard look review, the agency may not simply invoke the existence of "'substantial uncertainty' as a justification for its actions." The agency instead "must explain the evidence which is available, and must offer a 'rational connection between the facts found and the choice made.'"[38] The need for reasoned explanation extends to the content of the rule that the agency ultimately chooses and to the plausible alternatives it decides to forego.[39] The process of notice and comment on the proposed rule is integral to the checks on agency arbitrariness. Public comment serves as the principal means by which interested persons may offer information and argument to shed doubt on the agency's proposed approach.

The key point about the later stages of the rulemaking process is this: They can form the vehicle for the law to deploy rivalries within the plaintiffs' bar in the service of rule design. To be sure, the idea that rival plaintiffs' lawyers might object to the content of the proposed rule operates in tension with one of the justifications for negotiated rulemaking in conventional regulation: the promise of greater efficiency in rule implementation when potential objections are worked out in advance. As noted earlier, however, the justifications for negotiated rulemaking in the mass tort area do not rest on gains in efficiency. The justifications instead speak to the capacity of negotiated rulemaking to expose peacemaking in mass tort litigation as a rival regime of law reform and, at the same time, to discipline that process through implementation of the leveraging proposal. The prospect that rival plaintiffs' lawyers outside of the rulemaking committee might object to the content of the proposed rule works in consonance with these justifications. Here, again, peacemaking cast as negotiated rulemaking would not so much transform mass tort litigation as it would expose its underlying anatomy.

The major instances in which peace arrangements for mass torts have met with successful challenge have involved the playing out of rivalries within the plaintiffs' bar. Examples include the fissures within the asbestos plaintiffs' bar that ultimately derailed the class settlements in *Amchem* and *Ortiz* as well as the successful effort by rival lawyers to challenge the class settlement originally proposed in the Sulzer hip implant litigation.[40] Two features of the regime I have sketched would accentuate the potential for rival plaintiffs' lawyers to serve as a source of discipline on negotiated rulemaking.

First, the leveraging proposal would apply to plaintiffs' lawyers on the negotiated rulemaking committee and to their rivals. The result would be to make the contingency fees that rival lawyers stand to gain from their

264 | CHAPTER XII

representation of present claimants dependent on the capacity of the peace arrangement actually to deliver equitable treatment for future claimants. Rival lawyers thus would have self-interested reasons to scrutinize with care the factual premises and policy choices behind the proposed rule.

Second, recall that the leveraging proposal would work in tandem with fee awards based on the overall value of the peace arrangement. In determining the size of the award, the rulemaking agency would act in much the same manner as a court in the class settlement context, evaluating fee requests by comparison to awards made in similar litigation.[41] The allocation of the award, however, need not follow the practices prevalent in class settlements.

The current framework for fee awards in class action litigation contemplates the possibility of awards to objectors, but that framework makes for perverse incentives of its own. As one commentator notes, "the objector's attorney can receive a fee award only when the objector's efforts 'improve' the settlement, but not when the objector's efforts cause the court to reject the settlement or decline to certify the class. This creates an obvious incentive for the objector to "'pull his punch' and prefer revision over objection."[42] Other scholars have voiced similar dismay upon finding "no case in which a court has awarded attorney's fees to objecting counsel for raising arguments that caused the court to disapprove a class action settlement."[43] One line of further commentary suggests that the successful derailing of a proposed class settlement should work to install the objecting law firm as a replacement for incumbent class counsel, whether literally or in practical operation.[44]

Whatever reforms the law of class actions might undertake within its own sphere, there is no reason why one should perpetuate its present deficiencies in negotiated rulemaking for mass torts. In allocating any fee award, the agency properly should reward rival plaintiffs' lawyers whose input in the public comment process results in either the tweaking or the replacement of the rule as originally framed by negotiation. Allocation of the fee award, in other words, could serve much the same goal — at least, financially speaking — as class action reforms that raise the potential for replacement of incumbent class counsel. Most importantly, rival plaintiffs' lawyers need not actually object to proposed rules in order to function as a desirable constraint on the rulemaking process. Rather, the *potential* for them to do so would operate to discipline the conduct of negotiations by the rulemaking committee.[45] This, too, is in keeping with my larger rethinking of mass torts as a problem of governance. As *Bi-Metallic* teaches, rulemaking does not require preservation of the kinds of individual autonomy regarded as the hallmarks of due process in litigation. The alternative, however, consists of an institutional structure that constrains the rule makers by threatening them with replacement. The prospect that rival plaintiffs' lawyers might capture the lion's share of the fee award associated with peacemaking would translate this threat of replacement into financial terms.

Judicial Review

Peace made binding through negotiated rulemaking also would have beneficial consequences for judicial review. At present, the court undertaking review of a proposed class settlement or reorganization plan is likely to be the same court that has overseen the painstaking efforts—often, over an extended time period—to design the peace. Having already invested that time, a judge understandably might feel reluctant to chuck the resulting deal. By contrast, judicial review of peace arrangements in the form of agency rules would take place in a forum with no particular investment in the brokering of the deal. To be sure, no court would lightly toss out a rule that promises peace in mass tort litigation any more than a court would lightly invalidate a conventional agency rule on a matter of high policy importance. The court simply would not have any special reason, aside from the general importance of the subject matter, to tread lightly in its review for arbitrariness.

The law, moreover, need not tolerate a scattering of litigation to challenge rules for mass torts any more than it does for rules on more familiar subjects like air pollution. Nor should the forum for judicial review be the product of a strategy to sue in a particular court thought to be usually hospitable to those who wish to overturn the rule. Rather, Congress might provide for judicial review only in a specified venue, much like some regulatory legislation today provides for review of implementing rules exclusively in the United States Court of Appeals for the District of Columbia Circuit.[46]

Constitutionality and the Treatment of Pending Cases

The replacement of rights to sue in tort with a new set of rights to compensation under an agency rule would call for careful constitutional analysis. Two strands bear discussion. The first concerns the judicial power granted to the federal courts under Article III of the Constitution. The second concerns the right to jury trial protected by the Seventh Amendment. To anticipate the argument to follow: Supreme Court decisions concerning both provisions strongly suggest that the replacement of tort rights of action along the lines suggested here would be constitutional. And any lingering uncertainty—specifically, with regard to the treatment of pending tort cases—would not undercut the proposal in practice.

The issue under Article III is easily stated. At the very least, negotiated rulemaking moves future cases concerning a given mass tort out of the courts and into the administrative regime described in the rule. Some of those disputes undoubtedly would lie between citizens of different states— that is, might otherwise have given rise to cases in federal court under what is commonly known as the grant of "diversity jurisdiction" in Article III.[47] The prospect that at least some of the litigation replaced by the agency rule otherwise might have been brought in an Article III court is what gives rise to constitutional concern.

In a long line of decisions, the Supreme Court has sought to delineate the outer bounds on the authority of Congress to switch matters within the Article III jurisdiction of the federal courts into non–Article III institutions—what scholars describe as "legislative courts."[48] The administrative regime envisioned here would follow the workers' compensation model and, as such, lies well within permissible bounds. In its 1932 decision in *Crowell v. Benson,* the Supreme Court turned away, in relevant part, an Article III challenge to the Longshoremen's and Harbor Workers' Compensation Act.[49] The Act replaced the common-law negligence action of seamen against their employers for work-related injuries with a no-fault administrative compensation regime. In essence, the Act was "designed to accomplish the same general purpose" within the realm of admiralty as state workers' compensation laws for ordinary industry.[50] Like other workers' compensation laws, the Act in *Crowell* "establishe[d] the measure of the employer's liability, . . . leaving open for determination the questions of fact as to the circumstances, nature, extent, and consequences of injuries sustained by the employee for which compensation is to be made in accordance with the prescribed standards."[51] That determination was to be made by an administrative body, not an Article III court.

Just as Article III encompasses actions at common law between diverse citizens, Article III also includes "all cases of admiralty and maritime jurisdiction."[52] The *Crowell* Court nonetheless noted that "the mode of proceeding in which that jurisdiction is to be exercised" remains "subject to the regulation of Congress," acting within its constitutional powers.[53] The Court turned away the Article III challenge to the treatment of fact finding under the compensation grid, observing that the Act preserved the "full authority" of Article III courts "to deal with matters of law" arising from compensation proceedings. The Court understood these "matters of law" to encompass review by an Article III court to ascertain whether a given compensation award was "not supported by evidence in the record."[54] In more recent times, the Court has continued to voice its adherence to the idea that judicial review for matters of law, as framed in *Crowell,* will suffice for Article III purposes when an administrative compensation regime replaces litigation at common law.[55] The negotiated rulemaking regime proposed here—like administrative agency action generally—would not purport to foreclose such review.

The Seventh Amendment mandates the preservation of "the right of trial by jury" in "suits at common law."[56] Whatever the outer parameters of the phrase "suits at common law," constitutional doctrine has long established that tort actions are among those that trigger the Seventh Amendment right to jury.[57] Nevertheless, as part of a series of cases that put to rest the constitutionality of state workers' compensation legislation, the Supreme Court in its 1917 decision in *Mountain Timber Co. v. Washington* turned away objections based on the Seventh Amendment.[58] The legislation that prompted the Court's holding was purely prospective in the sense of abolishing rights of action in tort between workers and their employers after a specified date. The Court reasoned that the legislation, at least as to the matters within its reach, had "abolishe[d] all right of recovery" at common law and thus left "nothing to be tried by jury." By contrast, actions "pending and existing" prior to the specified date were "expressly saved" from workers' compensation legislation, and nothing therein purported to deny the right to jury trial in those cases.[59]

Taken on its own terms, the holding in *Mountain Timber* does not squarely resolve whether law reform on the workers' compensation model could move pending tort cases into a jury-less compensation scheme. The Court has since made clear that Congress, acting within its constitutional authority, may alter the content of substantive law in a manner that affects the treatment of pending cases, as long as Congress does not disturb any final judgments entered therein.[60] The implication is that, even though workers' compensation legislation did not reach pending cases short of final judgment, it could have done so, such that the logic of *Mountain Timber* would apply there as well. That result would be consistent with the holding of *Crowell* that fact finding in a workers' compensation–type regime may take place through administrative channels that do not involve juries.[61]

Any lingering uncertainty in constitutional doctrine aside, the implementation of the leveraging proposal through agency rulemaking does not depend in practice on the assertion of authority to reach pending tort claims. Any disinclination to do so—whether for legal or pragmatic reasons—actually would increase the desirability of the leveraging proposal.

If the agency rule would not reach pending cases, then those cases would have to be resolved separately—in all likelihood, through the sorts of aggregate settlements that accompanied the class settlements for future asbestos claims in *Amchem* and *Ortiz* or the original §524(g) trust for future claims in *Combustion Engineering*. The fear, as in those cases, would be that the resolution of pending cases would take place on terms designed to funnel resources to present claimants as a way to induce their lawyers' assent to a peace plan that would shortchange future claimants.

The crucial point is that the leveraging proposal could override the contingency fee arrangements for pending cases and thereby inhibit misallocation in a manner independent from the chosen reach of the compensation grid. Put differently, application of the leveraging proposal need not be coextensive with the category of mass tort claims subject to the agency rule. Unlike plucking pending cases themselves from the tort system, regulation of the fee contracts associated with them would involve no conceivable trampling upon the right to jury trial or, for that matter, Article III. With the leveraging proposal in place, it would not matter whether the agency rule encompassed pending tort cases. Even if they were to be resolved separately, the leveraging proposal would restructure the incentives of plaintiffs' lawyers for the protection of the future claimants who stand to be governed by the rule.

CONCLUSION

As the twenty-first century unfolds, the major theme for mass torts is one of convergence. Litigation brought by private lawyers on behalf of private claimants has come to operate, in practice, in the manner of public administration. The process involves the design of rules to govern large numbers of claims expected to stretch years into the future. Making peace means wielding coercive power so that the rules selected shall have the binding force of law. Peace, in other words, calls for private litigation to alter the rights of claimants on a prospective basis, much like workers' compensation legislation replaced tort litigation over workplace injuries at the dawn of the twentieth century. The story of mass torts today is the story of this rival regime of law reform.

In this study, I have argued for a "bottom-up" approach to mass torts. The most constructive step the law could take today would be to expose and to acknowledge forthrightly what mass tort litigation actually does. It is less a form of litigation and more an occasion for a series of miniaturized, privatized workers' compensation programs. The hard questions surrounding mass torts are questions of institutional design. They ask how the law might empower the making of peace and, at the same time, discipline the peacemakers themselves.

The meandering path of the law since the Supreme Court's 1997 decision in *Amchem* reflects a deep disjunction between the operation of mass tort litigation as a rival regime of law reform and the framework currently used to think about its workings. The vocabulary of mass torts today is the inherited vocabulary of litigation. It speaks in terms of lawyers and clients, not rule makers and rule subjects. It ties the financial rewards for the rule makers to the outcomes generated for persons the law regards as their clients. It bemoans conflicts of interest and, in their place, prescribes homogeneity as the main source of protection for future claimants against the demands of present ones upon available resources. The vocabulary of litigation, however, is not the only vocabulary available. To acknowledge the reality of mass torts today—to see them as presenting problems of governance, not of civil procedure or even of tort doctrine—would be to change the prevailing vocabulary.

Understood as problems of governance, mass torts call for a sharp break from entrenched suppositions. The impetus for that break rests on the need to bring institutional arrangements into line with the reality of peacemaking as a process for law reform. Any peace negotiation involves a kind of leveraging on the part of mass tort plaintiffs' lawyers. They use their representation of present claimants to support the assertion of a broader power to bargain over the fate of future ones. Instead of insisting on the separate representation of present and future claimants to avoid a conflict of interest, the law should leverage that conflict itself into a source of constraint. Instead of permitting contingency-fee arrangements for present claimants to separate the risks and rewards of peacemaking, the law should override those contracts for the protection of future claimants. Specifically, the law should restructure fee arrangements to correspond less with lawyer-client relationships and more with the leveraging that underlies the bargaining power of the peacemaking lawyers.

Overriding fee contracts, in turn, calls for a break from the institutions currently used to broker peace. Here, too, the law must build from the bottom up. It should draw its prescriptions from observed practice. To address the convergence of private negotiation with public lawmaking in the mass tort area, the law should look to the treatment of a similar convergence in the modern administrative state. Negotiated rulemaking offers a model for the integration of private negotiation with public authority—and, not incidentally, for the coupling of coercive power with responsibility in its exercise. This should not come as a surprise. When peacemaking for mass torts involves the making of rules for the future, we should not be startled to find that developments in agency rulemaking might offer a way beyond the impasse that has emerged in the law since *Amchem*.

Reform along the foregoing lines does not require a vast new public bureaucracy. Nor does it require that the government dictate the peace terms for mass tort disputes. Enforcement of the leveraging proposal I have sketched would cast the government in a much more modest role. The proposal would bring to bear upon private peacemakers the broader risks and costs that their activities pose—especially for persons who are not now and may never be their clients. In this regard, efforts to improve the connection between the risks and rewards of peacemaking draw upon much the same rationale as modern regulation. Both seek to impress upon the holders of private power the social costs of their activities but, otherwise, to leave those private actors with ample latitude to apply their creative talents.

All of this sounds thoroughly contemporary. It should not. Viewed from a longer historical perspective, the changes I have described would bring the law of large-scale civil litigation full circle with its ancestral past. In a leading historical account, Stephen Yeazell traces the origins of the modern class action to medieval group litigation. To the modern eye, the most remarkable thing about medieval group litigation consists of its "singular lack of attention to issues that lie close to the heart of the modern legal and social debate" over the class action device. "Manorial, royal, and ecclesiastical courts heard suits by and against collectivities of people without any apparent concern for the adequacy of the group's representation by those speaking for it, for conflicts of interest within the represented group, or even for the exact contours of the group itself."[1] The reason for this inattention lies in the unquestioned authority of medieval groups—the villages, merchant guilds, and other bodies that wielded powers of governance, albeit in premodern form. What Yeazell describes as "the matter-of-fact quality of medieval group litigation" stemmed from the "place of the group at the foundations of the social order."[2] In such a setting, litigation on a group basis simply did not seem like an anomaly in need of justification. Medieval group litigation, in short, reflected a convergence of litigation on a collective basis with the organization of government at the time.

We have come far from the medieval world. Our modern conception of rights to sue as a form of private property means that efforts to alter those rights must put forward some justification in order to be regarded as legitimate. The steps I have urged here, nonetheless, draw more than passing inspiration from the connection between mass litigation and institutions of governance in medieval times. What is needed to break the impasse in mass torts today is a renewed convergence of litigation and governance, just one in keeping with government as we now know it.

The leveraging proposal I have sketched builds on the insight of the Supreme Court's decision in *Bi-Metallic*, legitimizing the making of binding, prospective rules by administrative agencies as a matter of constitutional due process. The legitimacy of agency rulemaking flows not from its preservation of individual autonomy in the way we conceive it in civil litigation. Rules are not binding because they give people the opportunity to opt out from their force. They comport with constitutional due process because of a commitment in the institutions of rulemaking to align — imperfectly, to be sure — the self-interest of the rule makers with the welfare over time of those who stand to be governed by the rules made. The rule makers operate based on an underlying delegation of power to promulgate rules. But that delegation does not occur in the manner of a private contract by which a client might empower a lawyer to act on her behalf. The delegation instead occurs at a much more ephemeral level. It takes place within a larger array of institutions that seek to combine power with responsibility — in sum, arrangements of good governance. Mass torts as a problem of governance demand no less.

The notion of clothing the deal-making lawyers in mass tort litigation with concepts of legitimacy drawn from administrative law may seem discomforting. By acknowledging the law reform power wielded by those lawyers and seeking to discipline its exercise, this study makes peace with the existence of that power in the first place. This, too, however, is in keeping with notions of government, as seen through modern eyes. As chapter 1 suggested, mass torts arose within the political context of the late twentieth century. Peacemakers in mass tort litigation could approach the law reform power of public legislation only because government itself had ceded that terrain — only because of the prevalent skepticism about the capacity of government to serve as the primary solution to complex problems. Mass tort litigation has emerged as a rival regime for law reform, because we have not turned over to the government alone the job of managing the consequences of mass production in a modern industrial economy. If anything, even legal cultures that have made different choices in that regard have shown signs of embracing private litigation on a collective basis as an adjunct to the administrative state. Spurred by legal disputes over the risks posed by mass marketed products, no less than France and Germany are now contemplating the importation of the class action device from across the Atlantic.[3]

Within Anglo-American legal culture, one important strand of scholarship defends tort law as an integral part of modern liberal democracy, precisely because tort law posits the existence of a private power to seek redress.[4] Tort law empowers private persons to sue in a manner independent from the government, without having to seek its permission and, potentially, in the face of shortfalls in regulation by the government in times past. To be sure, this remains a much-disputed account among tort scholars. I suggest simply that it is consonant with the recognition that our world is not that of the medieval village, with trust reposed in a group of elders to govern wisely. If democracy today comes only along with distrust,[5] then it remains all the more important for private persons to have an alternative avenue for redress.

At the same time, however, our world is not one of thoroughgoing individualism. It is not the case that private persons have the capacity to wield on their own the rights that they hold independently from government. Enabling tort law to function as a meaningful avenue for redress necessarily means making use of agents—specialists adept in tort litigation in the same way that real estate agents are skilled at selling houses. It should not surprise us, then, that a world in which "the era of Big Government is over" is also a world in which big litigation has emerged over mass torts.[6]

The hard work for the law of mass torts today consists of harnessing the potential for peacemaking to generate tremendous social gains. Peace for defendants is what holds the potential to increase the availability of resources to fund any compensation grid. And peace for claimants holds the promise of streamlined payment with a minimum of wasteful transaction costs. In a world of scarce resources, this value-creating dimension of peacemaking is a considerable virtue. The job of unlocking those social gains takes creativity, savvy, and no small degree of risk taking. A world in which government is not a dictator of solutions is a world that needs the deal-making abilities of sophisticated, well-capitalized plaintiffs' lawyers and their defense counterparts. On this view, Joe Rice and the other leaders of the mass tort plaintiffs' bar are the latter-day descendants of the entrepreneurs who took the risks and crafted the complex business deals to unleash the modern industrial economy in the late nineteenth century. But just as the administrative state emerged to temper the self-interest of modern industrial enterprise, so, too, does the administrative state have a role to play now to discipline the "enterprise" of tort liability.[7] Peacemaking as a form of governance calls for sound governing arrangements for the making of peace.

ACKNOWLEDGMENTS

The completion of this book would not have been possible without the intellectual and personal support of many people. Three extraordinary scholars I am fortunate to count as friends—John Goldberg, Samuel Issacharoff, and Robert Rasmussen—gave generously of their scarce time to read the manuscript. I am grateful for their faith in me and in the project—especially for their willingness to push me hard about the arguments advanced in the book. I am indebted, in addition, to several scholars who enabled me to draw on their expertise in particular subject areas: Lisa Schultz Bressman on administrative law, Paul Edelman on the quantitative aspects of aggregation, Chris Guthrie on the cognitive psychology of litigation, Steven Hetcher on tort theory, Suzanna Sherry on the law of federal courts, and Charles Silver on the theory and practice of aggregate litigation. Howard Erichson, David Rosenberg, and an anonymous reviewer provided extensive comments on the entire manuscript in connection with the editorial process. Still others in the academy and the practicing bar—Timothy Lytton and Mark Plevin, respectively—assisted me in assembling relevant information for the book. I also benefited from the opportunity to present portions of the book at Stephen Bundy and Eleanor Swift's civil justice workshop at Boalt Hall School of Law and other portions at a Vanderbilt University Law School faculty workshop. Finally, two exceptional deans—Kent Syverud and, now, Edward Rubin—have created a dynamic, supportive environment for scholarship at Vanderbilt and accommodated me with the time needed to work intensively on the book.

My thinking about mass torts has been sharpened immeasurably by the opportunity to teach the subject over the past decade to the talented, energized students at both Vanderbilt University Law School and the University of Georgia School of Law. I am especially grateful for the fine research assistance I received from several Vanderbilt law students: Wendy Ertmer, David Housholder, Allison Small, and Stephanie Wolfe.

Portions of this book stand as revised versions of my earlier writings on mass torts and class actions. To describe anything found here as a "revised" form of those writings, nonetheless, is an understatement. Readers familiar with those works will find that relatively few sentences, much less broader arguments, have made their way into the book without significant revision. Portions of chapters 1, 2, and 12 build on ideas originally aired in a much more preliminary form in "Turning from Tort to Administration," 94 Michigan Law Review 899 (1996). The intellectual history of tort law presented in chapter 1 generalizes points that I first raised in "Gun Litigation in the Mass Tort Context," itself a chapter within a larger collection, *Suing the Gun Industry* (Timothy D. Lytton ed., University of Michigan Press 2005). Chapter 3 applies to the mass tort context observations about the broader phenomenon of class settlement pressure initially set forth in "Aggregation and Its Discontents: Class Settlement Pressure, Class-Wide Arbitration, and CAFA," 106 Columbia Law Review 1872 (2006). Chapter 4 builds on ideas originally set forth in "Future Mass Tort Claims and the Rule-Making/Adjudication Distinction," 74 Tulane Law Review 1781 (2000). Portions of chapters 5 and 8 extend, with substantial modification, the analysis first offered in "Autonomy, Peace, and Put Options in the Mass Tort Class Action," 115 Harvard Law Review 747 (2002), and "The Preexistence Principle and the Structure of the Class Action," 103 Columbia Law Review 149 (2003). Chapter 7 draws, in part, on ideas initially sketched in "Punitive Damage Class Actions and the Baseline of Tort," 36 Wake Forest Law Review 943 (2001).

NOTES

INTRODUCTION

1. John C. P. Goldberg et al., Tort Law: Responsibilities and Redress 3 (2004).

2. Palsgraf v. Long Island R.R. Co., 162 N.E. 99 (N.Y. 1928).

3. Brown v. Kendall, 60 Mass. 292 (1850).

4. Escola v. Coca-Cola Bottling Co., 150 P.2d 436 (Cal. 1944).

5. Oliver Wendell Holmes, *The Path of the Law*, 10 Harv. L. Rev. 457, 467 (1897).

6. *See* Samuel Issacharoff & John Fabian Witt, *The Inevitability of Aggregate Settlement: An Institutional Account of American Tort Law*, 57 Vand. L. Rev. 1571, 1577–99 (2005).

7. Michael J. Saks, *Do We Really Know Anything about the Behavior of the Tort Litigation System—And Why Not?*, 140 U. Pa. L. Rev. 1147, 1212 (1992).

8. *See* James S. Kakalik & Nicholas M. Pace, Costs and Compensation Paid in Tort Litigation 96 (1986) (96 percent of individual plaintiffs in tort litigation as a whole paid counsel on a contingent fee basis).

9. *E.g.*, Peter H. Schuck, Agent Orange on Trial (enlarged ed. 1987); Marcia Angell, Science on Trial (1996) (discussing silicone gel breast implant litigation); Michael D. Green, Bendectin and Birth Defects (1996); Joseph Sanders, Bendectin on Trial (2001).

10. Jack B. Weinstein, Individual Justice in Mass Tort Litigation (1995). For an instructional casebook in the area, *see* Linda S. Mullenix, Mass Tort Litigation (1996).

11. On the concept of relative risk, *see* Michael D. Green et al., Reference Guide on Epidemiology, in Federal Judicial Center, Reference Manual on Scientific Evidence 348–49 (2000).

12. Deborah R. Hensler & Mark A. Peterson, *Understanding Mass Personal Injury Litigation: A Socio-Legal Analysis*, 59 Brook. L. Rev. 961, 967 (1993).

13. The most significant exception consists of bankruptcy proceedings, a subject discussed in greater depth in chapter 9.

14. 521 U.S. 591 (1997); 527 U.S. 815 (1999).

15. *See* chapter 5.

16. *E.g.*, David Rosenberg, *The Causal Connection in Mass Exposure Cases: A "Public Law" Vision of the Tort System*, 97 Harv. L. Rev. 851 (1984).

17. *E.g.*, Ariel Porat & Alex Stein, Tort Liability under Uncertainty (2001); Wendy

E. Wagner, *Choosing Ignorance in the Manufacture of Toxic Products*, 82 Cornell L. Rev. 773 (1997); Heidi Li Feldman, *Science and Uncertainty in Mass Exposure Litigation*, 74 Tex. L. Rev. 1 (1995).

18. *See* Francis E. McGovern, *Resolving Mature Mass Tort Litigation*, 69 B.U. L. Rev. 659 (1989).

19. 509 U.S. 579 (1993).

CHAPTER 1

1. *See, e.g.,* Jon D. Hanson & Douglas A. Kysar, *Taking Behaviorism Seriously: The Problem of Market Manipulation*, 74 N.Y.U. L. Rev. 630 (1999); Jon D. Hanson & Douglas A. Kysar, *Taking Behaviorism Seriously: Some Evidence of Market Manipulation*, 112 Harv. L. Rev. 1420 (1999).

2. Asbestos litigation remains the leading example. *See* Paul Brodeur, Outrageous Misconduct (1985).

3. *See* Basic, Inc. v. Levinson, 485 U.S. 224, 243 (1988).

4. For an illustrative exposition, *see* Donald C. Langevoort, *Theories, Assumptions, and Securities Regulation: Market Efficiency Revisited*, 140 U. Pa. L. Rev. 151 (1992).

5. *See Basic*, 485 U.S. at 245–47.

6. *Id.*

7. John Fabian Witt, The Accidental Republic (2004).

8. *Id.*, ch. 3.

9. *E.g.*, G. Edward White, Tort Law in America: An Intellectual History 197–207 (expanded ed. 2003); James R. Hackney Jr., *The Intellectual Origins of American Strict Products Liability: A Case Study in American Pragmatic Instrumentalism*, 39 Am. J. Legal Hist. 443 (1995); George L. Priest, *The Invention of Enterprise Liability*, 14 J. Legal Stud. 461 (1985); William L. Prosser, *The Fall of the Citadel (Strict Liability to the Consumer)*, 50 Minn. L. Rev. 791 (1966).

10. *Id.* at 791 (discussing Henningsen v. Bloomfield Motors, Inc., 161 A.2d 69 (N.J. 1960)).

11. Restatement (Second) of Torts § 402A(1) (1964).

12. These aspects of the defect concept would emerge with sufficient clarity as to warrant articulation in the Restatement (Third) of Torts: Products Liability § 2 (1997).

13. James A. Henderson Jr. & Aaron D. Twerski, *Doctrinal Collapse in Products Liability: The Empty Shell of Failure to Warn*, 65 N.Y.U. L. Rev. 265, 325 (1990).

14. Restatement (Third) of Torts: Products Liability § 2 cmt. d (adopting "risk-utility balancing" as "the standard for judging the defectiveness of product design").

15. For criticism of this dominant view, *see* John C. P. Goldberg, *Unloved: Tort in the Modern Legal Academy*, 55 Vand. L. Rev. 1501, 1510–11 (2002).

16. For an exposition as to mass torts specifically, *see* David Rosenberg, *Mandatory-Litigation Class Action: The Only Option for Mass Tort Cases*, 115 Harv. L. Rev. 831 (2002).

17. William L. Prosser, Handbook on the Law of Torts 15 (1941). I am indebted to others for highlighting this passage from Prosser. *See* John C. P. Goldberg & Benjamin C. Zipursky, *The Moral of* MacPherson, 146 U. Pa. L. Rev. 1733, 1764–65 (1998).

18. Leon Green, *Tort Law as Public Law in Disguise (Part I)*, 38 Tex. L. Rev. 1 (1959).

19. Richard A. Posner, Economic Analysis of Law § 4.2, at 69 (1972).

20. United States v. Carroll Towing Company, 159 F.2d 169, 173 (2d Cir. 1947).

21. *See* Guido Calabresi, The Costs of Accidents 135–43 (1970).

22. On Traynor's intellectual contribution to modern products liability law, *see* White, *supra* note 9, ch. 6.

23. Michael L. Wells, *Scientific Policymaking and the Torts Revolution: The Revenge of the Ordinary Observer*, 26 Ga. L. Rev. 725, 727 (1992).

24. *E.g.*, Arthur Ripstein, Equality, Responsibility, and the Law (1999); Ernest J. Weinrib, The Idea of Private Law (1995); Jules Coleman, Risk and Wrongs (1992).

25. *E.g.*, Judith Resnik, *Trial as Error, Jurisdiction as Injury: The Transformation of Article III*, 113 Harv. L. Rev. 924 (2000).

26. Fed. R. Civ. P. 16 (authorizing the court "in its discretion" to hold pretrial conferences to "facilitate[e] the settlement of the case").

27. *E.g.*, Owen Fiss, *Against Settlement*, 93 Yale L.J. 1073 (1984).

28. Samuel R. Gross & Kent D. Syverud, *Don't Try: Civil Jury Verdicts in a System Geared to Settlement*, 44 UCLA L. Rev. 1, 3 (1996).

29. *See* Judith Resnik, *Managerial Judges*, 96 Harv. L. Rev. 376 (1982).

30. Additional amendments to Rule 23 in 2003 flesh out the basic structure created in 1966.

31. *See* Stephen C. Yeazell, From Medieval Group Litigation to the Modern Class Action (1987).

32. Fed. R. Civ. P. 23(b)(3).

33. *See* Fed. R. Civ. P. 23(b)(1)(B).

34. *See* Linda S. Mullenix, *Problems in Complex Litigation*, 10 Rev. Litig. 213, 215 (1991).

35. Fed. R. Civ. P. 23(b)(3) advisory committee's note.

36. Stephen C. Yeazell, *Re-Financing Civil Litigation*, 51 DePaul L. Rev. 183, 194 (2001).

37. *Id.* at 195.

38. Fed. R. Civ. P. 23(a).

39. As formulated in 1966, Rule 23(e) provided that "[a] class action may not be . . . compromised without the approval of the court."

40. *See* 18 Charles Alan Wright et al., Federal Practice and Procedure §4402, at 12 (2d ed. 2002).

41. 1 Public Papers of the Presidents of the United States: Ronald Reagan 1981, at 1 (1982).

42. 1 Public Papers of the Presidents of the United States: William J. Clinton 1996, at 79 (1997).

43. Both President Reagan and President Clinton would issue executive orders calling for cost-benefit analysis of regulatory initiatives. *See* Exec. Order No. 12291, 3 C.F.R. 127 (1981); Exec. Order No. 12866, 3 C.F.R. 638 (1993).

44. On the relationship between civil litigation in the United States and attitudes toward the role of government, *see* Robert A. Kagan, Adversarial Legalism 34–58 (2001).

CHAPTER II

1. *See* Francis E. McGovern, *Resolving Mature Mass Tort Litigation*, 69 B.U. L. Rev. 659 (1989).

2. *See* Daniel L. Rubinfeld & Suzanne Scotchmer, *Contingent Fees*, in 1 The New Palgrave Dictionary of Economics and Law 415, 417 (Peter Newman ed. 1998).

3. *E.g.*, Model Rules of Professional Conduct, Rule 1.7 (2003). Additional ethical prohibitions against the splitting of fees between lawyers and nonlawyers, subject to narrow exceptions, also affect the financing of mass tort litigation. *Id.*, Rule 5.4. The fee-splitting

stricture largely inhibits plaintiffs' law firms from providing to lending institutions or venture capitalists the sorts of security interests typically demanded in exchange for infusions of cash to support a new entrepreneurial venture.

4. *See* Paul Brodeur, Outrageous Misconduct 73 (1985) (crediting the plaintiff's victory in Borel v. Fibreboard Paper Products Corp., 493 F.2d 1076 (5th Cir. 1973), with triggering the "avalanche" of litigation over asbestos).

5. On the doctrinal difficulties raised by the public nuisance theory in the mass tort context, *see* chapter 10; Donald G. Gifford, *Public Nuisance as a Mass Products Liability Tort*, 71 U. Cin. L. Rev. 741 (2003).

6. *See, e.g.*, Sterling v. Velsicol Chem. Corp., 855 F.2d 1188, 1200 (6th Cir. 1988).

7. *E.g.*, Heather Won Tesoriero, *Vioxx "Trial in a Box" Cuts Cost of Filing Suit*, Wall St. J., Apr. 17, 2006, at B1.

8. McGovern, *supra* note 1, at 659.

9. Deborah R. Hensler & Mark A. Peterson, *Understanding Mass Personal Injury Litigation: A Socio-Legal Analysis*, 59 Brook. L. Rev. 961, 1045 (1993).

10. *See* Karen Dillon, *Only $1.5 Million a Year*, Am. Lawyer, Oct. 1989, at 38, 40–41 (profiling South Carolina firm known at the time as Ness, Motley, Loadholt, Richardson & Poole); Gary Taylor, *Outspoken Texan, Baron Establishes Toxic Tort Domain*, Legal Times, Nov. 21, 1983, at 1, 11 (profiling Dallas firm of Baron & Budd).

11. 28 U.S.C. § 1407 (2000).

12. *See* Howard M. Erichson, *Informal Aggregation: Procedural and Ethical Implications of Coordination among Counsel in Related Lawsuits*, 50 Duke L.J. 381, 398 (2000).

13. *See* American Bar Association, Commission on Asbestos Litigation, Report to the House of Delegates 8–9 (Feb. 2003).

14. Erichson, *supra* note 12.

15. Alex Berenson, *First Vioxx Lawsuit: Entryway into a Legal Labyrinth?*, N.Y. Times, July 11, 2005, at C5 (approximately 4,000 individual cases on file at the time of the first Vioxx trial).

16. *See, e.g.*, Benjamin C. Zipursky, *Civil Recourse, Not Corrective Justice*, 91 Geo. L.J. 695 (2003).

17. *See* Cimino v. Raymark Indus., 151 F.3d 297, 319–21 (5th Cir. 1998); *In re* Fibreboard Corp., 893 F.3d 706, 710–12 (5th Cir. 1990).

18. *See* Cimino v. Raymark Indus., 751 F. Supp. 649, 651–52 (E.D. Tex. 1990).

19. On the limits of preclusion doctrines in the asbestos litigation, *see* Michael D. Green, *The Inability of Offensive Collateral Estoppel to Fulfill Its Promise: An Examination of Estoppel in Asbestos Litigation*, 70 Iowa L. Rev. 141 (1984). On the problems of preclusion where informal aggregation of litigation has occurred, *see* Erichson, *supra* note 12, at 448–64.

20. 18 Charles Alan Wright et al., Federal Practice and Procedure § 4406, at 140 (2d ed. 2002).

21. *Id.* § 4417, at 412.

22. *See In re* Joint E. & S. Dist. Asbestos Litig., 129 B.R. 710, 746–47 (E. & S.D.N.Y. 1991) ("In part as a result of the known backlog of cases, only a trial date will generate sufficient incentive to compel the parties to settle or result in a trial verdict that terminates the case.").

23. Howard M. Erichson, *A Typology of Aggregate Settlements*, 80 Notre Dame L. Rev. 1791 (2005).

24. *See* W. Kip Viscusi, *Alternative Institutional Responses to Asbestos*, 12 J. Risk & Uncertainty 147, 160–61 (1996).

25. For discussion of how the asbestos litigation is both typical and atypical in the annals of mass torts, *see* Michelle J. White, *Asbestos and the Future of Mass Torts*, 18 J. Econ. Persp. 183 (2004).

26. *See* Report of the Judicial Conference Ad Hoc Committee on Asbestos Litigation 5 (Mar. 1991) ("[I]t is estimated that as many as 3.5 million workers are exposed to some extent to asbestos fibers, as are many more in the general population.").

27. Ortiz v. Fibreboard Corp., 527 U.S. 815, 821 (1999).

28. *See* W. Kip Viscusi, Smoking 7 (1992) ("Whereas the best scientific estimates of the lifetime lung cancer risks from smoking range from .05 to .10, individual perceptions of the risk are much greater. The entire population assesses this risk at .43, and even current smokers have a substantial risk perception of .37."). This is not to deny the existence of other significant health risks associated with smoking, only to use its most salient risk to illustrate the difference in absolute numbers between impaired and unimpaired persons among all those exposed.

29. Mark D. Plevin, Paul W. Kalish & Leslie A. Epley, *Where Are They Now, Part Three: A Continuing History of the Companies That Have Sought Bankruptcy Protection Due to Asbestos Claims*, Mealey's Asbestos Bankr. Rep., Nov. 2005, at 9−10.

30. 11 U.S.C. § 1126(c) (2000).

31. *See* James A. Henderson Jr. & Aaron D. Twerski, *Asbestos Litigation Gone Mad: Exposure-Based Recovery for Increased Risk, Mental Distress, and Medical Monitoring*, 53 S.C. L. Rev. 815, 818 (2002).

32. 45 U.S.C. § 51 (2000).

33. Consolidated Rail Corp. v. Gottshall, 512 U.S. 532, 544 (1994).

34. 521 U.S. 424, 432 (1997).

35. *Id.* at 440.

36. *Id.* at 426.

37. Christopher F. Edley Jr. & Paul C. Weiler, *Asbestos: A Multi-Billion-Dollar Crisis*, 30 Harv. J. on Legis. 383, 393 (1993).

38. Stephen J. Carroll et al., Asbestos Litigation 76 (2005). *See also id.* at 20 ("[W]e use the term *unimpaired* to refer to someone who experiences no decrease in the ability to perform the activities of daily life."). This final version of the RAND report seemingly goes out of its way to confuse matters, however. The report repeatedly suggests that unimpaired persons under its own definition suffer a legally cognizable injury under current tort doctrine. *See, e.g., id.* at xxv, xxx, 8. These passages do not seem to be the products of casual drafting. A 2002 interim draft of the RAND report contained no similar assertions, suggesting that the passages in the 2005 final version are conscious additions. *See* Stephen J. Carroll et al., Asbestos Litigation Costs and Compensation: An Interim Report (2002). The most startling thing about the final 2005 version of the report is this: Its suggestion that unimpaired persons have cognizable injuries in tort is at odds with the analysis of prevailing doctrine presented by the Supreme Court, hardly an obscure or ill-informed institution. For its part, the final RAND report contains no mention of the Supreme Court's FELA decisions. Nor does the report present its own analysis of prevailing tort doctrine.

39. *See In re* Joint E. & S. Dist. Asbestos Litig., 129 B.R. 710, 737−42 (E. & S.D.N.Y. 1991).

40. Peter H. Schuck, *The Worst Should Go First: Deferral Registries in Asbestos Litigation*, 15 Harv. J.L. & Pub. Pol'y 541, 547−48, 550 (1992).

41. 538 U.S. 135, 142 n.2 (2003).

42. *Id.* at 156. *See also id.* at 155 (describing asbestosis as a "painful and concrete reminder" to workers of their asbestos exposure).

43. *Id.* at 156 (quoting Henderson & Twerski, *supra* note 31, at 830).

44. *In re* Diet Drugs (Phentermine, Fenfluramine, Dexfenfluramine) Prods. Liab. Litig., MDL No. 1203, Civil Action No. 99–20593, 2000 U.S. Dist. LEXIS 12275, *29 (E.D. Pa. Aug. 28, 2000).

45. Chris Guthrie, *Framing Frivolous Litigation: A Psychological Theory*, 67 U. Chi. L. Rev. 163, 169 (2000).

46. *Id.* at 168–69.

47. *See, e.g.*, State ex rel., Mobil Corp. v. Gaughan, 565 S.E.2d 793, 794 (W. Va. 2002) (Maynard, J., concurring) (suggesting that consolidation of "thousands of dissimilar and unrelated asbestos claimants into a single trial" might violate the due process rights of defendants).

48. *See* Fairness in Asbestos Compensation Act of 1999: Hearing on H.R. 1283 before the House Comm. on the Judiciary, 106th Cong. 97–99 (1999) (statement of Professor William N. Eskridge Jr., Yale Law School). *See generally* Michelle J. White, *Resolving the "Elephantine Mass,"* Reg., summer 2003, at 48, 50 (estimating that consolidation increases plaintiffs' probability of winning at trial by 11–16 percent based on empirical study of all asbestos trials from 1987 to 2002); Michelle J. White, *Asbestos Litigation: Procedural Innovations and Forum Shopping*, 35 J Legal Stud. 365, 384 (2006) ("[Empirical data] support the hypothesis that consolidating [asbestos] cases for trial increases the degree of correlation of outcomes and therefore makes going to trial more risky. In fact, they suggest that the increase in risk due to consolidation is extremely large.").

49. *See* Richard A. Posner, *An Economic Approach to Legal Procedure and Judicial Administration*, 2 J. Legal Stud. 399, 448 (1973) (analogizing the creation of more courts to the construction of more highways). *See also* George L. Priest, *Private Litigants and the Court Congestion Problem*, 69 B.U. L. Rev. 527 (1989) (empirical study suggesting an interactive relationship between changes in the extent of court congestion and changes in the volume of litigation).

50. The discussion here draws on Kenneth S. Abraham, *The Maze of Mega-Coverage Litigation*, 97 Colum. L. Rev. 2102, 2103–05 (1997); James M. Fisher, *Insurance Coverage for Mass Exposure Tort Claims: The Debate over the Appropriate Trigger Rule*, 45 Drake L. Rev. 625, 633–51, 668–69 (1997). *See also* 2 Jeffrey W. Stempel, Stempel on Insurance Contracts § 14.09[B] (3d ed. 2006).

51. This approach traces its lineage to Keene Corp. v. Insurance Co. of North America, 667 F.2d 1034 (D.C. Cir. 1981).

52. *See* Fisher, *supra* note 50, at 636–37.

53. *See* James M. Fisher, *Insurer or Policyholder Control of the Defense and the Duty to Fund Settlements*, 2 Nev. L.J. 1, 6 n.14 (2002) ("[A] significant difference between excess insurance policies and primary insurance policies is that the latter contain first dollar exposure, invariably coupled with a duty to defend the policyholder.").

54. This discussion draws on Michelle J. White, *Why the Asbestos Genie Won't Stay in the Bankruptcy Bottle*, 70 U. Cin. L. Rev. 1319, 1335 (2002).

55. One commentator makes a similar observation about the use of class settlements in the mass tort area, though without the crucial link to stages of mass tort litigation. *See* George L. Priest, *Procedural versus Substantive Controls of Mass Tort Class Actions*, 26 J. Legal Stud. 521, 545 (1997).

CHAPTER III

1. 509 U.S. 579 (1993) [*Daubert I*].

2. The literature on *Daubert* is vast. *See, e.g.,* David H. Kaye et al., The New Wigmore: A Treatise on Evidence: Expert Evidence (2004); David L. Faigman et al., Modern Scientific Evidence: The Law and Science of Expert Testimony (2d ed. 2002); Erica Beecher-Monas, *The Heuristics of Intellectual Due Process: A Primer for Triers of Science,* 75 N.Y.U. L. Rev. 1563 (2000); Scott Brewer, *Scientific Expert Testimony and Intellectual Due Process,* 107 Yale L.J. 1535 (1998); Brian Leiter, *The Epistemology of Admissibility: Why Even Good Philosophy of Science Would Not Make for Good Philosophy of Evidence,* 1997 B.Y.U. L. Rev. 803.

For thoughtful discussions of aggregation and settlement pressure, *see, e.g.,* Randy J. Kozel & David Rosenberg, *Solving the Nuisance-Value Settlement Problem: Mandatory Summary Judgment,* 90 Va. L. Rev. 1849 (2004); Charles Silver, *We're Scared to Death: Does Class Certification Subject Defendants to Blackmail?,* 78 N.Y.U. L. Rev. 1357 (2003); J. B. Heaton, *The Risk Finance of Class Action Settlement Pressure,* 4 J. Risk Finance 75 (2003); Robert G. Bone & David S. Evans, *Class Certification and the Substantive Merits,* 51 Duke L.J. 1251 (2002); Warren F. Schwartz, *Long-Shot Class Actions: Toward a Normative Theory of Legal Uncertainty,* 8 Legal Theory 297 (2002).

3. 51 F.3d 1293 (7th Cir. 1995).

4. U.S. Const. amend. VII; Curtis v. Loether, 415 U.S. 189, 195-96 (1974).

5. *E.g.,* Russell B. Korobkin & Chris Guthrie, *Psychological Barriers to Litigation Settlement: An Experimental Approach,* 93 Mich. L. Rev. 107 (1994); Jeffrey J. Rachlinski, *Gains, Losses, and the Psychology of Litigation,* 70 S. Cal. L. Rev. 113 (1996); Russell B. Korobkin & Chris Guthrie, *Psychology, Economics, and Settlement: A New Look at the Role of the Lawyer,* 76 Tex. L. Rev. 77 (1997); Jeffrey J. Rachlinski, *A Positive Psychological Theory of Judging in Hindsight,* 65 U. Chi. L. Rev. 571 (1998) [Rachlinski, *Hindsight*]; Chris Guthrie, *Better Settle Than Sorry: The Regret Aversion Theory of Litigation Behavior,* 1999 U. Ill. L. Rev. 43; Chris Guthrie, *Framing Frivolous Litigation: A Psychological Theory,* 67 U. Chi. L. Rev. 163 (2000).

6. *See* Daniel Kahneman & Amos Tversky, *Prospect Theory: An Analysis of Decisions under Risk,* 47 Econometrica 263 (1979).

7. *See* Amos Tversky & Daniel Kahneman, *Judgment under Uncertainty: Heuristics and Biases,* 185 Sci. 1124 (1974). For further development, *see* Daniel Kahneman et al., eds., Judgment Under Uncertainty: Heuristics and Biases (1982).

8. *See* Baruch Fischhoff, *Hindsight ≠ Foresight: The Effect of Outcome Knowledge on Judgment under Uncertainty,* 1 J. Exper. Psych. 288 (1975).

9. For experimental evidence of hindsight bias among mock jurors in tort litigation, *see* Kim A. Kamin & Jeffrey J. Rachlinski, *Ex Post ≠ Ex Ante: Determining Liability in Hindsight,* 19 Law & Hum. Behav. 89 (1995).

10. *See* Neal Feigenson, Legal Blame 88-95, 116-23 (2000). The tendency to integrate a known outcome into a larger, coherent story may itself be a cause of hindsight bias, *see* Rachlinski, *Hindsight, supra* note 5, at 584.

11. *See* Nancy Pennington & Reid Hastie, *A Cognitive Theory of Juror Decision Making: The Story Model,* 13 Cardozo L. Rev. 519 (1991). *See also* Nancy Pennington & Reid Hastie, *Explaining the Evidence: Tests of the Story Model for Juror Decision Making,* 62 J. Pers. & Soc. Psych. 189 (1992).

12. Joseph Sanders, Bendectin on Trial 130-39 (1998).

13. Cass R. Sunstein, *Probability Neglect: Emotions, Worst Cases, and Law,* 112 Yale L.J. 61, 82 (2002).

14. 519 U.S. 172, 186–89 (1997).

15. *Id.* at 187.

16. *See* Feigenson, *supra* note 10, chs. 5–6.

17. *See* Arvin Maskin, *Litigating Claims for Punitive Damages: The View from the Front Line,* 31 Loy. L.A. L. Rev. 489, 493–94 (1998).

18. For the amplification metaphor, I am indebted to commentary on class actions. *See* Richard A. Epstein, *Class Actions: Aggregation, Amplification, and Distortion,* 2003 U. Chi. Legal F. 475.

19. *See, e.g.,* Hall v. Baxter Healthcare Corp., 947 F. Supp. 1387, 1401–2 (D. Or. 1996).

20. *See* Sherine E. Gabriel et al., *Complications Leading to Surgery after Breast Implantation,* 336 New Eng. J. Med. 677, 681 (1997) (finding that nearly 24 percent of women with implants suffer local complications serious enough to warrant reoperation within five years).

21. Marcia Angell, Science on Trial 111–12 (1996) (basing the 10,000 estimate on a rough estimate of 100 million adult women in the United States).

22. For details of these cases, *see* John A. Byrne, Informed Consent 93–107, 165–71 (1996).

23. Angell, *supra* note 21, at 120–22. *See also* Hopkins v. Dow Corning Corp., 33 F.3d 1116, 1123–25 (9th Cir. 1994).

24. *See* Byrne, *supra* note 22, at 175–77; *Hopkins,* 33 F.3d at 1119, 1127.

25. *See* Byrne, *supra* note 22, at 103–4.

26. *See* Michael D. Green, Bendectin and Birth Defects 35–36 (1996).

27. *See* Byrne, *supra* note 22, at 105.

28. *See Hopkins,* 33 F.3d at 1119–20.

29. Angell, *supra* note 21, at 53.

30. On the grounds for the moratorium, *see* David A. Kessler, *The Basis of the FDA's Decision on Breast Implants,* 326 New Eng. J. Med. 1713 (1992). On the unsuccessful effort to lift the moratorium in 2004, *see* Gina Kolata, *F.D.A. Defers Final Decision about Implants,* N.Y. Times, Jan. 9, 2004, at A1.

31. Kessler, *supra* note 30, at 1713.

32. PBS Frontline: Breast Implants on Trial (PBS television broadcast, Feb. 27, 1996).

33. Angell, *supra* note 21, at 112

34. Max Boot, *Queen of Torts,* Wall St. J., May 16, 1996, at A14.

35. Gina Kolata & Barry Meier, *Implant Lawsuits Create a Medical Rush to Cash In,* N.Y. Times, Sept. 18, 1995, at A1.

36. Gina Kolata, *Details of Implant Settlement Announced by Federal Judge,* N.Y. Times, Apr. 5, 1994, at A16.

37. *See In re* Dow Corning Corp., 86 F.3d 482, 485, 486 n.2 (6th Cir. 1996).

38. *See* Alison Frankel, *Dow Corning Goes for Broke,* Am. Lawyer, Jan.–Feb. 1996, at 78.

39. *In re* Dow Corning Corp., 187 B.R. 919, 929 (Bankr. E.D. Mich. 1995).

40. *See In re* Dow Corning Corp., 244 B.R. 634, 641 (Bankr. E.D. Mich. 1999). On the tendency of reorganization plans in bankruptcy to allocate resources to unimpaired claimants, *see* chapter 9.

41. *See* Barbara G. Silverman et al., *Reported Complications of Silicone Gel Breast Implants: An Epidemiological Review*, 124 Annals Internal Med. 744 (1996).

42. *See* Betty A. Diamond et al., *Silicone Breast Implants in Relation to Connective Tissue Diseases and Immunologic Dysfunction* (Nov. 17, 1998), available at http://earth.fjc.gov/BREIMLIT/SCIENCE/report.htm.

43. *See* Committee on the Safety of Silicone Breast Implants, National Academy of Sciences, Safety of Silicone Breast Implants (Stuart Bondurant et al., eds. 2000).

44. *See* Kaye et al., *supra* note 2; Faigman et al., *supra* note 2.

45. 509 U.S. at 597.

46. *Id.* at 590.

47. *Id.* at 588–89 (holding that the *Frye* "general acceptance" test did not survive the enactment of Rule 702 in 1975).

48. 293 F. 1013, 1014 (D.C. Cir. 1923).

49. *Daubert I,* 509 U.S. at 585.

50. *See, e.g.,* Kenneth J. Chesebro, *Taking* Daubert*'s "Focus" Seriously: The Methodology/Conclusion Distinction*, 15 Cardozo L. Rev. 1745 (1994).

51. *Daubert I,* 509 U.S. at 595 (stating that "[t]he focus [of the Rule 702 inquiry], of course, must be solely on principles and methodology, not on the conclusions that they generate").

52. *Hopkins,* 33 F.3d at 1124–25.

53. 522 U.S. 136, 146 (1997).

54. Kumho Tire Co., Ltd. v. Carmichael, 526 U.S. 137, 152–53 (1999).

55. *E.g., Hall,* 947 F. Supp. 1387; *In re* Breast Implant Cases, 942 F. Supp. 958 (E. & S.D.N.Y. 1996).

56. *See Daubert I,* 509 U.S. at 582.

57. Sanders, *supra* note 12, at 40, 146–49.

58. *See Daubert I,* 509 U.S. at 583.

59. Daubert v. Merrell Dow Pharmaceuticals, Inc. 43 F.3d 1311, 1322 (9th Cir. 1995) [*Daubert II*].

60. *Id.* at 1318.

61. Lloyd Dixon & Brian Gill, Changes in the Standards for Admitting Expert Evidence in Federal Civil Cases since the *Daubert* Decision 61–62 (2001).

62. David E. Bernstein & Jeffrey D. Jackson, *The* Daubert *Trilogy in the States,* 44 Jurimetrics J. 351 (2004).

63. David E. Bernstein, Frye, Frye *Again: The Past, Present and Future of the General Acceptance Test,* 41 Jurimetrics J. 385, 388 (2001).

64. *Kumho Tire,* 526 U.S. at 141.

65. For an interesting discussion of how this approach to tort elements deviates from the product rule in mathematics, *see* Saul Levmore, *Conjunction and Aggregation,* 99 Mich. L. Rev. 723, 724–26 (2001).

66. *Daubert II,* 43 F.3d at 1316. For an insightful statement of this concern from a philosophical standpoint, *see* Leiter, *supra* note 2.

67. *E.g.,* Laurens Walker & John Monahan, *Scientific Authority: The Breast Implant Litigation and Beyond,* 86 Va. L. Rev. 801 (2000); Stephen Breyer, *The Interdependence of Science and Law,* 280 Sci. 537 (1998).

68. On law and science as competing institutions for truth seeking, each with its own set of intellectual norms, *see* Peter H. Schuck, *Multi-Culturalism Redux: Science, Law, and Politics,* 11 Yale L. & Pol'y Rev. 1 (1993).

69. *See* Erica Beecher-Monas, *A Ray of Light for Judges Blinded by Science: Triers of Science and Intellectual Due Process,* 33 Ga. L. Rev. 1047, 1072-76 (1999). *See also* Eileen A. Scallen & William E. Weithoff, *The Ethos of Expert Witnesses: Confusing the Admissibility, Sufficiency, and Credibility of Expert Testimony,* 49 Hastings L.J. 1143 (1998).

70. *See* Schrott v. Bristol-Myers Squibb Co., 403 F.3d 940, 943 (7th Cir. 2005); 19 Charles Alan Wright et al., Federal Practice and Procedure §4512, at 405 (2d ed. 2002).

71. 304 U.S. 64, 78 (1938). On the tension between *Daubert* and *Erie, see* Lisa Heinzerling, *Doubting* Daubert, 14 J.L. & Pol'y 65, 78 (2006).

72. *Daubert II,* 43 F.3d at 1315.

73. 51 F.3d 1293 (7th Cir. 1995).

74. *E.g.,* West v. Prudential Securities, Inc., 282 F.3d 935, 937 (7th Cir. 2002); *In re* Bridgestone/Firestone, Inc., 288 F.3d 1012, 1015-16 (7th Cir. 2002).

75. *See* Henry J. Friendly, Federal Jurisdiction: A General View 120 (1973) (citing Milton Handler, *The Shift from Substantive to Procedural Innovations in Antitrust Suits,* 71 Colum. L. Rev. 1, 9 (1971)).

76. For delineation of the different versions of the settlement pressure argument, *see* Silver, *supra* note 2, at 1360-84.

77. Bone & Evans, *supra* note 2.

78. Silver, *supra* note 2; Schwartz, *supra* note 2; Kozel & Rosenberg, *supra* note 2.

79. 51 F.3d at 1296. For criticism of the blood products industry in connection with the HIV crisis, *see* George W. Conk, *Is There a Design Defect in the Restatement (Third) of Torts: Products Liability,* 109 Yale L.J. 1087, 1007-17 (2000).

80. *See* 51 F.3d at 1300-04 (pointing to obstacles grounded in choice of law and the Reexamination Clause of the Seventh Amendment).

81. *Id.* at 1299-1300.

82. *Id.* at 1299.

83. Jay Tidmarsh, Mass Tort Settlement Class Actions: Five Case Studies 92 (1998).

84. Silver, *supra* note 2, at 1379.

85. *In re* Factor VIII or IX Concentrate Blood Prods. Litig., 59 F.3d 1016, 1018 (7th Cir. 1998). *See also* Tidmarsh, *supra* note 83, at 93.

86. *Blood Prods. Litig.,* 159 F.3d at 1018.

87. *See* Silver, *supra* note 2, at 1408-9; Schwartz, *supra* note 2, at 306-9; Heaton, *supra* note 2, at 77-78.

88. I spotlight the consequences of defendants' risk aversion by assuming no difference in the absolute number of claims litigated by way of individual lawsuits, as compared to the class action, if certified. For his part, Judge Posner believed that, as a practical matter, defendants would face substantially fewer claims in individual litigation as compared to class action litigation. *See Rhone-Poulenc,* 51 F.3d at 1298.

89. Heaton, *supra* note 2, at 78.

90. *See* Silver, *supra* note 2, at 1414-15.

91. Heaton, *supra* note 2, at 79.

92. Schwartz, *supra* note 2, at 308.

93. Silver, *supra* note 2, at 1419.

94. *Rhone-Poulenc,* 51 F.3d at 1300.

95. *See* Silver, *supra* note 2, at 1421.

96. *E.g.,* Bernard Grofman & Scott L. Feld, *Rousseau's General Will: A Condorcertian*

Perspective, 82 Am. Pol. Sci. Rev. 567 (1988); Michael Abramowicz, *En Banc Revisited,* 100 Colum. L. Rev. 1600 (2000); Kevin A. Kordana & Eric A. Posner, *A Positive Theory of Chapter 11,* 74 N.Y.U. L. Rev. 161 (1999).

97. Paul H. Edelman, *On Legal Interpretations of the Condorcet Jury Theorem,* 31 J. Legal Stud. 327, 328 (2002).

98. *Id.* at 329.

99. Fed. R. Civ. P. 23(b)(3). Rule 23 states explicitly this requirement only as for opt-out classes authorized under its subsection (b)(3). But the superiority of the class action, relative to other procedural alternatives, is also implicit — indeed, conceptually essential — to the notion of mandatory classes under subsections (b)(1) and (b)(2). One hardly would want to require membership in the class were it not superior to other procedural modes for the adjudication of the dispute.

100. A theoretical version of this argument appears in Kozel & Rosenberg, *supra* note 2. For another version built on empirical research showing that courts already tend to decide summary judgment motions prior to class certification motions, *see* Silver, *supra* note 2, at 1393–96.

101. E.g., Bone & Evans, *supra* note 2, at 1328–30.

102. In a much-parsed passage in its 1974 decision in *Eisen v. Carlisle & Jacquelin,* the Supreme Court stated that it could "find nothing in the language or history of Rule 23 that gives a court any authority to conduct a preliminary inquiry into the merits of a suit in order to determine whether it may be maintained as a class action." 417 U.S. 156, 177 (1974). Later, however, the Court would add that "sometimes it may be necessary for the court to probe behind the pleadings before coming to rest on the certification question." *General Telephone Co. v. Falcon,* 457 U.S. 147, 160 (1982). On what to make of *Eisen* and *General Telephone, see* Geoffrey P. Miller, *Review of the Merits in Class Action Certification,* 33 Hofstra L. Rev. 51 (2004).

103. For a discussion of cognitive biases that favor plaintiffs and those that favor defendants, *see* Feigenson, *supra* note 10, at 98–104.

104. *See* Fed. R. Evid. 606.

105. Unlike settlements in nonclass lawsuits, class settlements must be judicially approved. *See* Fed. R. Civ. P. 23(e).

CHAPTER IV

1. For a detailed typology of the various ways in which aggregate settlements might be structured, *see* Howard M. Erichson, *A Typology of Aggregate Settlements,* 80 Notre Dame L. Rev. 1791 (2005).

2. Phillips Petroleum Co. v. Shutts, 472 U.S. 797, 807 (1985); Mullane v. Central Hanover Bank & Trust Co., 339 U.S. 306, 313 (1950).

3. For an illuminating comparison of agency relationships in real estate markets and civil litigation, *see* Saul Levmore, *Commissions and Conflicts in Agency Arrangements: Lawyers, Real Estate Brokers, Underwriters, and Other Agents' Rewards,* 36 J.L. & Econ. 503 (1993).

4. Charles Silver & Lynn Baker, *I Cut, You Choose: The Role of Plaintiffs' Counsel in Allocating Settlement Proceeds,* 84 Va. L. Rev. 1465, 1507 (1998).

5. For an argument that use of a standard contingency fee percentage or standard brokerage commission reduces interclient conflicts, *see* Levmore, *supra* note 3, at 505–11.

6. Model Rule 1.8(g) provides: "A lawyer who represents two or more clients shall

not participate in making an aggregate settlement of the claims of . . . the clients . . . unless each client consents after consultation, including disclosure of the existence and nature of all the claims involved and of the participation of each person in the settlement." Model Rules of Professional Conduct, Rule 1.8(g) (2003). As currently interpreted, Model Rule 1.8(g) calls for "disclosure of all settlement terms to all clients, including disclosure to each of what other plaintiffs are to receive." Charles Silver & Lynn Baker, *Mass Lawsuits and the Aggregate Settlement Rule,* 32 Wake Forest L. Rev. 733, 734 (1997).

7. *Compare id.* at 768–79 (arguing for waivability), *with* Nancy J. Moore, *The Case against Changing the Aggregate Settlement Rule in Mass Tort Lawsuits,* 41 S. Tex. L. Rev. 149, 174–81 (1999) (defending current principle of nonwaivability).

8. *See, e.g.,* Ortiz v. Fibreboard Corp., 527 U.S. 815, 846 (1999).

9. *See, e.g., id.* at 867–68 (Breyer, J., dissenting); David Rosenberg, *Adding a Second Opt-Out to Rule 23(b)(3) Class Actions: Cost without Benefit,* 2003 U. Chi. Legal F. 19, 50–51.

10. U.S. Const., amend. V ("nor shall private property be taken for public use, without just compensation").

11. The discussion here focuses on legislative rules as distinct from interpretative rules, which are not legally binding on the public of their own force but serve merely to inform the public about the agency's view as to the meaning of an underlying statutory provision. *See generally* 1 Richard J. Pierce Jr., Administrative Law Treatise § 6.4, at 324–49 (4th ed. 2002).

12. *Id.* § 11.5, at 817.

13. *See, e.g.,* United States Dept. of the Treasury v. FLRA, 995 F.2d 301, 302–4 (D.C. Cir. 1993) (reversing and remanding an agency order on the ground that the agency had not explained two apparently contrary orders in earlier adjudications, but emphasizing that the agency, on remand, retained the legal authority to change its position, as long as it explained the reasons for the change).

14. *See* Arizona Grocery Co. v. Atchison, Topeka & Santa Fe Ry., 284 U.S. 370, 389 (1932) (holding that an agency "may not in a subsequent proceeding, acting in its quasi-judicial capacity, ignore its own pronouncement promulgated in its quasi-legislative capacity" but may "substitute a new rule of conduct" to apply prospectively).

15. U.S. Const., art. I, § 8, cl. 3.

16. *See generally* Price V. Fishback & Shawn Everett Kantor, A Prelude to the Welfare State: The Origins of Workers' Compensation (2000).

17. *See* John Fabian Witt, The Accidental Republic, ch. 3 (2004).

18. *See* S. 852, 109th Cong. § 131(b) (2005) (setting specific compensation amounts for different categories of asbestos claims).

19. *See* Air Transportation Safety and Stabilization Act, Pub. L. No. 107–42, § 404, 115 Stat. 230, 237–38 (2001). For Special Master Feinberg's rules governing compensation, see September 11th Victim Compensation Fund of 2001, 28 C.F.R. pt. 104 (2003).

20. George L. Priest, *Procedural versus Substantive Controls of Mass Tort Class Actions,* 26 J. Legal Stud. 521, 551 (1997).

21. *See* Ortiz v. Fibreboard Corp., 527 U.S. 815, 821 (1999) ("[T]he elephantine mass of asbestos cases . . . defies customary judicial administration and calls for national legislation."); *id.* at 865 (Rehnquist, C.J., concurring) (calling for "a legislative solution"); Amchem Prods., Inc. v. Windsor, 521 U.S. 591, 622 (1997) ("The benefits asbestos-exposed persons might gain from the establishment of a grand-scale compensation

scheme is a matter fit for legislative consideration."); *id.* at 628–29 (acknowledging that "a nationwide administrative claims processing regime would provide the most secure, fair, and efficient means of compensating victims of asbestos exposure," but noting that "Congress . . . has not adopted such a solution").

22. *See* Geoffrey C. Hazard Jr., *The Futures Problem,* 148 U. Pa. L. Rev. 1901, 1916 (2000).

23. The phrase stems from Charles Reich, *The New Property,* 73 Yale L.J. 733 (1964).

24. 461 U.S. 458, 459–60 (1983) (citing 42 U.S.C. §423(d)(1)).

25. *Id.* at 461.

26. Jerry L. Mashaw et al., Administrative Law: The American Public Law System: Cases and Materials 455 (5th ed. 2003) (discussing 20 C.F.R. pt. 404, subpt. P, app. 2).

27. *Heckler,* 461 U.S. at 467. The same principle holds with regard to the administration of regulatory programs. *See id.* (citing illustrative cases).

28. 332 U.S. 194, 203 (1947). For an insightful analysis of this decision, *see* M. Elizabeth Magill, *Agency Choice of Policymaking Form,* 71 U. Chi. L. Rev. 1383 (2004).

29. *See* Christopher F. Edley Jr. & Paul C. Weiler, *Asbestos: A Multi-Billion-Dollar Crisis,* 30 Harv. J. on Legis. 383, 398 n.27 (1993); Glen O. Robinson & Kenneth S. Abraham, *Collective Justice in Tort Law,* 78 Va. L. Rev. 1481, 1500 n.58 (1992).

30. *Heckler,* 461 U.S. at 467 n.11.

31. *See* 4 Arthur Larson & Lex K. Larson, Larson's Workers' Compensation Law §86.02 (2002).

32. On the content and operation of the tort regime for workplace injuries prior to the adoption of workers' compensation legislation, *see* Fishback & Kantor, note 16, ch. 2; Witt, *supra* note 17, ch. 2.

33. *See id.* at 163–86.

34. *See* Fishback & Kantor, *supra* note 16, at 13–14.

35. *See* John Fabian Witt, *The Long History of State Constitutions and American Tort Law,* 36 Rutgers L.J. 1159, 1187 (2005).

36. 751 F. Supp. 649 (E.D. Tex. 1990), *rev'd,* 151 F.3d 297 (5th Cir. 1998).

37. *Id.* at 651–52.

38. *Id.* at 653.

39. *Id.* at 659–66. Even scholarly commentary that applauds the use of sampling techniques as a general matter has challenged the particulars of the statistical analysis in *Cimino. See* Michael J. Saks & Peter David Blanck, *Justice Improved: The Unrecognized Benefits of Aggregation and Sampling in the Trial of Mass Torts,* 44 Stan. L. Rev. 815, 842–43 (1992) (identifying errors in Judge Parker's understanding of statistical analysis). For other endorsements of statistical sampling techniques, *see* Laurens Walker & John Monahan, *Sampling Liability,* 85 Va. L. Rev. 329 (1999); Laurens Walker & John Monahan, *Sampling Damages,* 83 Iowa L. Rev. 545 (1998). For a normative critique, *see* Robert G. Bone, *Statistical Adjudication: Rights, Justice, and Utility in a World of Process Scarcity,* 46 Vand. L. Rev. 561 (1993).

40. 151 F.3d at 313.

41. *See id.* (citing *In re* Fibreboard Corp., 893 F.2d 706, 711–12 (5th Cir. 1990)). The earlier trial plan invalidated in *Fibreboard* had called for determination of the damage award for each disease category by reference to the average damage verdict in fifteen cases selected by plaintiffs and fifteen selected by defendants. *See Fibreboard,* 893 F.2d at

709. There was little reason to believe that the cases selected by each side would comprise a representative sampling of all pending cases within the relevant disease category.

42. *See* Samuel Issacharoff & John Fabian Witt, *The Inevitability of Aggregate Settlement: An Institutional Account of American Tort Law,* 57 Vand. L. Rev. 1571, 1626 (2005).

43. *Cimino,* 151 F.3d at 303.

44. *See id.* at 305. One cannot explain the similarity in dollar amounts for pleural disease cases, on the one hand, and those for asbestosis and asbestos-related lung cancer cases, on the other, by reference to some manner of discounting to account for the uncertainty about whether a given pleural disease case involves impairment. Such a discount would push the dollar amounts for pleural disease cases below those for asbestosis or asbestos-related lung cancer.

CHAPTER V

1. On the history of the modern class action, *see* Stephen C. Yeazell, From Medieval Group Litigation to the Modern Class Action (1987).

2. Hansberry v. Lee, 311 U.S. 32, 40 (1940).

3. *See id.* at 41.

4. Fed. R. Civ. P. 23(c)(1) & (e).

5. The court also determines the fee award to class counsel for the representation. *See* Fed. R. Civ. P. 23(h). The authority of the court over fees is the rough analogue to rate regulation for a monopoly, such as a public utility.

6. *See* Fed. R. Civ. P. 23(a)–(b).

7. *Compare* Fed. R. Civ. P. 23(c)(2) (opportunity to opt out required as to classes certified under subsection (b)(3)), *with* Fed. R. Civ. P. 23(c)(3) (no requirement that members of classes certified under subsection (b)(1) or (b)(2) be afforded the opportunity to opt out).

8. Fed. R. Civ. P. 23(e)(1)(C). The mantra "fair, reasonable, and adequate" was added to Rule 23 in 2003 so that the rule text would reflect the standard for class settlement approval already applied by courts under the predecessor version of subsection (e). *See id.,* advisory committee's note.

9. Fed. R. Civ. P. 23(b)(3) advisory committee's note.

10. *See* John C. Coffee Jr., *Class Wars: The Dilemma of the Mass Tort Class Action,* 95 Colum. L. Rev. 1343, 1357–58 (1995).

11. 521 U.S. 591 (1997).

12. 527 U.S. 815 (1999).

13. *See In re* "Agent Orange" Prod. Liab. Litig., 818 F.2d 145, 148–52 (2d Cir. 1987) (summarizing multiple opinions on settlement); Peter H. Schuck, Agent Orange on Trial (enlarged ed. 1987).

14. *See id.,* ch. 8. *See also* Richard L. Marcus, *Apocalypse Now?,* 85 Mich. L. Rev. 1267, 1289–95 (1987) (book review of Schuck, *supra* note 13); Kenneth A. Cohen, *Class Actions, Toxic Torts, and Legal Rules,* 67 B.U. L. Rev. 581, 586–94 (1987) (same).

15. *See* Schuck, *supra* note 13, 118–19.

16. *See id.* at 159.

17. *See id.* at 212 (noting that the special master "receive[d] "constant guidance' from [Judge] Weinstein").

18. *Cf.* Martha Minow, *Judge for the Situation: Judge Jack Weinstein, Creator of Temporary Administrative Agencies,* 97 Colum. L. Rev. 2010 (1997).

19. *See In re* Agent Orange Prod. Liab. Litig., 611 F. Supp. 1396, 1400 (E.D.N.Y. 1985). The ten-year period appears to reflect a rough sense that manifestations of disease thereafter — by then, roughly two decades after the last alleged exposure of class members — were highly unlikely to be the causal result of Agent Orange. *See* Richard A. Nagareda, *Administering Adequacy in Class Representation*, 82 Tex. L. Rev. 287, 322 (2003).

20. *See Agent Orange*, 818 F.2d 145.

21. *See* Coffee, *supra* note 10, at 1349–50.

22. *See* Report of the Judicial Conference Ad Hoc Committee on Asbestos Litigation (Mar. 1991).

23. *See In re* Asbestos Prods. Liab. Litig., 771 F. Supp. 415 (J.P.M.L. 1991).

24. *See* Kane v. Johns-Manville Corp., 843 F.2d 636 (2d Cir. 1988).

25. *See In re* Joint E. & S. Dist. Asbestos Litig., 129 B.R. 710, 754–62 (E. & S.D.N.Y. 1991); Frank J. Macchiarola, *The Manville Personal Injury Settlement Trust: Lessons for the Future*, 17 Cardozo L. Rev. 583 (1996).

26. *See* Ralph R. Mabey & Peter A. Zisser, *Improving Treatment of Future Claims: The Unfinished Business Left by the Manville Amendments*, 69 Am. Bankr. L.J. 487, 495–96 (1995).

27. 11 U.S.C. §524(g) (2000).

28. *See* Mabey & Zisser, *supra* note 26, at 497–500.

29. *See* 11 U.S.C. §1129(b)(2).

30. The class definition in *Amchem* spoke specifically of occupational exposure. 521 U.S. at 602. Although the class definition in *Ortiz* contained no such express limitation, the nature of Fibreboard's products was such that the bulk of claims against that firm arose from "industrial applications." 527 U.S. at 822.

31. *Amchem*, 521 U.S. at 601. *See Ortiz*, 527 U.S. at 826 n.5.

32. *Amchem*, 521 U.S. at 608. The Court referred in dicta to the potential difficulties associated with a notice campaign to class members in the asbestos context. *See id.* at 628 ("Many persons in the exposure-only category . . . may not even know of their exposure, or realize the extent of the harm they may incur. . . . [T]hose without current afflictions may not have the information or foresight needed to decide, intelligently, whether to stay in or opt out.").

33. *Ortiz*, 527 U.S. at 828.

34. *Id.* at 859.

35. *Amchem*, 521 U.S. at 603–4.

36. *Id.* at 633 (Breyer, J., dissenting).

37. *Id.* at 604.

38. *See* Georgine v. Amchem Prods., Inc., 157 F.R.D. 246, 292 (E.D. Pa. 1994), *vacated on other grounds*, 83 F.3d 610 (3d Cir. 1996), *aff'd sub nom. Amchem*, 521 U.S. 591.

39. *See Ortiz*, 527 U.S. at 824–25. The *Ortiz* class settlement would have made a $1.535 billion fund available to class members. *Id.* The settlement in the insurance coverage litigation provided $1.525 billion of this total, with Fibreboard adding the remaining $10 million — "all but $500,000 of it from other insurance proceeds." *Id.* at 825.

40. The *Ortiz* settlement did provide class members with a right to sue the trust — not Fibreboard itself — upon dissatisfaction with the compensation provided. 527 U.S. at 847 n.23. This right was severely limited, however. The class settlement required claimants first to exhaust a process of alternative dispute resolution, and any damage award ultimately made against the trust would have been spread over time and capped at an amount well below the high end of awards in asbestos litigation. *See id.* (limiting dam-

ages against the trust "to $500,000, to be paid out in installments over 5 to 10 years . . . despite multimillion-dollar jury verdicts sometimes reached in asbestos suits").

41. *See, e.g., Amchem,* 521 U.S. at 600–601.

42. *See Georgine,* 157 F.R.D. at 295–96 (finding that the *Amchem* defendants resolved on similar terms inventory cases represented by both class counsel and other asbestos plaintiffs' law firms); George M. Cohen, *The "Fair" Is the Enemy of the Good: Ortiz v. Fibreboard Corporation and Class Action Settlements,* 8 S. Ct. Econ. Rev. 23, 30 (2000) (noting that the inventory settlement with the class counsel in *Ortiz* "allegedly served as a model for settling the inventory cases of other plaintiffs' firms").

43. *See* Coffee, *supra* note 10, at 1397 (estimating that an aggregate settlement covering the inventory cases of one firm among the *Amchem* class counsel amounted to 54 percent more in dollar terms than the same cases would have received immediately under the class settlement); Susan P. Koniak, *Feasting While the Widow Weeps:* Georgine v. Amchem Products, Inc., 80 Cornell L. Rev. 1045, 1067 n.104 (1995) (detailing the same estimate in chart form).

44. *See* Richard A. Nagareda, *Turning from Tort to Administration,* 94 Mich. L. Rev. 899, 965 n.249 (1996) (comparing cash amounts paid to inventory cases of *Amchem* class counsel with the average annual cost of health insurance for American workers).

45. *See* Georgine v. Amchem Prods., Inc., 157 F.R.D. 246 (E.D. Pa. 1994), *rev'd,* 83 F.3d 610 (3d Cir. 1996), *aff'd sub nom. Amchem,* 521 U.S. 591; Ahearn v. Fibreboard Corp., 162 F.R.D. 505 (E.D. Tex. 1995), *aff'd sub nom. In re* Asbestos Litig., 90 F.3d 963 (5th Cir. 1996), *vacated and remanded for further consideration in light of* Amchem, 521 U.S. 1114 (1997), *aff'd,* 134 F.3d 668 (5th Cir. 1998), *rev'd sub nom. Ortiz,* 527 U.S. 815.

46. *Amchem,* 521 U.S. at 603; *Ortiz,* 527 U.S. at 824–25.

47. 521 U.S. at 620–22.

48. Fed. R. Civ. P. 23(b)(3).

49. 521 U.S. at 619.

50. *Id.* at 622.

51. *Id.* (emphasis added).

52. *Id.* at 623 (emphasis added).

53. Phillips Petroleum Co. v. Shutts, 472 U.S. 797, 809 (1985).

54. 5 U.S.C. §706(2)(A) (2000). The Act distinguishes this ground for invalidation of agency action from invalidation based on the assertion of agency power "in excess of statutory jurisdiction, authority, or limitations." *Id.* §706(2)(C).

55. *Ortiz,* 527 U.S. at 835 (discussing Dickinson v. Burnham, 197 F.2d 973 (2d Cir. 1952)).

56. *Id.* at 836 (discussing Guffanti v. Nat'l Sur. Co., 90 N.E. 174 (N.Y. 1909)).

57. *Id.* at 837 (discussing Ross v. Crary, 1 Paige Ch. 416 (N.Y. Ch. 1829)).

58. *Id.* at 842–43.

59. *See id.* at 848.

60. *Id.* at 843.

61. Air Transportation Safety and System Stabilization Act, Pub. L. No. 107-42, §406(b), 115 Stat. 230, 240 (2001).

62. 28 U.S.C. §2072(a)–(b) (2000).

63. *Compare* Hanna v. Plumer, 380 U.S. 460, 472 (1965) (recognizing "congressional power to make rules governing the practice and pleading in [the federal] courts, which in turn includes a power to regulate matters which, though falling within the uncertain

area between substance and procedure, are rationally capable of classification as either"), *with* Sibbach v. Wilson & Co., 312 U.S. 1, 14 (1941) ("The test must be whether a rule really regulates procedure,—the judicial process for enforcing rights and duties recognized by substantive law and for justly administering remedy and redress for disregard or infraction of them."). *See, e.g.,* Stephen B. Burbank, *The Rules Enabling Act of 1934,* 130 U. Pa. L. Rev. 1015, 1025–26 (1982); John Hart Ely, *The Irrepressible Myth of Erie,* 87 Harv. L. Rev. 693, 695 (1974); Paul J. Mishkin, *Some Further Last Words on Erie — The Thread,* 87 Harv. L. Rev. 1682, 1686 (1974); Peter Westen & Jeffrey S. Lehman, *Is There Life for Erie after the Death of Diversity?,* 78 Mich. L. Rev. 311, 315 (1980).

64. *See* Stephen Skowronek, Building a New American State: The Expansion of National Administrative Capacities, 1877–1920, at 13 (1982) ("Providing the national institutional capacities commensurate with the demands of an industrial society required nothing less than building a different kind of state organization.").

65. For arguments to revive the nondelegation doctrine, *see, e.g.,* David Schoenbrod, Power without Responsibility (1993); Marci A. Hamilton, *Representation and Nondelegation: Back to Basics,* 20 Cardozo L. Rev. 807 (1999).

66. 298 U.S. 238, 283–84 (1936).

67. Louis L. Jaffe, *Law Making by Private Groups,* 51 Harv. L. Rev. 201, 205 (1937).

68. *Id.* at 220–21.

69. David M. Lawrence, *Private Exercise of Governmental Power,* 61 Ind. L.J. 647, 648–49 (1986).

70. Lisa Schultz Bressman, Schechter Poultry *at the Millennium: A Delegation Doctrine for the Administrative State,* 109 Yale L.J. 1399, 1428 (2000).

71. Lisa Schultz Bressman, *Disciplining Delegation after* Whitman v. American Trucking Ass'ns, 87 Cornell L. Rev. 452, 454–55 (2002).

72. Jody Freeman, *The Private Role in Public Governance,* 75 N.Y.U. L. Rev. 543, 584 (2000).

73. *Id.* at 586.

74. Gillian E. Metzger, *Privatization as Delegation,* 103 Colum. L. Rev. 1367, 1437–45 (2003).

75. *Id.* at 1456.

76. Whitman v. American Trucking Associations, 531 U.S. 457, 472–75 (2001) (reaffirming the "intelligible principle" standard for delegations).

77. *Amchem,* 521 U.S. at 621–22. *See also* Fed. R. Civ. P. 23(c)(4) ("When appropriate . . . a class may be divided into subclasses and each subclass treated as a class, and the provisions of this rule shall then be construed and applied accordingly.").

78. 521 U.S. at 622–23.

79. *Id.* at 626.

80. 521 U.S. 424 (1997).

81. John C. Coffee Jr., *Class Action Accountability: Reconciling Exit, Voice, and Loyalty in Representative Litigation,* 100 Colum. L. Rev. 370, 394 (2000). The *Ortiz* Court deemed impermissible not only the conflation of impaired and unimpaired claimants in a single plaintiff class but also the amalgamation of claims with varying legal strength due to differences in Fibreboard's insurance coverage during different time periods. 527 U.S. at 856–57. The Court noted that "[p]re-1959 claimants . . . had more valuable claims than post-1959 claimants" due to differences in Fibreboard's insurance coverage and that these differences stood as "a second instance of disparate interests" warranting

subclassing. *Id.* at 857. *But see id.* at 881 (Breyer, J., dissenting) (citing the district court's finding that the purported distinction between pre- and post-1959 claimants was "not significant," because the insurance coverage settlement had made money "available equally" to sets of persons).

82. The requirement of adequate class representation stems not only from the text of Rule 23(a)(4) but also from the constitutional due process standard by which absent class members may be bound by the results of class litigation. *See Hansberry,* 311 U.S. at 44–46 (holding, in a pre-Rule 23 decision, that due process demands adequate representation before absent parties may be bound to a class judgment).

83. *See Ortiz,* 527 U.S. at 852–53.

84. *Id.* at 852 (emphasis added).

85. *Id.* at 863. *See also id.* at 852–53 ("In this case, certainly, any assumption that plaintiffs' counsel could be of a mind to do their simple best in bargaining for the benefit of the settlement class is patently at odds with the fact that at least some of the same lawyers representing plaintiffs and the class had also negotiated the separate settlement of 45,000 pending claims, the full payment of which was contingent on a successful Global Settlement Agreement or the successful resolution of the insurance coverage dispute.").

86. For an overview of the ossification literature, *see* William S. Jordan III, *Ossification Revisited: Does Arbitrary and Capricious Review Significantly Interfere with Agency Ability to Achieve Regulatory Goals through Informal Rulemaking?,* 94 Nw. U.L. Rev. 393 (2000).

87. 527 U.S. at 878 (Breyer, J., dissenting). *See also* Coffee, *supra* note 82, at 388 ("Typically, experienced class counsel in a mass tort class action may have a large inventory of individual actions pending against the same defendants. . . . [A]lthough disqualifying class counsel on this basis after *Ortiz* may be justified, the impact of such disqualifications on the plaintiffs' bar with experience in these actions may be fairly sweeping.").

88. Geoffrey C. Hazard Jr., *The Settlement Black Box,* 75 B.U. L. Rev. 1257, 1267–68 (1995).

89. Kamilewicz v. Bank of Boston Corp., 100 F.3d 1348, 1352 (7th Cir. 1996) (Easterbrook, J., dissenting from denial of rehearing en banc). The *Amchem* Court quoted with approval this passage. *See* 521 U.S. at 621.

90. *Id.* at 617.

91. *In re* Rhone-Poulenc Rorer, Inc., 51 F.3d 1293, 1300 (7th Cir. 1995).

92. *Ortiz,* 527 U.S. at 822.

93. *See* Nagareda, *supra* note 44, at 962–63 (discussing campaign against *Amchem* class settlement by Dallas law firm of Baron & Budd).

94. *See id.* at 936–37.

95. On the lack of repeated interactions in the class action context, *see* Stephen C. Yeazell, *Collective Litigation as Collective Action,* 1989 U. Ill. L. Rev. 43, 45–46.

CHAPTER VI

1. For a description of the Owens Corning NSP, *see* Fairness in Asbestos Compensation Act of 1999, Hearing Before the House Comm. on the Judiciary, 106th Cong. 137–42 (1999) (statement of Maura J. Albern, Senior Vice President, General Counsel, and Secretary, Owens Corning) [Albern Testimony].

2. *E.g.,* David Rosenberg, *Mandatory-Litigation Class Action: The Only Option for Mass Tort Cases,* 115 Harv. L. Rev. 831 (2002).

3. *In re* Simon II Litig., 407 F.3d 125 (2d Cir. 2005) (overturning certification of mandatory punitive damage class action against the tobacco industry).

4. *In re* Diet Drugs (Phentermine/Fenfluramine/Dexfenfluramine) Prods. Liab. Litig., MDL No. 1203, Civ. No. 99-20593, 2000 U.S. Dist. LEXIS 12275 (E.D. Pa. 2000), *aff'd without opinion*, 275 F.3d 34 (3d Cir. 2001).

5. Roughly one-half of all asbestos-related bankruptcies have occurred post-*Amchem*. *See* Stephen J. Carroll et al., Asbestos Litigation 152–53 (2005).

6. *See* chapter 2.

7. For a prominent exposition, *see* Christopher H. Schroeder, *Corrective Justice and Liability for Increased Risk*, 37 UCLA L. Rev. 439 (1990). For additional accounts, *see, e.g.,* Claire Finkelstein, *Is Risk a Harm?*, 151 U. Pa. L. Rev. 963 (2003); Andrew R. Klein, *A Model for Enhanced Risk Recovery in Tort*, 56 Wash. & Lee L. Rev. 1173 (1999).

8. *See* Rosenberg, *Mandatory-Litigation Class Action, supra* note 2; David Rosenberg, *The Regulatory Advantage of Class Action*, in Regulation through Litigation 244 (W. Kip Viscusi, ed. 2002); David Rosenberg, *Mass Tort Class Actions: What Defendants Have and Plaintiffs Don't*, 37 Harv. J. on Legis. 393 (2000); David Rosenberg, *Individual Justice and Collectivizing Risk-Based Claims in Mass-Exposure Cases*, 71 N.Y.U. L. Rev. 210 (1996); David Rosenberg, *The Causal Connection in Mass Exposure Cases: A "Public Law" Vision of the Tort System*, 97 Harv. L. Rev. 849 (1984).

9. *See* Rosenberg, *Mandatory-Litigation Class Action, supra* note 2, at 831–32.

10. *See, e.g.,* John C. P. Goldberg & Benjamin C. Zipursky, *Unrealized Torts*, 88 Va. L. Rev. 1625 (2002); James A. Henderson & Aaron D. Twerski, *Asbestos Litigation Gone Mad: Exposure-Based Recovery for Increased Risk, Mental Distress, and Medical Monitoring*, 53 S.C. L. Rev. 815 (2002).

11. An important early collection of essays on the legislation appears in Symposium, *After Disaster: The September 11th Compensation Fund and the Future of Civil Justice*, 53 DePaul L. Rev. 205 (2003).

12. Robert S. Peck, *The Victim Compensation Fund: Born from a Unique Confluence of Events Not Likely to Be Duplicated*, 53 DePaul L. Rev. 209, 217 (2003).

13. Samuel Issacharoff & Anna Morawiec Mansfield, *Compensation for the Victims of September 11th*, in The Handbook of Reparations 284, 285 (Pablo De Greiff, ed. 2006).

14. Air Transportation Safety and System Stabilization Act, Pub. L. No. 107-42, §403, 115 Stat. 230, 237 (2001) (declaring the purpose of the 9/11 Fund legislation "to provide compensation to any individual (or relatives of a deceased individual) who was physically injured or killed as a result of the terrorist-related aircraft crashes of September 11, 2001").

15. United States Department of Justice, Final Report of the Special Master for the September 11th Victim Compensation Fund of 2001, at 79 (2004) [Special Master's Final Report].

16. *Id.* at 71.

17. Air Transportation Safety and System Stabilization Act, Pub. L. No. 107-42, §405(b)(1)(B)(ii), 115 Stat. 230, 238 (2001).

18. September 11th Victim Compensation Fund of 2001, 67 Fed. Reg. 11,233, 11,236–37 (2002) (discussing "presumed award charts" used by Special Master).

19. *See* Peter H. Schuck, Agent Orange on Trial 144–45 (enlarged ed. 1987). For criticism of the sweeping discretion exercised by Special Master Feinberg, *see* Elizabeth Berkowitz, *The Problematic Role of the Special Master: Undermining the Legitimacy of the September 11th Victim Compensation Fund*, 24 Yale L. & Pol'y Rev. 1 (2006).

20. *See* Anthony J. Sebok, *What's Law Got to Do with It? Designing Compensation Schemes in the Shadow of the Tort System*, 53 DePaul L. Rev. 501, 504–17 (2003). Tort claims arising from the deaths of persons on the ground did manage to survive the defendant airlines' motion to dismiss. *In re* September 11 Litig., 280 F. Supp. 2d 279 (S.D.N.Y. 2003). For criticism of the analysis of New York tort doctrine in this decision, *see* Sebok, *supra*, at 517–23.

21. Robert L. Rabin, *September 11 through the Prism of Victim Compensation*, 106 Colum. L. Rev. 464, 467 (2006).

22. *Id.* at 473.

23. Special Master's Final Report, *supra* note 15, at 8 (noting that presumed awards under Special Master's grid extended "only to income levels up to the 98th percentile of individual income in the United States").

24. *See* Kenneth R. Feinberg, What Is Life Worth? 47 (2005) (recounting advice from one Senator to "make sure that 15 percent of the families don't receive 85 percent of the taxpayers' money"). Special Master Feinberg goes on to note that the average award for a death claim was approximately $2 million and the median award $1.7 million. As he observes: "[I]f extremely large payments to wealthy families had been made, they would have skewed the average such that the gap between average and median would have been much higher. I avoided this." *Id.* at 156–57.

25. Special Master's Final Report, *supra* note 15, at 82.

26. *Id.* at 1.

27. S. 852, 109th Cong. (2005).

28. *Id.* § 121(d)(1) (defining "Level I" of compensation grid to include persons with asbestos-related disease but without impairment), 131(b)(1) (providing that claimants at Level I shall receive only medical monitoring benefits, not immediate cash compensation), 132 (defining reimbursable medical monitoring costs to include "the costs of a claimant not covered by health insurance for an examination by the claimant's physician, x-ray tests, and pulmonary function tests every 3 years").

29. Paul Brodeur, Outrageous Misconduct 193–94, 250 (1985).

30. On the operations of the CCR, *see* Lawrence Fitzpatrick, *The Center for Claims Resolution*, 53 Law & Contemp. Probs. 13 (Autumn 1990).

31. Kenneth R. Meyer et al., *Emerging Trends in Asbestos Premises Liability Claims*, 72 Def. Counsel J. 241, 243 (2005).

32. Stephen Labaton, *Asbestos Bill Is Sidelined by the Senate*, N.Y. Times, Feb. 15, 2006, at C1.

33. Some scholarly treatments have included brief discussions of the Owens Corning NSP. *See* Samuel Issacharoff, *"Shocked": Mass Torts and Aggregate Asbestos Litigation after Amchem and Ortiz*, 80 Tex. L. Rev. 1925, 1937–38 (2002); Deborah R. Hensler, *As Time Goes By: Asbestos Litigation after Amchem and Ortiz*, 80 Tex. L. Rev. 1899, 1907 (2002); Richard A. Nagareda, *Future Mass Tort Claims and the Rule-Making/Adjudication Distinction*, 74 Tul. L. Rev. 1781, 1801–3 (2000).

34. Owens Corning, Financial Reorganization, Asbestos Chronology, *available at* http://www.owenscorning.com/finre/asbestos.html [OC Asbestos Chronology].

35. *Id.* (describing Owens Corning as "becom[ing] a target defendant" after *Amchem* and *Ortiz* injunctions and bankruptcies of leading asbestos companies).

36. On the CCR and the Owens Corning acquisition of Fibreboard as different means of litigation coordination on the defense side of the asbestos litigation, *see* Issacharoff, *supra* note 33, at 1937.

37. Albern Testimony, *supra* note 1, at 139; OC Asbestos Chronology, *supra* note 34.

38. Albern Testimony, *supra* note 1, at 139.

39. Issacharoff, *supra* note 33, at 1937.

40. Model Rules of Professional Conduct, Rule 1.2 (2003).

41. *Id.* Rule 5.6.

42. The principal question is whether the contracts used in the Owens Corning NSP would trigger the per se prohibition against agreements among would-be competitors not to compete — what antitrust law describes as "horizontal" agreements. For an overview of this prohibition, *see* 12 Herbert Hovencamp, Antitrust Law ¶ 2030b (1999). To be sure, the agreements used in the NSP did not, on their face, run horizontally between would-be competitors within the asbestos plaintiffs' bar. It remains unclear, however, whether the assent of each such firm occurred independently or pursuant to some manner of tacit agreement, with each firm signing a deal with Owens Corning based on an understanding that its rivals would do so as well. *Cf.* Toys "R" Us, Inc. v. FTC, 221 F.3d 928, 934–36 (7th Cir. 2000) (invalidating agreements between a major toy retailer and various toy manufacturers on the ground that any given manufacturer's assent stemmed from an implicit understanding that other manufacturers would enter into similar arrangements with the retailer).

43. Albern Testimony, *supra* note 1, at 134.

44. Carroll et al., *supra* note 5, at 23–24.

45. Asbestos Litigation, Hearing Before the Senate Comm. on the Judiciary, 107th Cong. 200–01 (2002) (statement of Steven J. Kazan, law firm of Kazan, McClain, Edises, Abrams, Fernandez, Lyons & Farrise).

46. Carroll et al., *supra* note 5, at 153.

CHAPTER VII

1. The title of one article in this series states Rosenberg's prescription. *See* David Rosenberg, *Mandatory-Litigation Class Action: The Only Option for Mass Tort Cases,* 115 Harv. L. Rev. 831 (2002).

2. *Id.* at 222.

3. Bruce L. Hay & David Rosenberg, *"Sweetheart" and "Blackmail" Settlements in Class Actions: Reality and Remedy,* 75 Notre Dame L. Rev. 1377 (2000).

4. David Rosenberg, *Mass Tort Class Actions: What Defendants Have and Plaintiffs Don't,* 37 Harv. J. on Legis. 393, 404 (2000).

5. Again, the title of one Rosenberg article states this contention. *See* David Rosenberg, *The Regulatory Advantage of Class Action,* in Regulation through Litigation 244 (W. Kip Viscusi, ed. 2002).

6. *See* Joseph A. Grundfest & Peter H. Huang, *The Unexpected Value of Litigation: A Real Options Perspective,* 58 Stan. L. Rev. 1267 (2006). For an earlier treatment of litigation investments as options as a way to analyze the bringing of low-probability or "frivolous" lawsuits, *see* Peter H. Huang, *Lawsuit Abandonment Options in Possibly Frivolous Litigation Games,* 23 Rev. Litig. 47 (2004).

7. Rosenberg, *supra* note 1, at 870–71. A similar argument appears in Michael A. Perino, *Class Action Chaos? A Theory of the Core and an Analysis of Opt-Out Rights in Mass Tort Class Actions,* 46 Emory L.J. 85, 104–5 (1997).

8. Rosenberg, *supra* note 1, at 871, 878.

9. David Rosenberg, *Individual Justice and Collectivizing Risk-Based Claims in Mass-Exposure Cases,* 71 N.Y.U. L. Rev. 210, 246 (1996).

10. Geoffrey C. Hazard, *The Settlement Black Box,* 75 B.U. L. Rev. 1257, 1267 (1995).

11. William B. Rubinstein, *A Transactional Model of Adjudication,* 89 Geo. L.J. 371, 434 (2001).

12. U.S. Const. preamble.

13. *See* John Rawls, A Theory of Justice (1971). Rosenberg appropriately points to the influence of Rawls on his conception of *ex ante* choice by would-be class members. Rosenberg, *supra* note 1, at 840; Rosenberg, *supra* note 9, at 210, 244 n.83 (1996).

14. Hay & Rosenberg, *supra* note 3, at 1394.

15. *Id.* at 1394, 1397.

16. 51 F.3d 1293, 1299–1300 (7th Cir. 1995).

17. A substantial literature draws on internal documents of the tobacco industry to reveal the conspiracy to mislead consumers. *E.g.,* Stanton A. Glantz et al., The Cigarette Papers (1996); Phillip J. Hilts, Smokescreen (1996).

18. 211 F.R.D. 86 (E.D.N.Y. 2002), *rev'd,* 407 F.3d 125 (2d Cir. 2005).

19. Some use the phrase "limited generosity" to describe the same idea. *See* Joan Steinman, *Managing Punitive Damages: A Role for Mandatory "Limited Generosity" Classes and Anti-Suit Injunctions?,* 36 Wake Forest L. Rev. 1043, 1047 (2001).

20. Oral argument took place on November 20, 2003. The Second Circuit did not issue its decision until May 6, 2005. *Simon II,* 407 F.3d 125.

21. The first such decision is *BMW of North America, Inc. v. Gore.* 517 U.S. 559 (1996).

22. *See* Pacific Mutual Life Ins. Co. v. Haslip, 499 U.S. 1, 26–27 (1991) (Scalia, J., concurring); TXO Production Corp. v. Alliance Resources Corp., 509 U.S. 443, 470 (1993) (Scalia, J., concurring); *Gore,* 517 U.S. at 599 (Scalia, J., dissenting, joined by Thomas, J.); State Farm Mut. Auto. Ins. Co. v. Campbell, 538 U.S. 408, 429–30 (2003) (Thomas, J., dissenting).

23. Roginsky v. Richardson-Merrell, Inc., 378 F.2d 832, 839 (2d Cir. 1967). Judge Weinstein himself echoed this concern in the Agent Orange litigation. *In re* "Agent Orange" Prod. Liab. Litig., 100 F.R.D. 718, 728 (E.D.N.Y. 1983).

24. Dunn v. Hovic, 1 F.3d 1371, 1400–05 (Weis, J., dissenting), *modified on other grounds,* 13 F.3d 58 (3d Cir. 1993); *id.* at 1405 (Becker, J., dissenting); Juzwin v. Amtorg Trading Corp., 705 F. Supp. 1053, 1060–64 (D.N.J. 1989), *modified,* 718 F. Supp. 1233 (D.N.J. 1989).

25. *Dunn,* 1 F.3d at 1386 (recognizing that "no single court can fashion an effective response"); *Juzwin,* 718 F. Supp. at 1236 (stating that "multiple awards of punitive damages for a single course of conduct violate the fundamental fairness requirement of the Due Process Clause," but adding that "equitable and practical concerns prevent [courts] from fashioning a fair and effective remedy").

26. 517 U.S. 559, 574 (1996). For earlier cases articulating the existence of a due process limit but ultimately upholding the particular awards at issue, *see TXO,* 509 U.S. 443; *Haslip,* 499 U.S. 1.

27. *Campbell,* 538 U.S. at 425.

28. The precise parameters of this limit remain somewhat uncertain, for the Court's analysis in *Gore* and *Campbell* under the Due Process Clause remains intertwined with additional considerations of federalism. Part of what doomed the punitive damage award

in *Gore,* said the Court, lay in a concern that the Alabama jury may have punished BMW based on the nationwide scope of its repainting policy, even though that conduct remained lawful in many other jurisdictions. This, the Court declared, amounted to "Alabama . . . infringing on the policy choices of other States." 517 U.S. at 572. Along similar lines, the Court in *Campbell* criticized the Utah trial judge for permitting the Campbells to present evidence of other purported misconduct on the part of State Farm nationwide. Much of that other conduct "was lawful where it occurred" and, in any event, "bore no relation" to the ways in which State Farm had mishandled the defense of the underlying lawsuit against the Campbells. 538 U.S. at 422. *Gore* and *Campbell* thus leave open the question whether the Due Process Clause would prohibit a series of punitive damage awards returned by juries in various states, each with a single-digit ratio and each based on only those aspects of the defendant's misconduct that affected the particular rendering state. For the most part, however, concern about multiple punitive damage awards in the tobacco litigation does not arise from such state-specific proceedings.

29. Castano v. American Tobacco Co., 84 F.3d 734 (5th Cir. 1996).

30. On the overlap between the "*Castano* group" of plaintiffs' lawyers and the lawyers retained to represent the states on a contingency fee basis in the Medicaid reimbursement litigation, *see Tobacco Litigation:* The American Lawyer*'s Guide to the Players,* Am. Lawyer, Mar. 1996, at 108, 109–13, 115–16.

31. On the attorneys involved in these trials, *see* Milo Geyelin, *California May Be Hazardous to Big Tobacco's Health,* Wall St. J., June 8, 2001, at B1 (profiling Michael J. Piuze, counsel for individual plaintiff awarded $3 billion in punitive damages in California trial); Milo Geyelin, *Suing Tobacco, Florida Firm Takes Own Path,* Wall St. J., May 15, 2000, at B1 (profiling Stanley and Susan Rosenblatt, counsel for a class of Florida smokers awarded $144.87 billion in punitive damages at trial); Bob Van Voris, *Big Bucks Guy Shows Little Ego,* Nat'l L.J., June 18, 2001, at A4 (same).

32. *Simon II,* 211 F.R.D. at 190.

33. *Simon II,* 407 F.3d at 137 (quoting *Ortiz,* 527 U.S. at 864).

34. *Id.* at 138 (quoting *Ortiz,* 527 U.S. 849).

35. *Id.*

36. *Id.*

37. *Ortiz,* 527 U.S. at 835–37 (discussing early equity cases relied upon by drafters of Rule 23(b)(1)(B)).

38. *Simon II,* 407 F.3d at 138.

39. *See* Lawrence Gene Sager, *Fair Measure: The Legal Status of Underenforced Constitutional Norms,* 91 Harv. L. Rev. 1212 (1978).

40. *Simon II* effectively sought to bring the choice of judicial forum (a single federal court) into line with the source of the constraint on punitive damages (federal constitutional law). *See generally* Samuel Issacharoff & Catherine M. Sharkey, *Backdoor Federalization,* 53 UCLA L. Rev. 1353, 1427–28 (2006).

41. *Simon II,* 211 F.R.D. at 192.

42. John C. Coffee Jr., *Tobacco Wars: Peace in Our Time?,* N.Y.L.J., July 20, 2000, at 1, 8.

43. *Ortiz,* 527 U.S. at 841.

44. *Id.* (quoting John Norton Pomeroy, Equity Jurisprudence §407, at 764–65 (4th ed. 1918)).

45. Cooper Indus., Inc. v. Leatherman Tool Group, Inc., 532 U.S. 424, 432 (2001).

46. *Id. See also Campbell*, 538 U.S. at 419 ("It should be presumed a plaintiff has been made whole for his injuries by compensatory damages, so punitive damages should only be awarded if the defendant's culpability, after having paid compensatory damages, is so reprehensible as to warrant the imposition of further sanctions to achieve punishment or deterrence.").

47. Recent scholarship questions the current characterization of punitive damages as distinct from compensatory damages. On the origins of modern punitive damages in earlier forms of relief designed to compensate the plaintiff for offenses to her dignity, above and beyond her concrete loss, *see* Anthony J. Sebok, *What Did Punitive Damages Do? Why Misunderstanding the History of Punitive Damages Matters Today*, 78 Chi.-Kent L. Rev. 163 (2003); Thomas B. Colby, *Beyond the Multiple Punishment Problem: Punitive Damages as Punishment for Individual, Private Wrongs*, 87 Minn. L. Rev. 583 (2003). One commentator questions the line between compensation and punishment, contending that the law should understand punitive damages as compensatory, but for wrongs to society generally rather than to the individual plaintiff. *See* Catherine M. Sharkey, *Punitive Damages as Societal Damages*, 113 Yale L.J. 347 (2003).

CHAPTER VIII

1. *In re* Diet Drugs (Phentermine/Fenfluramine/Dexfenfluramine) Prods. Liab. Litig., MDL No. 1203, Civ. No. 99-20593, 2000 U.S. Dist. LEXIS 12275, *140 (E.D. Pa. Aug. 28, 2000), *aff'd without opinion*, 275 F.3d 34 (3d Cir. 2001) [Fen-Phen Class Settlement Approval Opinion].

2. *Id.* at *7.

3. *Id.* at *30 (quoting record from hearing on fairness of class settlement).

4. 4 David L. Faigman et al., Modern Scientific Evidence § 39-2.5.4, at 393 (2d. ed. 2002) ("[It] is not clear that patients with mild or less severe regurgitation will develop serious heart disease because even patients with severe aortic regurgitation can remain stable and asymptomatic for years.").

5. *See* Laura Johannes & Robert Langreth, *Fen-Phen Defense: Marketer of Redux, Mulling Settlement, Sees Plaintiffs' Hand*, Wall St. J., Sept. 28, 1999, at A1. On the indications of heart valve problems from diet drug users in Belgium, *see* Laura Johannes & Steve Stecklow, *Early Warning: Heart-Valve Problem That Felled Diet Pills Had Arisen Previously*, Wall St. J., Dec. 11, 1997, at A1.

6. Jim Yardley, *$23 Million Awarded in Suit against Maker of Diet Drug*, N.Y. Times, Aug. 7, 1999, at A7. The plaintiff's "own cardiologist testified that her heart problems predated her use of fen-phen." *Id.* The plaintiff's counsel nonetheless "made a case that [Wyeth] attempted to minimize the possible risks of the diet drugs by trying to limit the warnings on side effects." Robert Langreth, *American Home Is Ordered to Pay $23.36 Million in Diet-Drug Suit*, Wall St. J., Aug. 9, 1999, at A4.

7. *See* David S. Cloud & Richard B. Schmitt, *FBI Looks into the Approval of Redux*, Wall St. J., Sept. 9, 1999, at A3; Gardiner Harris, *Grand Jury Probes American Home on Reporting of Drugs' Side Effects*, Wall St. J., May 16, 2000, at B14.

8. *In re* Diet Drugs (Phentermine/Fenfluramine/Dexfenfluramine) Prods. Liability Litig., 226 F.R.D. 498, 501–02 (E.D. Pa. 2005) [Fen-Phen Seventh Amendment Opinion].

9. *Id.* at 503.

10. Richard A. Brealey et al., Fundamentals of Corporate Finance §24.1, at 697 (3d ed. 2001).

11. Fen-Phen Class Settlement Approval Opinion, 2000 U.S. Dist. LEXIS 12275, *52–53.

12. *Id., aff 'd without opinion*, 275 F.3d 34 (3d Cir. 2001).

13. *Id.* at *140–42.

14. *Id.* at *152 n.22.

15. David J. Morrow, *American Home to Settle Some 1,400 Fen-Phen Suits*, N.Y. Times, Dec. 23, 1999, at C2. A rival pharmaceutical firm, Pfizer, Inc., sued to prevent the merger and subsequently completed its own hostile takeover of Warner-Lambert. Jeffrey H. Dyer et al., *When to Ally and When to Acquire*, Harv. Bus. Rev. (July–Aug. 2004), at 108, 113–14.

16. U.S. Const. amend. V ("[N]or shall any person be subject for the same offense to be twice put in jeopardy of life or limb."). "The underlying idea [of the Double Jeopardy Clause] . . . is that the State . . . should not be allowed to make repeated attempts to convict an individual for an alleged offense, thereby subjecting him to embarrassment, expense and ordeal and compelling him to live in a continuing state of anxiety and insecurity." United States v. Green, 355 U.S. 184, 187 (1957). On the kinship between the problem of multiple punitive damage awards in tort litigation and the concerns underlying the Double Jeopardy Clause in criminal prosecutions, *see* Richard W. Murphy, *Superbifurcation: Making Room for State Prosecution in the Punitive Damages Process*, 76 N.C. L. Rev. 463, 544–45 (1998); Malcolm E. Wheeler, *The Constitutional Case for Reforming Punitive Damages Procedures*, 69 Va. L. Rev. 269, 345–51 (1983).

17. United States v. Halper, 490 U.S. 435, 451 (1989).

18. U.S. Const. amend. VI ("In all criminal prosecutions, the accused shall enjoy the right to a speedy . . . trial."). On the length of delay permissible under the Speedy Trial Clause, *see* Wayne R. LaFave et al., Criminal Procedure §18.2, at 862–67 (4th ed. 2004).

19. Dan B. Dobbs, The Law of Torts §381, at 1063 (2000); Restatement (Second) of Torts §908 cmt. c (1977).

20. Looking to the common law of torts to inform the standards for federal civil rights litigation, the Supreme Court has observed that "punitive damages . . . are never awarded as of right, no matter how egregious the defendant's conduct." Rather, "the question whether to award punitive damages is left to the jury, which may or may not make such an award." By contrast, the jury is "required" to award compensatory damages "once liability is found." Smith v. Wade, 461 U.S. 30, 52 (1983) (quoting Dan B. Dobbs, Handbook on the Law of Remedies §3.9, at 204 (1973)).

21. *See* chapter 7.

22. For defenses of back-end opt-out rights on grounds of procedural legitimacy, with favorable reference to the fen-phen class settlement, *see* Richard A. Nagareda, *Autonomy, Peace, and Put Options in the Mass Tort Class Action*, 115 Harv. L. Rev. 747, 796–822 (2002), John C. Coffee Jr. *Class Action Accountability: Reconciling Exit, Voice, and Loyalty in Representative Litigation*, 100 Colum. L. Rev. 370, 432–33 & n.158 (2000). In addition to Coffee, other prominent scholars testified in favor of the fen-phen class settlement before the district court. *See* Fen-Phen Class Settlement Approval Opinion, 2000 U.S. Dist. LEXIS 12275, *22 (citing supportive testimony by Arthur R. Miller, among others).

23. I am grateful to David Rosenberg for an insight along these lines in a detailed response to my earlier article on the fen-phen class settlement. *See* David Rosenberg, *Mandatory-Litigation Class Action: The Only Option for Mass Tort Cases,* 115 Harv. L. Rev. 831, 880 n.93 (2002).

24. *Id.* at 891 n.119; Michael A. Perino, *Class Action Chaos? A Theory of the Core and an Analysis of Opt-Out Rights in Mass Tort Class Actions,* 46 Emory L.J. 85, 125 (1997).

25. Fen-Phen Class Settlement Approval Opinion, 2000 U.S. Dist. LEXIS 12275, *86.

26. Fen-Phen Seventh Amendment Opinion, 226 F.R.D. at 506-7.

27. Reed Abelson & Jonathan D. Glater, *Tough Questions Are Raised on Fen-Phen Compensation,* N.Y. Times, Oct. 7, 2003, at C1, C10.

28. Fen-Phen Seventh Amendment Opinion, 226 F.R.D. at 510-11.

29. Victor E. Schwartz & Leah Lorber, *Twisting the Purpose of Pain and Suffering Awards: Turning Compensation into "Punishment,"* 54 S.C. L. Rev. 47 (2002).

30. *In re* Diet Drugs (Phentermine/Fenfluramine/Dexfenfluramine) Prods. Liab. Litig., 369 F.3d 293, 303 (3d Cir. 2004).

31. *Id.* at 300.

32. *Id.* at 312-15.

33. Fen-Phen Seventh Amendment Opinion, 226 F.R.D. at 522 (60,000 back-end opt-outs); *How Deep Do Merck's Wounds Go?,* Wall St. J., Sept. 30, 2006 ($21 billion cost of fen-phen litigation to Wyeth).

34. Fen-Phen Class Settlement Approval Opinion, 2000 U.S. Dist. LEXIS 12275,*85.

35. *Field of Dreams* (Universal 1989).

36. Stephen J. Carroll et al., Asbestos Litigation 12 (2005).

37. Fen-Phen Seventh Amendment Opinion, 226 F.R.D. at 506. *See also* Alison Frankel, *Still Ticking,* Am. Lawyer, Mar. 2005, 92, 98.

38. Anders Zitting, *Prevalence of Radiographic Small Lung Opacities and Pleural Abnormalities in a Representative Adult Population Sample,* 107 Chest 126 (1995).

39. Carroll et al., *supra* note 36, at 76.

40. Joseph N. Gitlin et al., *Comparison of "B" Readers' Interpretations of Chest Radiographs for Asbestos Related Changes,* 11 Acad. Radiology 843 (2004).

41. *In re* Silica Prods. Liab. Litig., 398 F. Supp. 2d 563, 620 (S.D. Tex. 2005).

42. *Id.* at 628.

43. *Id.* at 633.

44. *Id.*

45. *Id.* at 633-34.

46. *Id.* at 635.

47. Fen-Phen Seventh Amendment Opinion, 226 F.R.D. at 507.

48. For clarity of presentation, I shall cite this early version as the "original" Sulzer class settlement to distinguish it from the "final" version that is different in content. For a summary of the original class settlement, *see In re* Inter-Op Hip Prosthesis Liab. Litig., 204 F.R.D. 330, 351-52 (N.D. Ohio 2001). For the original settlement agreement, *see* Class Action Settlement Agreement among Sulzer Orthopedics and Affiliated Entities Including Sulzer Medica Ltd. and Class Counsel on Behalf of Class Representatives (Aug. 23, 2001), Inter-Op Hip Prosthesis (MDL Docket No. 01-CV-9000) [Original Sulzer Class Settlement].

For a summary of the final version of the class settlement, *see In re* Sulzer Hip Prosthesis & Knee Prosthesis Liab. Litig., MDL Docket No. 1401, Case No. 1:01-CV-9000, slip op. at 3 (N.D. Ohio Mar. 14, 2002), available at http://www.hipimplantlaw .com/pdf/20020314_memo_and_order.pdf [Sulzer Summary]. For the final settlement agreement, *see* Class Action Settlement Agreement among Sulzer Orthopedics Inc., Sulzer Medica AG, Sulzer AG, and Class Counsel on Behalf of Class Representatives (Mar. 13, 2002), Sulzer Hip Prosthesis (MDL Docket No. 01-CV-9000), available at http://www.sulzerimplantsettlement.com/classactionsettlement.htm [Final Sulzer Class Settlement].

49. *Inter-Op Hip Prosthesis*, 204 F.R.D. at 335.

50. Amy Schatz, *Sulzer Medica Distances Itself from Faulty Hip Implants*, Austin Am.-Statesman, July 18, 2001, at D1, *available at* 2001 WL 4581554.

51. *Inter-Op Hip Prosthesis*, 204 F.R.D. at 348.

52. Jess Bravin, *Sulzer Medica Reaches Novel Class-Action Pact*, Wall St. J., Aug. 16, 2001, at A3.

53. *Inter-Op Hip Prosthesis*, 204 F.R.D. at 351–52.

54. *Id.* at 352.

55. Original Sulzer Class Settlement, *supra* note 48, § 2.8(f).

56. U.C.C. § 9–320(a) (2002).

57. Bravin, *supra* note 52, at A3.

58. U.C.C. § 9–102(72)(A).

59. 50 C.J.S. Judgment § 554, at 108 (1997).

60. U.C.C. § 9–322(a)(1) (setting priorities among perfected security interests in same collateral).

61. 527 U.S. 815, 838, 839 (1999).

62. *Inter-Op Hip Prosthesis*, 204 F.R.D. at 356.

63. *Id.* at 344.

64. Petitioners' Consolidated Brief in Support of Appeal Pursuant to FRCP 23(f) and FRAP 5 at 3–4, *In re* Inter-Op Hip Prosthesis Prod. Liab. Litig. (6th Cir. Feb. 2002) (Nos. 01–303 & 01–304).

65. Drummer v. Sulzer Orthopedics Inc., 2001 U.S. App. LEXIS 25910, *5 (6th Cir. Oct. 29, 2001).

66. *In re* Inter-Op Hip Prosthesis Prod. Liab. Litig., MDL Docket No. 1401, Case No. 1:01-CV-9000, slip op. (N.D. Ohio May 8, 2002), available at http://www.ohnd .uscourts.gov/Clerk_s_Office/Notable_Cases/01cv9000-fairness-ord.PDF.

67. Sulzer Summary, *supra* note 48, at 3.

68. Goran Mijuk, *Sulzer Medica's Stock Jumps on Proposed Legal Settlement*, Wall St. J. Eur., Feb. 5, 2002, at 16.

69. *In re* Telectronics Pacing Sys., Inc., 221 F.3d 870, 880–81 (6th Cir. 2000).

70. *In re* Telectronics Pacing Sys., Inc., 137 F. Supp. 2d 985, 1002–3 (S.D. Ohio 2001) (comparing original mandatory class settlement with final opt-out class settlement).

CHAPTER IX

1. Stephen J. Carroll et al., Asbestos Litigation 118 (2005).

2. 391 F.3d 190 (3d Cir. 2004).

3. 11 U.S.C. §§ 1101–74 (2000).

4. *E.g.*, Douglas G. Baird, *The Uneasy Case for Corporate Reorganizations*, 15 J. Legal Stud. 127 (1986); Michael Bradley & Michael Rosenzweig, *The Untenable Case for Chapter 11*, 101 Yale L.J. 1043 (1992).

5. *E.g., In re* SGL Carbon Corp., 200 F.3d 154, 163 (3d Cir. 1999).

6. 11 U.S.C. §105(a) (broadly authorizing the bankruptcy court to "issue any order, process, or judgment that is necessary or appropriate to carry out the provisions of [the Bankruptcy Code]").

7. *In re* Joint Eastern & Southern Dist. Asbestos Litig., 982 F.2d 721, 725–26 (2d Cir. 1992).

8. In the Matter of Johns-Manville Corp., 68 B.R. 618, 628–29 (Bankr. S.D.N.Y. 1986).

9. 11 U.S.C. §1126(c) (2000).

10. *Johns-Manville*, 68 B.R. at 631.

11. Kane v. Johns-Manville Corp., 843 F.2d 636, 646–48 (2d Cir. 1988).

12. Paul Brodeur, Outrageous Misconduct 283–85, 323–24 (1985).

13. *See* H.R. Rep. No. 103–835, at 40–41 (1994). *See also* The Need for Supplemental Permanent Injunctions in Bankruptcy, Hearing before the Subcomm. on Courts & Admin. Practice of the Senate Comm. on the Judiciary, 103d Cong. (1993); Injunctions in Mass Tort Cases in Bankruptcy, Hrg. Before the Subcomm. on Econ. & Commercial Law of the House Comm. on the Judiciary, 102d Cong. (1992). For a concise overview of the relationship between the Manville bankruptcy and the enactment of §524(g), *see* Mark D. Plevin et al., *The Future Claims Representative in Prepackaged Asbestos Bankruptcies: Conflicts of Interest, Strange Alliances, and Unfamiliar Duties for Burdened Bankruptcy Courts*, 62 N.Y.U. Ann. Surv. Am. L. 271, 275–80 (2006).

14. 11 U.S.C. §514(g)(5) (2000).

15. *Id.* §524(g)(2)(B)(ii)(V).

16. *Id.* §524(g)(4)(B)(i).

17. *Id.* §524(g)(2)(B)(ii)(IV)(bb).

18. *Id.* §524(g)(4)(ii)-(iii).

19. *See* Brodeur, *supra* note 12, at 283.

20. Michael C. Jensen, A Theory of the Firm: Governance, Residual Claims, and Organizational Forms 74–77 (2000).

21. New Generation Research, Inc., The 2004 Bankruptcy Yearbook & Almanac 163 (2004) (empirical data on use of prepacks from 1986 forward).

22. Anup Malani & Charles Mullin, *Assessing the Merits of Reallocation under Joint and Several Liability, with an Application to Asbestos Litigation* (Dec. 21, 2004), available at http://www.law.virginia.edu/home2002/pdf/malani/asbestos.pdf.

23. Carroll et al., *supra* note 1, at 110.

24. Ronald Barliant et al., *From Free-Fall to Free-for-All: The Rise of Pre-Packaged Asbestos Bankruptcies*, 12 Am. Bankr. Inst. L. Rev. 441, 446 (2004) (listing a total of eight asbestos-related prepacks).

25. *Combustion Engineering*, 391 F.3d at 201–8.

26. *In re* Combustion Engineering, 295 B.R. 459, 477 (Bankr. D. Del. 2003), *rev'd*, 391 F.3d 190 (3d Cir. 2004). For a judicial recognition of the same point in connection with another asbestos-related prepack, *see In re* Congoleum Corp., 426 F.3d 675, 679–80 (3d Cir. 2005).

27. *Combustion Engineering*, 295 B.R. at 476–77.

28. Roger Parloff, *Tort Lawyers: There They Go Again!*, Fortune, Sept. 6, 2004, at 186;

Barliant et al., *supra* note 24; Alex Berenson, *A Caldron of Ethics and Asbestos*, N.Y. Times, Mar. 12, 2003, at C1, C22; Mark D. Plevin et al., *Pre-Packaged Asbestos Bankruptcies: A Flawed Solution*, 44 S. Tex. L. Rev. 883 (2003). For discussion of a broadly similar attorney conflict involving another prepack, *see Congoleum*, 426 F.3d at 690.

29. Pope v. Rice, No. 04-Civ.-4171, 2005 U.S. Dist. LEXIS 4011 (S.D.N.Y. Mar. 14, 2005).

30. *Combustion Engineering*, 391 F.3d at 204–5.

31. *Id.* at 205.

32. *Id.* at 244.

33. *Id.* at 208, 245.

34. *Id.* at 235.

35. *Id.* at 237.

36. Findings of Fact and Conclusions of Law Regarding Confirmation of Combustion Engineering, Inc.'s Plan of Reorganization, as Modified through Oct. 7, 2005, In re *Combustion Engineering*, No. 03-10495-JKF, at 26 (Bank. D. Del. Dec. 19, 2005) [Modified Plan Opinion], *aff'd* Misc. No. 06-21(JEI) (D. Del. Mar. 1, 2006).

37. *Combustion Engineering*, 391 F.3d at 242.

38. Brief for Appellees Combustion Engineering, Inc. and Asea Brown Boveri Inc., at 73, *In re* Combustion Engineering, 391 F.3d 190 (3d Cir. 2004), *available at* 2003 WL 23976712.

39. Insurers also objected to the plan confirmation, on the apparent premise that its generosity toward lower-value claimants would increase the overall price tag associated with the reorganization. The Third Circuit concluded that insurers, for the most part, lacked standing to challenge the plan confirmation. The court reasoned that plan confirmation did not alter the terms of insurer's preexisting contracts with Combustion Engineering and related companies, thereby leaving insurers free to contest coverage for claims paid by the §524(g) trust. *Combustion Engineering*, 391 F.3d at 215–23. This stance is consistent with a significant subsequent ruling arising from another prepackaged reorganization under §524(g). Fuller-Austin Insulation Co. v. Highlands Ins. Co., 38 Cal. Rptr. 3d 716 (Cal. Ct. App. 2006). *But see* UNR Indus., Inc. v. Continental Casualty Co., 942 F.2d 1101 (7th Cir. 1991) (pre-524(g) decision treating confirmation of reorganization plan itself as triggering insurance coverage obligations).

40. *Combustion Engineering*, 391 F.3d at 244.

41. *Id.* (quoting S. Elizabeth Gibson, *Symposium—Mass Torts: A Response to Professor Resnick: Will This Vehicle Pass Inspection?*, 148 U. Pa. L. Rev. 2095, 2112 (2000)).

42. *Id.* at 245.

43. Modified Plan Opinion, *supra* note 36, at 17.

44. *Id.* at 28.

45. *Id.* at 4, 33.

46. The modified plan, for example, provided that "all diagnoses must be based upon a physical examination of the claimant by the physician providing the diagnosis" and imposed specifications for the professional qualifications of physicians diagnosing asbestos-related disease. *Id.* at 19.

47. *Id.*

48. *Id.* at 22.

49. Yair Listokin & Kenneth Ayotte, *Protecting Future Claimants in Mass Tort Bankruptcies*, 98 Nw. U.L. Rev. 1435, 1451–52 (2004).

50. *Combustion Engineering*, 391 F.3d at 206 n.10.

51. 11 U.S.C. §524(g)(4)(B)(i) (calling for appointment of futures representative "as part of the proceedings leading to issuance of [a channeling] injunction").

52. *Id.* §547(b)(4)(A).

53. *Id.* §303(b)(1).

54. Plevin et al., *supra* note 28, at 916–17.

55. Listokin & Ayotte, *supra* note 49, at 1457.

56. *Id.* at 1457–60.

57. *See* Plevin et al., *supra* note 13, at 292–93.

58. Green also served as the futures representative in non-prepack reorganizations involving asbestos defendants Federal-Mogul Corp. and Babcock & Wilcox Co. Schiro so served for the reorganization of Swan Transportation Co.; Fitzpatrick for the reorganization of Pittsburgh Corning Corp.; and Austern for the reorganization of W. R. Grace & Co. For identification of the prepacks through 2004, I draw on the listing in Carroll et al., *supra* note 1, at 120, with updating based on Mark D. Plevin et al., *Where Are They Now, Part Three: A Continuing History of the Companies That Have Sought Bankruptcy Protection Due to Asbestos Claims,* Mealey's Asbestos Bankr. Rep., Nov. 2005, 1.

59. *In re* Kensington Int'l, Ltd., 368 F.3d 289, 308–9 (3d Cir. 2004). There, the federal judge responsible for five asbestos-related reorganizations—Judge Alfred Wolin— had appointed as his advisors both the futures representative in a similar reorganization pending in another court and that representative's local counsel. The Third Circuit found itself "hard pressed to overstate the importance of the Advisors' role" vis-à-vis Judge Wolin. The advisors "had a unique level of influence over Judge Wolin, given the role they played . . . in educating [him] (a self-admitted neophyte) on all of the key asbestos-related issues." *Id.* at 304.

60. Mark J. Roe, *Bankruptcy and Mass Tort,* 84 Colum. L. Rev. 846 (1984); Thomas A. Smith, *A Capital Markets Approach to Mass Tort Bankruptcy,* 104 Yale L.J. 367 (1994).

61. Roe, *supra* note 60, at 871–73.

62. Smith, *supra* note 60, at 392; Listokin & Ayotte, *supra* note 49, at 1453.

63. Smith, *supra* note 60, at 394–401.

64. *Id.* at 406.

65. Listokin & Ayotte, *supra* note 49, at 1455.

66. *Id.* at 1460.

67. *Id.* at 1492.

CHAPTER X

1. For a detailed estimate of the payments required under the MSA, *see* W. Kip Viscusi, Smoke-Filled Rooms 43 (2002).

2. A complete list of the plaintiffs' lawyers representing the various states appears as an exhibit to the MSA. *See* Multistate Settlement Agreement, Exh. S, available at http://www.naag.org/upload/1109185724_1032468605_cigmsa.pdf.

3. *See* Viscusi, *supra* note 1, at 52–54.

4. Ian Ayres, *Using Tort Settlements to Cartelize,* 34 Val. U.L. Rev. 595, 595 (2000).

5. I draw here—albeit with some alteration of terminology—on the discussion in William B. Rubenstein, *On What a "Private Attorney General" Is—and Why It Matters,* 57 Vand. L. Rev. 2129, 2140–41 (2004).

6. A. D. Bedell Wholesale Co. v. Philip Morris Inc., 263 F.3d 239, 259 (3d Cir. 2001).

7. Donald W. Gardner, *Cigarettes and Welfare Reform*, 26 Emory L.J. 269, 314 (1977).

8. *E.g.*, Robert L. Rabin, *The Third Wave of Tobacco Tort Litigation*, in Regulating Tobacco 176 (Robert L. Rabin & Stephen D. Sugarman, eds. 2001) [Rabin, *Third Wave*]; Robert L. Rabin, *Institutional and Historical Perspectives on Tobacco Tort Liability*, in Smoking Policy: Law, Politics, & Culture 110 (Robert L. Rabin & Stephen D. Sugarman, eds. 1993); Gary T. Schwartz, *Tobacco Liability in the Courts*, in Smoking Policy, 131.

9. Peter Pringle, Cornered 7 (1998).

10. Haines v. Liggett Group, Inc., 814 F. Supp. 414, 421 (D.N.J. 1993) (quoting internal memorandum from R. J. Reynolds attorney J. Michael Jordan).

11. Pringle, *supra* note 9, at 26.

12. *See, e.g., id.*, ch. 1; Michael Orey, Assuming the Risk 256–63 (1999).

13. Castano v. American Tobacco Co., 84 F.3d 734 (5th Cir. 1996).

14. Engle v. Liggett Group, Inc., 945 So. 2d 1246 (Fla. 2006).

15. The argument here about government reimbursement litigation as both an implicit aggregation device and a means to shift attention from the individual choices of smokers draws upon Howard M. Erichson, *Private Lawyers, Public Lawsuits: Plaintiffs' Attorneys in Municipal Gun Litigation*, in Suing the Gun Industry 140–43 (Timothy D. Lytton, ed. 2005).

16. A significant early trove consisted of internal documents from Brown & Williamson Tobacco Company and its corporate affiliates, brought to light as a result of their unauthorized release by a paralegal on the defense side. The documents are analyzed in Stanton A. Glantz et al., The Cigarette Papers (1996).

17. FDA v. Brown & Williamson Tobacco Corp., 529 U.S. 120 (2000).

18. Helpful works untangling the tort and nontort concepts in government reimbursement litigation against the tobacco industry include Anthony J. Sebok, *Pretext, Transparency and Motive in Mass Restitution Litigation*, 57 Vand. L. Rev. 2177 (2004); Hanoch Dagan & James J. White, *Governments, Citizens, and Injurious Industries*, 75 N.Y.U. L. Rev. 334 (2000); Doug Rendelman, *Common Law Restitution in the Mississippi Tobacco Settlement: Did Smoke Get in Their Eyes?*, 33 Ga. L. Rev. 847 (1999).

19. William Prosser et al., Prosser & Keeton on the Law of Torts §86, at 616 (5th ed. 1984).

20. Restatement (Second) of Torts §821B (1979). The notion that localities might draw on the tort concept of a public nuisance to sue the firearms industry stems from scholarly writing. *E.g.*, David Kairys, *Legal Claims of Cities against the Manufacturers of Handguns*, 71 Temp. L. Rev. 1, 14 (1998). For a more skeptical assessment of the public nuisance claim, *see* Donald G. Gifford, *Public Nuisance as a Mass Products Liability Tort*, 71 U. Cin. L. Rev. 741 (2003).

21. Restatement (Second) of Torts §821B, cmt. g, 92.

22. *E.g.*, City of Chicago v. Beretta U.S.A. Corp., 821 N.E.2d 1099, 1114–16 (Ill. 2004) (citing similar decisions from other states).

23. A roadmap to the various allegations made in the firearms litigation appears in Timothy D. Lytton, *Introduction: An Overview of Lawsuits against the Gun Industry*, in Suing the Gun Industry 5–15 (Timothy D. Lytton, ed. 2005).

24. Gary T. Schwartz, *Cigarette Litigation's Offspring: Assessing Tort Issues Related to Guns, Alcohol, & Other Controversial Products in Light of the Tobacco Wars*, 74 Pepp. L. Rev. 751, 754, (2000).

25. Even scholars not averse to the general notion of tobacco litigation point to

the weakness of the state reimbursement actions in these regards. *E.g.*, Rabin, *Third Wave, supra* note 8, at 190 (characterizing the states' arguments for the independence of their reimbursement actions as resting on "a shaky foundation" and as sounding "suspiciously circular").

26. *E.g.*, Camden County Bd. of Chosen Freeholders v. Beretta U.S.A. Corp., 273 F.3d 536, 540 (3d Cir. 2001).

27. *E.g.*, *City of Chicago*, 821 N.E.2d at 1126.

28. *E.g.*, People ex rel. Spitzer v. Sturm, Ruger & Co., 761 N.Y.S.2d 192, 201 (N.Y. App. Div. 2003); *Camden County Bd.*, 273 F.3d at 541. *See also* Ganim v. Smith & Wesson Corp., 780 A.2d 98, 132–33 (Conn. 2001) (casting causation problems as indicating the plaintiff city's lack of standing to sue).

29. Erichson, *supra* note 15, at 140.

30. *Recent Legislation — Tort Law — Civil Immunity — Congress Passes Prohibition of Qualified Civil Claims against Gun Manufacturers and Distributors,* 119 Harv. L. Rev. 1939, 1939 n.30 (2006).

31. Protection of Lawful Commerce in Arms Act, Pub. L. No. 109-92, §§3 & 4(5)(A), 119 Stat. 2095, 2096–97 (2005).

32. Judge Jack Weinstein reasoned that New York City's public nuisance lawsuit came within the statutory exception for actions predicated upon "knowing" violation of a state statute applicable to the sale or marketing of firearms, where that violation is a "proximate cause" of the harm for which relief is sought. City of New York v. Beretta U.S.A. Corp., 401 F. Supp. 2d 244, 258–71 (E.D.N.Y. 2005) (interpreting Pub. L. No. 109-92, §4(5)(A)(iii), 119 Stat. 2097–98). An interlocutory appeal is pending before the Second Circuit.

33. Peter Harry Brown & Daniel G. Abel, Outgunned 206–14 (2003).

34. *Id.* at 298–99.

35. For an argument to expand this category of torts, where the defendant's lack of reasonable care enables a criminal offender to harm the victim, *see* Robert L. Rabin, *Enabling Torts,* 49 DePaul L. Rev. 435 (1999).

36. *See* Rabin, *Third Wave, supra* note 8, at 191–92; Dagan & White, *supra* note 18, at 380.

37. *See* chapter 3.

38. On the structure of the tobacco industry, *see* Kevin M. Walsh, *Corporate Spinoffs and Mass Tort Liability,* 1995 Colum. Bus. L. Rev. 675, 684–87.

39. Tom Diaz, Making a Killing 5 (1999).

40. *Id.* at 213 n.10.

41. On the contested cultural meaning of smoking, *see* Richard Klein, Cigarettes Are Sublime 181–93 (1993). On the contested cultural meaning of firearms and its significance for litigation, *see* Dan M. Kahan et al., *A Cultural Critique of Gun Litigation,* in Suing the Gun Industry 105 (Timothy D. Lytton ed. 2005).

42. Important early accounts of the historical evidence include Nelson Lund, *The Second Amendment, Political Liberty, and the Right to Self-Preservation,* 39 Ala. L. Rev. 103, 111–16 (1987); Sanford Levinson, *The Embarrassing Second Amendment,* 99 Yale L.J. 637, 648–51 (1989).

43. The proposal is reproduced in Mealey's Litigation Report: Tobacco, July 3, 1997, at A-1.

44. Dagan & White, *supra* note 18, at 368.

45. Viscusi, *supra* note 1, at 26.

46. Major Garrett & Kenneth T. Walsh, *Congress Snuffs Out the Tobacco Bill*, U.S. News & World Rep., June 29, 1998, 32 (quoting industry advertisement).

47. Thomas A. Schmeling, *Stag Hunting with the State AG: Anti-Tobacco Litigation and the Emergence of Cooperation among State Attorneys General*, 25 L. & Pol'y 429, 450 (2003).

48. For a more nuanced exposition of cartel theory, *see* Richard A. Posner, Antitrust Law 60–69 (2d ed. 2001).

49. Jeremy Bulow & Paul Klemperer, *The Tobacco Deal*, 1998 Brookings Papers on Econ. Activity, Microeconomic 323, 351.

50. Viscusi, *supra* note 1, at 45–49.

51. *Bedell*, 263 F.3d at 246.

52. Viscusi, *supra* note 1, at 41.

53. Frank J. Chaloupka et al., *Taxing Tobacco: The Impact of Tobacco Taxes on Cigarette Smoking and Other Tobacco Use*, in Regulating Tobacco 53 (Robert L. Rabin & Stephen D. Sugarman, eds. 2001) (associating 10 percent price increase with 2.5 to 5 percent reduction in overall consumption); Viscusi, *supra* note 1, at 19 (associating 10 percent price increase with 4 to 7 percent reduction in overall consumption).

54. For an overview of the literature, *see* Frank J. Chaloupka et al., *Policy Levers for the Control of Tobacco Consumption*, 90 Ky. L.J. 1009, 1023–25 (2002).

55. Centers for Disease Control, *Cigarette Use among High School Students — United States, 1991–2003*, 53 Morbidity & Mortality Wkly. Rep. 499, 499 (2004).

56. Centers for Disease Control, *Cigarette Smoking among Adults — United States, 2003*, 54 Morbidity & Mortality Wkly. Rep. 509, 510 (2005).

57. Bulow & Klemperer, *supra* note 49, at 348.

58. For a side-by-side comparison of the advertising restrictions in the proposed federal legislation and those in the MSA, *see* Michael Givel & Stanton A. Glantz, *The "Global Settlement" with the Tobacco Industry: 6 Years Later*, 94 Am. J. Pub. Health 218, 219–20 (2004).

59. Jeremy Bulow, *Profiting from Smokers*, 69 So. Econ. J. 736, 739 (2003) (book review of Viscusi, *supra* note 1).

60. Roger Parloff, *Is the $200 Billion Tobacco Deal Going Up in Smoke?*, Fortune, Mar. 7, 2005, at 136.

61. MSA, *supra* note 2, Exh. T.

62. Parloff, *supra* note 60, at 134.

63. MSA, *supra* note 2, §IX(d)(2)(B).

64. Parloff, *supra* note 60, at 136.

65. Dagan & White, *supra* note 18, at 381 (estimating that a 10 percent loss of market share by signatory firms to nonsignatories could lead to a reduction in MSA payments to the states of up to 24 percent). In 2006, an independent arbitrator ruled that the MSA was a "factor" in the loss of market share by the major tobacco firms, a conclusion that positions the industry to reduce its payments to the states. Vanessa O'Connell, *Big Tobacco Gets Favorable Ruling*, Wall St. J., Mar. 29, 2006, at B3.

66. Parloff, *supra* note 60, at 136–38.

67. *E.g.*, NCAA v. Board of Regents of the Univ. of Oklahoma, 468 U.S. 85, 100 (1984).

68. Freedom Holdings, Inc. v. Spitzer, 357 F.3d 225, 226 (2d Cir. 2004).

69. 317 U.S. 341 (1943).

70. 445 U.S. 97, 105 (1980).

71. Patrick v. Burget, 486 U.S. 94, 101 (1988).

72. *Bedell*, 263 F.3d at 264.

73. *Freedom Holdings*, 357 F.3d at 231-32.

74. Eastern R.R. Presidents Conference v. Noerr Motor Freight, Inc., 365 U.S. 127 (1961); United Mine Workers v. Pennington, 381 U.S. 657 (1965).

75. *Bedell*, 263 F.3d at 253.

76. *Id.* at 251.

77. In the popular business press, Roger Parloff has noted in general terms the possibility that the MSA ultimately might not garner antitrust immunity. *See* Parloff, *supra* note 60.

78. *Freedom Holdings*, 357 F.3d at 229 ("[I]t is questionable whether *Parker* immunity extends to a cartel arrangement supported by a state solely to allow the state to share the monopoly profits as state revenues.").

79. *E.g.*, City of Columbia v. Omni Outdoor Advertising, 499 U.S. 365, 370 (1991) (citing other similar decisions).

80. *E.g.*, Walter K. Olson, The Rule of Lawyers, ch. 1 (2003); Catherine Crier, The Case against Lawyers 184-85 (2002).

81. For a sympathetic assessment of cost-benefit analysis in the regulatory process, *see* Matthew D. Adler & Eric A. Posner, eds., Cost-Benefit Analysis: Legal, Economic, and Philosophical Perspectives (2001). For a more skeptical assessment, *see* Frank Ackerman & Lisa Heinzerling, Priceless: On Knowing the Price of Everything and the Value of Nothing (2004).

82. Viscusi, *supra* note 1, at 217.

83. *Id.* at 195.

84. *E.g.*, Stephen P. Teret & Michael Jacobs, *Prevention and Torts: The Role of Litigation in Injury Control*, 17 L., Med. & Health Care 17 (1989).

85. David Kessler, A Question of Intent 392-93 (2001).

86. David A. Dana, *Public Interest and Private Lawyers: Toward a Normative Evaluation of Parens Patriae Litigation by Contingency Fee*, 51 DePaul L. Rev. 315, 328 (2001).

87. United States v. Philip Morris Inc., 116 F. Supp. 2d 131 (D.D.C. 2000).

88. *Id.* at 136.

89. United States v. Philip Morris USA, Inc., 396 F.3d 1190, 1198 (D.C. Cir. 2005) (discussing 18 U.S.C. § 1964(a)).

90. *Id.* at 1198.

91. *Id.* at 1200-01 (discussing 18 U.S.C. § 1963(a)).

92. *See* United States v. Philip Morris USA, Inc., 449 J. Supp. 2d 1, 938-45 (D.D.C. 2006) (ordering forward-looking remedies consisting primarily of the issuance of corrective statements and the disclosure of industry documents concerning the conspiracy). On the rise in Altria Group shares, see Vanessa O'Connell et al., *Cigarette Companies Escape Major Financial Penalty in Suit*, Wall St. J., Aug. 18, 2006, at A3.

93. On the use of MSA payments by the various states, *see* General Accounting Office, Tobacco Settlement: States' Allocations of Fiscal Year 2003 and Expected Fiscal Year 2004 Payments (2004); American Heart Association et al., A Broken Promise to Our Children: The 1998 State Tobacco Settlement Six Years Later (2004).

94. *E.g.*, Viscusi, *supra* note 1, at 35.

95. *Id.* at 26-27.

CHAPTER XI

1. Samuel Issacharoff & John Fabian Witt, *The Inevitability of Aggregate Settlement: An Institutional Account of American Tort Law,* 57 Vand. L. Rev. 1571, 1584–99 (2004).

2. 11 U.S.C. §524(g)(2)(B)(ii)(IV)(bb) (conditioning confirmation of asbestos-related reorganization plan on vote by those whose claims the plan would resolve and calling for a favorable vote by "75 percent of those voting"); *id.* §1126(c) (deeming a class of claims to have accepted a reorganization plan under general Chapter 11 "if such plan has been accepted by creditors . . . that held at least two-thirds in amount and more than one-half in number of the allowed claims of such class"); *id.* §1129(a)(8)(A) (conditioning confirmation of reorganization plan on acceptance by each class of claims) (2000).

3. *See* chapter 3.

4. *E.g.,* John C. Coffee Jr., *Class Wars: The Dilemma of the Mass Tort Class Action,* 95 Colum. L. Rev. 1343, 1373–76 (1995); Susan P. Koniak, *Feasting While the Widow Weeps:* Georgine v. Amchem Products, Inc., 80 Cornell L. Rev. 1045, 1051–86 (1995).

5. Stephen C. Yeazell, *Re-Financing Civil Litigation,* 51 DePaul L. Rev. 183, 198–205 (2001).

6. *See* chapter 5.

7. *In re* Diet Drugs (Phentermine/Fenfluramine/Dexfenfluramine) Prods. Liab. Litig., 226 F.R.D. 498, 506–8 (E.D. Pa. 2005).

8. For a similar observation about risk allocation in the context of mass tort-related reorganization plans in bankruptcy, *see* Yair Listokin & Kenneth Ayotte, *Protecting Future Claimants in Mass Tort Bankruptcies,* 98 Nw. U.L. Rev. 1435, 1460 (2004).

9. Fed. R. Civ. P. 23(a).

10. *See* chapter 7.

11. One commentator recognizes that, "in many circumstances, current claimants are the best proxies for future claimants." Deborah R. Hensler, *Bringing* Shutts *into the Future: Rethinking the Protection of Future Claimants in Mass Tort Class Actions,* 74 UMKC L. Rev. 585, 588 (2006). But the same source stops short of questioning the conventional wisdom that simultaneous representation of present and future claimants is something that the law should avoid.

12. Amchem Prods., Inc. v. Windsor, 521 U.S. 591, 626–27 (1997).

13. Ortiz v. Fibreboard, Inc., 527 U.S. 815, 856 (1999).

14. 11 U.S.C. §524(g)(4)(B)(i) (2000).

15. Listokin & Ayotte, *supra* note 8, at 1451–52.

16. National Bankruptcy Review Commission, Bankruptcy: The Next Twenty Years 332 (1997).

17. *Amchem,* 521 U.S. at 601; *Ortiz,* 527 U.S. at 825.

18. *Ortiz,* 527 U.S. at 852.

19. *In re* Combustion Engineering, 391 F.3d 190, 244 (3d Cir. 2004).

20. Model Rules of Professional Responsibility, Rule 1.7 (2004) [Model Rule 1.7]. *See also* Restatement of the Law Governing Lawyers §121 (2000) (defining a conflict of interest as involving a "substantial risk" that the representation of one client "would be materially and adversely affected" by the lawyer's representation of another client). Even client consent will not suffice if the lawyer "reasonably believes" that she will be unable to provide "competent and diligent representation to each affected client." Model Rule 1.7(b)(1). *See also* Restatement of the Law Governing Lawyers §122(2)(c) (prohibiting joint

representation, even with client consent, where "it is not reasonably likely that the lawyer will be able to provide adequate representation to one or more of the clients").

21. Charles Silver & Lynn Baker, *I Cut, You Choose: The Role of Plaintiffs' Counsel in Allocating Settlement Proceeds,* 84 Va. L. Rev. 1465, 1507 (1998).

22. *See Ortiz,* 527 U.S. at 878 (Breyer, J., dissenting).

23. *See* chapter 9.

24. *E.g.,* F. H. Buckley, *The Bankruptcy Priority Puzzle,* 92 Va. L. Rev. 1393, 1415–19 (1986); David W. Leebron, *Limited Liability, Tort Victims, and Creditors,* 91 Colum. L. Rev. 1565, 1643–50 (1991).

25. For recent commentary emphasizing this dimension of elections, *see* Richard A. Posner, Law, Pragmatism, and Democracy, ch. 5 (2003).

26. For a typology of these measures, *see* Reinier R. Kraakman et al., The Anatomy of Corporate Law, ch. 2 (2004).

27. The *Amchem* class settlement, for example, capped the contingency fees for claims filed thereunder at 20 to 25 percent, markedly below the usual fee percentages in asbestos litigation of 33 to 40 percent. Georgine v. Amchem Prod. Inc., 157 F.R.D. 246, 285 (E.D. Pa. 1994).

28. Charles Silver, *A Restitutionary Theory of Attorneys' Fees in Class Actions,* 76 Cornell L. Rev. 656, 664–65 (1991).

29. The usual principle holds that a fee award for creation of a common fund is independent even of whether class members exercise their rights under the settlement to make claims against the fund. *See* Boeing Co. v. Van Gemert, 444 U.S. 472, 480 (1980) (holding that the right of class members "to share the harvest of the [class] litigation . . . whether or not they exercise it, is a benefit in the fund created by the efforts of the class representatives and their counsel").

30. *See* Fed. R. Civ. P. 23(e).

31. *See* chapter 5.

32. 11 U.S.C. §503(b)(3)(D) & (4) (2000).

33. *In re* United States Lines, Inc., 103 B.R. 427, 429 (S.D.N.Y. 1989). *See also, e.g., In re* Baldwin-United Corp., 79 B.R. 335, 338 (S.D. Ohio 1987).

34. *E.g., In re* Celotex Corp., 227 F.3d 1336, 1340 (11th Cir. 2000).

35. Bankruptcy courts routinely consider twelve factors set forth in a prominent class action case from the civil rights context involving a fee award determined by the lodestar method: Johnson v. Georgia Highway Express, Inc., 448 F.2d 714 (5th Cir. 1974).

36. 472 U.S. 797, 812 (1985).

37. John Bronsteen & Owen Fiss, *The Class Action Rule,* 78 Notre Dame L. Rev. 1419, 1446–47 (2003).

38. *See* chapter 6 (discussing the 9/11 Fund legislation).

39. 210 U.S. 373 (1908); 239 U.S. 441 (1915).

40. United States v. Florida East Coast Railway, 410 U.S. 224, 244–45 (1973), states most crisply this widely accepted reading of *Londoner* and *Bi-Metallic.* In describing the requisite "opportunity to be heard" in agency adjudication, the *Londoner* Court spoke of a "hearing" short of that afforded in "strictly judicial proceedings" — just an opportunity "to support [one's] allegations by argument however brief, and if need be, by proof, however informal." 210 U.S. at 386.

41. 239 U.S. at 445.

42. On the style and rhetoric of Justice Holmes's opinions, *see* Richard A. Posner, *Introduction,* in The Essential Holmes (Richard A. Posner ed., 1992).

43. See Adam F. Scales, *Against Settlement Factoring? The Market in Tort Claims Has Arrived*, 2002 Wisc. L. Rev. 859, 961.

44. Memorandum and Pretrial Order No. 2622, at 25, *In re* Diet Drugs (Phentermine/Fenfluramine/Dexfenfluramine) Prods. Liab. Litig., Civ. No. 99-20593 (E.D. Pa. Oct. 3, 2002), available at http://fenphencentral.com/feeaward.pdf.

45. *See* chapter 10.

46. The most detailed expositions in the mass tort setting appear in the work of David Rosenberg. *See, e.g.,* David Rosenberg, *The Causal Connection in Mass Exposure Cases: A "Public Law" Vision of the Tort System*, 97 Harv. L. Rev. 849 (1984) [Rosenberg, *Causal Connection*]; David Rosenberg, *Mandatory-Litigation Class Actions: The Only Option for Mass Tort Cases*, 115 Harv. L. Rev. 831 (2002) [Rosenberg, *Mandatory-Litigation Class Actions*].

47. Rosenberg, *Causal Connection, supra* note 46, at 920.

48. See Rosenberg, *Mandatory-Litigation Class Actions, supra* note 46.

49. Bruce L. Hay & David Rosenberg, *"Sweetheart" and "Blackmail" Settlements in Class Actions: Reality and Remedy*, 75 Notre Dame L. Rev. 1377, 1398 (2000).

CHAPTER XII

1. The bankruptcy court in the Dalkon Shield contraceptive litigation drew upon class action precedents to approve a 10 percent cap on contingency fees associated with pro rata distributions to tort creditors late in the life of the A. H. Robins bankruptcy trust. *See In re* A. H. Robins Co., 182 B.R. 128, 137-38 (Bankr. E.D. Va. 1995). These pro rata distributions came from funds that had accumulated unexpectedly in the trust over the course of its operation and represented a "bonus distribution" to tort creditors on top of earlier payouts that resolved their claims against A. H. Robins. *See id.* at 131. Even while upholding the cap on fees associated with this bonus distribution, however, the court took care to avoid the assertion of authority to regulate the contingency fees associated with the earlier payouts that resolved tort claims. *See id.* at 139.

2. A detailed exposition of the various sources of authority appears in *In re* Joint E & S. Dist. Asbestos Litig., 878 F. Supp. 473, 558-62 (E. & S.D.N.Y. 1995), which involved the use of a class settlement to restructure the Manville bankruptcy trust.

3. U.S. Const. art. I, §8, cl. 4.

4. G. Marcus Cole, *A Calculus without Consent: Mass Tort Bankruptcies, Future Claimants, and the Problem of Third Party Non-Debtor "Discharge,"* 84 Iowa L. Rev. 753, 757 (1999).

5. For a leading exposition of this point, *see* Thomas H. Jackson, The Logic and Limits of Bankruptcy 49 (1986).

6. 11 U.S.C. §524(g)(5) (defining a "demand" as "a demand for payment, present or future, that . . . was not a claim during the proceedings leading to the confirmation of a plan of reorganization" but that arises out of the same underlying events and will be paid under the reorganization plan).

7. *In re* SGL Carbon Corp., 200 F.3d 154, 163 (3d Cir. 1999).

8. *Id.* at 160-62.

9. The shorthand "reg-neg" stems from the term "regulatory negotiation" originally used to describe what is now called "negotiated rulemaking." *See, e.g.,* Regulatory Negotiation: Joint Hearings before the Select Subcomm. on Small Bus. & the Subcomm. on Oversight of Gov't Mgmt. of the Senate Comm. on Governmental Affairs, 96th Cong. (1980).

10. *See* 5 U.S.C. §553 (2000).

11. *See* Phillip J. Harter, *Negotiating Regulations: A Cure for Malaise,* 71 Geo. L.J. 1, 19–22 (1982).

12. *See id.*; Lawrence Susskind & Gerard McMahon, *The Theory and Practice of Negotiated Rulemaking,* 3 Yale J. Reg. 133 (1985); Henry H. Perritt Jr., *Negotiated Rulemaking before Federal Agencies: Evaluation of Recommendations by the Administrative Conference of the United States,* 74 Geo. L.J. 1625 (1986); Peter H. Schuck, *Litigation, Bargaining, and Regulation,* Reg., July–Aug. 1979, at 26.

13. 5 U.S.C. §§ 561–70 (2000).

14. *Id.* § 563 (a)(2) & (a)(3)(A).

15. *Id.* § 564(a). Those who stand to be significantly affected by the rulemaking but "who believe that their interests will not be adequately represented by any person" on the committee may apply, or nominate a person, for membership. *Id.* § 564(b).

16. *Id.* § 566(b).

17. *Id.* § 562(2). *See also id.* § 566(f) (issuance of committee report containing proposed rule based on "consensus").

18. *Id.* § 563(a)(7).

19. *Id.* § 570.

20. Phillip J. Harter, *Assessing the Assessors: The Actual Performance of Negotiated Rulemaking,* 9 N.Y.U. Envtl. L.J. 32, 37–38 (2000) (citing examples).

21. *See* Laura I. Langbein & Cornelius M. Kerwin, *Regulatory Negotiation versus Conventional Rule Making: Claims, Counterclaims, and Empirical Evidence,* 10 J. Pub. Admin. Research & Theory 599, 629–30 (2000).

22. Exec. Order No. 12866, § 6(a)(1), 3 C.F.R. 638, 645 (1993) (Clinton order, directing agencies "to explore and, where appropriate, use consensual mechanisms for developing regulations, including negotiated rulemaking"); Exec. Order No. 13258, 3 C.F.R. 204 (2002) (Bush order, retaining provision of Clinton order concerning negotiated rulemaking).

23. William Funk, *When Smoke Gets in Your Eyes: Regulatory Negotiation and the Public Interest — EPA's Woodstove Standards,* 18 Envtl. L. 55, 96 (1987).

24. *Compare* Cary Coglianese, *Assessing Consensus: The Promise and Performance of Negotiated Rulemaking,* 46 Duke L.J. 1255, 1292–1302 (1997), *with* Harter, *supra* note 20, at 39–41; Jody Freeman & Laura I. Langbein, *Regulatory Negotiation and the Legitimacy Benefit,* 9 N.Y.U. Envtl. L.J. 60, 127–30 (2000).

25. *See* Susan Rose-Ackerman, *Consensus versus Incentives: A Skeptical Look at Regulatory Negotiation,* 43 Duke L.J. 1206, 1211 (1994).

26. Negotiated Rulemaking Act of 1990, Pub. L. No. 101-648, § 5, 104 Stat. 4969, 4976–77. *See also* Administrative Dispute Resolution Act of 1996, Pub. L. No. 104-320, § 11, 110 Stat. 3870, 3873–74 (repealing six-year sunset provision in original Negotiated Rulemaking Act).

27. Helpful overviews of the issues surrounding postmarketing surveillance by the FDA include Catherine T. Struve, *The FDA and the Tort System: Postmarketing Surveillance, Compensation, and the Role of Litigation,* 5 Yale J. Health Pol'y, L. & Ethics 587, 598–606 (2005); U.S. Department of Health and Human Services, Food and Drug Administration, Managing the Risks from Medical Product Use — Creating a Risk Management Framework 51–70 (May 1999); Timothy Brewer & Graham A. Colditz, *Postmarketing Surveillance and Adverse Drug Reactions,* 281 JAMA 824 (1999).

28. *E.g.,* Peter Juni et al., *Risk of Cardiovascular Events and Rofecoxib: Cumulative Meta-Analysis,* 364 Lancet 2021 (2004).

29. *How Deep Do Merck's Wounds Go?*, Wall St. J., Sept. 30, 2006, at B14 (reporting that "27,000 people were suing Merck over [Vioxx] as of June 30," 2006); *In re* Vioxx Prods. Liab. Litig., 360 F. Supp. 2d 1352 (J.P.M.D.L. 2005) (consolidating 148 actions pending in 41 federal courts).

30. Barry Meier, *Merck Canceled an Early Study of Vioxx*, N.Y. Times, Feb. 8, 2005, at C1; Barbara Martinez, *Merck Documents Shed Light on Vioxx Legal Battles*, N.Y. Times, Feb. 7, 2005, at A1; Barry Meier, *Early Merck Study Indicated Risks of Vioxx*, N.Y. Times, Nov. 18, 2004, at C1; Alex Berenson et al., *In Face of Warnings, Drug Giant Took Long Path to Vioxx Recall*, N.Y. Times, Nov. 14, 2004, § 1, at 1; Anna Wilde Mathews & Barbara Martinez, *E-Mails Suggest Merck Knew Vioxx's Dangers at Early Stage*, Wall St. J., Nov. 1, 2004, at A1.

31. David Armstrong, *How the New England Journal Missed Warning Signs on Vioxx*, Wall St. J., May 15, 2006, at A1. *See also* Andrew Pollack & Reed Abelson, *Why the Data Diverge on the Dangers of Vioxx*, N.Y. Times, May 22, 2006, at C1.

32. Richard A. Epstein, Overdose 209–13 (2006).

33. *See* The FDA's Drug Approval Process, Hearing before the Senate Comm. on Education, Labor and Pensions, 109th Cong. (2005); FDA, Merck, and Vioxx: Putting Patient Safety First, Hearing before the Senate Comm. on Finance, 109th Cong. (2004). In February 2005, the FDA announced its establishment of a new Drug Safety Oversight Board to advise the agency on the safety of drugs already approved. Anna Wilde Mathews & Leila Abboud, *New FDA Board Set Up to Review Approved Drugs*, Wall St. J., Feb. 16, 2005, at A1.

34. Barry Meier et al., *Medicine Fueled by Marketing Intensified Trouble for Pain Pills*, N.Y. Times, Dec. 19, 2004, § 1, at 1.

35. 28 U.S.C. § 1407(a) (2000).

36. *Id. See also* Lexecon, Inc. v. Milberg Weiss Bershad Hynes & Lerach, 523 U.S. 26 (1998) (overturning the practice of "self-transfer" whereby transferee courts had retained MDL-consolidated cases beyond pretrial proceedings).

37. 5 U.S.C. § 706 (2000).

38. Motor Vehicle Manufacturers Assoc. v. State Farm Mutual Automobile Ins. Co., 463 U.S. 29, 52 (1983) (quoting Burlington Truck Lines, Inc. v. United States, 371 U.S. 156, 168 (1962)).

39. In *State Farm*, the Court overturned the National Highway Traffic Safety Administration's rescission of a rule that would have required the inclusion of airbags in new automobiles. The Court concluded that the agency had scrapped the airbag rule as a whole without a reasoned explanation of why the alternative of rule modification would not have been a superior approach in light of the underlying statutory objective to advance auto safety. 463 U.S. at 46.

40. For *Amchem* and *Ortiz*, see chapter 5; for the Sulzer hip replacement, *see* chapter 8.

41. For an illustration of this approach from outside the mass tort context, *see In re* Cendent Corp. PRIDES Litig., 243 F.3d 722 (3d Cir. 2001).

42. John C. Coffee Jr., *Class Action Accountability: Reconciling Exit, Voice, and Loyalty in Representative Litigation*, 100 Colum. L. Rev. 370, 423 (2000).

43. Susan P. Koniak & George M. Cohen, *Under Cloak of Settlement*, 82 Va. L. Rev. 1051, 1107 n.184 (1996).

44. *See* Geoffrey P. Miller, *Competing Bids in Class Action Settlements*, 31 Hofstra L. Rev. 633 (2003); Richard A. Nagareda, *Administering Adequacy in Class Representation*, 82 Tex. L. Rev. 287 (2003).

45. The argument here parallels the theory of "contestable markets" in the regulation of monopolies. In simplified form, the theory posits that the potential for rival firms to enter the market of an incumbent monopolist will operate to restrain the latter from wielding its monopoly power to the detriment of consumers. For application of the theory to problems of class representation, *see* Richard A. Nagareda, *The Preexistence Principle and the Structure of the Class Action*, 103 Colum. L. Rev. 149, 168–74 (2003).

46. *E.g.*, 42 U.S.C. §7607(b)(1) (Clean Air Act); *id.* §9613(a) (Comprehensive Environmental Response, Compensation, and Liability Act); 47 U.S.C. §402(b) (Federal Communications Act).

47. U.S. Const. art. III, §2 (providing that the federal judicial power "shall extend to . . . controversies . . . between citizens of different states").

48. For an overview of these decisions, *see* Richard H. Fallon Jr. et al., Hart & Wechsler's The Federal Courts and the Federal System 362–418 (5th ed. 2003). For critical analysis, *see, e.g.*, Richard H. Fallon Jr., *Of Legislative Courts, Administrative Agencies, and Article III*, 101 Harv. L. Rev. 915 (1988). The reason for constitutional concern is that Article III affords to judges within its aegis the protections of life tenure and a prohibition against salary reduction. U.S. Const. art. III, §1. The framework suggested here, like other administrative schemes, lacks these insulations from the political branches of government.

49. 235 U.S. 22 (1932).

50. *Id.* at 40.

51. *Id.* at 54.

52. U.S. Const. art. III, §2.

53. 235 U.S. at 53.

54. *Id.* at 48. Here, the Court reasoned that "[a]n award not supported by evidence in the record is not in accordance with law." *Id. See also* Fallon, *supra* note 48, at 988 n.392 (observing that the "clear implication" of *Crowell* is that "there must be enough review of fact-finding to establish the lawfulness of an administrative order").

The *Crowell* Court went on to distinguish between review on the administrative record of facts concerning the application of the compensation grid and review of facts that are "jurisdictional" in the sense of bringing the matter within federal authority in the first place — specifically, that the injury occurred within the navigable waters of the United States and arose in the context of a master-servant relationship. These jurisdictional facts, the *Crowell* Court held, called for de novo review by an Article III court. 235 U.S. at 54–65. The continued vitality of this further holding in *Crowell* remains uncertain. *See* Henry P. Monaghan, *Constitutional Fact Review*, 85 Colum. L. Rev. 229, 255–63 (1985). In any event, any remaining uncertainty on this point concerns facets of workers' compensation in admiralty that have no bearing on mass torts.

55. Thomas v. Union Carbide Agricultural Prods. Co., 473 U.S. 568, 586–87 (1985) (confirming the continued vitality of *Crowell* in relevant part). In *Thomas*, the Court noted that Congress enjoys even greater flexibility when addressing matters other than actions at common law. *See id.* at 587 (noting that "[t]he extent of judicial review afforded by the legislation reviewed in *Crowell* does not constitute a minimal requirement of Article III without regard to the origin of the right at issue").

56. U.S. Const. amend. VII.

57. *See* Curtis v. Loether, 415 U.S. 189, 195–96 (1974). Unlike most of the protections in the Bill of Rights, the Seventh Amendment right to jury trial has not been incorpo-

rated against the states. *See* Minneapolis & St. Louis R.R. Co. v. Bombolis, 241 U.S. 211, 217 (1916). Any potential Seventh Amendment objection to the displacement of pending tort actions by agency rulemaking thus would be limited to cases pending in the federal courts. Federal agency rulemaking with the force of law would override any guarantees of jury trial in state courts pursuant to state constitutional provisions.

58. 243 U.S. 219 (1917).

59. *Id.* at 235–36.

60. *See* Plaut v. Spendthrift Farm, Inc., 514 U.S. 211, 226–27 (1995) (distinguishing between permitted application of amendment to federal securities law in cases "still on appeal" and prohibited application in cases where final judgments had been entered).

61. When discussing the replacement of a common-law right of action with a statutory right of action against the federal government, the Court has gone so far as to say that, "if Congress may assign the adjudication of a statutory cause of action to a non–Article III tribunal, then the Seventh Amendment poses no independent bar to the adjudication of that action by a nonjury factfinder." Granfinanciera, S.A. v. Nordberg, 492 U.S. 52, 53–54 (1989). The Court's continued adherence to *Crowell* suggests that the same would hold true where the statutory cause of action does not run against the federal government but, rather, against a private party.

For commentary suggesting that Article III and the Seventh Amendment instead call for distinct lines of analysis with regard to legislative courts, *see* Ellen E. Sward, *Legislative Courts, Article III, and the Seventh Amendment*, 77 N.C. L. Rev. 1037 (1999); Martin H. Redish & Daniel J. LaFave, *Seventh Amendment Right to Jury Trial in Non–Article III Proceedings: A Study in Dysfunctional Constitutional Theory*, 4 Wm. & Mary Bill Rts. J. 407 (1995).

CONCLUSION

1. Stephen C. Yeazell, From Medieval Group Litigation to the Modern Class Action 39 (1987).

2. *Id.* at 271.

3. Bob Sherwood & Nikki Tait, *Class Actions across the Atlantic*, Fin. Times, June 16, 2005, at 14.

4. On this conception of tort law and its significance for contemporary debates over tort reform, *see* John C. P. Goldberg, *The Constitutional Status of Tort Law: Due Process and the Right to a Law for the Redress of Wrongs*, 115 Yale L.J. 524 (2005).

5. *Cf.* John Hart Ely, Democracy and Distrust (1980).

6. My argument here extends the connection drawn by one observer between the waning of the political consensus for direct government regulation and the rise of government reimbursement litigation. *See* Robert B. Reich, *Regulation Is Out, Litigation Is In*, USA Today, Feb. 11, 1999, at 15A.

7. On tort litigation as a form of business enterprise, *see* Anita Bernstein, *The Enterprise of Liability*, 39 Val. U.L. Rev. 27 (2004).

INDEX

comparison to, 156–57; 9/11
Fund, comparison to, 83; *Simon II,*
comparison to, 130
ossification, 90
Owens Corning National Settlement
Program (NSP), 98, 108–12, 143, 168

pacemaker litigation, 159
Parker, Robert, 67, 90
Philip Morris, 213
Phillips Petroleum Co. v. Shutts, 234
plaintiffs' bar, competition in, ix, xiv, 93,
225, 243, 263
pleural thickening, 24
Posner, Richard, 6, 30, 43, 92, 123
postmarketing surveillance of
pharmaceutical products, 259
preclusion of litigation, 9, 19
privatization, 86
prospect theory, 31
Prosser, William, 4, 6
public-private distinction, xi
punitive damages: allocation of, 128,
130–34; class action treatment of,
123–29; constitutional limitations on,
124; mass tort litigation, prevalence
in, 32–33; option premium, use as,
140–42; settlement, effect on, 126

Racketeer Influenced and Corrupt
Organization Act (RICO), 192, 212
RAND Institute for Civil Justice, 23
Rawls, John, 122
Reagan, Ronald, 10
reinsurance, 27
relative risk, xii
Restatement (Second) of Torts, 5, 192
restitution, 191
Rhone-Poulenc Rorer, Inc., In re, 30, 43–45,
52–53, 123
Rice, Joseph, 169–70, 182, 184, 273
risk-based torts: academic debate over,
xvi, 100; legislation, comparison to,
100; leveraging proposal, comparison
to, 245–49; Rosenberg and, 99;
theories of liability, xv–xvi; tort
doctrine, status in, 22–24

risk regulation, 5
R.J. Reynolds Tobacco Company, 188
Roe, Mark, 179
Rosenberg, David: *ex ante* perspective of,
115–16; fee proposal, 122; insurance
markets and, 120–21; mandatory class
actions, 116
Rules Enabling Act, 84

Schmeling, Thomas, 199
Schuck, Peter, 74
Schwartz, Gary, 193
Schwartz, Warren, 48
Scirica, Anthony, 171
Scruggs, Richard, 152, 157, 169, 184, 188
Sebok, Anthony, 104
*Securities and Exchange Commission v. Chenery
Corp.,* 65
securities fraud, 2
securitization of legal fees, 239
security interests, use in hip implant class
settlement, 154–56
Sentelle, David, 212
settlement: bankruptcy as alternative to,
76; class actions and, 72–73; market
capitalization and, x; prevalence of,
ix; promotion by civil procedure, 7;
value-creating potential of, x–xi
silica litigation, medical diagnosis in, 149
silicone gel breast implant litigation: class
settlement, 35–36; doctors, role of,
35; Dow Corning reorganization, 36;
history of, 29, 33–36; moratorium on
sales, 35
Silver, Charles, 48, 59
Simon II Litigation, In re, 124, 128–29,
268; fen-phen class settlement,
comparison to, 142–43; *Ortiz,*
comparison to, 130
Smith, Thomas, 179
Smith & Wesson Corporation, 194
smoking, health risks of, 21
Souter, David, 32, 82
Specter, Arlen, 106
*State Farm Mutual Automobile Insurance Co. v.
Campbell,* 126
statistical sampling, xvii, 58, 67–70